Microsoft® Publisher 2002

Illustrated Introductory

Elizabeth Eisner Reding
and
Michael Reding

Australia • Canada • Mexico • Singapore • Spain • United Kingdom • United States

Microsoft Publisher 2002, Illustrated Introductory
Elizabeth Eisner Reding and Michael Reding

Managing Editor:
Nicole Jones Pinard

Production Editors:
Catherine DiMassa
Kristen Guevara

QA Manuscript Reviewers:
Maxwell Prior, Alex White

Product Managers:
Rebecca Berardy
Jennifer T. Campbell

Developmental Editor:
Jennifer T. Campbell

Text Designer:
Joseph Lee, Black Fish Design

Associate Product Manager:
Emeline Elliott

Editorial Assistant:
Christina King Garrett

Composition House:
GEX Publishing Services

COPYRIGHT © 2002 Course Technology, a division of Thomson Learning™. Thomson Learning™ is a trademark used herein under license.

Printed in the United States of America

1 2 3 4 5 6 7 8 9 BM 05 04 03 02 01

For more information, contact Course Technology, 25 Thomson Place, Boston, Massachusetts, 02210.

Or you can visit us on the World Wide Web at www.course.com

ALL RIGHTS RESERVED. No part of this work covered by the copyright hereon may be reproduced or used in any form or by any means - graphic, electronic, or mechanical, including photocopying, recording, taping, Web distribution, or information storage and retrieval systems - without the written permission of the publisher.

For permission to use material from this text or product, contact us by
Tel (800) 730-2214
Fax (800) 730-2215
www.thomsonrights.com

Trademarks
Some of the product names and company names used in this book have been used for identification purposes only and may be trademarks or registered trademarks of their respective manufacturers and sellers.

Some of the images used in this book are property of Rubber Ball Productions and PhotoDisc™.

Microsoft and the Office logo are either registered trademarks or trademarks of Microsoft Corporation in the United States and/or other countries. Course Technology is an independent entity from Microsoft Corporation, and not affiliated with Microsoft in any manner.

ISBN 0-619-04516-7

The Illustrated Series Vision

Teaching and writing about computer applications can be extremely rewarding and challenging. How do we engage students and keep their interest? How do we teach them skills that they can easily apply on the job? As we set out to write this book, our goals were to develop a textbook that:

- works for a beginning student
- provides varied, flexible and meaningful exercises and projects to reinforce the skills
- serves as a reference tool
- makes your job as an educator easier, by providing resources above and beyond the textbook to help you teach your course

Our popular, streamlined format is based on advice from instructional designers and customers. This flexible design presents each lesson on a two-page spread, with step-by-step instructions on the left, and screen illustrations on the right. This signature style, coupled with high-caliber content, provides a comprehensive yet manageable introduction to Microsoft Publisher 2002 — it is a teaching package for the instructor and a learning experience for the student.

ACKNOWLEDGMENTS

Creating a book is a team effort: We wish to thank Jennifer Campbell, the project manager and development editor. Her patience and wisdom have been invaluable. The suggestions made by our reviewers, Rick Sheridan at California State University and Joanne Storch at Santa Fe Community College, made this a much better book. We would also like to thank the production and editorial staff for all of their hard work, which made this project a reality.

Preface

Welcome to Microsoft Publisher 2002–Illustrated Introductory. Each lesson in the book contains elements pictured to the right.

▶ How is the book organized?

The book is organized into ten units on Publisher, covering creating a publication, formatting text, working with art, enhancing a publication, working with multiple pages, using special features, working efficiently, and working on the Web.

▶ What kinds of assignments are included in the book? At what level of difficulty?

The lesson assignments use Image Magic, a small advertising agency, as the case study. The assignments on the blue pages at the end of each unit increase in difficulty. Project files and case studies, with many international examples, provide a great variety of interesting and relevant business applications for skills. Assignments include:

- **Concepts Reviews** include multiple choice, matching, and screen identification questions.
- **Skills Reviews** provide additional hands-on, step-by-step reinforcement.
- **Independent Challenges** are case projects requiring critical thinking and application of the skills learned in the unit. The Independent Challenges increase in difficulty, with the first Independent Challenge in each unit being the easiest (most step-by-step with detailed instructions). Independent Challenges 2 and 3 become increasingly open-ended, requiring more independent thinking and problem solving.
- **E-Quest Independent Challenges** are case projects with a Web focus. E-Quests require the use of the World Wide Web to conduct research to complete the project.
- **Visual Workshops** show a completed file and require that the file be created without any step-by-step guidance, involving problem solving and an independent application of the unit skills.

Each two-page spread focuses on a single skill.

Concise text that introduces the basic principles in the lesson and integrates the brief case study (indicated by the paintbrush icon).

Using Layout Guides

Publisher 2002 — Unit C

When correctly laid out, elements in a publication are placed to achieve a balanced and consistent look. This balance and consistency occurs only with careful planning and design. **Layout guides** and **margin guides**, horizontal and vertical lines visible only on the screen, help you accurately position objects on a page and across pages in a publication. Layout guides are created on the **Master Page**, the background that is the same for all pages within a publication.

 Mike's assignment is to create a flyer for an upcoming design clinic. He will use a publication from the Publication Gallery, then set up the layout guides to help plan for future placement of objects in the publication. Mike will also experiment with a different color scheme.

Steps

1. Start Publisher, click **Flyers** in the By Publication Type list, click **Informational**, then click **Bars Informational Flyer** in the Informational Flyers list

   The flyer appears on the screen and the Flyer Options task pane opens. You want to change from the Wildflower to the Bluebird color scheme in the Personal Information Set. The Bluebird color scheme uses the same colors as the Wildflower scheme but applies them differently.

   QuickTip — Color schemes are listed in alphabetical order.

2. Click **Edit** on the menu bar, click **Personal Information**, click **Secondary Business**, if necessary type **Mike Mendoza** in the Name text box, type **Account Executive** in the Job or position title text box, type **Image Magic** in the Address text box, press **[Enter]**, type **214 Old Spanish Trail**, press **[Enter]**, type **Santa Fe, New Mexico 87501**, in the Phone/fax/e-mail text box type **Phone: 505-555-5555**, press **[Enter]**, type **Fax: 505-555-4444**, press **[Enter]**, type **E-mail: mikemendoza@imagemagic.com**, type **Image Magic** in the Organization name text box, type **Your Image! Our Magic!** in the Tag line or motto text box, click the **Color Schemes list arrow**, click **Bluebird**, then click **Update**

   The task pane is not necessary for the remainder of the flyer you are designing.

3. Click the **Close button** on the Flyer Options task pane, then save the publication to the drive and folder where your Project Files are stored as **Design Clinic Flyer**

   QuickTip — Ruler coordinates are given as follows: **4" H / 5" V**. This means that the coordinate is at 4" on the horizontal ruler, and 5" on the vertical ruler.

4. Right-click the graphic placeholder at **4" H / 5" V**, click **Delete Object**, click **Yes** in the warning box, right-click the text box at **4" H / 5" V**, then click **Delete Object**

   The image and text box are deleted from the flyer.

5. Click **Arrange** on the menu bar, then click **Layout Guides**

   The Layout Guides dialog box opens. You use the Layout Guides dialog box to change the margin dimensions.

6. If necessary, click the **Left down arrow** until **0.5** appears in the text box, click the **Right down arrow** until **0.5** appears in the text box, click the **Top down arrow** until **0.5** appears in the text box, select the text **1** in the **Bottom text box**, then type **0.66** in the text box if necessary

   The top and bottom margins are small enough to allow lots of information to be placed on each page. Layout guides create a grid to help you line up design elements, such as images and text boxes, on the page.

7. Click the **Columns up arrow** until **3** appears in the text box, click the **Rows up arrow** until **3** appears in the text box as shown in Figure C-1, then click **OK**

   The pink lines represent the column guides, and the blue lines represent the column guide margins. The guides appear on the screen, as shown in Figure C-2, but do not print on the page.

8. Click the **Save button** on the Standard toolbar

▶ PUBLISHER 50 **WORKING WITH TEXT**

Hints as well as troubleshooting advice, right where you need it — next to the step itself.

▶ IV

Every lesson features large, full-color representations of what the screen should look like as students complete the numbered steps.

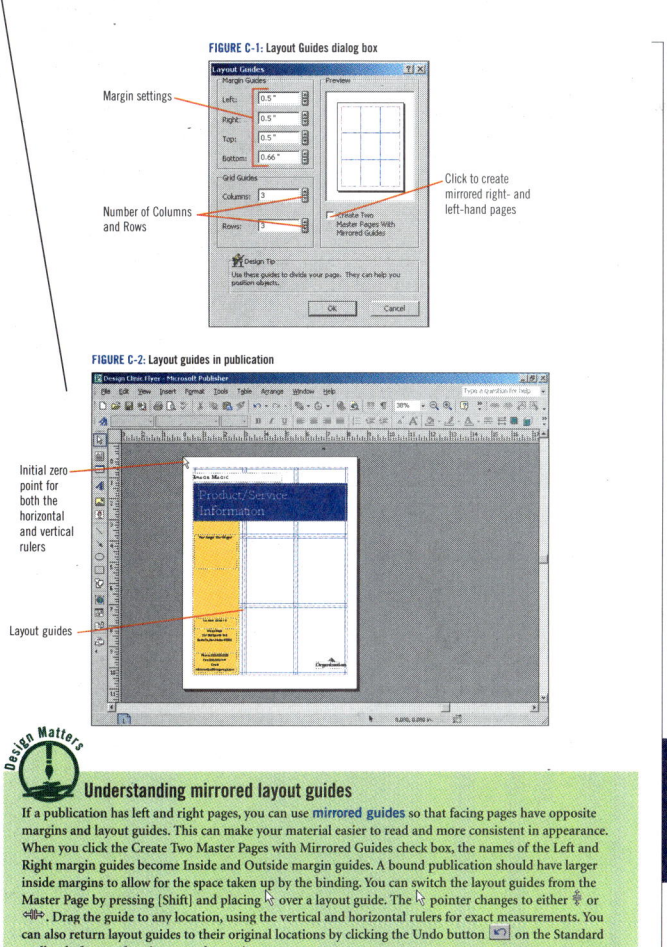

Design Matters boxes help students apply smart design principles to their Web sites. Each Design Matters deals exclusively with design considerations, such as ease of use, navigation and appeal, for Web pages and Web sites.

- **Capstone Projects** are additional exercises at the end of each unit that allow students to practice skills learned in the unit, with special emphasis on reinforcing the design concepts behind the skills.

▶ What distance learning options are available to accompany this book?

Visit *www.course.com* for more information on our Distance Learning materials to accompany Illustrated titles. Options include:

MyCourse.com

Need a quick, simple tool to help you manage your course? Try MyCourse.com, the easiest to use, most flexible syllabus and content management tool available. MyCourse.com offers you brand new content, including Topic Reviews, Extra Case Projects, and Quizzes, to accompany this book.

WebCT

Course Technology and WebCT have partnered to provide you with the highest quality online resources and Web-based tools for your class. Course Technology offers content for this book to help you create your WebCT class, such as a suggested Syllabus, Lecture Notes, Practice Test questions, and more.

Blackboard

Course Technology and Blackboard have also partnered to provide you with the highest quality online resources and Web-based tools for your class. Course Technology offers content for this book to help you create your Blackboard class, such as a suggested Syllabus, Lecture Notes, Practice Test questions, and more.

Instructor Resources

The Instructor's Resource Kit (IRK) CD is Course Technology's way of putting the resources and information needed to teach and learn effectively into your hands. All the components are available on the IRK, (pictured below), and many of the resources can be downloaded from *www.course.com*.

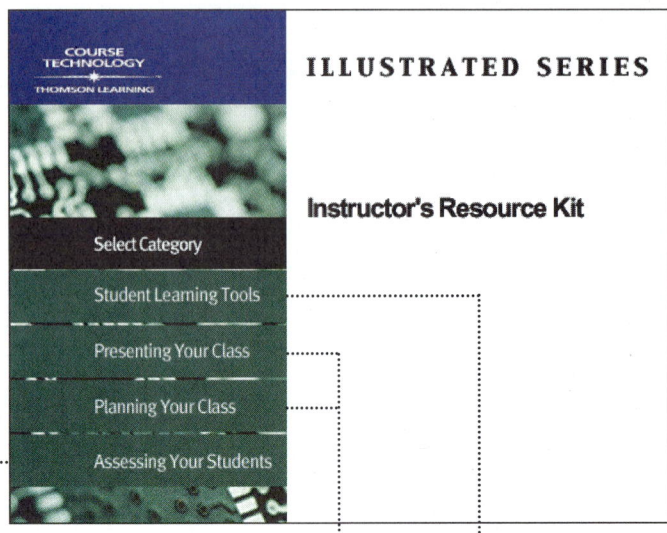

ASSESSING YOUR STUDENTS

Solution Files
Solution Files are Project Files completed with comprehensive sample answers. Use these files to evaluate your students' work. Or, distribute electronically or in hard copy so students can verify their own work.

ExamView
ExamView is a powerful testing software package that allows you to create and administer printed, computer (LAN-based), and Internet exams. ExamView includes hundreds of questions that correspond to the topics covered in this text, enabling students to generate detailed study guides that include page references for further review. The computer-based and Internet-testing components allow students to take exams at their computers, and also save you time by grading each exam automatically.

PRESENTING YOUR CLASS

Figure Files
Figure Files contain all the figures from the book in .jpg format. Use the figure files to create transparency masters or in a PowerPoint presentation.

STUDENT TOOLS

Project Files and Project Files List
To complete most of the units in this book, your students will need **Project Files**. Put them on a file server for students to copy. The Project Files are available on the Instructor's Resource Kit CD-ROM, the Review Pack, and can also be downloaded from *www.course.com*.

Instruct students to use the **Project Files List** at the end of the book. This list gives instructions on copying and organizing files.

PLANNING YOUR CLASS

Instructor's Manual
Available as an electronic file, the Instructor's Manual is quality-assurance tested and includes unit overviews, detailed lecture topics for each unit with teaching tips, comprehensive sample solutions to all lessons and end-of-unit material, and extra Independent Challenges. The Instructor's Manual is available on the Instructor's Resource Kit CD-ROM, or you can download it from *www.course.com*.

Sample Syllabus
Prepare and customize your course easily using this sample course outline (available on the Instructor's Resource Kit CD-ROM).

Brief Contents

The Illustrated Series Vision   III
Preface   IV
Read This Before You Begin   XIV

Publisher 2002		
	Getting Started with Microsoft Publisher 2002	PUBLISHER 1
	Creating a Publication	PUBLISHER 25
	Working with Text	PUBLISHER 49
	Working with Art	PUBLISHER 75
	Enhancing a Publication	PUBLISHER 99
	Improving a Publication	PUBLISHER 125
	Working with Multiple Pages	PUBLISHER 145
	Using Special Features	PUBLISHER 169
	Working Efficiently	PUBLISHER 193
	Working on the Web	PUBLISHER 217

Project Files List   PUBLISHER 241
Glossary   PUBLISHER 245
Index   PUBLISHER 250

Contents

The Illustrated Series Vision III
Preface IV
Read This Before You Begin XIV

Publisher 2002

Getting Started with Microsoft Publisher 2002 — PUBLISHER 1
Defining Publication Software ....PUBLISHER 2
Starting Publisher 2002 ....PUBLISHER 4
   Using the New Publication task pane ....PUBLISHER 5
Viewing the Publisher Window ....PUBLISHER 6
   Using task panes ....PUBLISHER 7
Opening and Saving a Publication ....PUBLISHER 8
   Using dialog box views ....PUBLISHER 9
Entering Text in a Text Box ....PUBLISHER 10
   Understanding objects ....PUBLISHER 11
Viewing and Printing a Publication ....PUBLISHER 12
Getting Help and Changing Personal Information ....PUBLISHER 14
   Opening a file created in the Publication Gallery ....PUBLISHER 15
Closing a Publication and Exiting Publisher ....PUBLISHER 16
   Microsoft Publisher World Wide Web site ....PUBLISHER 17
✓ Capstone Project: Study Abroad Flyer ....PUBLISHER 18
Concepts Review ....PUBLISHER 20
Skills Review ....PUBLISHER 22
Independent Challenges ....PUBLISHER 23
Visual Workshop ....PUBLISHER 24

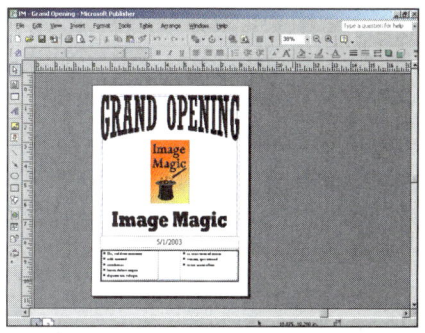

Creating a Publication — PUBLISHER 25
Planning a Publication ....PUBLISHER 26
   Developing design sense ....PUBLISHER 27
Designing a Publication ....PUBLISHER 28
   Recognizing bad design ....PUBLISHER 29
Creating a Publication with the Task Pane ....PUBLISHER 30
   Publication Gallery options ....PUBLISHER 31
Replacing Text ....PUBLISHER 32
   Resizing a frame ....PUBLISHER 33
Adding a Graphic Image ....PUBLISHER 34
Adding a Sidebar ....PUBLISHER 36
   Using templates ....PUBLISHER 37
Using the Design Gallery ....PUBLISHER 38
Grouping Objects ....PUBLISHER 40
✓ Capstone Project: College Brochure ....PUBLISHER 42
Concepts Review ....PUBLISHER 44

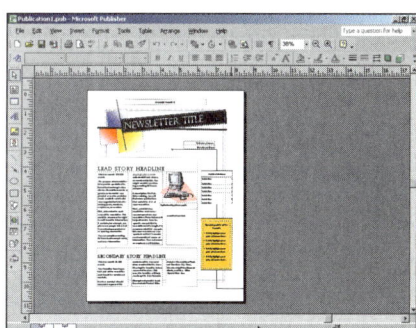

IX

Contents

Skills Review ....PUBLISHER 45
Independent Challenges ....PUBLISHER 46
Visual Workshop ....PUBLISHER 48

Working with Text — PUBLISHER 49

Using Layout Guides ....PUBLISHER 50
   Understanding mirrored layout guides ....PUBLISHER 51
Using Ruler Guides ....PUBLISHER 52
   Choosing measurement tools ....PUBLISHER 53
Formatting a Text Box ....PUBLISHER 54
   Making use of margins ....PUBLISHER 55
Adding Bullets and Numbering ....PUBLISHER 56
Checking Spelling ....PUBLISHER 58
Modifying a Smart Object ....PUBLISHER 60
   Nudging an object ....PUBLISHER 61
Painting Formats ....PUBLISHER 62
   Creative deletion ....PUBLISHER 63
Adding a Table ....PUBLISHER 64
   Using AutoFormat ....PUBLISHER 65
Capstone Project: College Brochure ....PUBLISHER 66
Concepts Review ....PUBLISHER 68
Skills Review ....PUBLISHER 69
Independent Challenges ....PUBLISHER 70
Visual Workshop ....PUBLISHER 74

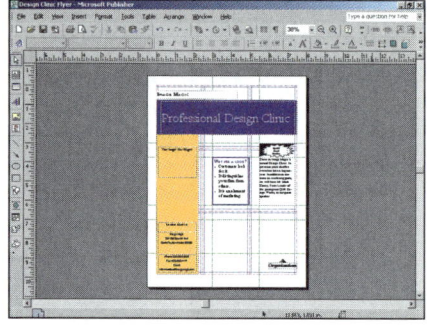

Working with Art — PUBLISHER 75

Inserting and Resizing Clip Art.....................................PUBLISHER 76
   Browsing the Design Gallery Live ....PUBLISHER 77
Copying and Moving an Object ....PUBLISHER 78
   Using the Office Clipboard ....PUBLISHER 79
Cropping an Image ....PUBLISHER 80
   Cropping as creative deletion ....PUBLISHER 81
Aligning and Grouping Images ....PUBLISHER 82
   Scanning artwork ....PUBLISHER 83
Layering Objects ....PUBLISHER 84
   Using the Bring Forward and
   Send Backward commands......................................PUBLISHER 85
Rotating Art ....PUBLISHER 86
   Using the Measurement toolbar ....PUBLISHER 87
Using Drawing Tools ....PUBLISHER 88
   Drawing perfect shapes and lines ....PUBLISHER 89
Fill Drawn Shapes ....PUBLISHER 90
Capstone Project: Flower Show Web Page ....PUBLISHER 92
Concepts Review ....PUBLISHER 94
Skills Review ....PUBLISHER 95
Independent Challenges ....PUBLISHER 96
Visual Workshop ....PUBLISHER 98

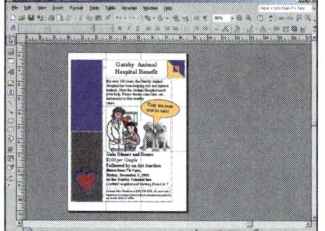

Enhancing a Publication — PUBLISHER 99

Defining Styles	PUBLISHER 100
Choosing fonts	PUBLISHER 101
Modifying and Applying a Style	PUBLISHER 102
Adjusting spaces between characters	PUBLISHER 103
Changing a Format into a Style	PUBLISHER 104
Horizontal text alignment	PUBLISHER 105
Creating Columns	PUBLISHER 106
Manually creating multiple columns	PUBLISHER 107
Adjusting Text Overflows	PUBLISHER 108
Adding Continued on/from Notices	PUBLISHER 110
Changing the style of continued notices	PUBLISHER 110
Adding Drop Caps	PUBLISHER 112
Font schemes	PUBLISHER 112
Creating Reversed Text	PUBLISHER 114
Attracting a reader's attention	PUBLISHER 115
Capstone Project: Solar System Newsletter	PUBLISHER 116
Concepts Review	PUBLISHER 118
Skills Review	PUBLISHER 119
Independent Challenges	PUBLISHER 121
Visual Workshop	PUBLISHER 124

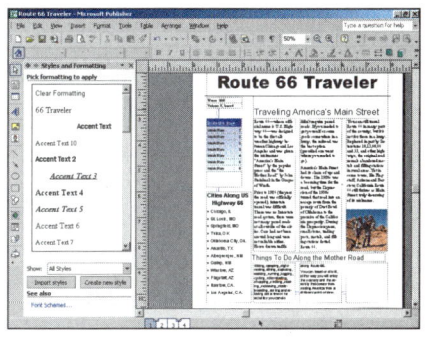

Improving a Publication — PUBLISHER 125

Critiquing a Publication	PUBLISHER 126
Using diplomacy	PUBLISHER 127
Strengthening a Masthead	PUBLISHER 128
Examine the components	PUBLISHER 129
Rearranging Elements	PUBLISHER 130
Overcoming the fear of white space	PUBLISHER 131
Modifying Objects	PUBLISHER 132
Refining a Page	PUBLISHER 134
Working with advertisements	PUBLISHER 135
Experimenting with Design Elements	PUBLISHER 136
Using contrast to add emphasis	PUBLISHER 137
Capstone Projects: Flower Shop Flyer	PUBLISHER 138
Concepts Review	PUBLISHER 140
Skills Review	PUBLISHER 141
Independent Challenges	PUBLISHER 142
Visual Workshop	PUBLISHER 144

Working with Multiple Pages — PUBLISHER 145

Adding Pages	PUBLISHER 146
Printing multi-page documents	PUBLISHER 147
Deleting Pages	PUBLISHER 148
Saving objects on a page	PUBLISHER 149
Working with a Master Page	PUBLISHER 150
Changing from double to single Master Pages	PUBLISHER 150

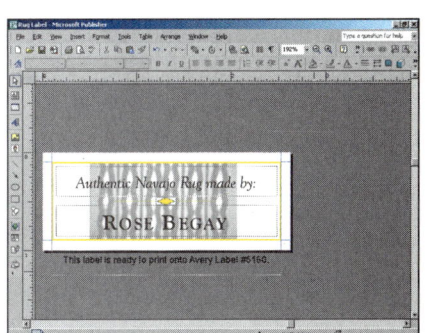

XI

Contents

Creating a Header and Footer	PUBLISHER 152
Adding Page Numbers	PUBLISHER 154
Editing a Story	PUBLISHER 156
Copyfitting text	PUBLISHER 156
Modifying a Table of Contents	PUBLISHER 158
Creating Labels	PUBLISHER 160
Capstone Project: Jewelry Tools Catalog	PUBLISHER 162
Concepts Review	PUBLISHER 164
Skills Review	PUBLISHER 165
Independent Challenges	PUBLISHER 166
Visual Workshop	PUBLISHER 168

Using Special Features — PUBLISHER 169

Adding Border Art	PUBLISHER 170
Creating custom BorderArt	PUBLISHER 170
Designing WordArt	PUBLISHER 172
Wrapping Text Around an Object	PUBLISHER 174
Editing shapes for text wrapping	PUBLISHER 174
Rotating a Text Box	PUBLISHER 176
Understanding Mail Merge	PUBLISHER 178
Catching costly errors	PUBLISHER 179
Creating a Mail Merge	PUBLISHER 180
Preparing for Commercial Printing	PUBLISHER 182
Using the Pack and Go Wizard	PUBLISHER 184
Taking files to another computer	PUBLISHER 184
Capstone Project: Automotive Gift Certificate	PUBLISHER 186
Concepts Review	PUBLISHER 188
Skills Review	PUBLISHER 189
Independent Challenges	PUBLISHER 190
Visual Workshop	PUBLISHER 192

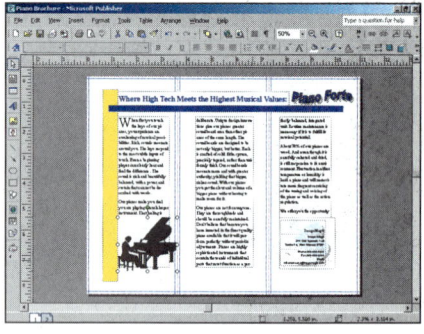

Working Efficiently — PUBLISHER 193

Integrating with Office Products	PUBLISHER 194
Importing a Word Document	PUBLISHER 196
Using AutoCorrect	PUBLISHER 198
Using tools wisely	PUBLISHER 199
Recording Images	PUBLISHER 200
Studying color	PUBLISHER 201
Embedding and Linking Objects	PUBLISHER 202
Using Design Checker	PUBLISHER 204
Working with Design Checker	PUBLISHER 205
Understanding Speech Recognition	PUBLISHER 206
Capstone Project: Dinner Invitation	PUBLISHER 208
Concepts Review	PUBLISHER 210
Skills Review	PUBLISHER 212
Independent Challenges	PUBLISHER 213
Visual Workshop	PUBLISHER 216

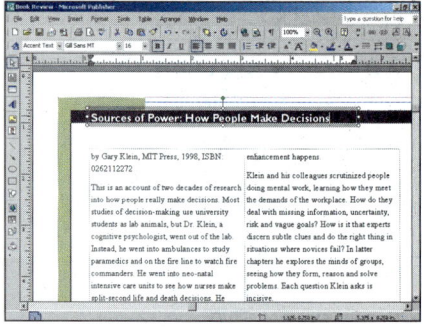

Working on the Web — PUBLISHER 217

Planning a Web Site ....PUBLISHER 218
   Planning for customer service ....PUBLISHER 219
Designing a Web Site ....PUBLISHER 220
Creating a Web Site ....PUBLISHER 222
Adding Hyperlinks ....PUBLISHER 224
   Adding a hyperlink to an e-mail address ....PUBLISHER 225
Modifying a Background ....PUBLISHER 226
   Creating a custom color scheme ....PUBLISHER 226
Testing a Web Site ....PUBLISHER 228
Publishing a Web Site ....PUBLISHER 230
   Adding design elements ....PUBLISHER 230
   Increasing Web site traffic ....PUBLISHER 231
Converting a Publication into a Web Site ....PUBLISHER 232
   Converting a Web site to a print publication ..PUBLISHER 233
Capstone Project: Personal Web Site ....PUBLISHER 234
Concepts Review ....PUBLISHER 236
Skills Review ....PUBLISHER 237
Independent Challenges ....PUBLISHER 238
Visual Workshop ....PUBLISHER 240

Project Files List — PUBLISHER 241
Glossary — PUBLISHER 245
Index — PUBLISHER 250

XIII

Read This Before You Begin

What are Project Files?

To complete many of the units in this book, you need to use Project Files. Your instructor will either provide you with a copy of the Project Files or ask you to make your own copy. Detailed instructions on how to organize your files, as well as a complete listing of all the files you'll need and will create, can be found in the back of the book (look for the yellow pages) in the Project Files List.

Personal Information Sets

Publisher uses **Personal Information Sets** to insert information, such as name, address, and e-mail, into publications. This feature allows you to quickly personalize a publication, and gives you a choice of four options—two business sets, a home/family set, and one for another organization. Throughout the lessons and exercises in this book you will be asked to use Personal Information Sets to enter appropriate information. Where it is relevant to the case scenario, we have provided you with the following steps:

In the Personal Information Set Wizard (click **Edit** on the menu bar, then click **Personal Information** if necessary), click **Secondary Business** if necessary, type **Mike Mendoza** in the Name text box, type **Account Executive** in the Job or position title text box, type **Image Magic** in the Address text box, press **[Enter]**, type **214 Old Spanish Trail**, press **[Enter]**, type **Santa Fe, New Mexico 87501**, in the Phone/fax/e-mail text box type **Phone 505-555-5555**, press **[Enter]**, type **Fax: 505-555-4444**, press **[Enter]**, type **E-mail: mikemendoza@imagemagic.com**, type **Image Magic** in the Organization name text box, type **Your Image! Our Magic!** in the Tag line or motto text box, click the **Include color scheme check box**, click the **Color Schemes list arrow**, click **Bluebird**, then click **Update**.

Depending on whether you are working on your own PC or in a lab, this step may not be necessary to repeat each time. We instruct you to use the Secondary Business Personal Information Set so as to not write over any information that may be inserted by your school, company, or for your personal use.

In the end-of-unit material you have the options of using Personal Information Sets for entering your own information, using Mike Mendoza's information as listed above, or making up a character and company as you choose.

Publisher 2002

Getting
Started with Microsoft Publisher 2002

Objectives

- ▶ Define publication software
- ▶ Start Publisher 2002
- ▶ View the Publisher window
- ▶ Open and save a publication
- ▶ Enter text in a text box
- ▶ View and print a publication
- ▶ Get Help and change Personal Information
- ▶ Close a publication and exit Publisher
- ▶ Capstone Project: Study Abroad Flyer

Microsoft Publisher 2002 is a popular desktop publishing program that uses the Windows operating system. In this unit, you will learn how to start Publisher and use elements found in the Publisher window and menus. You will also learn how to open and save existing files, enter text in a publication, view and print a publication, use the extensive Help system, and change Personal Information. Mike Mendoza is an account executive at Image Magic, a small advertising agency. Mike will use Publisher to create a flyer announcing the location of the agency's new office. Image Magic wants this flyer to reflect the company's color palette, have their logo, and express their excitement about the new office.

Defining Publication Software

Publisher is a **desktop publishing program**, a software program that lets you combine text and graphics, as well as worksheets and charts created in other programs, to produce typeset-quality documents for output on a computer printer, or for commercial printing. A document created in Publisher is called a **publication**. Table A-1 contains examples of the types of publications you can create. Mike enjoys using Publisher because he can generate a variety of professional-looking custom publications quickly and easily. The benefits of using Publisher include the ability to:

► Create professional publications
Publisher comes with a **Publication Gallery**, a collection of often used publications that let you choose the type of publication you want to develop, help you decide on its appearance, then suggest text and graphic image placement to complete the publication. The New Publication task pane and Publication Gallery create complete publications that you can modify easily to meet specific needs.

► Use clip art
Artwork not only makes any publication appear more vibrant and interesting, but also helps to explain your ideas with visual images. Publisher comes with more than 15,000 pieces of artwork that can be incorporated into publications. In addition, other illustrations, sound files, video clips, and photographs can be imported into the **Office Collections**, which is the artwork library that all Office applications share.

► Create logos
Most organizations use a recognizable symbol, shape, color, or combination of these to attach to their name. This distinctive shape, called a **logo**, can be created using Publisher's Design Sets, or by designing your own artwork and text. Figure A-1 illustrates a sample flyer created in Publisher that contains a logo formed by combining clip art and text.

► Make your work look consistent
Publisher has many tools to help you create consistent publications that have similar design elements. You can use **design sets** to create different types of stylized publications. When creating work from scratch, you might, for example, want to have an information box in the lower-left corner on the back page of all Image Magic brochures. Using rulers and layout guides, you can create grids to help position graphics and text on a page. You can also save a publication as a **template**, a specially formatted publication with placeholder text that serves as a master for other, similar publications.

► Work with multiple pages
Publisher makes it easy to work with multi-page publications. Pages can be added, deleted, and moved easily within a publication. Text that flows from one page to another can be connected with continued on and continued from notices.

► Emphasize special text
Even great writing can seem boring if all the text looks the same. Using varied text styles to express different meanings and convey messages can add interest. You can use headlines to grab readers and lead them to stories of specific significance. You can use a sidebar to make a short statement more noticeable, or a pull quote to make an important story stand out and grab a reader's attention. Altering the appearance of text by making it bold, italics, or underlined can emphasize or lessen the significance of text.

► Publish to the Internet
Publisher can be used to create Web sites. Menus, design elements, and commands specifically designed for **Web sites** make it easy to include links and graphics. Page backgrounds and animated GIFs add color and motion to your pages. A **Web Publishing Wizard** helps you make your Web site available to a local network drive, an intranet, or an Internet Service Provider for worldwide viewing.

FIGURE A-1: Sample flyer

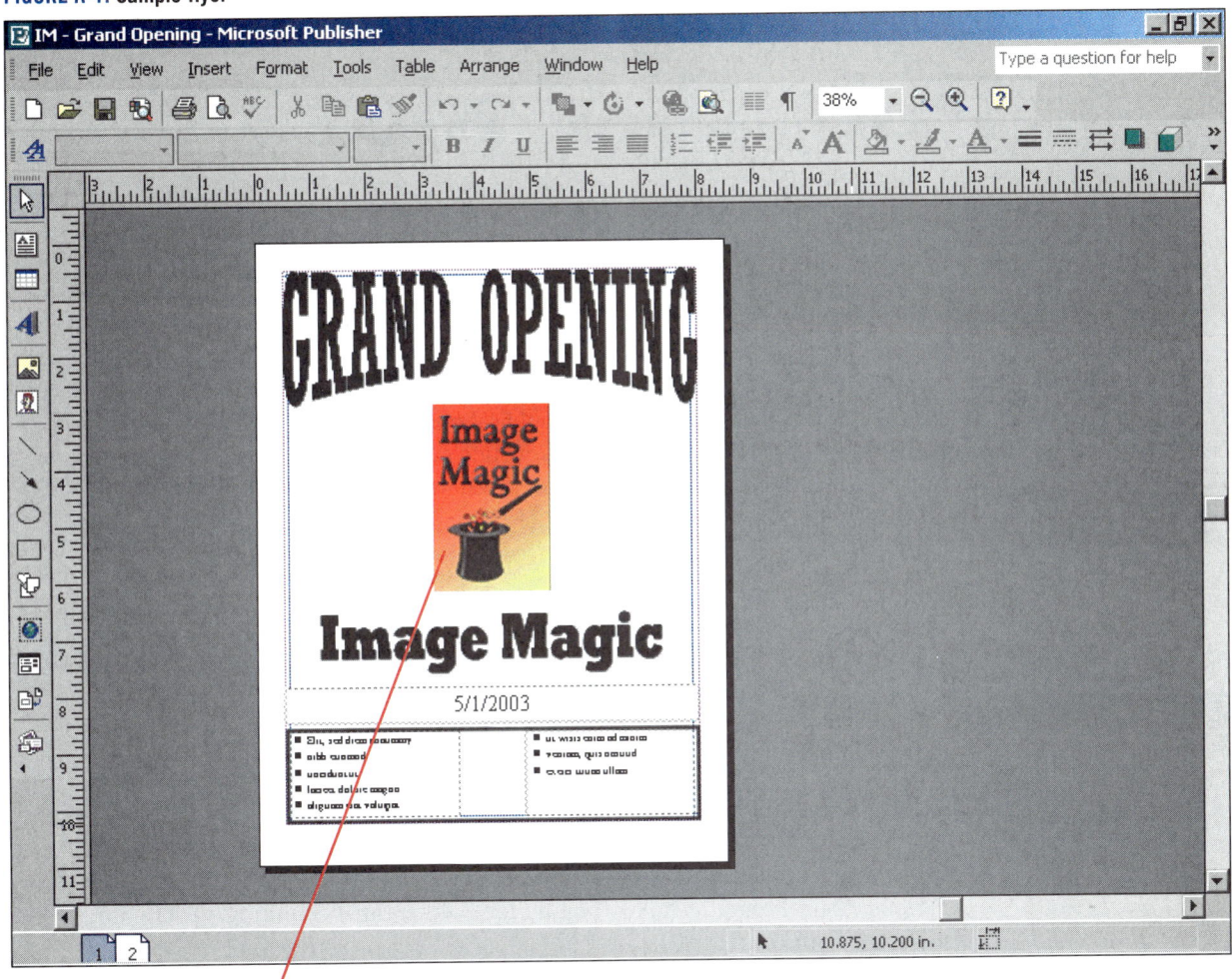

Logo consists of text and graphic image

TABLE A-1: Common publications

publication type	example
Informational	Brochures, signs, calendars, forms
Periodical	Newsletters, catalogs
Promotional	Advertisements, flyers, press releases
Stationery	Letterhead, labels, business cards, envelopes, postcards, invitations
Specialty	Banners, airplanes, origami, resumes, award certificates, gift certificates

GETTING STARTED WITH MICROSOFT PUBLISHER 2002 PUBLISHER 3

Starting Publisher 2002

To start Publisher, you click the Start button on the taskbar to access the Start menu. A slightly different procedure might be required for computers on a network, and those that use utility programs to enhance Windows. If you need assistance, ask your instructor or technical support person for help. When you start Publisher, the program displays a list of publication types and file options on the left, and samples of publication types on the right. You can use the **New Publication task pane** on the left side of the screen to select a publication type. The **task pane** is an area of the Publisher window that is used to organize design templates, color schemes, font schemes, and other layout tools in a visual gallery, which appears alongside your publications. The task pane lets you select a publication by design, open a new publication, or open an existing publication. The selected publication type displays available samples on the right side of the screen in the Publication Gallery. Before he can create his publication, Mike must start Publisher and open a new document.

1. **Locate the Start button** 🏁Start **on the taskbar**
   The Start button is on the left side of the taskbar and is used to start programs on your computer.

   QuickTip
   Microsoft Publisher 2002 can be used with versions of Windows 98 or higher.

2. **Click** 🏁Start
   Microsoft Publisher is located in the Programs group, located near the top of the Start menu.

3. **Point to Programs**
   All of the programs on your computer, including Microsoft Publisher, can be found in this area of the Start menu. You can see the Microsoft Publisher icon 📘 and the icons of other programs. Your Programs menu might look different, depending which programs are installed on your computer.

   Trouble?
   If you don't see the Microsoft Publisher icon, look in a folder called Microsoft Office or Office 2002, or ask your instructor or technical support person for help.

4. **Click the Microsoft Publisher program icon** 📘, **as shown in Figure A-2**
   Publisher opens and the New Publication task pane appears on the left side of the screen. The Quick Publications task pane appears on the right side of the screen in the Publication Gallery.

5. **Position** ↖ **over Blank Publication in the New section of the task pane, but do not click**
   The pointer turns to 👆 when positioned over Blank Publication, as shown in Figure A-3. Because you have not yet clicked on Blank Publication, the Quick Publications samples are still visible.

6. **Click Blank Publication in the New section of the task pane**
   A blank full-page publication appears on the screen.

▶ PUBLISHER 4 GETTING STARTED WITH MICROSOFT PUBLISHER 2002

FIGURE A-2: Start menu and Programs menu

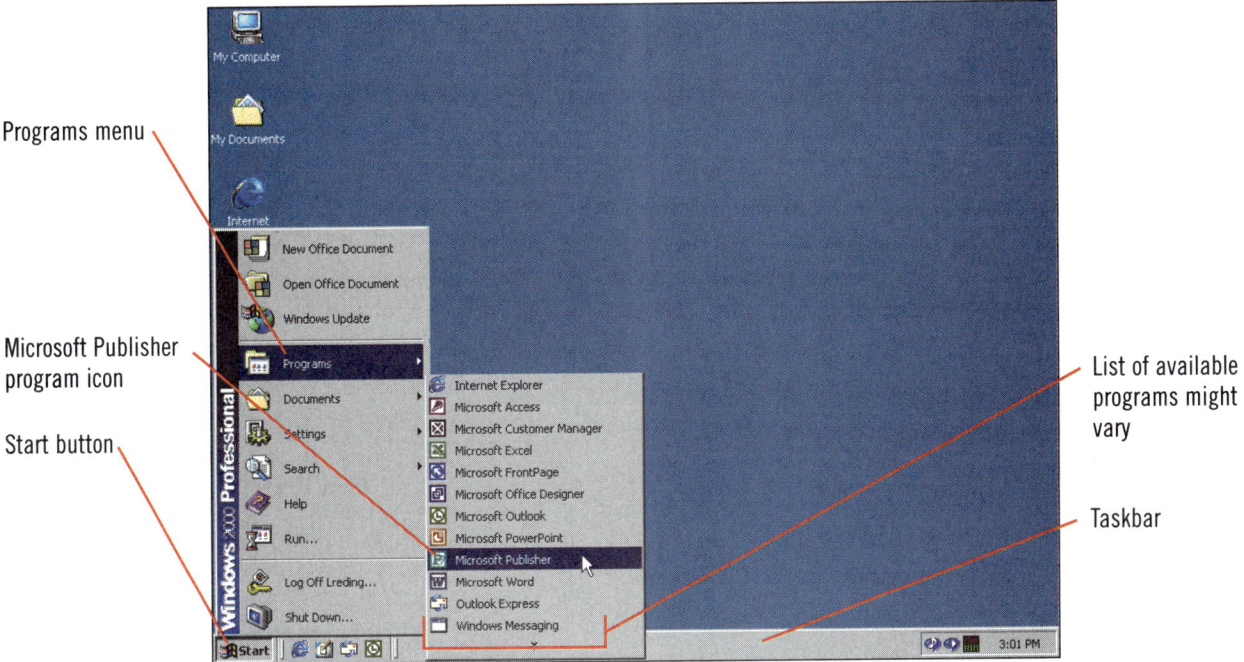

Programs menu

Microsoft Publisher program icon

Start button

List of available programs might vary

Taskbar

FIGURE A-3: Pointing to Blank Publication

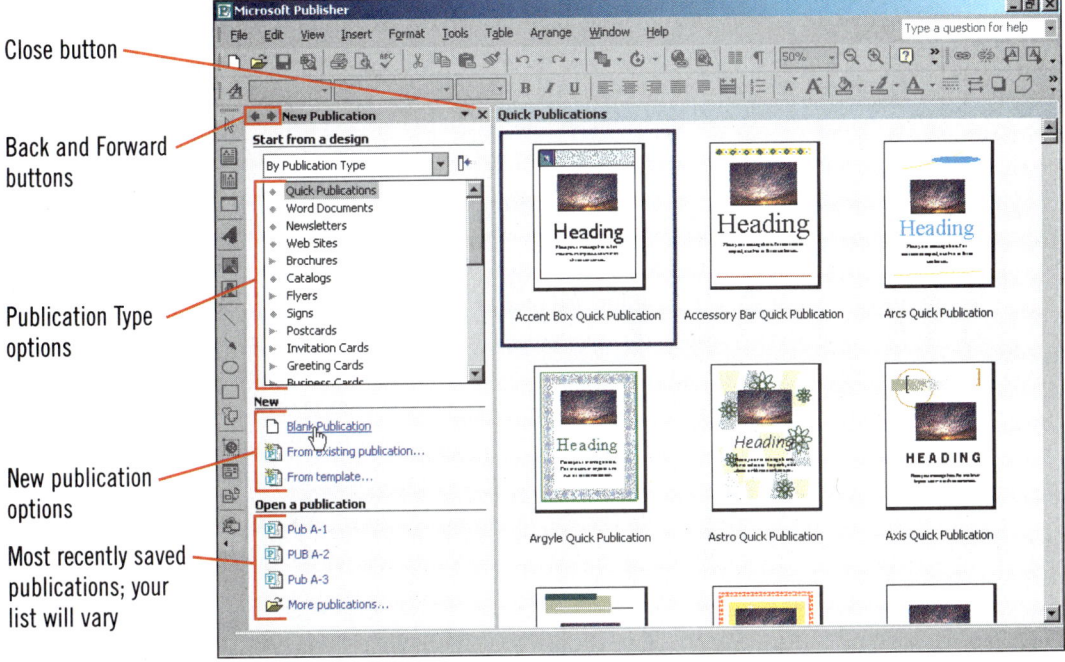

Close button

Back and Forward buttons

Publication Type options

New publication options

Most recently saved publications; your list will vary

Using the New Publication task pane

When you first open Publisher, the New Publication task pane appears on the left side of the screen. It has three sections: Start from a design, New, and Open a publication. The Start from a design section guides you through the creation of a new publication using either a publication type, a design set, or different kinds of blank publications. The New section allows you to create new publications, and the Open a publication section allows you to open one of the three most recently used publications, or to search for more publications. To close the task pane, click the Close button in the upper-right corner of the task pane. To open the task pane, click View on the menu bar, then click Task Pane.

GETTING STARTED WITH MICROSOFT PUBLISHER 2002   PUBLISHER 5

Viewing the Publisher Window

The area where a new or existing publication appears is called the **workspace**, which includes both the publication page and the scratch area. The workspace is where you actually work on a publication, and each page within a publication is viewed here. The workspace is bordered above and on the left by horizontal and vertical rulers that help you position text and graphics in your publications. The workspace is also bordered by horizontal and vertical scroll bars that allow you to view different areas of the workspace. Mike takes some time to familiarize himself with the Publisher workspace and its elements before he works on the flyer. Compare the descriptions below to Figure A-4.

Details

▶ The **title bar** is at the top of the window, and displays the program name (Microsoft Publisher) and the filename of the open publication. In Figure A-4, the file name is Publication1, the default, because the file has not yet been named and saved. The title bar also contains a Control menu box, a Close button, and resizing buttons.

▶ The **menu bar** contains menus that list commands, organized in categories such as View and Format. As with all Windows programs, you can choose a menu command by clicking it with the mouse, or by pressing [Alt] plus the underlined letter in the menu name. A menu containing a down arrow at its lower edge contains additional commands. As you use Publisher, unused commands will be hidden, and only the frequently used commands will appear on the menu. To see these hidden commands, click the down arrow, or wait several seconds and the commands will appear. Once you select a previously hidden command, it will appear on the menu going forward. The Publisher Help feature can also be accessed by typing a question in the box on the right of the menu bar.

▶ The **toolbars** contain buttons for frequently used Publisher commands. The **Standard toolbar** is located just below the menu bar and contains buttons for the most frequently used Publisher features. Place the pointer over each button to display the ScreenTip, a label that describes what each button does. To select a button, click it with the left mouse button. The face of any button has a graphic representation of its function; for instance, the Print button has a printer on its face. The **Objects toolbar** is on the left side of the screen next to the vertical ruler, and contains buttons used to insert the most frequently used objects (text boxes, clip art, geometric shapes, etc.) into Publications. The **Formatting toolbar** appears just above the horizontal ruler and contains buttons for often used text formatting commands such as bold, italics, or underlining. Toolbars can be opened or closed by clicking View on the menu bar, pointing to Toolbars, and clicking to select or deselect the particular toolbar.

▶ **Rulers** let you precisely measure the size of objects, as well as place objects in exact locations on a page. They can be moved from the edge of the workspace to more convenient positions. Your rulers may have different beginning and ending numbers, depending on the size of your monitor, the resolution of your display, and the positioning of the page on the workspace. The units of measurement displayed in rulers can be changed to show inches, centimeters, picas, or points.

▶ The workspace contains the currently displayed page and the scratch area.

▶ The **status bar** is located at the bottom of the Publisher window. On the left side of the status bar are **page navigation icons**, which show you the number of pages in a publication, and are used to navigate from page to page. Click the icon for the page you want to view. In a multi-page publication, an icon is displayed for each page; the icon for the current page appears in light blue. The right side of the status bar shows the object status, which includes the size and position of selected objects.

▶ The **scratch area** is the gray area that surrounds the publication page, and can be used to store objects.

▶ **PUBLISHER 6   GETTING STARTED WITH MICROSOFT PUBLISHER 2002**

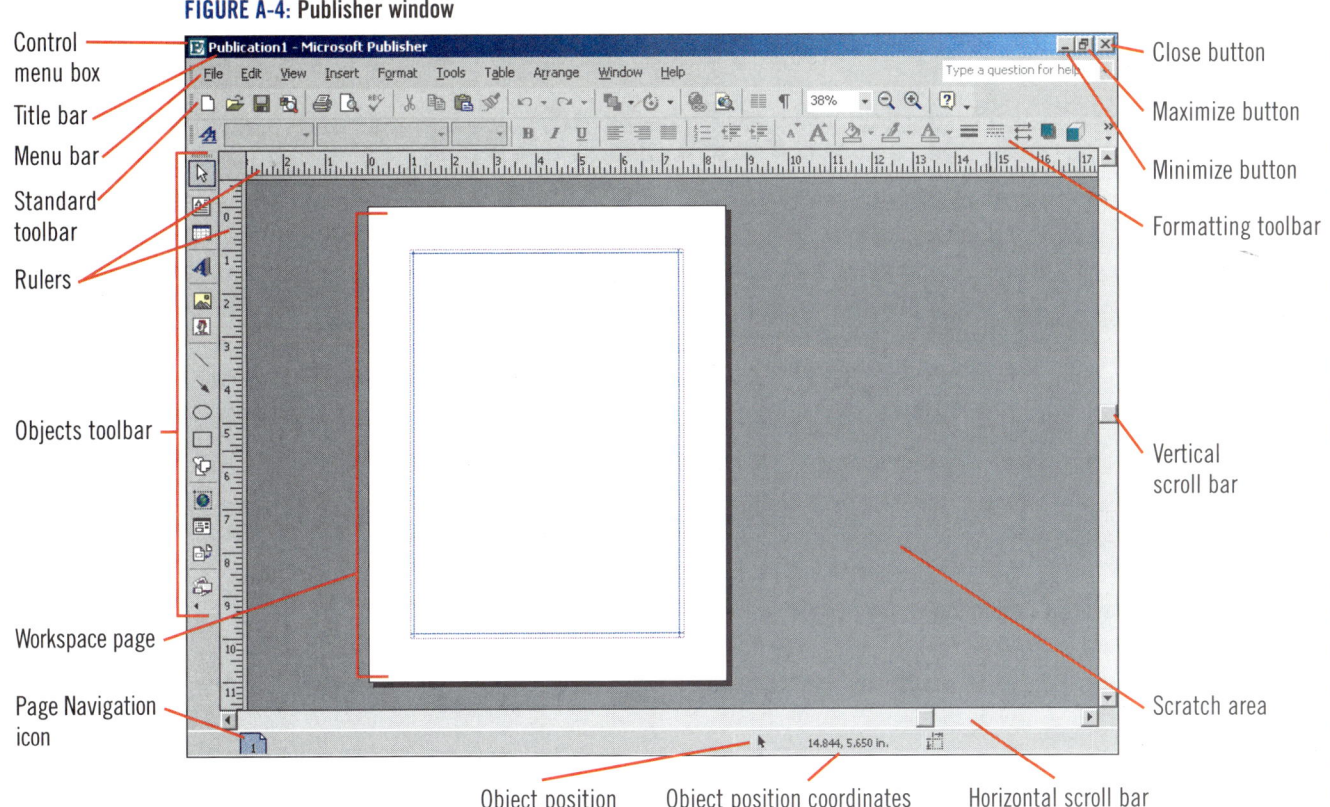

FIGURE A-4: Publisher window

Using task panes

In addition to the New Publication task pane, you will see a variety of task panes on either the left or right side of the screen. The task panes feature can be turned on or off from the View menu on the menu bar, and can be moved to different locations on the screen by clicking and dragging the title bar to a new location. There are task panes for new publications, color schemes, font schemes, publication designs, styles and formatting, mail merge, and for various types of publications. You can move back and forth between open task panes by clicking the Forward or Back buttons in the upper-left corner of the task pane window. You can see more task pane options by clicking the Other Task Panes list arrow in the task pane title bar. You can also close the task pane by clicking the Close button in the upper-right corner of the task pane.

GETTING STARTED WITH MICROSOFT PUBLISHER 2002   PUBLISHER 7

Opening and Saving a Publication

Often a project is completed in stages: you start working on a publication, save it, and then stop to do other work or take a break. Later, you open the publication and resume working on it. Sometimes you will open a file and save it under another name because it is more efficient to create a new publication by modifying one that already exists. This approach saves you from having to re-create existing information, and preserves the designs already chosen. Throughout this book, you will be instructed to open a file from the drive and folder where your Project Files are stored, use the Save As command to create a copy of the file with a new name, then modify the new file by following the lesson steps. Saving the files with new names keeps your original Project Files intact in case you have to start the lesson over again, or you wish to repeat an exercise.

 Mike started the Image Magic flyer and is ready to finish it. He opens the file, then uses the Save As command to create a copy of the file with a new name.

QuickTip
If you click the Views list arrow, then select Preview, the Preview pane shows a reduced image of the selected publication.

1. **Click the Open button 📂 on the Standard toolbar**
   The Open Publication dialog box opens. A dialog box is a window that opens when more information is needed to carry out a command. A list of the available folders and publications appears.

2. **Click the Look in list arrow**
   A list of the available drives appears. The files that you need for these lessons are located where your Project Files are stored.

3. **Click the drive and folder where your Project Files are located**
   A list of the Project Files appears, as shown in Figure A-5.

Trouble?
If you receive a message that the printer cannot be initialized, click OK to change to your default printer.

4. **Click the file PUB A-1, then click Open**
   The file PUB A-1 opens. You could also double-click the filename in the Open Publication dialog box to open the file. You want to save a copy of the file with a new name.

5. **Click File on the menu bar, then click Save As**
   The Save As dialog box opens.

6. **Make sure that the drive and folder where your Project Files are stored appear in the Save in list box**
   You should save all your files in the drive and folder where your Project Files are stored, unless instructed otherwise.

7. **Select the current filename in the File name text box if necessary, then type Grand Opening Flyer**
   See Figure A-6.

QuickTip
Use the Save As command to create a new publication from an existing one. Use the Save command to store any changes made to an existing file on your disk.

8. **Click Save**
   The Save As dialog box closes, the file PUB A-1 closes, and a duplicate file named Grand Opening Flyer is now open, as shown in Figure A-7. Changes made to Grand Opening Flyer will not be reflected in the file PUB A-1. To save the publication in the future, you can click File on the menu bar, then click Save, or click the Save button 💾 on the Standard toolbar.

FIGURE A-5: Open Publication dialog box

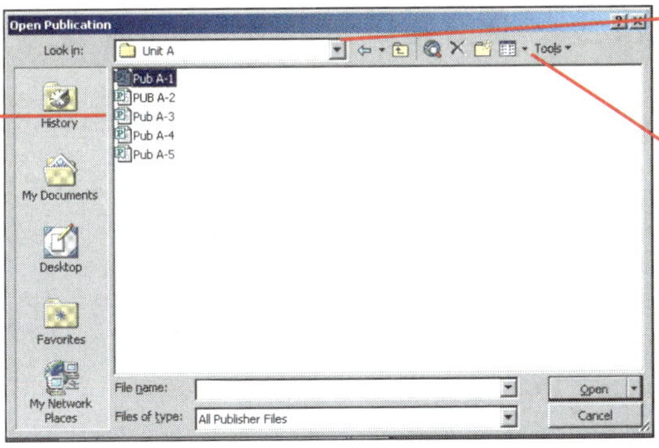

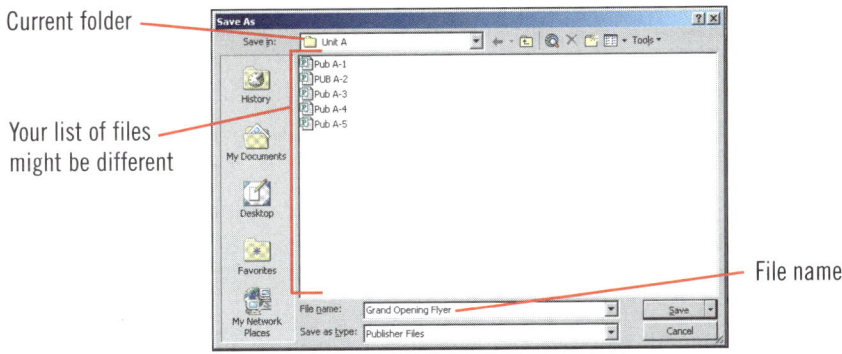

- Look in list arrow
- Available files and folders display here; yours may be different
- Views list arrow

FIGURE A-6: Save As dialog box

- Current folder
- Your list of files might be different
- File name

FIGURE A-7: Grand Opening Flyer publication

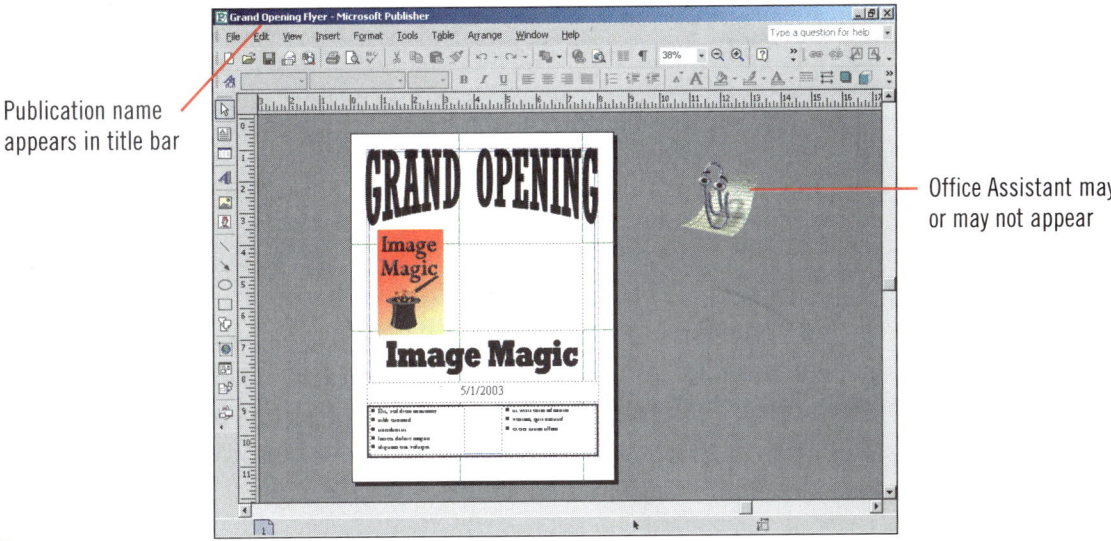

- Publication name appears in title bar
- Office Assistant may or may not appear

Using dialog box views

You may notice that the information in the Open and Save As dialog boxes varies depending on the view selected. There are eight views: Large Icons, Small Icons, List, Details, Properties, Preview, Thumbnails, and WebView. The Large and Small Icon Views show the file type, and the name of the file. The List View displays the names of the contents of a given folder. The Details View displays the same information as the List View, but includes the size, the last date and time the file was saved, and the file type. The Properties View displays detailed information on the file size and when it was modified (when available). The Preview View displays an image of the file, although previews are not always available. The Thumbnail View shows the file type with the filename underneath. To select a different view, click the Views list arrow in a dialog box, then click the view you want.

GETTING STARTED WITH MICROSOFT PUBLISHER 2002

Entering Text in a Text Box

In word processing, text is entered directly on a page and is the main element of a document. In desktop publishing, text is only a part of a publication, since graphic objects add significantly to the layout. Text in a publication must be entered into a text box. A **text box** is an object into which text is typed so it can be easily resized and repositioned in relation to the graphic images and other elements on a page. **Point size** is the unit of measurement for fonts, and the space between paragraphs and text characters. There are 72 points in each inch. Because stories are often continued onto another page, text boxes can even be connected to other text boxes. You can select a text box by clicking anywhere within it. When selected, small hollow circles called **handles** appear at eight points around its perimeter. This publication also includes **placeholders**, which are reminders of where information should be inserted. **Ruler guides** are green horizontal and vertical lines that appear on the screen to help you position objects on a page, but do not print in the publication. Mike creates some text boxes and enters additional text in the flyer.

1. Click the **Text Box button** on the Objects toolbar

   The pointer changes to +. You want to create a rectangular text box that is slightly shorter than the Image Magic logo and located to its right. You can use the object coordinates (displayed in inches on the status bar) to size and position the text box. Ruler guides have been placed in the publication to help you line up the text box.

2. Position + so that the object position coordinates are **3.500, 4.000 in.**, press and hold the **left mouse button**, drag + to create a rectangle that has object size coordinates of **4.000 × 2.750 in.**, then release the mouse button

   As you drag the text box, the coordinates on the status bar change to display the object size and the position of the pointer in the workspace. When the mouse button is released, the text box appears as a selected object surrounded by handles, with the insertion point blinking in the upper-left corner, as shown in Figure A-8. Additional buttons appear on the Standard and Formatting toolbars when the text box is selected. This means that Publisher is ready for you to type text, and has made the relevant tools available to you. Before typing the text, however, you want to make the text readable on the screen.

   QuickTip
   You can zoom in and out of a page using the View menu, the Zoom In and Zoom Out buttons on the Standard toolbar, or the [F9] keyboard shortcut.

3. Press [F9], type **We are excited about our new office space. Here, we will offer expanded services in a professional atmosphere. Please join us at our Grand Opening celebration on Friday, August 1, 2003, from 1 to 5 pm.**, press [Enter] twice, type **Our new address is:**, press [Enter], type **214 Old Spanish Trail**, press [Enter], then type **Santa Fe, New Mexico 87501**

   You decide to enlarge the text to make it easier to read.

   Trouble?
   Wavy red lines under typed text indicate words that may be misspelled. Correct any spelling errors you may have typed.

4. Press [Ctrl][A] to select all the text in the box, click the **Font Size list arrow** on the Formatting toolbar, then click **16**

   The font size makes the text stand out and it is more legible. You are finished editing the text box, so you want to deselect it.

5. Click anywhere on the **scratch area** to deselect the text box

   You could also press [Esc] twice to deselect the text box. Compare your screen to Figure A-9. You want to change the zoom level to see as much of the publication as possible.

6. Click the **Zoom list arrow**, then click **Whole Page**

   The magnification adjusts so that the entire page is in view on the screen.

7. Click the **Save button** on the Standard toolbar

   It is a good idea to save your work early and often in the creation process, especially before making significant changes to the publication, or before printing.

PUBLISHER 10 GETTING STARTED WITH MICROSOFT PUBLISHER 2002

FIGURE A-8: Text box in publication

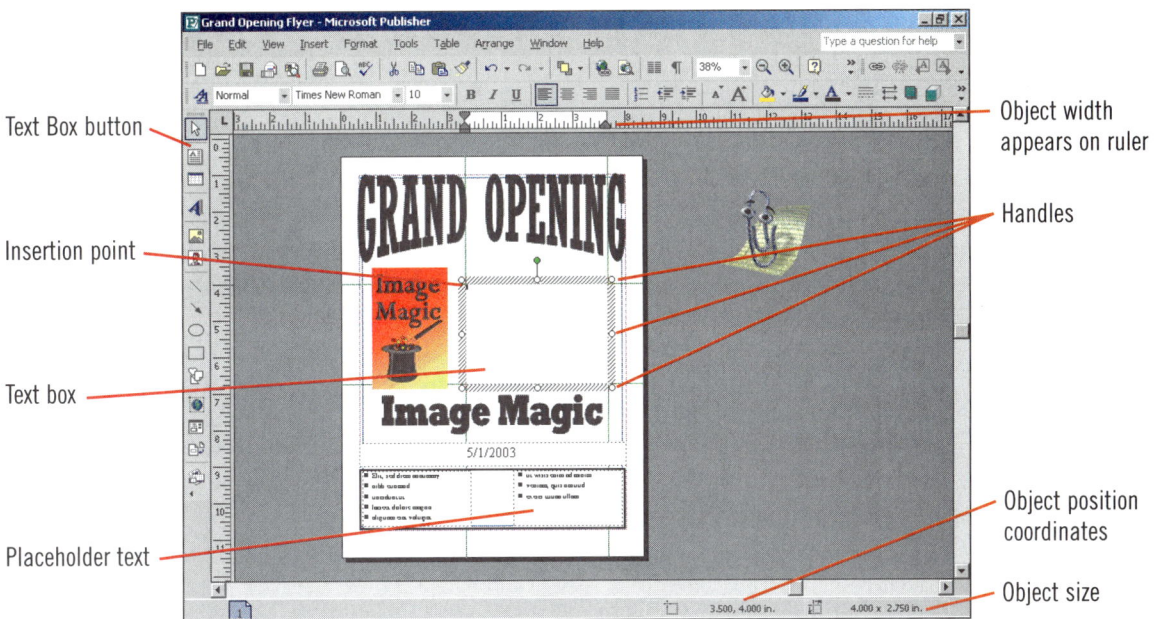

- Text Box button
- Insertion point
- Text box
- Placeholder text
- Object width appears on ruler
- Handles
- Object position coordinates
- Object size

FIGURE A-9: Completed text in text box

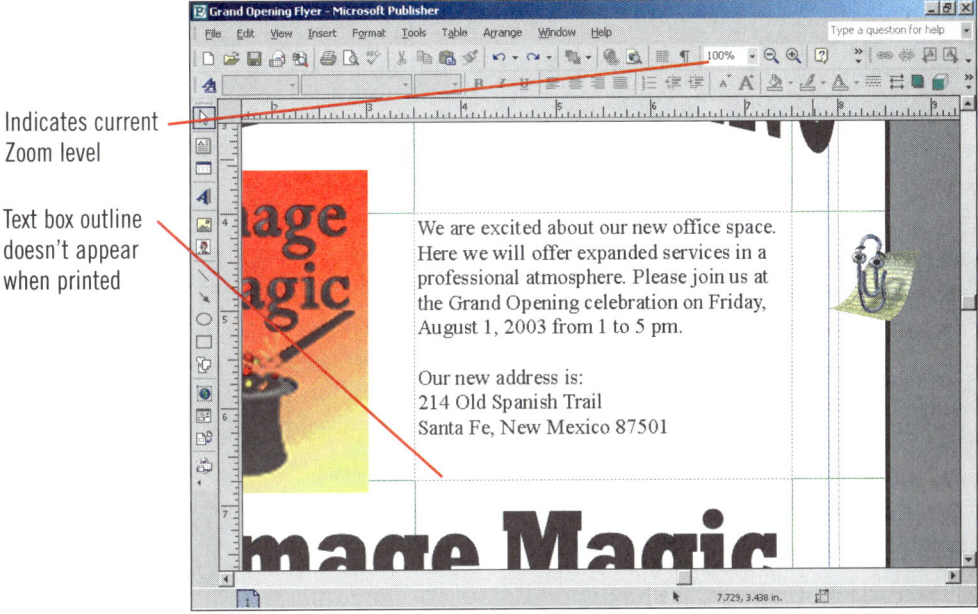

- Indicates current Zoom level
- Text box outline doesn't appear when printed

Understanding objects

Objects are elements such as tables, text boxes, geometric shapes, clip art, and picture frames that can be resized, moved, joined, or organized so that one object appears to be in front of another. In addition, text boxes can be wrapped around other objects. The advantage to using text boxes is that the contents within the box can be easily moved anywhere within a publication. Figure A-10 shows text wrapped around a graphic image.

FIGURE A-10: Text wrapped around a picture

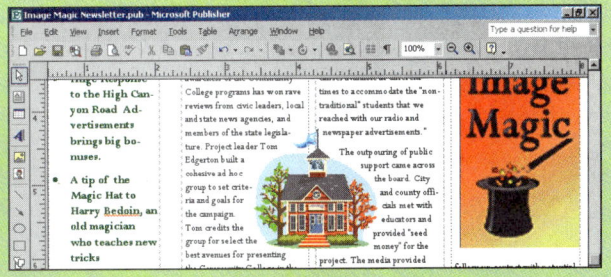

GETTING STARTED WITH MICROSOFT PUBLISHER 2002

Viewing and Printing a Publication

Printing is the conversion of a publication from an electronic form into a paper document. When a publication is completed, you can print it to have a paper copy to reference, file, or send to others. You can also print specific pages from a publication that is not complete so that you can review it or work on it when you are not at a computer. Before you print a publication, you should use the **Print Preview** feature to make sure that it fits on a page and looks the way you want. You cannot make changes to your publication when in Print Preview, but it will allow you to see how it will look when printed. Publisher's Print Preview feature will show your publication in either grayscale or in color, depending upon the type of printer that is selected. Table A-2 provides printing tips. ✍ Mike prints a copy of the Image Magic flyer to show to a coworker.

Trouble?
If a file is sent to print and the printer is off, an error message appears.

1. Make sure the printer is on and contains paper
First you will view the document in Print Preview to check the flyer's overall appearance and see how it will look when it is printed.

2. Click the **Print Preview button** 🔍 on the Standard toolbar
If your printer allows both black and white and color printing, you can change the display from black and white to color to see how it will appear using different printers.

Trouble?
If your selected printer is not a color printer, Print Preview will only appear in grayscale.

3. If necessary, click the **Color/Grayscale button** 🖼 on the Print Preview toolbar to change the display to color
The page appears in color, as shown in Figure A-11. If there were multiple pages, you could preview them individually by clicking the Page Up 🔼 and Page Down buttons 🔽 on the Print Preview toolbar, or see as many as six pages at once by clicking the Multiple Pages button ⊞ on the Print Preview toolbar.

4. Click the **Close Preview button** [Close] on the Print Preview toolbar
Now that you have previewed the publication, you will add your name to it.

5. Click the **Text Box button** 🔤 on the Objects toolbar, position + so that the object position coordinates are **0.500, 8.000 in.**, press and hold the **left mouse button**, drag + to create a rectangular text box that has object size coordinates of **2.000 × 0.400 in.**, release the mouse button, press [F9], then type **your name**
You should always save a publication before printing it.

6. Press [F9], then click the **Save button** 💾 on the Standard toolbar
Now that the publication is saved, you can print it.

QuickTip
You can also print using the Print button 🖨 on the Standard toolbar, but doing so will print all the pages of a publication.

7. Click **File** on the menu bar, then click **Print**
The Print dialog box opens, as shown in Figure A-12. You can use this dialog box to control the number of pages that are printed.

8. Make sure that the **All option button** is selected for print range, and that **1** appears in the Number of copies text box, then click **OK**
Review the publication to see if it printed as expected.

▶ PUBLISHER 12   **GETTING STARTED WITH MICROSOFT PUBLISHER 2002**

FIGURE A-11: Whole page in Print Preview window

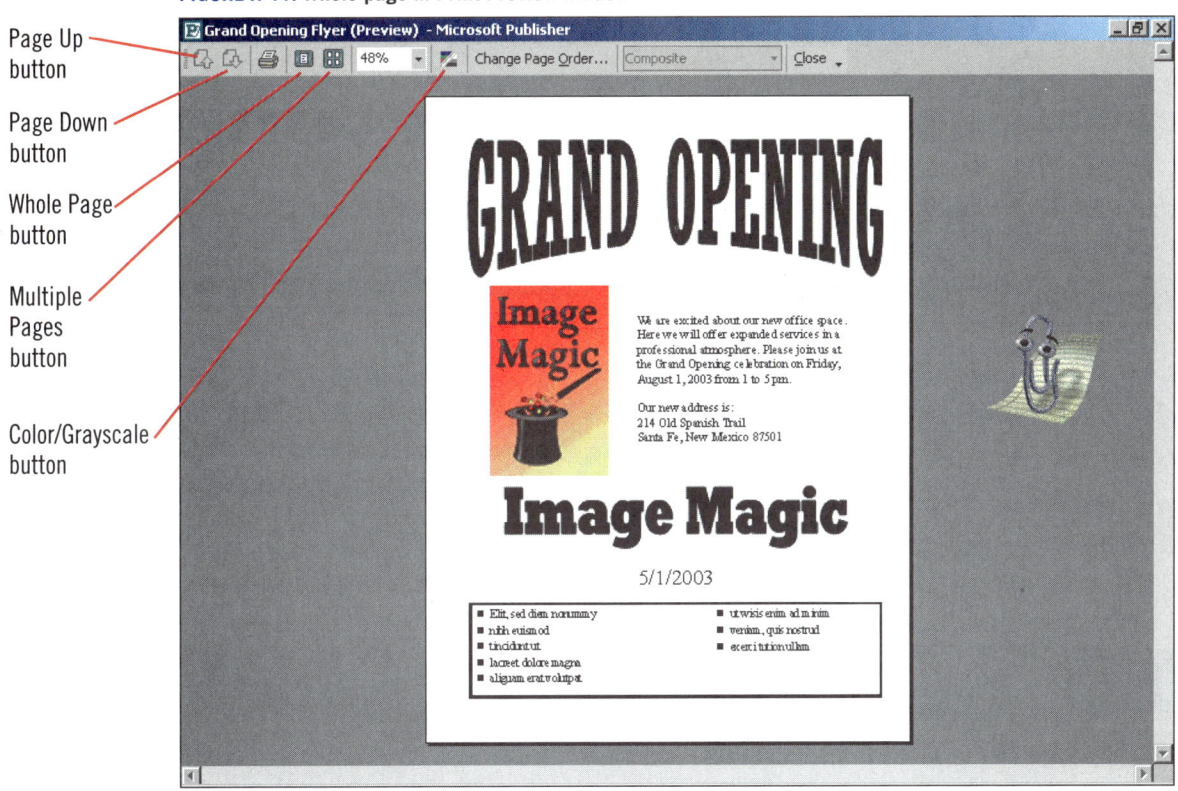

FIGURE A-12: Print dialog box

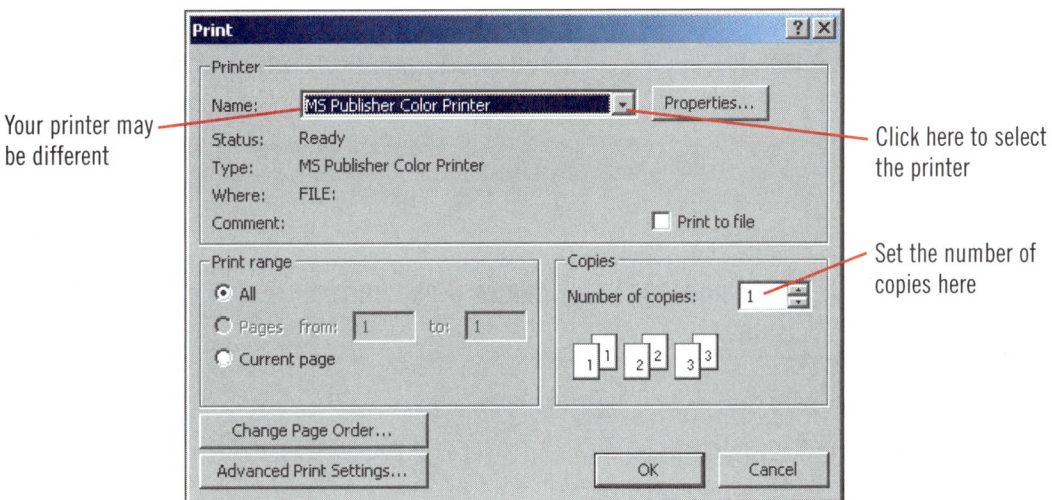

TABLE A-2: Publication printing tips

before you print	recommendation
Check the printer	Make sure that the printer is turned on and online, that it has paper, and that there are no error messages or warning signals
Check the printer selection	In the Printer section of the Print dialog box, select the correct printer from the Name list arrow to make sure that the correct printer is selected

GETTING STARTED WITH MICROSOFT PUBLISHER 2002 PUBLISHER 13

Getting Help and Changing Personal Information

Publisher offers extensive **Help** features that give you immediate access to definitions, explanations, and useful tips. The Help window is displayed along the right side of the workspace and contains pages of documentation and examples to assist you in your work. When opened, the window can be resized or moved for your purposes, and can remain on the screen so you can refer to it as you work. Help can be accessed at any time while Publisher is open. Because you probably create publications for yourself, or your business or organization, Publisher makes it easy for you to store frequently used information about these entities. This feature, called **Personal Information Sets**, means that you won't have to enter this information each time. You can store up to four Personal Information Sets: for your primary and secondary businesses, another organization, and your home or family. The information in the Primary Business set is applied by default, but you can easily apply the information in any of the other sets.  Mike decides to use Help to find out about Personal Information and how it can be modified. He wants to find out how to create a Personal Information Set for Image Magic that he can use to easily insert company information into publications.

Steps

Trouble?
To display the Office Assistant, click Help on the menu bar, then click Show the Office Assistant, if necessary.

1. **Click the Office Assistant**
   The Office Assistant Help window opens. It will help you learn about modifying Personal Information Sets.

2. **Type How do I change Personal Information?, then click Search**
   The Office Assistant displays topics about Personal Information, as shown in Figure A-13.

QuickTip
Click the Show All down arrow to read additional information.

3. **Click Add, change, or remove personal information data**, the Microsoft Publisher Help window opens, click **Add or change information within a personal information set** from the Help window choices, then read about making modifications
   The Help window has the same functionality of other windows. You can print the information in any Help window by clicking the Print button on the Publisher Help window toolbar. The window can be closed using the Close button, and the Office Assistant can be hidden at any time.

4. **Click the Publisher Help window Close button**, right-click the **Office Assistant**, then click **Hide**
   The Office Assistant is hidden. Any Personal Information Set can be modified, and the changes can be used in future publications.

Trouble?
If Personal Information does not appear on the menu, click the down arrow at the bottom of the menu, or wait several seconds, and the command will appear.

5. **Click Edit on the menu bar, then click Personal Information**
   To modify a Personal Information Set, you replace existing data with new text.

6. **Click the Secondary Business information set in the Personal Information dialog box**
   The information in the dialog box is for the current secondary business.

7. **Press [Tab] to select the name in the Name text box, type Mike Mendoza, press [Tab]**, then refer to Figure A-14 to type the rest of the information in the Personal Information dialog box including job title, phone numbers, e-mail, and color scheme
   The information set modifications take effect when they have been updated.

8. **Click Update**

PUBLISHER 14 GETTING STARTED WITH MICROSOFT PUBLISHER 2002

FIGURE A-13: Office Assistant Help topics

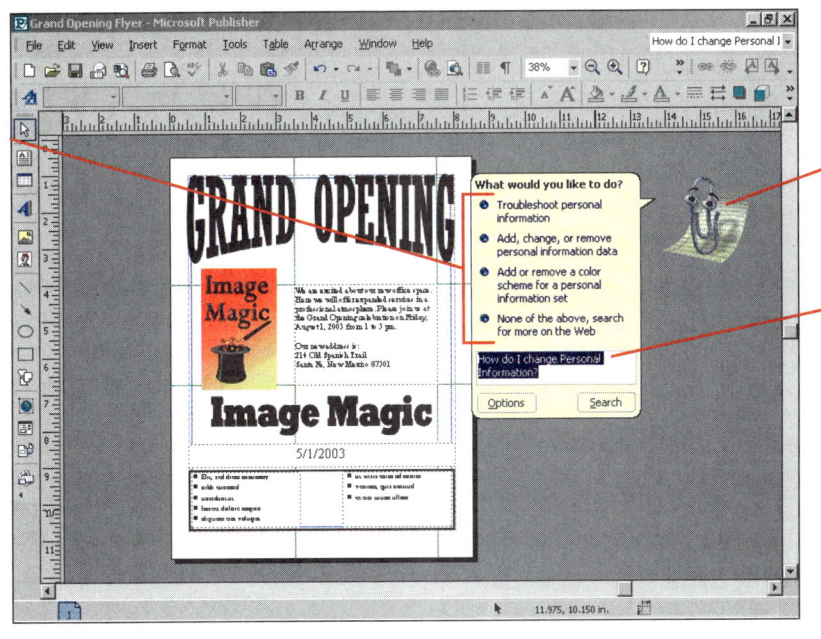

Click a topic to get more information

The size, shape, and location of your Office Assistant may differ

Question posed to the Office Assistant

FIGURE A-14: Personal Information dialog box

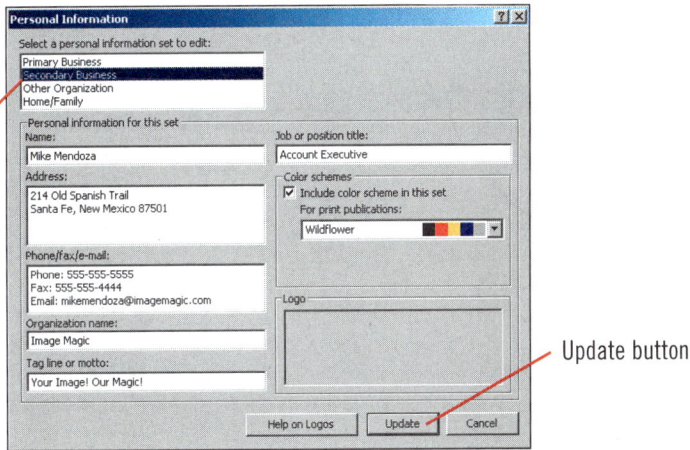

Information displayed is for the Secondary Business information set

Update button

Opening a file created in the Publication Gallery

When you open a file created with the New Publication task pane and the Publication Gallery, a specific task pane associated with that publication also opens. For example, when you open a newsletter you created using the New Publication task pane and the Publication Gallery, the Newsletter Options task pane opens. The specific task pane associated with the publication you created has options that make it easy to modify the publication.

GETTING STARTED WITH MICROSOFT PUBLISHER 2002   PUBLISHER 15

Closing a Publication and Exiting Publisher

When you finish working on a publication, you should save the file and close it. **Closing** a file puts away a publication so you can no longer work on it, but leaves Publisher running so you can work on other publications. When you complete all your work in Publisher, you want to exit the program. **Exiting** puts away any open publication files and returns you to the desktop, where you can choose to run another program. Mike finished adding the information to the Image Magic flyer and needs to attend a meeting, so he closes the publication and then exits Publisher.

Steps

1. **Click File on the menu bar**
   The File menu opens. See Figure A-15.

2. **Click Close**
   You could also click the Close button on the title bar instead.

3. **If asked if you want to save your work, click Yes**
   Publisher closes the publication and a blank publication appears on the workspace.

4. **Click File on the menu bar, then click Exit**
   You could also double-click the program control menu box to exit the program. Publisher closes, and computer memory is freed up for other computing tasks.

> **QuickTip**
> To exit Publisher and close an open publication, click the Close button on the upper-right corner of the window. Publisher will prompt you to save any unsaved changes before closing.

PUBLISHER 16 GETTING STARTED WITH MICROSOFT PUBLISHER 2002

FIGURE A-15: Closing a publication using the File menu

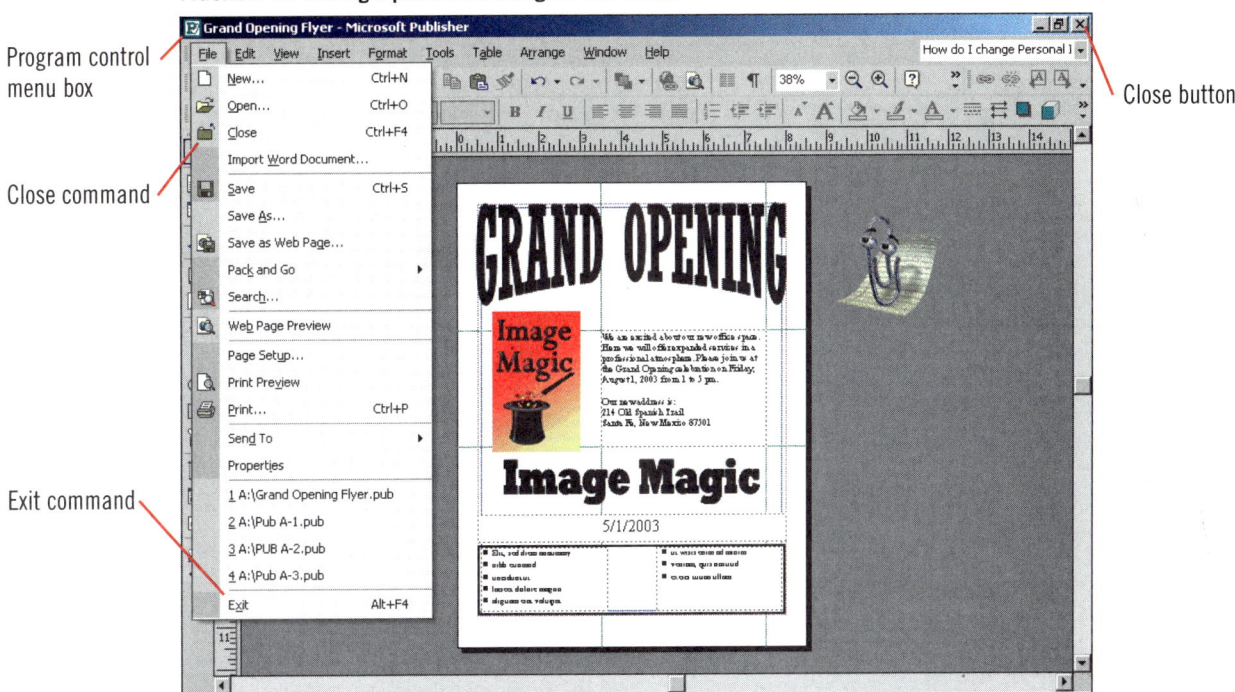

Microsoft Publisher World Wide Web site

You can get even more information about Microsoft Publisher by accessing the Microsoft Publisher Web site. This constantly changing site offers tips, upgrades, sales promotions, and information on new developments in Publisher. By clicking on the blue underlined links, you'll be able to find additional information on the Microsoft product line. Figure A-16 shows http://microsoft.com/office/publisher/default. It may look different on your screen, because the site changes often and sales promotions end. To find even more information, you can search the Internet using your favorite search engine for any sites about Microsoft Publisher.

FIGURE A-16: Microsoft Publisher World Wide Web site

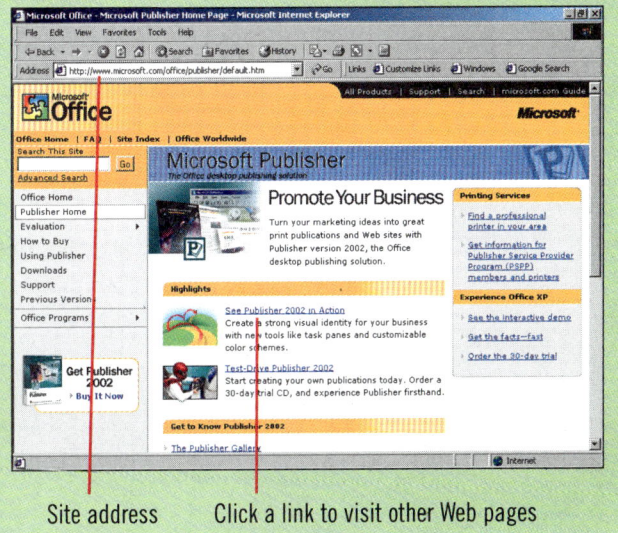

GETTING STARTED WITH MICROSOFT PUBLISHER 2002   PUBLISHER 17

Publisher 2002

Capstone Project: Study Abroad Flyer

You have learned the basic skills necessary to modify an existing publication. You can open a file and save it under a different name. You know how to create a text box, insert text, zoom, and reduce the font size so you can add additional text. Once your work is complete, you can preview the flyer in both black and white and in color, then print it. Using the Publication Gallery, Mike started a flyer for the Community College Council that advertises a one-credit course in Mexico. Additional work is needed to complete the project.

Steps

1. Start Publisher, click the **Open button** on the Standard toolbar, open the file **PUB A-2** from the drive and folder where your Project Files are stored, then save the publication as **Study Abroad Flyer**
   You need to create a text box to hold some additional information.

2. Click the **Text Box button** on the Objects toolbar, then use + to create a rectangular text box that has object coordinates of **1.200, 9.000 in.**, with the dimensions **4.300 × 0.900 in.**
   Zooming in helps you see your work more clearly.

3. Press **[F9]** to zoom in to the text box
   Many publications are very brief; their purpose is to convey a limited amount of information and to stimulate interest. It is a good idea to give the reader a specific way to obtain more information, or make contact with an organization.

4. Type **For more information, contact:**, press **[Enter]**, type **your name**, press **[Enter]**, then type **Extension 3210**
   Since you are requesting a response from the reader, it is helpful to make the text larger so it attracts more attention and is easier to read. Compare your publication to Figure A-17.

5. Press **[Ctrl][A]** to select the contents of the text box, click the **Font Size list arrow** on the Formatting toolbar, then click **14**
   You want to examine the publication for its overall design and for any errors that need correction.

6. Press **[Esc]** twice, press **[F9]** to zoom out, then click the **Save button** on the Standard toolbar
   The publication looks very good. Make any corrections that you think are necessary.

7. Click the **Print Preview button** on the Standard toolbar
   The publication appears on the screen as it will appear printed. You cannot see the outlines of text boxes, or other non-printing characters. You check to make sure that everything looks correctly positioned on the page.

8. Click the **Color/Grayscale button** to change the view from black and white to color
   As you will be printing in color, you want to make sure that the colors are complementary. Compare your publication to Figure A-18.

9. Close the Preview window, click the **Print button** on the Standard toolbar, then exit Publisher

FIGURE A-17: Contact information inserted in Study Abroad Flyer

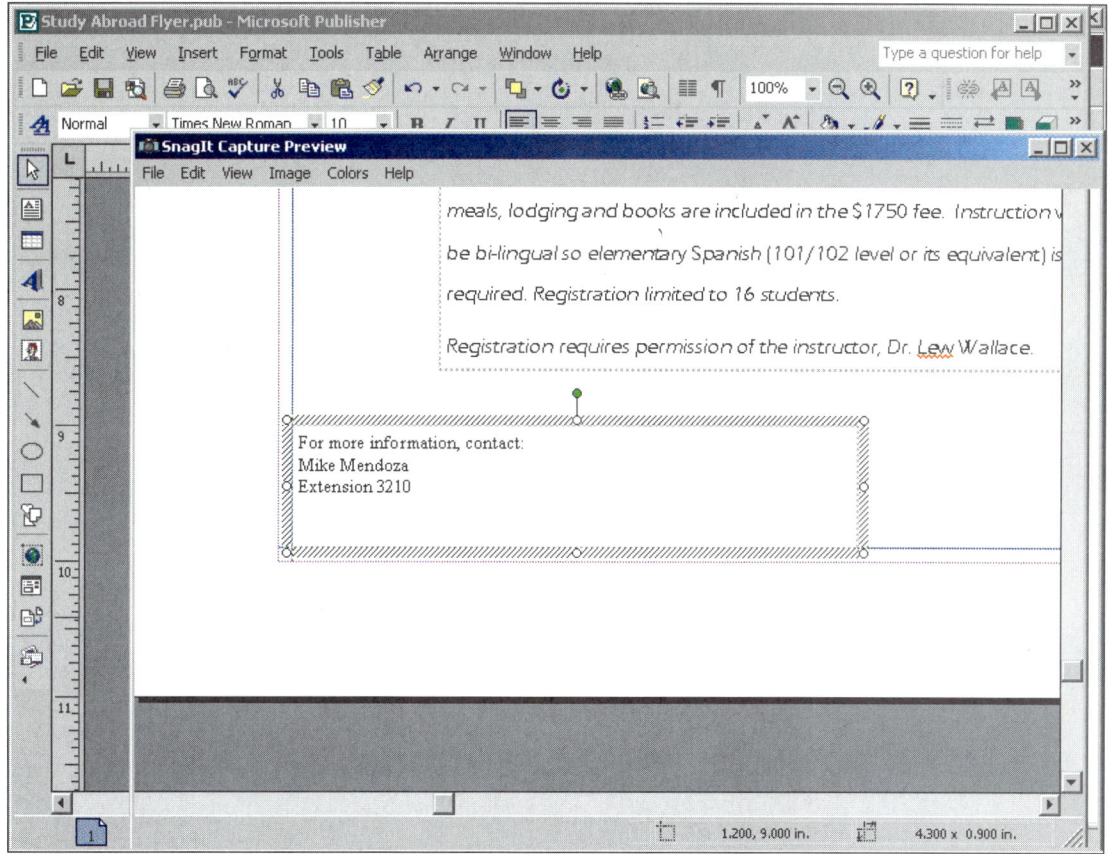

FIGURE A-18: Color Print Preview of Study Abroad Flyer

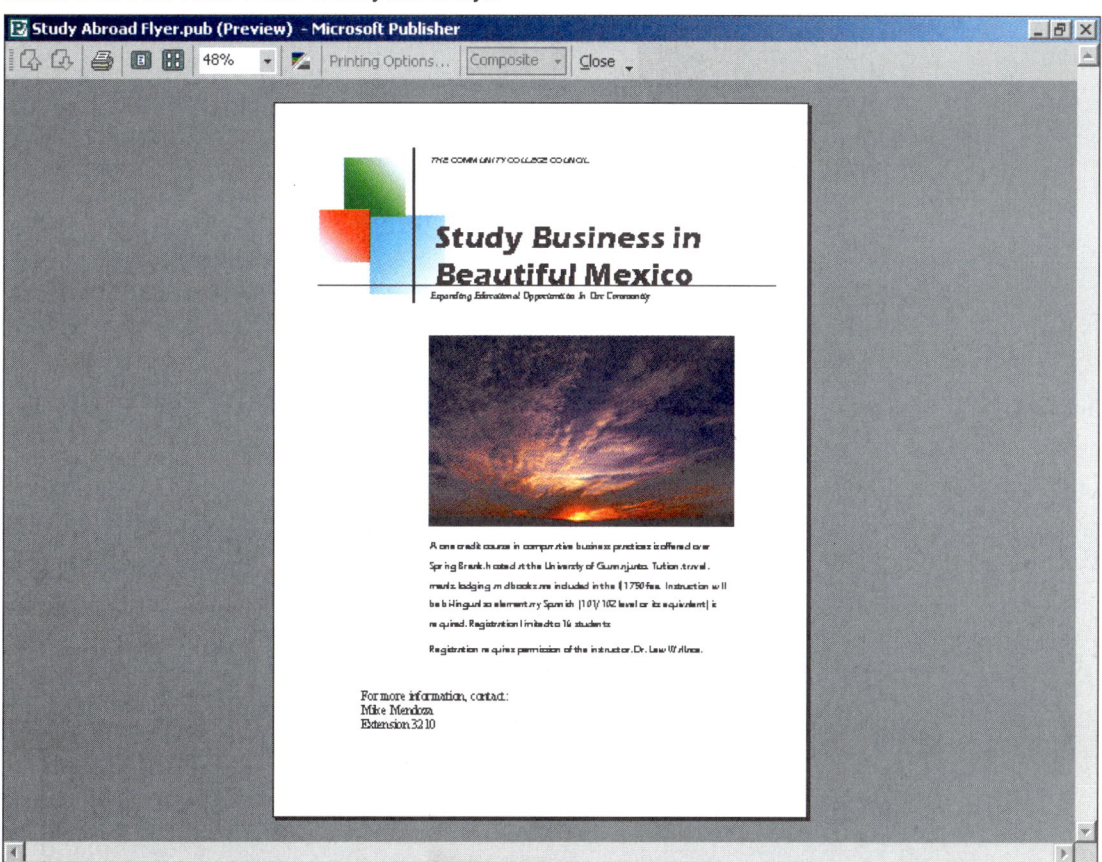

GETTING STARTED WITH MICROSOFT PUBLISHER 2002 PUBLISHER 19

Publisher 2002 Practice

▶ Concepts Review

Label each of the elements in the Publisher window shown in Figure A-19.

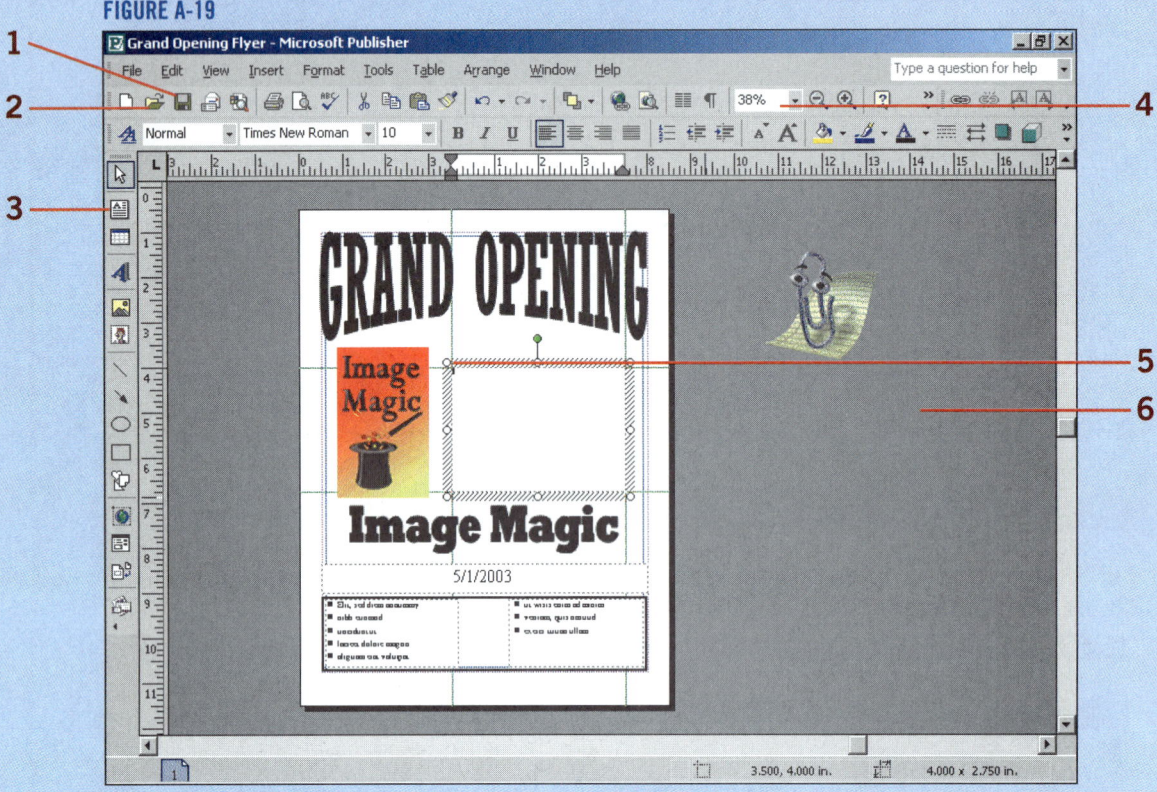

FIGURE A-19

Match each of the terms or buttons with the statement that describes its function.

7. 📂
8. 💾
9. **Text box**
10. 🖨
11. **Handles**
12. **Status bar**

a. Used to save a publication to a disk
b. Small black circles surrounding an object
c. Shows size and position of selected object
d. Contains typed text
e. Opens an existing publication
f. Prints every page in the publication

Select the best answer from the list of choices.

13. A document created in Publisher is called a:
    a. Booklet.
    b. Notebook.
    c. Publication.
    d. Brochure.

PUBLISHER 20   GETTING STARTED WITH MICROSOFT PUBLISHER 2002

14. Which of the following statements about text boxes is false?
    a. They can be moved.
    b. They can be resized.
    c. They aren't very useful.
    d. They can be connected to other frames.
15. Which key is pressed to zoom into a selected area?
    a. [F8]
    b. [F2]
    c. [F6]
    d. [F9]
16. A template is:
    a. A publication that serves as a master for other publications.
    b. A short statement placed off to the side to grab a reader's attention.
    c. An online artwork organizer.
    d. A distinctive shape in a publication.
17. Which of the following is considered an object?
    a. Text box
    b. Pictures
    c. Tables
    d. All of the above
18. Which button is used to create a text box?
    a.
    b.
    c.
    d.
19. Which feature is used to magnify the view?
    a. Magnify
    b. Enlarge
    c. Amplify
    d. Zoom In
20. Each of the following is found in the status bar, except:
    a. A selected object's position.
    b. The name of the current publication.
    c. Page icons.
    d. A selected object's size.
21. Which is not a type of Personal Information set?
    a. Primary Business
    b. Secondary Business
    c. Home/Family
    d. Colleague

Publisher 2002 Practice

▶ Skills Review

1. **Start Publisher 2002.**
   a. Start Publisher.
   b. Open a new blank publication.
   c. Try to identify as many elements in the Publisher window as you can without referring to the unit material.
2. **Open and save a publication.**
   a. Open the file PUB A-3. If you get a message to initialize the default printer, click OK.
   b. Save the publication as **Sample Business Card**.
   c. Click the Business Card Options task pane Close button, if necessary.
3. **Enter text in a text box.**
   a. Create a text box with the size coordinates 2.000 × 0.500 in. for your name, using Figure A-20 as an example. The top-left corner should be placed at 1.250, 0.500 in. (ruler guides were inserted to make this placement easier). Type your name using a 16 point font size or larger.
   b. Create a text box with the size coordinates 2.000 × 0.750 in. for your address, using Figure A-20 as a guide. The top-left corner should be placed at 1.250 in., 1.250 in. Substitute your address for the text shown using a 10-point text size.
   c. Save the publication.
4. **View and print a publication.**
   a. Zoom out.
   b. Zoom in.
   c. Use the Print button to print one copy of the publication.
5. **Get Help and change Personal Information.**
   a. Click Help on the menu bar, if necessary, then click Show the Office Assistant to display the Office Assistant.
   b. Click the Office Assistant.
   c. Find information on text boxes. (*Hint:* Use keywords "text boxes," then read several of the search result topics.)
   d. Click the Print button above the Help window to print the information you find.
   e. Close the Help window.
   f. Hide the Office Assistant.
   g. Open the Personal Information dialog box.
   h. Select the Secondary Business information set.
   i. Change the Color Scheme for the Secondary Business to Wildflower.
6. **Close the publication and exit Publisher.**
   a. Save and close your publication.
   b. Exit Publisher.

FIGURE A-20

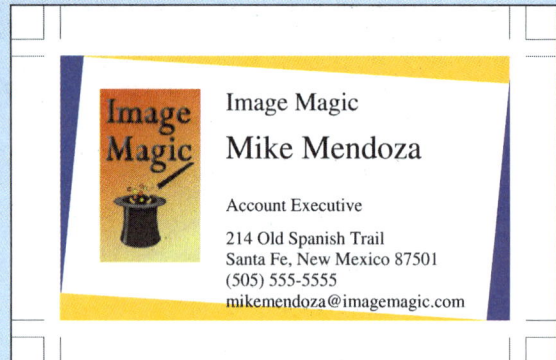

Practice

▶ Independent Challenge 1

The Publisher Help feature provides definitions, explanations, procedures, and other helpful information. It also provides examples and demonstrations to show how Publisher features work. You need to add a page to a brochure you are working on for your new client, Mangez!, a French importer of baked goods and cheeses. Open any existing publication, and explore Help using the Office Assistant. Find out how to add a page to a publication. Print out the information.

▶ Independent Challenge 2

Desktop publishing programs can be used to create many types of publications. Some examples of how Publisher can be used are discussed at the beginning of this unit. Publisher can be used in many ways in business and education. If you were teaching a class, how could you use Publisher to your advantage as a teaching aid?

   a. Think of three types of publications you could create with Publisher that would be effective in a classroom.
   b. Sketch a sample of each publication.
   c. Open a blank publication for each sample. Using text boxes, re-create your sketches. (These publications do not need to be fancy; they can just contain text boxes.) Your three publications should be named **Suggestion 1**, **Suggestion 2**, and **Suggestion 3**.
   d. In a separate blank publication, use text boxes to explain why each of your suggestions would be an effective use of Publisher. Name this publication **Explanation**.
   e. Be sure to include your name in a text box in each publication, then print each one.
   f. Save and close the publications, then exit Publisher.

▶ Independent Challenge 3

You are selected as the Image Magic Employee of the Month. You're being honored because you always come up with creative ways of accomplishing tasks. When you are given your award, you are asked for ways to improve the certificate. To complete the certificate, more text is needed.

   a. Start Publisher, if necessary, open the file PUB A-4, then save it as **Image Magic Award**.
   b. If necessary, close the task pane.
   c. Use Zoom as needed. In the space above the Name of Recipient placeholder, insert a text box that contains an explanation of why you are being given this award.
   d. Replace the Name of Recipient placeholder with your name.
   e. Print the final publication.
   f. Save your work.
   g. Close the publication, then exit Publisher.

Publisher 2002 *Practice*

e Independent Challenge 4

The World Wide Web is a rich resource for individuals and businesses. You examine the possibility of starting your own desktop publishing business. The advantages include: flexible hours, low start-up costs, having an outlet for artistic impulses, the ability to conduct business remotely over the Internet, contact with other business people, and being your own boss. On the negative side, you have no formal education in design. You decide to look on the Internet to learn something about design.

a. Start Publisher, if necessary, then open a new blank publication.
b. Save the publication as **Graphic Ideas** to the drive and folder where your Project Files are stored.
c. Connect to the Internet, then use a search engine to go find information on design basics.
d. Click the topics listed to find articles on design basics.
e. Create text boxes in the blank publication and type brief descriptions of some of your findings.
f. Disconnect from the Internet, if necessary.
g. Complete your publication. Be sure to include your name in the publication.
h. Print the publication, then exit Publisher.

▶ Visual Workshop

Open the publication PUB A-5 from the drive and folder where your Project Files are stored, and add the text shown in Figure A-21 using the skills you learned in this unit. The font size in the text box is 16 point. Save the publication as **Image Magic Gift Card**. Be sure to include your name in the publication. Print the publication.

FIGURE A-21

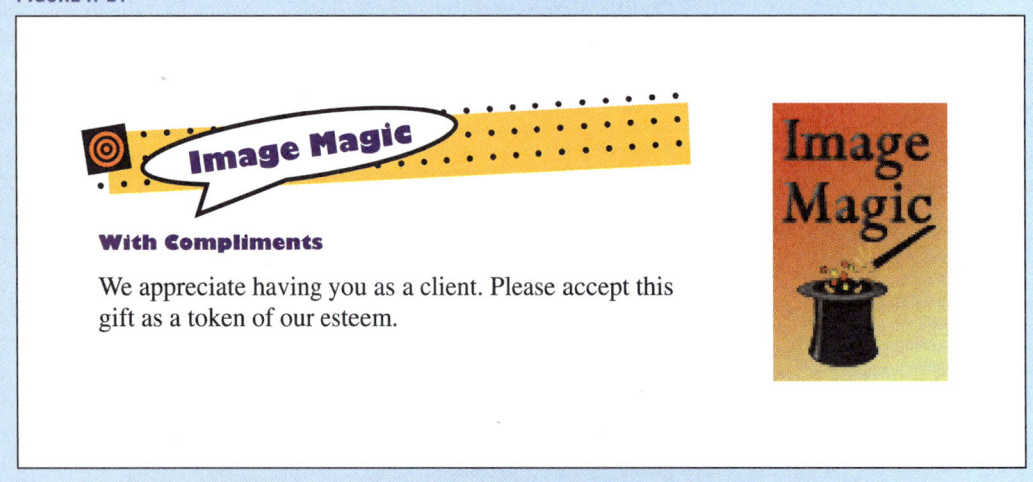

Image Magic

With Compliments

We appreciate having you as a client. Please accept this gift as a token of our esteem.

Image Magic

▶ PUBLISHER 24   **GETTING STARTED WITH MICROSOFT PUBLISHER 2002**

Publisher 2002

Unit B

Creating
a Publication

Objectives

- Plan a publication
- Design a publication
- Create a publication with the task pane
- Replace text
- Add a graphic image
- Add a sidebar
- Use the Design Gallery
- Group objects
- Capstone Project: College Brochure

Now that you are familiar with the Publisher window and understand how to open and save a file, you are ready to create your own publication. It is important to think about the objectives of your publication, as well as the design goals, before starting a publication. Once you establish the message and layout of your publication, you must add text and graphics, as well as ensure objects are in the correct places. Marjorie Raynovich, an intern at Image Magic, is learning how to use Publisher. She is on the newsletter team and is working on the latest issue.

Planning a Publication

Publisher 2002 — Unit B

To create an effective publication, you should do some planning. Planning a publication has at least three steps: determining what you want to achieve, deciding what information to include, and figuring out how to best present it. Knowing the goals of your publication helps you determine what form it should take. Keeping in mind the content of the message and your audience helps you to decide how the publication should be written, and how it should look. While there are many ways to plan a publication, it's best to start by determining the purpose of the publication. See Figure B-1 for an illustration of this process. Marjorie's assignment is to create a one-page newsletter. Before starting, she answers these questions: Who is the audience? What is the message? What form should the message take? She knows that the newsletter will be read by employees and by clients. The purpose of the newsletter is to inform the employees of news within the company, to make them feel important and included, and to recognize business and personal achievements.

Details

Answering the following questions is the key to planning the publication:

▶ **What is the desired effect of the publication?**
Are you trying to inform, motivate, sell, inspire confidence, raise morale, solicit a vote, or solicit a contribution of time or money?

▶ **What response do you want?**
Do you intend this to be a one-way communication, or do you desire feedback? If you want feedback, what form should it take? Do you want volunteers, attendance at an event, and/or inquiries for additional information via phone or e-mail? Do you want visits to a Web site; registrations; contracts signed and returned; payments by check, cash or credit card; or RSVPs, for example?

▶ **What are you going to do with the responses you requested?**
If you solicit inquiries for additional information via mail or e-mail, but don't prepare a polite, informative response to send, you risk alienating your audience. If you solicit information, but neglect to gather it, interpret it, or fail to use it, you wasted time and effort, and lost an opportunity.

▶ **Who is the target audience?**
The more narrowly you can define the characteristics of your target audience, the more you can tailor the content and appearance of the message to appeal to that group. For instance, a colorful comic book publication would be right for trying to educate fourth graders, but not appropriate for informing cardiologists of newly identified risk factors for heart disease.

Some of the possible ways to identify a group are by age, sex, geography, reading level, educational background, first language, hobbies, nationality, ethnicity, religion, culture, political affiliation, employment, income level, taste in music and art, home ownership, and health or ill health.

FIGURE B-1: Planning process

Developing design sense

Designing publications is a skill that can be learned through thoughtful practice and critical observation. Just as artists gather ideas from trips to museums, and musicians gather ideas from attending concerts, you can sharpen your design skills by looking at publications created by others. Start with a visit to a library or a magazine stand, observing the overall design of the publications. Gauge your overall reaction to a publication, and judge for yourself what you find appealing and what you find distracting or offensive. Concentrate on how your eye moves across a page. What combinations of design elements (balance, color, consistency, contrast, and white space) are you drawn to, and what do you find unappealing?

Designing a Publication

Publisher 2002 — Unit B

Just as form follows function in the old adage, planning should always precede design. The elements of design— unity, balance, color, consistency, contrast, and white space—should be combined to support the objectives of the publication. This is why design follows planning because it must support the goals identified in the planning stages. After planning, Marjorie knows she wants the newsletter to catch the eye of the readers, be easy to read, and look professional to clients. She wants to include the company logo to identify the newsletter as Image Magic's, and she wants to call attention to specific text to be sure it is seen and understood. She also wants the newsletter to display a tasteful sense of humor.

Details

▶ View the document as a whole
The publication needs enough contrast to be interesting, but must be consistent to help the audience find the meaning without confusion or unnecessary effort.

▶ Use placeholders for text and graphics to create an effective layout
Placeholder text and graphics are objects that are inserted into a publication to illustrate how the finished product will appear when replaced with more significant materials at a later time. Publisher uses placeholder text boxes and graphics extensively in the Publication Gallery to demonstrate how the combined design elements in a publication will look.

▶ Use graphics to add interest and present ideas
Graphics can efficiently communicate feelings and ideas. Use of artwork not only adds interest, but also is a means to communicate ideas and feelings that can reinforce text.

▶ Use white space liberally
White space, also known as negative space, describes the open space between design elements. It can be between elements of text (letters or paragraphs), in between and surrounding graphics, and between all other objects on the page. It is crucial for providing spatial relations between visual items, and actually guides the reader's eye from one point to another. Without sufficient white space, text is unreadable, graphics lose emphasis, and there is no balance between the elements on a page. White space tells you where one section ends and another begins.

▶ Prominently feature the company logo
The Image Magic logo appears on all its print material—letterhead, envelopes, business cards, and advertisements—to reinforce the identity of the company. It boosts morale for employees and associates to see the logo displayed with pride, and enhances clients' perception of the firm.

▶ Emphasize certain text
Some text on a page should stand out. See Figure B-2. For example, **sidebars** are text related to the story but not vital to it. They are placed adjacent to the story to add emphasis and pique the interest of readers. Usually sidebars have a different background color, font, or point size to set them apart from the story.

FIGURE B-2: Sample newsletter

— Masthead

— Date and Issue Number

— Pull quote text is taken from an article

— Graphic image

— Sidebar is a related story with formatting to add emphasis

Design Matters

Recognizing bad design

Thoughtful practice and critical observation are the keys to learning good design. But how can you recognize bad design? First, always look at a publication from the reader's point of view, by trying to find what is of interest in the publication. If you don't spot something of interest right away, do you think the typical reader is going to pursue it or set it aside? Nothing discourages a reader more than long columns of dull gray type, unless it is long columns of dull gray type that are hard to read. Ornate type that might look stylish on the sample sheet in the print shop with great lighting may be very hard to read elsewhere. Is the artwork carefully chosen and well placed to generate interest, or is the publication too cluttered with fluff so that the reader may be distracted rather than enlightened? In a nutshell, bad design is anything that fails to capture or sustain a reader's interest.

Creating a Publication with the Task Pane

Publisher 2002 — Unit B

The New Publication task pane makes it easy to choose the kind of publication you want by choosing a publication type or a design set, and then selecting from the samples in the Publication Gallery. This feature helps you get started by letting you choose among the Start from a design, New, or Open a publication options. The Start from a design option is organized By Publication Type, By Design Sets, and By Blank Publications, with a list arrow that switches between them. The By Publication Type option includes Quick Publications, Word Documents, Newsletters, Web Sites, and more. The By Design Sets option includes Master Sets, Special Events Sets, Holiday Sets, and Restaurant Sets that are further organized by design schemes such as Accent Box, Accessory Bar, Arcs, Bars, or Bubbles, etc. The menu choices you select help create all the necessary features you need to get started quickly. Marjorie uses the New Publication option to create a newsletter.

Steps

Trouble?
If Publisher is already open but you don't see the New Publication task pane, click File on the menu bar, then click New. If the task pane does not appear on the left side of your screen, see your instructor or technical support person for help.

1. **Start Publisher**
   The New Publication task pane opens. You want to create a newsletter so you start with this Publication Type.

2. **Click Newsletters in the By Publication Type list**
   The Publication Gallery displays different newsletter designs, as shown in Figure B-3.

3. **Scroll down if necessary, then click Blends Newsletter**
   The Newsletter layout appears on the right of the screen. The Newsletter Options task pane opens on the left. This is where you can specify some features of your publication. You want to accept the defaults of two-sided printing and no customer address.

4. **Click the Close button on the Newsletter Options task pane**
   You now have a clear view of the newsletter, which appears in the workspace.

QuickTip
These changes may have already been made.

5. **Click Edit on the menu bar, click Personal Information, click Secondary Business** if necessary, type **Mike Mendoza** in the Name text box, type **Account Executive** in the Job or position title text box, type **Image Magic** in the Address text box, press **[Enter]**, type **214 Old Spanish Trail**, press **[Enter]**, type **Santa Fe, New Mexico 87501**, in the Phone/fax/e-mail text box type **Phone: 505-555-5555**, press **[Enter]**, type **Fax: 505-555-4444**, press **[Enter]**, type **E-mail: mikemendoza@imagemagic.com**, type **Image Magic** in the Organization name text box, type **Your Image! Our Magic!** in the Tag line or motto text box, click the **Color Schemes list arrow**, click **Wildflower**, then click **Update**
   The Wildflower color scheme provides an array of bright colors. The newsletter appears in the workspace, as shown in Figure B-4.

6. **Click the Save button 💾 on the Standard toolbar, click the Save in list arrow**, locate the drive and folder where your Project Files are stored, type **IM Newsletter** in the File name text box, then click **Save**

PUBLISHER 30   CREATING A PUBLICATION

FIGURE B-3: New Publication task pane and Publication Gallery

- Newsletters option
- Publication types
- Publications displayed in the Publication Gallery

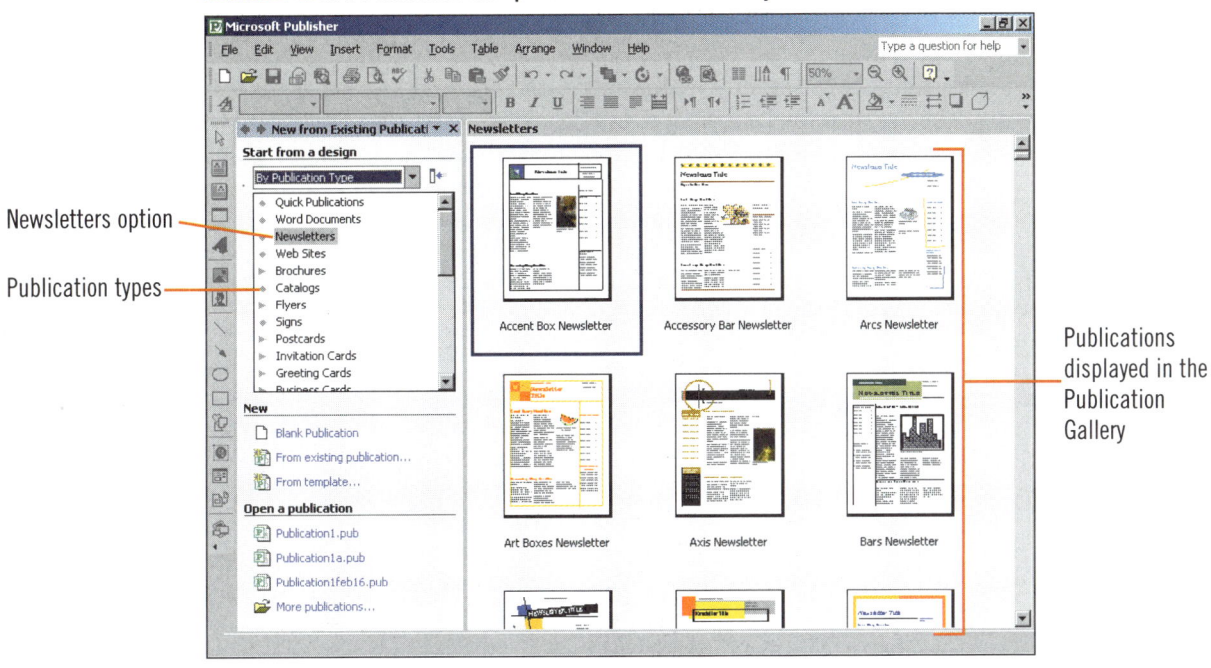

FIGURE B-4: Newsletter with the Wildflower color scheme

- The Wildflower color scheme was selected in the Personal Information dialog box

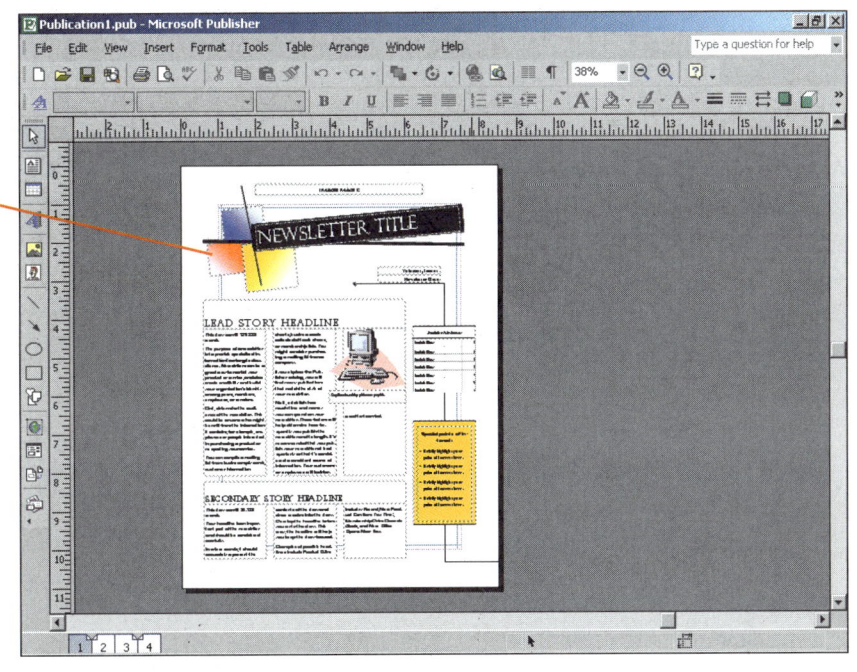

Publication Gallery options

The Publication Gallery is a visual directory of more than 1600 different publications. It is organized into three sections: By Publication Type, By Design Sets, and By Blank Publications. To switch between them, click the By Publication Type list arrow. Each selection offers a variety of choices within its particular category. Brochures, for example, are available in many different styles and layout schemes. Labels can be created for computer disks, binders, audiocassettes, videocassettes, and CD case liners. Publications created using the Publication Gallery can be easily modified.

CREATING A PUBLICATION PUBLISHER 31

Replacing Text

Publisher 2002 — Unit B

You can either type text directly into a text box, or you can insert documents created with a word processor, such as Microsoft Word, into your publication. The Publication Gallery inserts placeholders in the publications for you to enter your own text. Marjorie needs to replace the placeholders in the newsletter she created earlier with the text she wrote. She inserts a Word document and types replacement text.

Steps

> **QuickTip**
> Hide the Office Assistant, if necessary.

1. **Click the Lead Story Headline text box, as shown in Figure B-5**
   Handles surround the selected text box, and its position and size appear on the status bar. The Formatting toolbar appears below the Standard toolbar. The text in this text box is just a placeholder provided by the Publication Gallery; you must type the text for this heading.

2. **Press [Ctrl][A] to select the text Lead Story Headline, then type New Location Opens Soon!**
   The placeholder text is deleted with the first keystroke of the new text. Because of the formatting in place, the text is automatically capitalized.

> **QuickTip**
> You can zoom by clicking the Select Zoom Mode button [100%], which always displays the Zoom factor, or clicking the Zoom In and Zoom Out buttons.

3. **Press [F9]**
   Zooming into the selected text can help you get a closer look.

4. **Click the placeholder text in the column below the new heading to select it**
   Clicking placeholder text, instead of the text box surrounding it, selects all the text, so there is no need to press [Ctrl][A]. Now that the placeholder text within the text box is selected, you can insert an existing Word document.

> **Trouble?**
> If you receive an error message advising you that Publisher can't import the specified format because this feature is not currently installed, and asking if you would like to install it now, insert the Office XP Disc 2 CD, then follow the instructions to install the feature. If you need further assistance, ask your instructor or technical support person.

5. **Click Insert on the menu bar, click Text File, locate the drive and folder where your Project Files are stored, click the file PUB B-1, then click OK**
   You might have to use the scroll buttons to see the new text. Compare your newsletter to Figure B-6. Instead of using the menu bar to insert text from a document file, you could right-click placeholder text, point to Change Text, then click Text File.

6. **Press [F9], then click the Save button on the Standard toolbar**

▶ PUBLISHER 32 CREATING A PUBLICATION

FIGURE B-5: Selected text box

- Handles surround selected text box
- Lead Story Headline placeholder text
- Placeholder graphic
- Lead Story placeholder text
- Coordinates of the upper-left corner of the selected text box

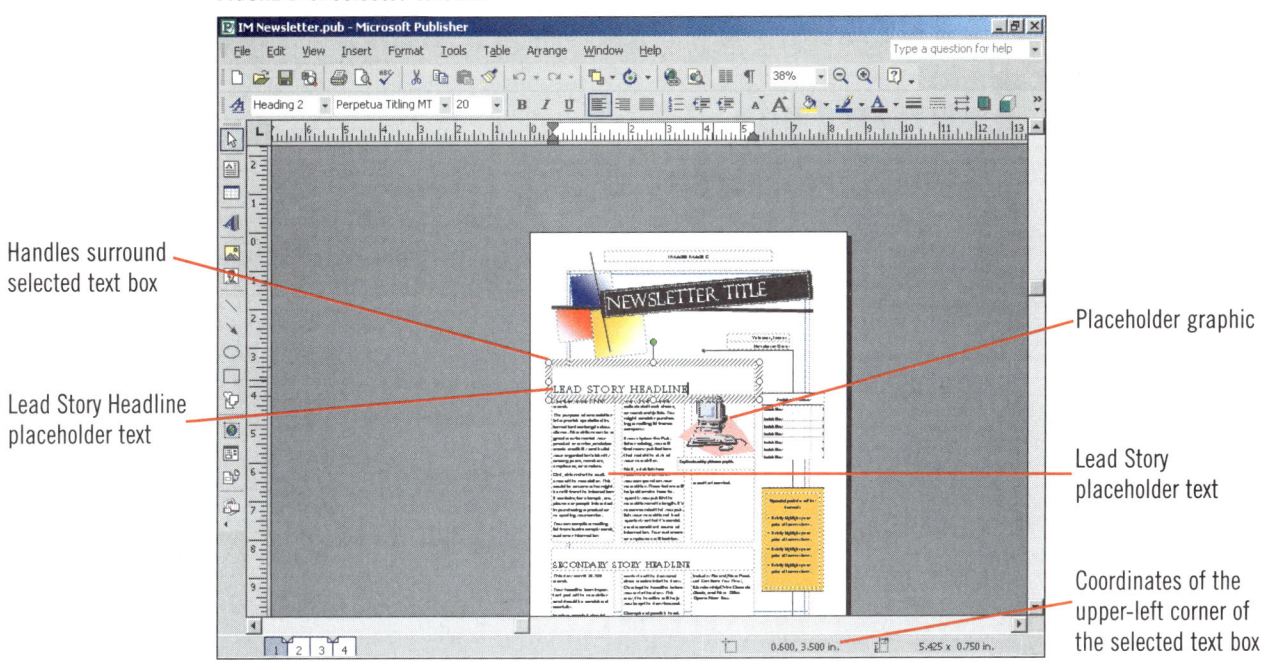

FIGURE B-6: Word document text in newsletter

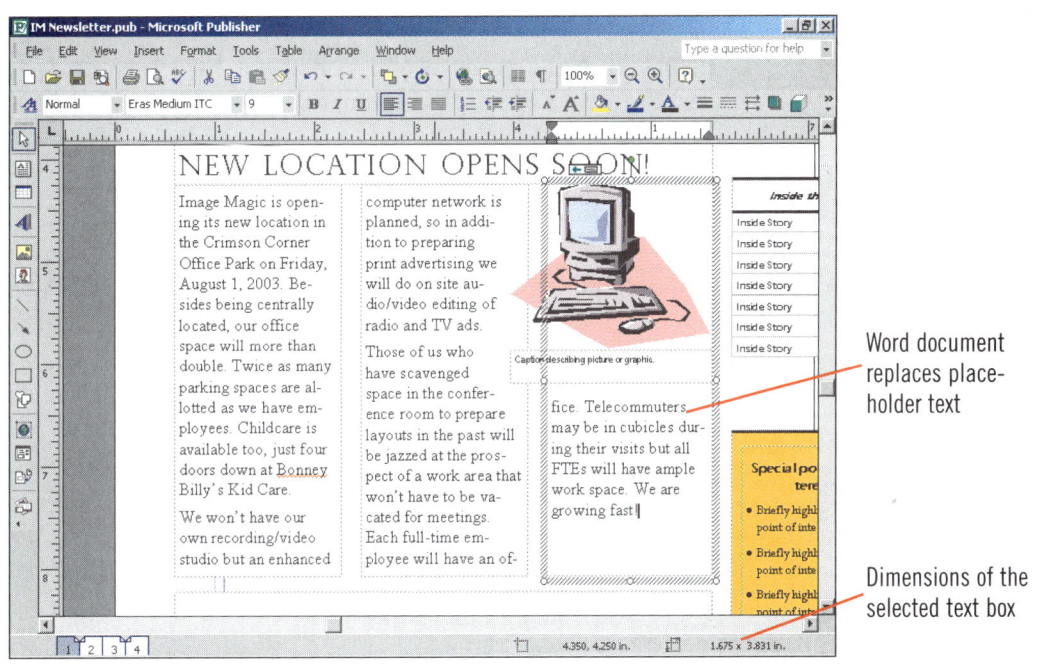

- Word document replaces placeholder text
- Dimensions of the selected text box

Clues to Use

Resizing a frame

A **frame**—whether it is a text box or contains an object—can be resized. Once a frame is selected, you can change its size by placing the mouse pointer over a handle, then dragging the handle. The pointer may change to ⬚, ⬚, ⬚, or ⬚, depending on which handle you place the pointer on. If, for example, the Text in Overflow button appears at the end of a selected frame, it may be possible to resize the frame, enabling the text to fit.

CREATING A PUBLICATION   PUBLISHER 33

Publisher 2002

Adding a Graphic Image

Publisher 2002

Artwork can express feelings and ideas that may be inexplicable with words. A picture, a piece of clip art, a graph, or a drawing is called a **graphic image**, or simply a **graphic**. **Clip art** is a collection of graphic images supplied on a disk or over the Web. Publisher comes with thousands of pieces of clip art. Artwork can also be scanned into your computer, created using drawing programs or a digital camera, or purchased separately on a disk or online. Table B-1 lists some of the common graphic image formats that can be used with Publisher. Marjorie incorporates the logo—already in electronic format—into her newsletter. She begins by selecting the graphic image of the computer and the associated text box, which are placeholders, and zooming to a better view of the image.

Steps

1. Click the **computer graphic image placeholder**, then press **[F9]**
   Handles surround both the placeholder clip art and the caption beneath it, indicating that both are selected. Underneath the selection is the Ungroup Objects button, which indicates that you selected objects that were purposely grouped together so that they can be treated as one unit.

2. Press **[Delete]**
   The graphic image and caption text box placeholders disappear, and the text box expands to replace them.

   > **QuickTip**
   > When looking for graphic files, you can change the view in the Insert Picture dialog box to Thumbnails so that it shows you a sample of the images available in the folder.

3. Click **Insert** on the menu bar, point to **Picture**, then click **From File**
   The Insert Picture dialog box opens. It opens to the My Pictures folder by default.

4. Click the **Look in list arrow**, locate the drive and folder where your Project Files are stored, click **Imlogo** as shown in Figure B-7, then click **Insert**
   The Image Magic logo appears.

5. Select the **Imlogo graphic image**, then use to drag it until the upper-left corner of the image is at coordinates **4.375, 4.375 in.**
   The repositioned image is near the upper-left portion of the column, as shown in Figure B-8. You want the image to be larger. Placing the pointer over a handle and then dragging the frame edge resizes an image. As you drag the pointer, the status bar reflects the object's size and position, using the ruler coordinates. To preserve an image's scale while increasing or decreasing its size, press and hold [Shift] while dragging the frame edge. The top-right corner of the image will change position, but the upper-left corner remains fixed in place.

6. Place the pointer over the lower-right handle of the image so it turns to , press and hold **[Shift]**, click the **left mouse button**, drag + down and to the right until the image has dimensions **1.563 × 2.500 in.**, release **[Shift]**, then release the mouse button
   The top-left corner of the image is now at coordinates 4.375, 4.375 in., and has dimensions 1.563 × 2.500 in., as shown in Figure B-9.

7. Press **[F9]**, then click on the **scratch area** to deselect the logo
   Pleased with how the image looks, you save your work.

8. Click the Save button

PUBLISHER 34   CREATING A PUBLICATION

FIGURE B-7: Insert Picture dialog box

- Available graphic images appear here
- Preview of selected file
- Publisher recognizes many picture file formats

FIGURE B-8: Repositioned graphic image

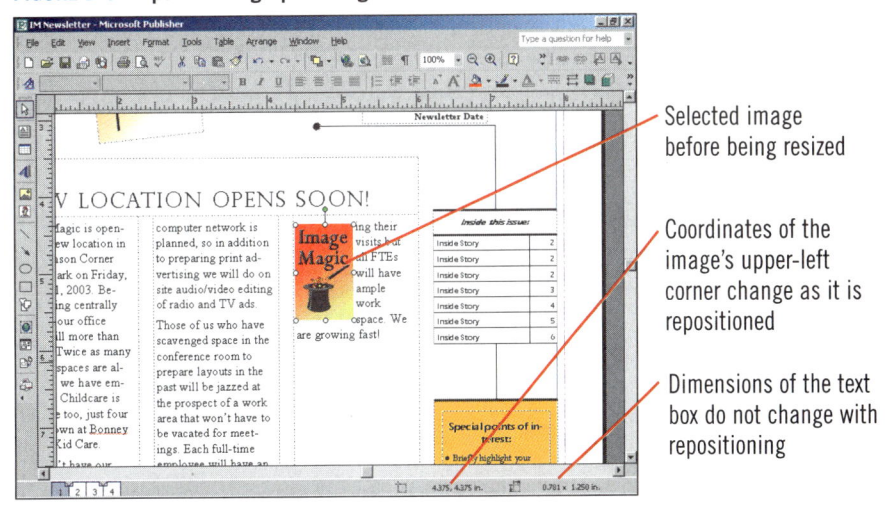

- Selected image before being resized
- Coordinates of the image's upper-left corner change as it is repositioned
- Dimensions of the text box do not change with repositioning

FIGURE B-9: Resized graphic image

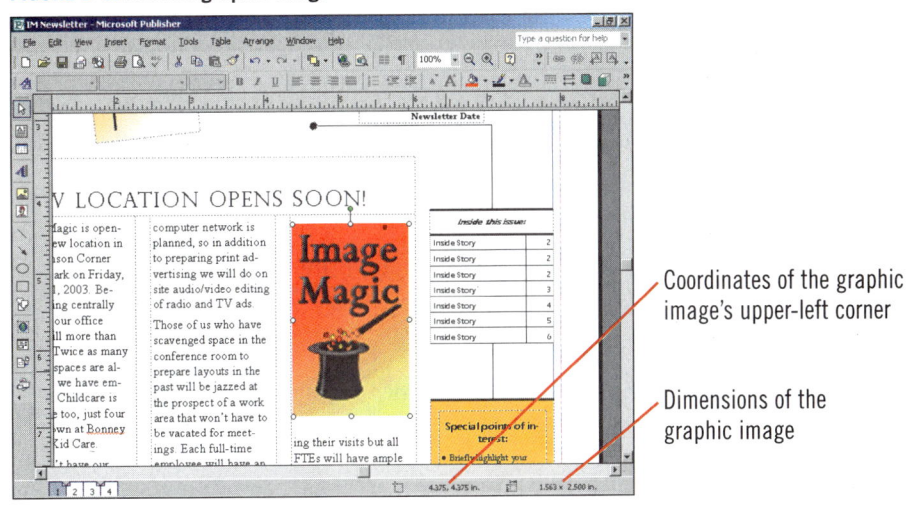

- Coordinates of the graphic image's upper-left corner
- Dimensions of the graphic image

TABLE B-1: Common graphic image formats

graphic image	extension	graphic image	extension
Bitmap	.BMP	Tagged Image File Format	.TIF
PC Paintbrush	.PCX	JPEG Picture Format	.JPG or .JPEG
Graphics Interchange Format	.GIF	Windows Metafile	.WMF
Encapsulated PostScript	.EPS	CorelDraw	.CDR

CREATING A PUBLICATION

Publisher 2002

Adding a Sidebar

Information not vital to a publication can make interesting reading when placed to the side of the regular text in a sidebar. A **sidebar** is a short news story containing supplementary information that is printed alongside a feature story. It can use the same font size as regular body text, but it may look better in a larger size or a different font. Adding a border or shading can dramatize sidebars. Marjorie replaces the sidebar placeholder with text in a Word document.

Steps

1. **Click inside the sidebar placeholder, then press [Ctrl][A] to select the text**
   Handles appear around the sidebar, as shown in Figure B-10. Underneath the selection, the Ungroup Objects button appears. In this case, the grouped objects are the title and the text of the sidebar, which were in different text boxes, and three geometric shapes. Now you insert the sidebar text prepared in Word.

2. **Press [F9], click Insert on the menu bar, click Text File, click the file PUB B-2 from the drive and folder where your Project Files are stored, then click OK**
   The new text appears in the text box. Notice the changes to the formatting. The bulleted list changed to plain text in Times New Roman font. The inserted Word document is not italicized, and the font size changed to fit the text in the frame. The heading is italicized, and is now in Eras Bold ITC font.

3. **Press [Esc] twice to deselect both the text and the text box, leaving the sidebar selected**
   You want to see what the sidebar looks like with a shadow.

4. **Click the Shadow Style button on the Formatting toolbar, click Shadow Style 1, then press [Esc] to deselect the frame**
   Compare your work to Figure B-11. A gray shadow is behind the gold background containing the text. The shadow effect is not as evident as in some styles, and you decide you prefer the way the sidebar looked without the shadow.

5. **Click the Undo button on the Standard toolbar, then click the scratch area to deselect the sidebar**
   The shadow is removed from the sidebar and it is deselected.

6. **Click the Save button on the Standard toolbar**
   You want to see the full-page image so you can check the overall appearance of the newsletter.

7. **Press [F9]**
   All the text fits nicely inside the frame.

FIGURE B-10: Sidebar placeholder selected

- Sidebar placeholder text
- Handles surround the text box
- The Ungroup Objects button

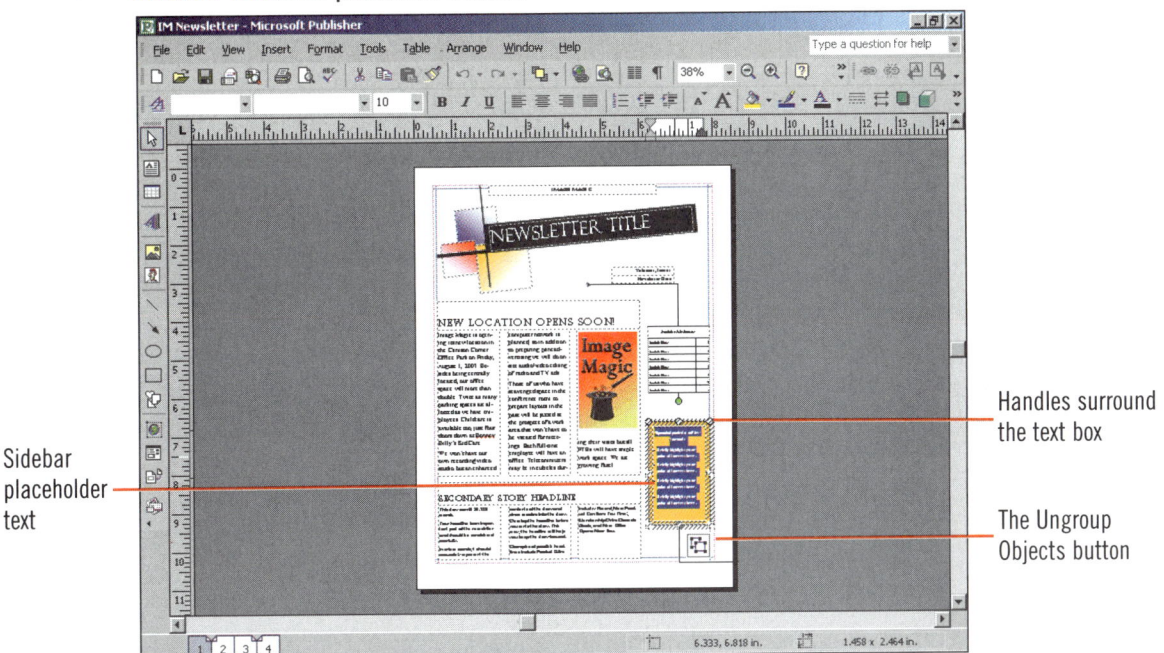

FIGURE B-11: Sidebar with shadow

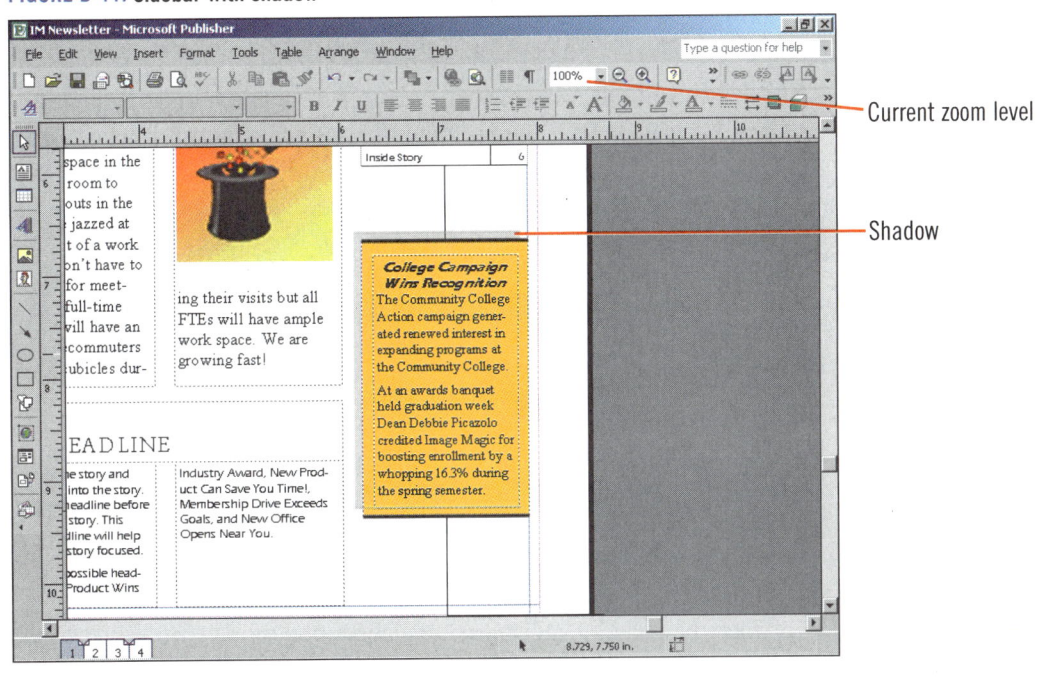

- Current zoom level
- Shadow

Design Matters

Using templates

Have you ever stared at a blank piece of paper or a blank screen not knowing where to begin? You can use templates as a starting point, particularly if you are just beginning in design. Just browsing through the Publication Gallery can spark your creativity and get you started down the path to creating your own masterpieces. And, there are occasions when even the best designers use templates. If you just need a routine expense form or an invoice, for example, if your client can't afford a "one-of-a-kind design," or just to save time. The important thing to remember about using a template is to choose one that is appropriate to the publication. A bad choice will require too many alterations so that the advantages of using a template are lost.

Using the Design Gallery

Unit B — Publisher 2002

The Design Gallery is a feature used to assemble a publication quickly. One element found in the Design Gallery is a pull quote. A **pull quote** is an excerpt pulled from the text and set next to it, usually in a different typeface. The purpose of a pull quote is to draw attention to the story from which it is quoted. Pull quotes should be short enough to be read easily, but long enough to capture interest. They should be on the same page as the story and placed close to it. The wording does not have to be identical to that found in the article, but should be similar. In addition to adding a pull quote, you can use the Design Gallery to easily insert a Publisher-designed object such as an ad, calendar, coupon, or logo. Marjorie inserts a pull quote near the article on new office space.

Steps

1. Click the **Table of Contents** at 7.000, 4.500 in., click **Edit** on the menu bar, then click **Delete Object**

   The Table of Contents is deleted, making more space available for design elements.

2. Click the **Design Gallery Object button** on the Objects toolbar

   The Design Gallery opens. The Design Gallery is organized into three tabs: Objects by Category, which lets you select the type of object to add to a publication; Objects by Design, which helps you organize your objects with a uniform design; and Your Objects, for special objects you create and save.

3. Click the **Objects by Category tab** if necessary, click **Pull Quotes** in the Categories list, click **Bars Pull Quote**, then click **Insert Object**

   You select the simple Bars Pull Quote because you used the colorful Blends Newsletter and you want the pull quote to have a plainer design. It is often best to use less ornate design elements to avoid distracting the reader. The pull quote placeholder appears on the first page of the publication, as shown in Figure B-12. Note that the Wizard Button appears underneath the pull quote. It indicates that the object is a Smart Object and is associated with a wizard. If you wished to replace this object with another similar object from the Design Gallery, you could click on the button to return to the Design Gallery to pick another design.

4. Place the pointer over the upper-left edge of the pull quote so it changes to , drag the upper-left corner to **6.225, 4.250 in.**, then press **[F9]**

   The pull quote sits just above the sidebar. Compare your pull quote text box to Figure B-13.

5. Click the **pull quote text** to select it, then type **"More Space, Childcare, Audio-video editing, and PARKING!"**

   When the pull quote is selected, the horizontal ruler becomes active, just as with any text box.

6. Press **[Ctrl][A]** to select the text, click **Format** on the menu bar, point to **AutoFit Text**, then click **Best Fit**

   Compare your pull quote to Figure B-14.

7. Press **[F9]**, then click the **scratch area** to deselect the pull quote

   Now you save your work.

8. Click the **Save button** on the Standard toolbar

PUBLISHER 38   CREATING A PUBLICATION

FIGURE B-12: Pull quote added

Pull quote placeholder text

Click Wizard button to change the pull quote format

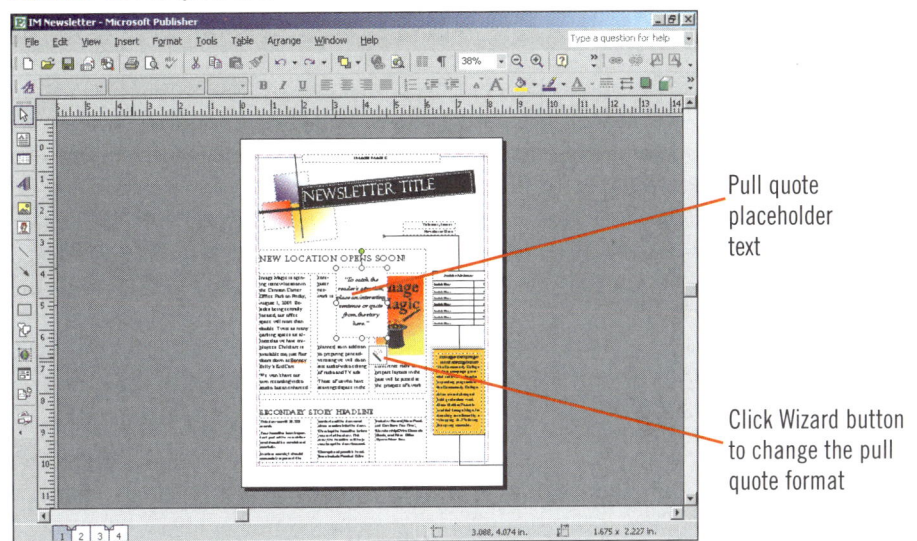

FIGURE B-13: Repositioned pull quote

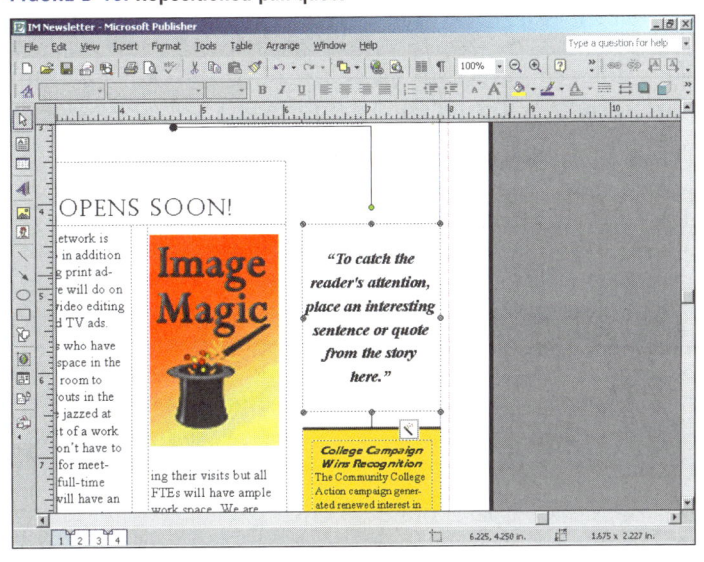

FIGURE B-14: Pull quote after AutoFit

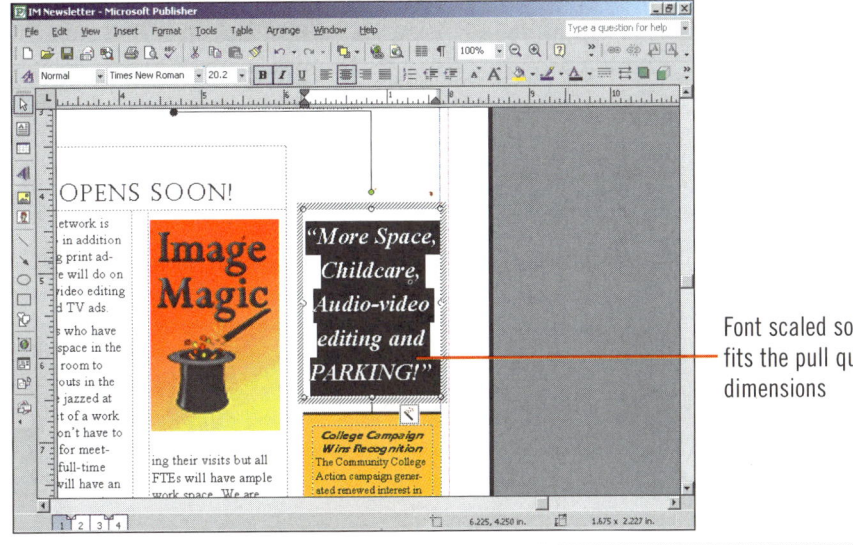

Font scaled so text fits the pull quote's dimensions

Publisher 2002

CREATING A PUBLICATION PUBLISHER 39

Publisher 2002

Grouping Objects

Once many objects are positioned on a page, you may find that you want to move one or more of them. Moving a single object is as simple as selecting it, then dragging it to a new location. But it gets more complicated when more than one object is involved, and you want them to retain their relative positions. **Grouping**, or turning several objects into one object, is an easy way to move multiple items. Later, you can always ungroup them for individual modifications, turning the combined objects back into individual objects. Marjorie wants to place a caption under the Image Magic logo. To change the size of the caption text box, she needs to ungroup the objects, make her modifications, then regroup the logo and caption.

Steps

1. Click the **Image Magic logo**, press **[F9]**, then press **[Esc]**
   You want to add text directly under the Image Magic logo so you insert a text box.

2. Click the **Text Box button**, draw a text box whose upper-left corner is at **4.313, 6.875 in.**, and whose dimensions are **1.625 × 0.313 in.**
   Now you will enter the Image Magic slogan and format it to fit the text box.

3. Type **Your Image! Our Magic!** in the text box, press **[Ctrl][A]**, click the **Bold button** on the Formatting toolbar, click **Format** on the menu bar, point to **AutoFit Text**, then click **Best Fit**
   The new caption appears beneath the logo and is now in Eras medium ITC font.

4. With the text box still selected, press and hold **[Shift]**, click the **Image Magic logo**, then release **[Shift]**
   The Group Objects button appears beneath the two selected objects, as shown in Figure B-15. Notice that both objects have handles surrounding them.

5. Click, position over the object, then drag the upper-left corner of the object to **4.375, 5.250 in.**
   You notice that the handles changed to a single set of handles surrounding both the combined objects. Compare your newsletter to Figure B-16.

6. Press **[Esc]** twice, scroll up to the text box whose top-left corner is at **2.00, 0.500 in.**, click inside the **text box**, press **[Ctrl][A]**, type **your name**, then press **[Esc]** twice
   You are finished working on the publication for now, so you decide to save your work.

7. Press **[F9]**, then click the **Save button** on the Standard toolbar
   You want to print the first page of the newsletter.

8. Click **File** on the menu bar, click **Print**, click the **Current page option button**, then click **OK**
   A copy of the publication is printed. You end your Publisher session.

9. Click **File** on the menu bar, then click **Exit**

▶ PUBLISHER 40 CREATING A PUBLICATION

FIGURE B-15: Preparing to group objects

Both objects are selected and appear with handles

Group Objects button

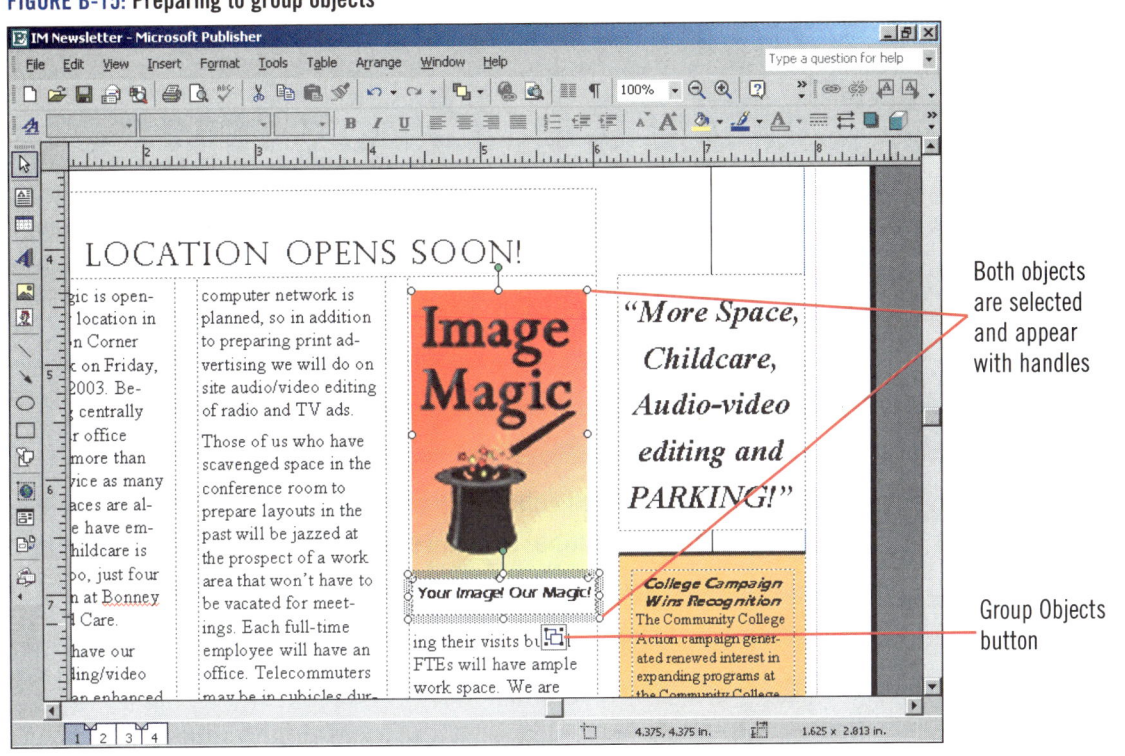

FIGURE B-16: Grouped and repositioned objects

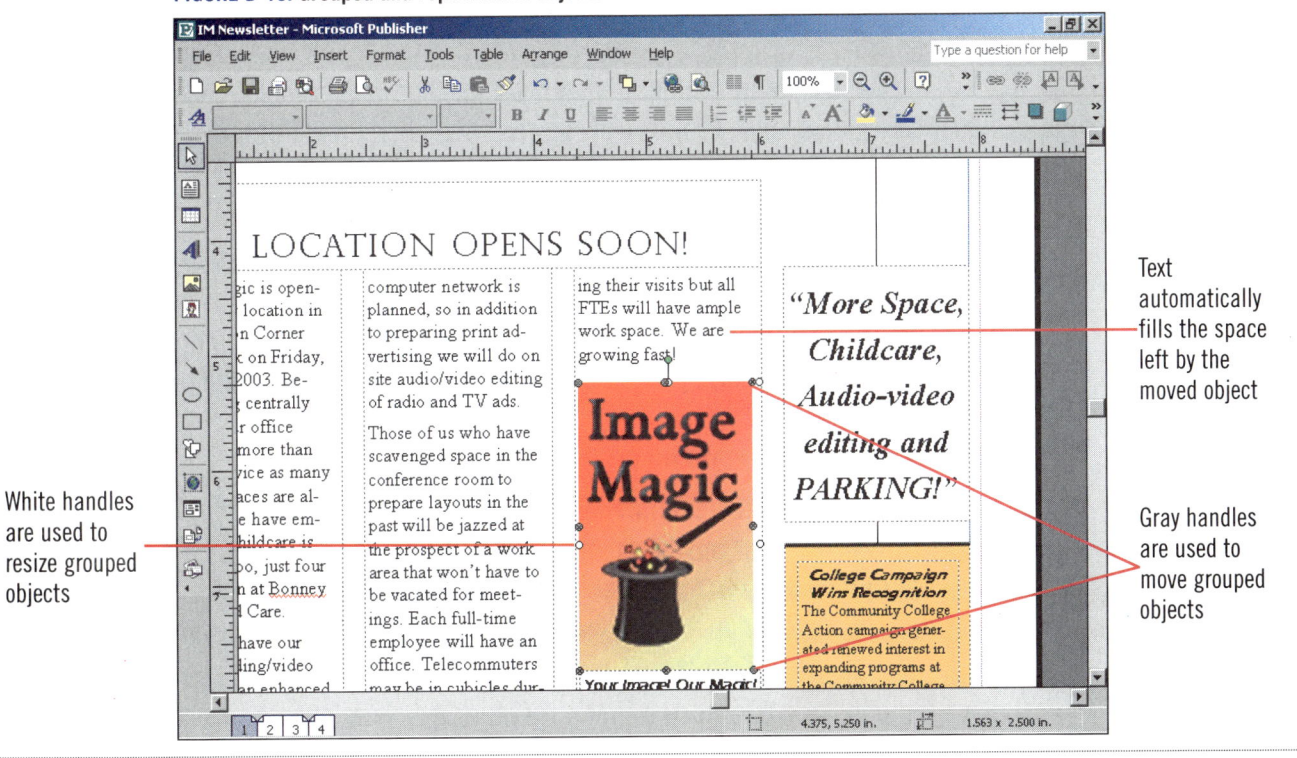

White handles are used to resize grouped objects

Text automatically fills the space left by the moved object

Gray handles are used to move grouped objects

CREATING A PUBLICATION

Capstone Project: College Brochure

Unit B — Publisher 2002

You have learned the skills necessary to plan, design, and create a new publication. You can find and open an existing file using the New Publication task pane and Publication Gallery, and save it under a different name. Using buttons on the Objects toolbar, you can create a text box, and add graphic images and sidebars, and using the Design Gallery, you can insert objects that enhance your publication. Once objects are placed in your publication, you can group them so they can be treated as a single object. Camelback Community College is one of Image Magic's local clients. Mike needs to create a brochure that promotes their courses.

Steps

1. Start Publisher, click **Brochures** from the By Publication Type list, click **Informational**, click **Blends Informational Brochure**, then save the publication to the drive and folder where your Project Files are stored as **Camelback Brochure**

   Mike will use the Image Magic Personal Information Set as placeholder text while preparing the brochure. He will substitute the college's information for the placeholder text before turning over the publication to the client.

2. Click **Edit** on the menu bar, click **Personal Information**, click **Secondary Business**, then click **Update**

   You want to replace some of the placeholder text.

3. Click the **Product/Service Information placeholder**, type **Camelback Community College**, press **[Esc]** twice, then close the task pane

   Now you will add a slogan for the college that will help attract students with its simple and powerful message.

4. Click the placeholder at **8.500, 4.000 in.**, press **[Ctrl][A]** to select the text, then type **Education You Can Use!**

   You think the center panel of the brochure needs some colorful objects so you will add a colorful pull quote. Then you will group it and move it and the graphic placeholder.

   > **Trouble?**
   > Move the pull quote to 6.775, 3.435 in., if necessary.

5. Click the **Design Gallery Object button** on the Objects toolbar, click **Pull Quotes** under Categories, click **Blends Pull Quote**, then click **Insert Object**

   The pull quote remains selected so grouping it with the graphic placeholder is easy. The pull quote is on the right panel, above the computer graphic image, as shown in Figure B-17.

6. Press **[Shift]**, click the object at **8.500, 5.000 in.**, then click the **Group Objects button**

   The objects grouped are as shown in Figure B-18.

7. Position the pointer over the grouped object, when the pointer changes to click and drag the grouped objects until the coordinates are **4.250, 2.000 in.**, then release the mouse button

   The grouped objects are now on the center panel of the brochure.

8. Click the **placeholder text** in the pull quote, replace it with **your name**, press **[Ctrl][A]**, click **Format** on the menu bar, point to **AutoFit Text**, click **Best Fit**, then press **[Esc]** three times

   Compare your publication with Figure B-19. With your name prominently placed on the publication, you are ready to print.

9. Save the publication, print the first page, then exit Publisher

FIGURE B-17: Inserted Design Gallery object

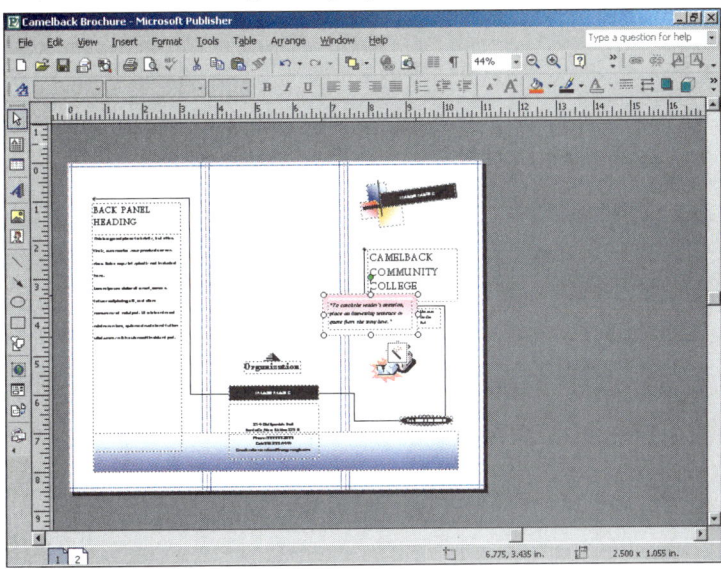

FIGURE B-18: Grouped objects

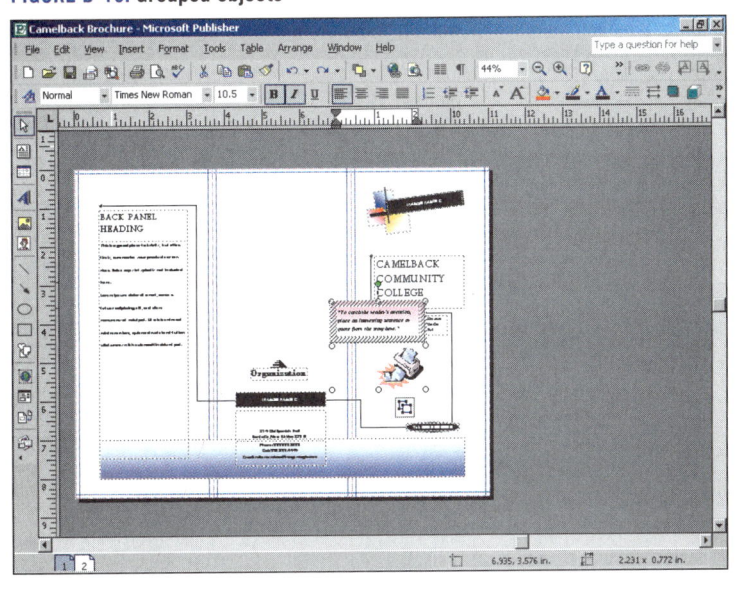

FIGURE B-19: Objects moved and text replaced

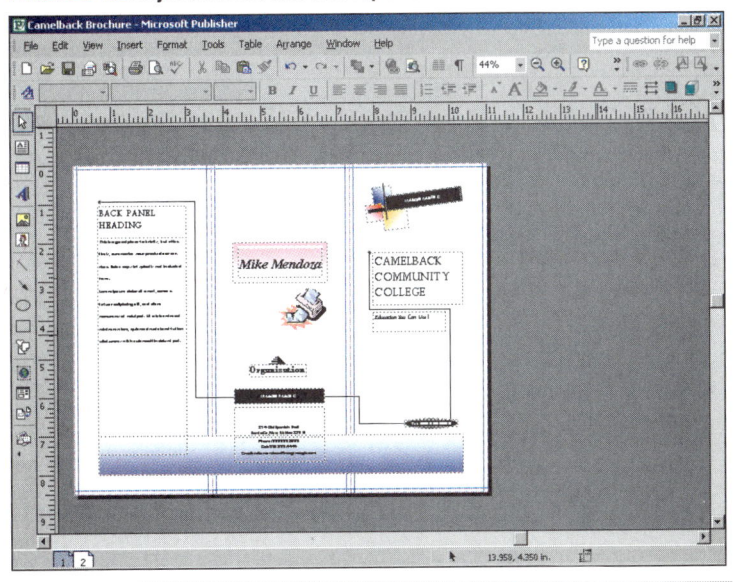

CREATING A PUBLICATION PUBLISHER 43

Publisher 2002

Practice

▶ Concepts Review

Label each of the elements of the Publisher window shown in Figure B-20.

FIGURE B-20

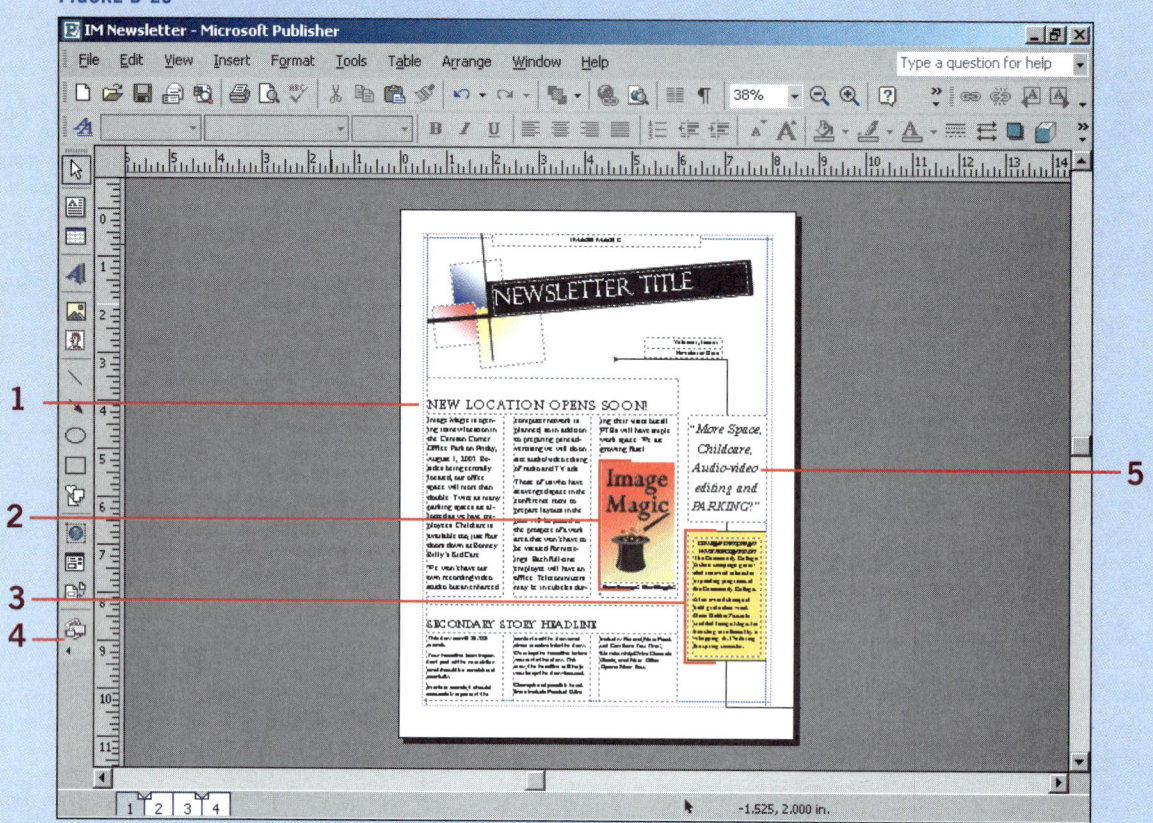

Match each of the terms or buttons with the statement that describes its function.

6.
7.
8. New Publication option
9. Publication Gallery
10.
11. Graphic image

a. Can be used to create an ad or logo, for example
b. A visual directory containing different publications
c. Resizes a frame vertically
d. Creates a text box
e. Artwork stored in an electronic file
f. Displays different shadows

Select the best answer from the list of choices.

12. Which menu is used to access the AutoFit text feature?
    a. Edit
    b. Format
    c. Tools
    d. Arrange

▶ PUBLISHER 44   CREATING A PUBLICATION

Practice

13. Maintain the scale of an image while resizing a graphic image by pressing:
    a. [Esc].
    b. [Alt].
    c. [Shift].
    d. The right mouse button.
14. Which of the following extensions does not indicate a common graphic image format?
    a. .GIF
    b. .TIF
    c. .CDR
    d. .GFX
15. Interesting information that invites you to read a story is called a:
    a. Placeholder.
    b. Sidebar.
    c. Pull quote.
    d. Side quote.
16. Which of the following statements about a pull quote is false?
    a. It should be on a different page from the actual text.
    b. It should be short and easy to read.
    c. It does not have to be identical to the text in the article.
    d. It should entice you to read the article.
17. Which of the following statements about graphic images is false?
    a. Scanned artwork can be used in Publisher.
    b. Artwork created in drawing programs can be used in Publisher.
    c. You can use only the artwork that comes with Publisher.
    d. You can use any electronic artwork in Publisher.
18. Which button is the Design Gallery button?
    a.
    b.
    c.
    d.
19. Which pointer is used to change the location of an object?
    a.
    b.
    c.
    d.
20. Group objects by holding and pressing [Shift], clicking each object, then clicking:
    a.
    b. Tools on the menu bar, then Group Objects.
    c.
    d. Objects on the menu bar, then Group.

▶ Skills Review

1. Create a publication with the New Publication option.
    a. Start Publisher, then select **Newsletters** from By Publications Type in the New Publication task pane.
    b. Create a publication that has the following options: Floating Oval Newsletter, two-sided printing, and no placeholder for the customer's address. Use the Personal Information Set of your choosing, or enter information for address, phone number, and other pertinent information.
    c. Change to the Monarch color scheme. In the Page Content section of the task pane, change to two columns.
    d. Save this publication as **Mock-up Newsletter** to the drive and folder where your Project Files are stored.
2. Replace text.
    a. Close the task pane.
    b. Click the Lead Story Headline placeholder, then zoom in.
    c. Replace the placeholder text with the following text: **Making the Workspace Work for You**
    d. Select the lead story text, then delete it.
    e. Insert the Word file PUB B-3 from the location where your Project Files are stored.
    f. Read the article, then zoom out, then save the publication.

CREATING A PUBLICATION

Publisher 2002 | Practice

3. **Add a graphic image.**
   a. Select the graphic image placeholder and its caption, then delete them.
   b. Insert the picture file **Imlogo** from the drive and folder where your Project Files are stored.
   c. Press and hold [Shift], resize the image to 1.563 × 2.500 in., then reposition it so that the upper-left corner is at 6.000, 5.000 in., then save the publication.

4. **Add a sidebar.**
   a. Select the sidebar placeholder in the left column above the Table of Contents, then select the text within it.
   b. Zoom in to view the Special Points of Interest placeholder text in the sidebar, then delete the text.
   c. Insert the Word file PUB B-4 from the drive and folder where your Project Files are stored.
   d. View and read the sidebar, zoom out so you can see the entire publication, then deselect the sidebar.
   e. Save the publication.

5. **Use the Design Gallery.**
   a. Click the Design Gallery Object button on the Objects toolbar, then click Pull Quotes.
   b. Add a Floating Oval pull quote, then zoom in to view the pull quote.
   c. Move the pull quote so the upper-left corner is at 2.500, 2.500 in.
   d. Replace the placeholder with: **You spend one-third of your day at work. Shouldn't you be comfortable?**
   e. Resize the pull quote frame so the dimensions are 4.360 × 0.375 in. It should be placed above the Making the Workspace Work for You text box.
   f. Click AutoFit Text on the Format menu, then click Best Fit.
   g. Zoom out so you can see the entire publication, deselect the pull quote, zoom in, then save the publication.

6. **Group objects.**
   a. Press and hold [Shift], then select both the volume and newsletter date text boxes in the left column.
   b. Group the two selected objects.
   c. Move the grouped object so the top-left corner of the combined object is at 0.500, 2.500 in.
   d. Ungroup the objects, deselect the objects, then replace the Newsletter Date text with **your name**.
   e. Save your work, print the first page of the publication, then exit Publisher.

▶ Independent Challenge 1

You volunteered to help the local Kiwanis Club design a flyer for its upcoming fund-raiser, a Fun Run. The organization is trying to raise money for victims of earthquakes in Central America. The funds will go toward medicine, building materials, food, clothing, and transportation costs for the material and some volunteers.

   a. Start Publisher if necessary, then create a flyer using the Charity Bazaar Fund-raiser Flyer.
   b. Save the publication in the folder where your Project Files are stored as **Fun Run Flyer**.
   c. Change the Color Scheme to Floral, then accept the default options on the Flyer Options task pane.
   d. Modify the Charity Bazaar text placeholder to say **Kiwanis Fun Run**, replace the five bulleted items with five of your own good reasons to attend this event, then include your name as the contact person for the event.
   e. Make up the necessary information, such as the location of the fund-raiser, the address of the Kiwanis Club, and the date and time of the event, to make sure all the text in the flyer relates to the Fun Run event.
   f. Save and print the publication, then close the publication and exit Publisher.

Practice

▶ Independent Challenge 2

You are a regular at the Get it While it's Hot luncheonette. They ask you to help create a menu for their new take-out division. Use the New Publication option to create this menu, and replace the existing text with your own.

   a. Start Publisher if necessary, then create a take-out menu by choosing the Gingham Take-Out Menu.
   b. Save the publication to the drive and folder where your Project Files are stored as **Take-Out Menu**.
   c. Change the Color Scheme to Bluebird, and accept the default options for Customer Address.
   d. Modify the placeholder company name and information for the Get it While it's Hot luncheonette.
   e. Replace the placeholder text under the restaurant's name with a description of the food served at this luncheonette.
   f. Include your name as the contact person for take-out orders.
   g. Make sure all the text in the flyer relates to the take-out menu.
   h. Make up your own menu items. (*Hint:* Click the Page 2 icon to access the second page.)
   i. Group two objects on the menu and move them.
   j. Save the publication, print the publication, then exit Publisher.

▶ Independent Challenge 3

The tenants in your rental property just gave you 30 days notice, so you must find new tenants. You need to create a sign in which you can describe the house in order to attract new tenants.

   a. Start Publisher if necessary, then use the New Publication option to create a sign using the For Rent Sign.
   b. Save the publication to the drive and folder where your Project Files are stored as **For Rent Sign**.
   c. Replace the bulleted items with your descriptions of the house for rent.
   d. Modify the telephone number placeholder using your number.
   e. Create a text box under the telephone number that says **Call your name for more information**.
   f. Select the text containing your name, then make the font size 18 points. (*Hint:* Resize the text box to fit the text if necessary.)
   g. Save the publication, print the publication, then exit Publisher.

e Independent Challenge 4

You are asked to create a Web page for your school's Publisher class. You will use the New Publication task pane and the Publication Gallery. This site should discuss what topics are covered in the class.

   a. Connect to the Internet and go to your school's Web site.
   b. Print out the home page and the page for the department offering this Publisher course.
   c. Start Publisher if necessary, then use the New Publication task pane and the Publication Gallery to create a Web site for your Publisher class.
   d. The Web page should consist of one page, using a style, color scheme, and background that complement the school's existing Web site.
   e. Save your publication as **Publisher Class Web Page** to the drive and folder where your Project Files are stored.
   f. Create a text box that lists you as the contact person if more information is necessary. Adding a telephone number, fax number, or e-mail address is optional.
   g. Replace the text placeholders with your own text, based on the topics that are covered in this class. (*Hint:* Consult your class syllabus.)
   h. Include your name in a text box in the lower-left corner of the Web page.
   i. Save and print your publication, then exit Publisher.

CREATING A PUBLICATION

Publisher 2002 | Practice

▶ Visual Workshop

Use the New Publication task pane and Publication Gallery to create an informational postcard for Image Magic that announces its new location. Save the publication as **IM Postcard** to the drive and folder where your Project Files are stored. Use the Borders Informational Postcard layout, the quarter-page format, and show only the address on the other side of the card. Add the Imlogo graphic image, apply the Wildflower color scheme, and replace the placeholder text and add new text in text boxes, as necessary, using Figure B-21 as a guide. Add a text box to the publication with your name, then print the page.

FIGURE B-21

We Are On The Move

Just another friendly reminder that we are moving to a more spacious, more centrally located facility.

We are expanding our services but continuing the same high quality products we are known for.

Image Magic

Image Magic
214 Old Spanish Trail
Santa Fe, New Mexico 87501

Phone: 505-555-5555
Fax: 505-555-4444
Email:
mikemendoza@imagemagic.co

Your Image! Our Magic!

PUBLISHER 48 CREATING A PUBLICATION

Publisher 2002

Unit C

Working
With Text

Objectives

- ▶ Use layout guides
- ▶ Use ruler guides
- ▶ Format a text box
- ▶ Add bullets and numbering
- ▶ Check spelling
- ▶ Modify a Smart Object
- ▶ Paint formats
- ▶ Add a table
- ▶ Capstone Project: College Brochure

Publisher has many powerful tools to help you design and lay out text and graphics. You will use Publisher's layout guides and rulers to assure that your layout is accurate and consistent. You will also check spelling, add objects, and apply formatting so that your finished publication is professional looking. Mike Mendoza is designing a flyer that will be used to promote Image Magic's Professional Design Clinic. Image Magic wants the flyer to be colorful and informative and to grab people's attention.

Using Layout Guides

Publisher 2002 — Unit C

When correctly laid out, elements in a publication are placed to achieve a balanced and consistent look. This balance and consistency occurs only with careful planning and design. **Layout guides** and **margin guides**, horizontal and vertical lines visible only on the screen, help you accurately position objects on a page and across pages in a publication. Layout guides are created on the **Master Page**, the background that is the same for all pages within a publication. Mike's assignment is to create a flyer for an upcoming design clinic. He will use a publication from the Publication Gallery, then set up the layout guides to help plan for future placement of objects in the publication. Mike will also experiment with a different color scheme.

Steps

1. Start Publisher, click **Flyers** in the By Publication Type list, click **Informational**, then click **Bars Informational Flyer** in the Informational Flyers list

   The flyer appears on the screen and the Flyer Options task pane opens. You want to change from the Wildflower to the Bluebird color scheme in the Personal Information Set. The Bluebird color scheme uses the same colors as the Wildflower scheme but applies them differently.

   QuickTip: Color schemes are listed in alphabetical order.

2. Click **Edit** on the menu bar, click **Personal Information**, click **Secondary Business**, if necessary type **Mike Mendoza** in the Name text box, type **Account Executive** in the Job or position title text box, type **Image Magic** in the Address text box, press **[Enter]**, type **214 Old Spanish Trail**, press **[Enter]**, type **Santa Fe, New Mexico 87501**, in the Phone/fax/e-mail text box type **Phone: 505-555-5555**, press **[Enter]**, type **Fax: 505-555-4444**, press **[Enter]**, type **E-mail: mikemendoza@imagemagic.com**, type **Image Magic** in the Organization name text box, type **Your Image! Our Magic!** in the Tag line or motto text box, click the **Color Schemes list arrow**, click **Bluebird**, then click **Update**

   The task pane is not necessary for the remainder of the flyer you are designing.

3. Click the **Close button** on the Flyer Options task pane, then save the publication to the drive and folder where your Project Files are stored as **Design Clinic Flyer**

   QuickTip: Ruler coordinates are given as follows: 4" H / 5" V. This means that the coordinate is at 4" on the horizontal ruler, and 5" on the vertical ruler.

4. Right-click the graphic placeholder at **4" H / 5" V**, click **Delete Object**, click **Yes** in the warning box, right-click the text box at **4" H / 5" V**, then click **Delete Object**

   The image and text box are deleted from the flyer.

5. Click **Arrange** on the menu bar, then click **Layout Guides**

   The Layout Guides dialog box opens. You use the Layout Guides dialog box to change the margin dimensions.

6. If necessary, click the **Left down arrow** until **0.5** appears in the text box, click the **Right down arrow** until **0.5** appears in the text box, click the **Top down arrow** until **0.5** appears in the text box, select the text **1** in the **Bottom text box**, then type **0.66** in the text box if necessary

   The top and bottom margins are small enough to allow lots of information to be placed on each page. Layout guides create a grid to help you line up design elements, such as images and text boxes, on the page.

7. Click the **Columns up arrow** until **3** appears in the text box, click the **Rows up arrow** until **3** appears in the text box as shown in Figure C-1, then click **OK**

   The pink lines represent the column guides, and the blue lines represent the column guide margins. The guides appear on the screen, as shown in Figure C-2, but do not print on the page.

8. Click the **Save button** on the Standard toolbar

▶ PUBLISHER 50 **WORKING WITH TEXT**

FIGURE C-1: Layout Guides dialog box

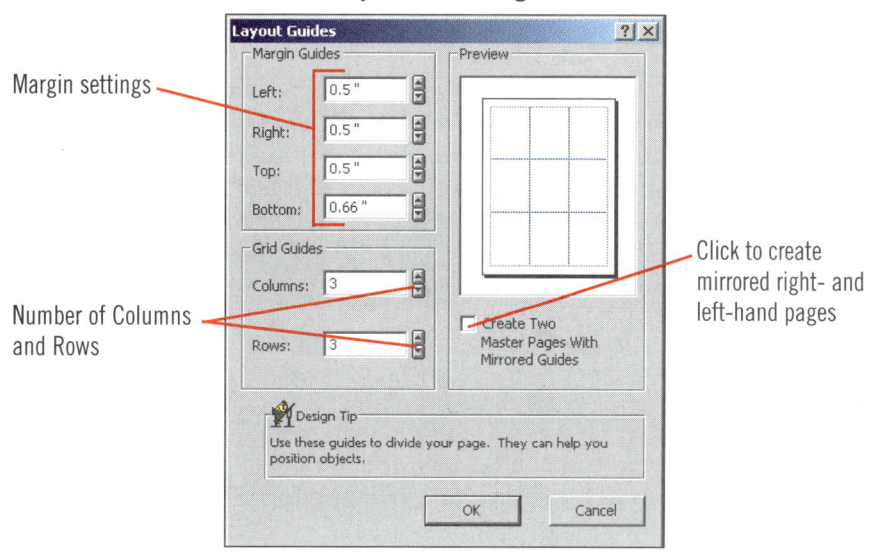

Margin settings → [Margin Guides section: Left: 0.5", Right: 0.5", Top: 0.5", Bottom: 0.66"]

Number of Columns and Rows → [Grid Guides: Columns: 3, Rows: 3]

Click to create mirrored right- and left-hand pages → [Create Two Master Pages With Mirrored Guides check box]

FIGURE C-2: Layout guides in publication

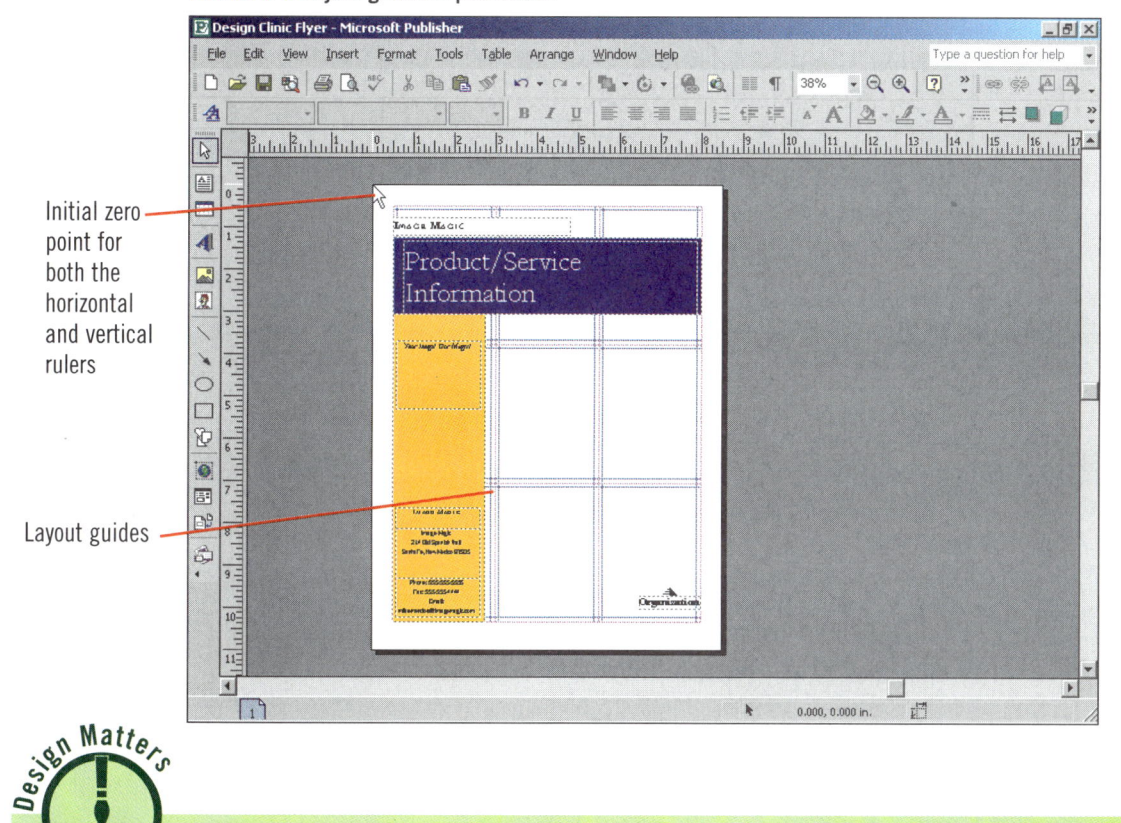

Initial zero point for both the horizontal and vertical rulers

Layout guides

Understanding mirrored layout guides

If a publication has left and right pages, you can use **mirrored guides** so that facing pages have opposite margins and layout guides. This can make your material easier to read and more consistent in appearance. When you click the Create Two Master Pages with Mirrored Guides check box, the names of the Left and Right margin guides become Inside and Outside margin guides. A bound publication should have larger inside margins to allow for the space taken up by the binding. You can switch the layout guides from the Master Page by pressing [Shift] and placing over a layout guide. The pointer changes to either or . Drag the guide to any location, using the vertical and horizontal rulers for exact measurements. You can also return layout guides to their original locations by clicking the Undo button on the Standard toolbar before performing any other action.

WORKING WITH TEXT

Publisher 2002 — Unit C

Using Ruler Guides

Publisher also lets you create individual page guides, called ruler guides. **Ruler guides** work just like layout guides, but are created in the foreground of individual pages, whereas layout guides are on the background of each page in a publication. Functionally, layout guides and ruler guides are the same, and neither is printed on the publication. Ruler guides are green horizontal and vertical lines that are dragged from the rulers into the workspace. The location of zero, the **zero point**, on both the vertical and horizontal rulers can be moved, giving you the flexibility to make precise measurements from any point on the page. Mike moves each ruler's zero point and adds ruler guides for the location of a graphic image on the first page. First, he moves the vertical ruler closer to the page.

Steps

1. Position ⇗ over the vertical ruler, when the pointer changes to ↔ press and hold the **left mouse button**, drag the **vertical ruler** to the left edge of the publication, then release the left mouse button

   The ruler is repositioned, as shown in Figure C-3. When you move a ruler, the zero point does not change; the ruler moves closer, making it easier to locate positions. You don't need to move the horizontal ruler since it sits just above the top of the page. Currently, the horizontal and vertical zero point is set at the top-left edge of the page. You want to change the horizontal and vertical zero point to the left edge and top margin so you can determine exact measurements from the top-left margin edge.

   Trouble?
   You can reset the zero point to its default settings by double-clicking each ruler, or by double-clicking the Move Both Rulers button.

2. Position ⇗ over the **Move Both Rulers button** ☐ at the intersection of the horizontal and vertical rulers, the pointer changes to ⇘, press and hold **[Shift]**, right-click ☐, drag ⇘ to ½" H / ½" V, release the mouse button, then release [Shift]

   You want to double-check that you moved the zero point correctly.

3. Place ⇗ at the top-left corner of the pink guides

   The coordinates in the object position on the status bar are 0.000, 0.000 in. To further help you position design elements, you can add ruler guides where you want a graphic image to appear.

   QuickTip
   Use the horizontal ruler to measure a vertical ruler guide; use the vertical ruler to measure a horizontal ruler guide.

4. Press and hold **[Shift]**, position the pointer anywhere over the vertical ruler, drag ⇔ to **3" H**, release [Shift], then release the mouse button

   A green vertical ruler guide appears on the screen at the 3" horizontal mark. You use the same techniques to create a horizontal ruler guide, using the horizontal adjust pointer.

5. Press and hold **[Shift]**, position the pointer over the horizontal ruler, drag ⇕ to **3½" V**, release [Shift], then release the mouse button

   After looking at the horizontal ruler guide, you realize its position is too high and that the ruler guide must be lowered.

6. Press and hold **[Shift]**, position the pointer over the horizontal ruler guide at **3"** until it changes to ⇕, drag the ruler guide to **3¾"** on the vertical ruler, release the mouse button, then release [Shift]

   The ruler guides appear only on this page and will be helpful when a text box is added.

7. Place ⇗ on the vertical ruler, press and hold **[Shift]**, drag ⇔ to create a vertical ruler guide at **5½" H**

8. Place ⇗ on the horizontal ruler, press and hold **[Shift]**, drag ⇕ to create three horizontal ruler guides: at **6¼" V, 7" V, and 8¾" V**

   Compare your ruler guides to those in Figure C-4.

9. Click the **Save button** 💾 on the Standard toolbar

▶ PUBLISHER 52   **WORKING WITH TEXT**

FIGURE C-3: Moving a ruler

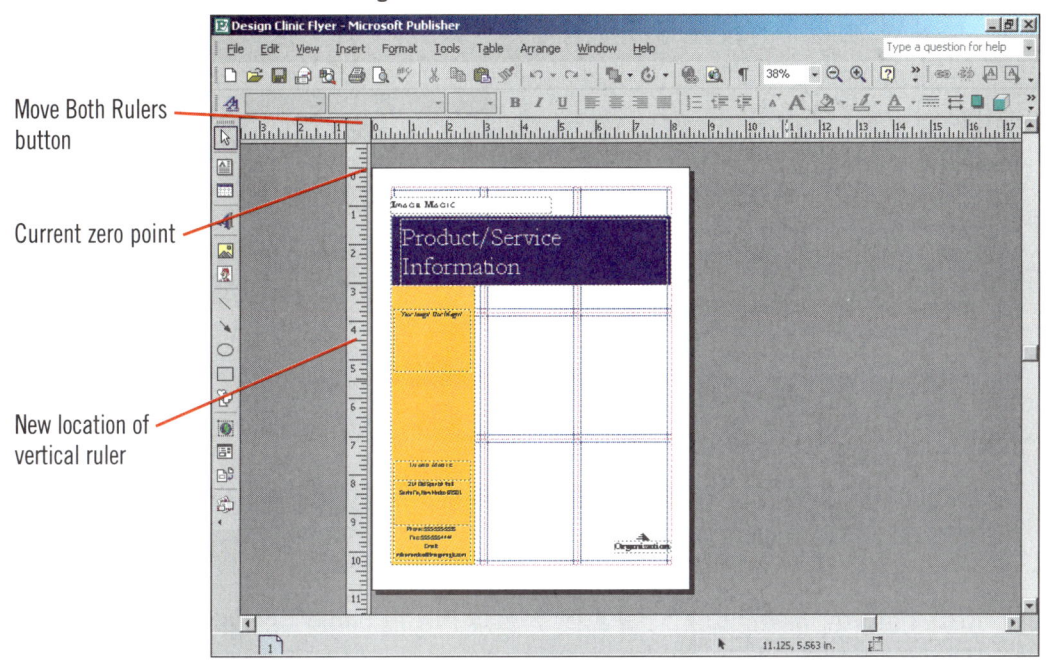

Move Both Rulers button

Current zero point

New location of vertical ruler

FIGURE C-4: Horizontal and vertical ruler guides added

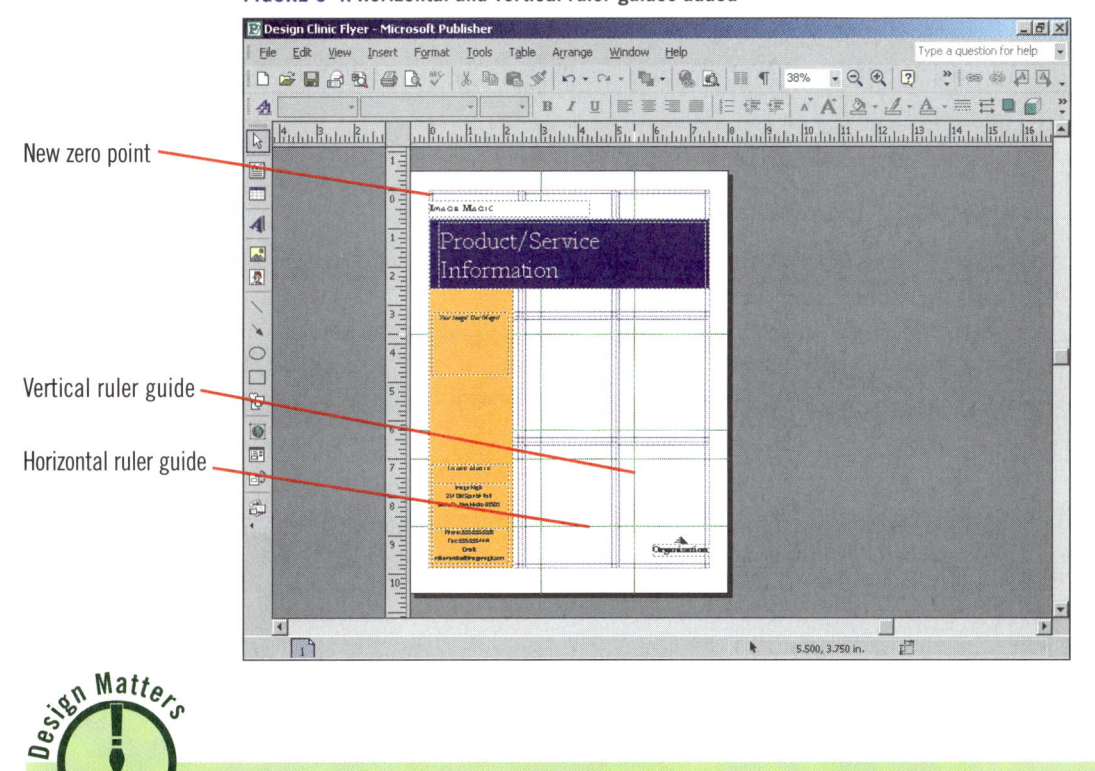

New zero point

Vertical ruler guide

Horizontal ruler guide

Choosing measurement tools

Publisher provides different ways to measure the dimensions and positions of objects. The Object Position and Object Size coordinates on the status bar are always visible, but it can be difficult to place and size objects using them. The **Measurement toolbar** is a direct way to precisely position and size objects to one 1/1000 of an inch accuracy. To open the Measurement toolbar, click View on the menu bar, point to Toolbars, then click Measurement. The Format *item* dialog boxes (where item stands for Text box, Object, Picture, Table, etc.) have tabs that let you position and size the item, but require you to shift from one tab of the dialog box to another. The horizontal and vertical rulers have the advantage of being the closest tools to the publication, and they are moveable so they can be even closer.

WORKING WITH TEXT PUBLISHER 53

Publisher 2002 — Unit C

Formatting a Text Box

Ruler guides help place objects accurately on a page. Objects can be placed freely on the page, or you can use Snap To commands to take advantage of the layout and ruler guides, which create a magnet-like effect, pulling whatever you're trying to line up toward the ruler, guide, or object. Once a text box is added to a page, it can be moved or resized. A border can be added and formatted to appear in any available color or line width you choose. The Formatting toolbar contains buttons for the most common commands used to improve the text box's appearance. Mike wants to add a text box that describes how to best use logos. He places the text box using the ruler guides, and then enhances it with formatting attributes. To begin, he moves the vertical ruler out of the way.

Steps

1. Position the pointer over the vertical ruler, then when the pointer changes to ↔ drag the **vertical ruler** to the left edge of the workspace
   The vertical ruler is now out of the way.

2. Click the flyer heading at **1" H / 1" V**, type **Professional Design Clinic**, then press **[Esc]** three times
   The new heading is in the deselected text box. Using the ruler and layout guides to place text boxes and other objects is extremely helpful, particularly when you use the Snap To feature.

3. Click **Arrange** on the menu bar, point to **Snap**, then click **To Ruler Marks** and **To Guides** to select them if necessary
   You will now add a text box.

4. Click the **Text Box button** on the Objects toolbar
   The pointer changes to +. The ruler guides help you easily place a text box.

   > **Trouble?**
   > A text box must be selected before it can be modified.

5. Drag + from **3" H / 3¾" V** to **5" H / 6¼" V**
   The text box automatically snapped to the ruler and layout guides. Compare your page to Figure C-5. You decide that a thicker, more colorful border would make the text box stand out.

6. Right-click the **text box**, click **Format Text Box**, click the **Line Color list arrow**, then click the **blue** (fourth from left) **color box**
   A sample of the color appears in the Format Text Box dialog box, as shown in Figure C-6. Since you selected a color scheme in the Personal Information dialog box, those colors are presented to you on this palette to help you retain design consistency in the publication. You could click More Colors from the Line Color drop down list if you wanted to work outside the color scheme.

7. Click the **Weight up Arrow** until **4 pt** appears in the text box, then click **OK**
   The text box that you placed on the page using the ruler guides appears with the thick blue border that matches the fill in the flyer heading, as shown in Figure C-7.

8. Click the **Save button** on the Standard toolbar

PUBLISHER 54   **WORKING WITH TEXT**

FIGURE C-5: Text box inserted

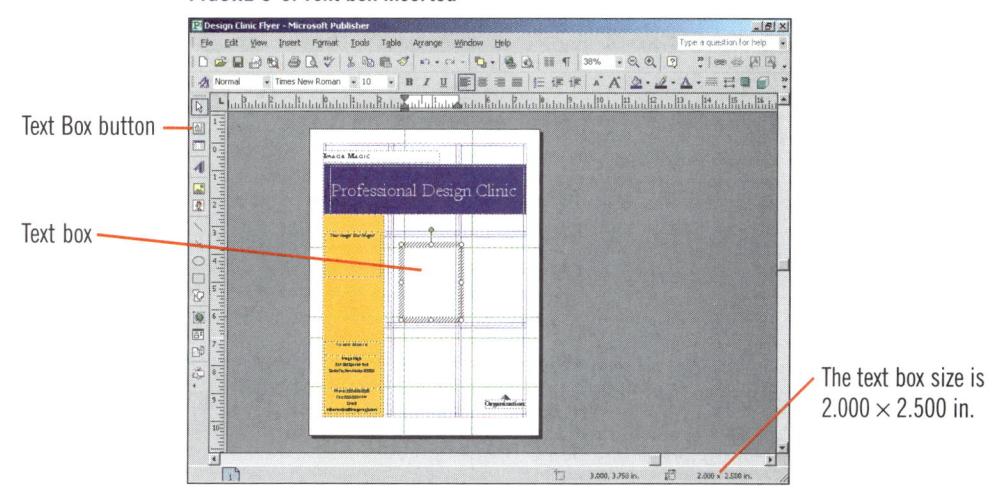

- Text Box button
- Text box
- The text box size is 2.000 × 2.500 in.

FIGURE C-6: Format Text Box dialog box

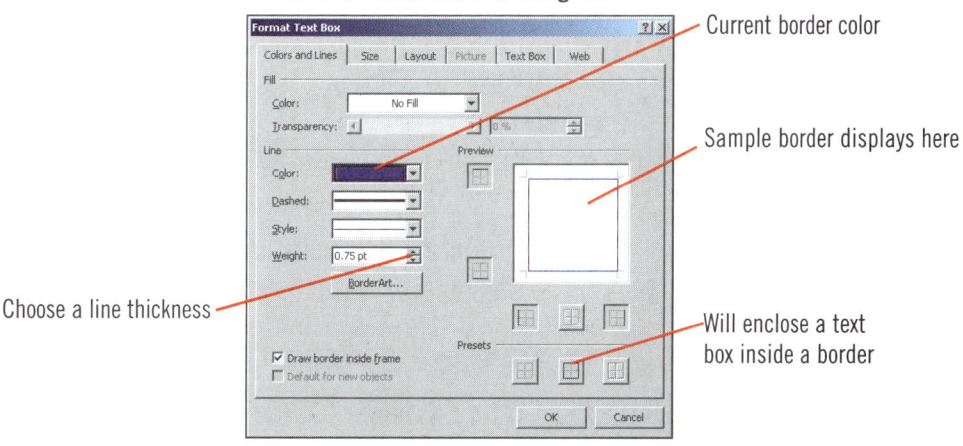

- Current border color
- Sample border displays here
- Choose a line thickness
- Will enclose a text box inside a border

FIGURE C-7: Text box with thick blue border

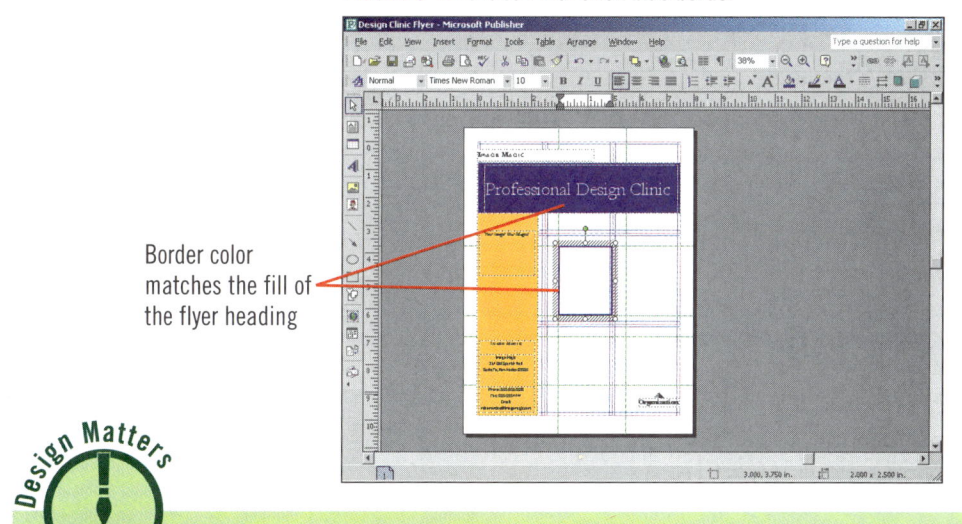

- Border color matches the fill of the flyer heading

Design Matters

Making use of margins

When you think of **margins**, you probably think of the space surrounding the four edges of a page. The term also applies to the space that surrounds any boundary, so each design object has margins. Margins are often used to create **white space**, the designer's term for space on a page that is not covered with printed or graphic material. The addition of white space is critical for clarity since without it the page looks cluttered and is difficult to read. Margins are used around graphic images, around each side of a column, and within a table or text box.

WORKING WITH TEXT   PUBLISHER 55

Adding Bullets and Numbering

Publisher 2002 — Unit C

When you need to display information in a list, you can add emphasis to the items by formatting them with bullets or numbers. A **bulleted list** is used to present a list of supporting or related points. A **numbered list** is generally used to present items that occur in a particular sequence, while items in a **bulleted list** can be in any order. Both numbered and bulleted list formats can be applied either before or after the text is typed. You can switch back and forth between numbers and bullets, trying different styles of numbers and bullets until you arrive at the right format. Mike adds a numbered list in the text box he just created.

Steps

1. Make sure that the text box with the blue border is still selected, then press **[F9]**
   The point size for a list can be larger than that in a paragraph because you have less text and want to emphasize each word. You add a heading to help identify the content in your list.

2. Click the **Font Size list arrow** on the Formatting toolbar, click **16**, type **Why use a logo?**, then press **[Enter]**
   The heading, which is not part of the numbered list, is entered first.

3. Click the **Numbering button** on the Formatting toolbar, **1.** appears in the text box, type **Customers look for it.**, press **[Enter]**, type **It distinguishes your firm from others.**, press **[Enter]**, then type **It is an element of marketing**
   Compare your text with Figure C-8. To apply numbers or bullets to existing text, or to change from numbers to bullets, or back again, you first must select the text you want to format.

4. Drag I to select the text from **Customers** to **marketing.** so that the three numbered sentences are selected, click **Format** on the menu bar, then click **Indents and Lists**
   The Indents and Lists dialog box opens. You can change the appearance of a numbered list, convert it to a bulleted list, or change the appearance of the bullets by using this dialog box.

5. Click the **Bulleted list option button** in the Indents and Lists dialog box
   Available bullet options appear in the Indents and Lists dialog box, as shown in Figure C-9. To enhance any list, you can change the appearance of the bullets. Publisher lets you use a variety of characters as bullets, as well as change the size (measured in points) of the bullets.

6. Click the **diamond bullet**, click **OK**, then press **[Esc]** twice
   Compare your work with Figure C-10. The numbered list has been converted to a bulleted list. You zoom out to see the full page.

7. Press **[F9]**
   The bulleted list fits nicely on the page.

8. Click the **Save button** on the Standard toolbar

▶ PUBLISHER 56 **WORKING WITH TEXT**

FIGURE C-8: Numbered list in a text box

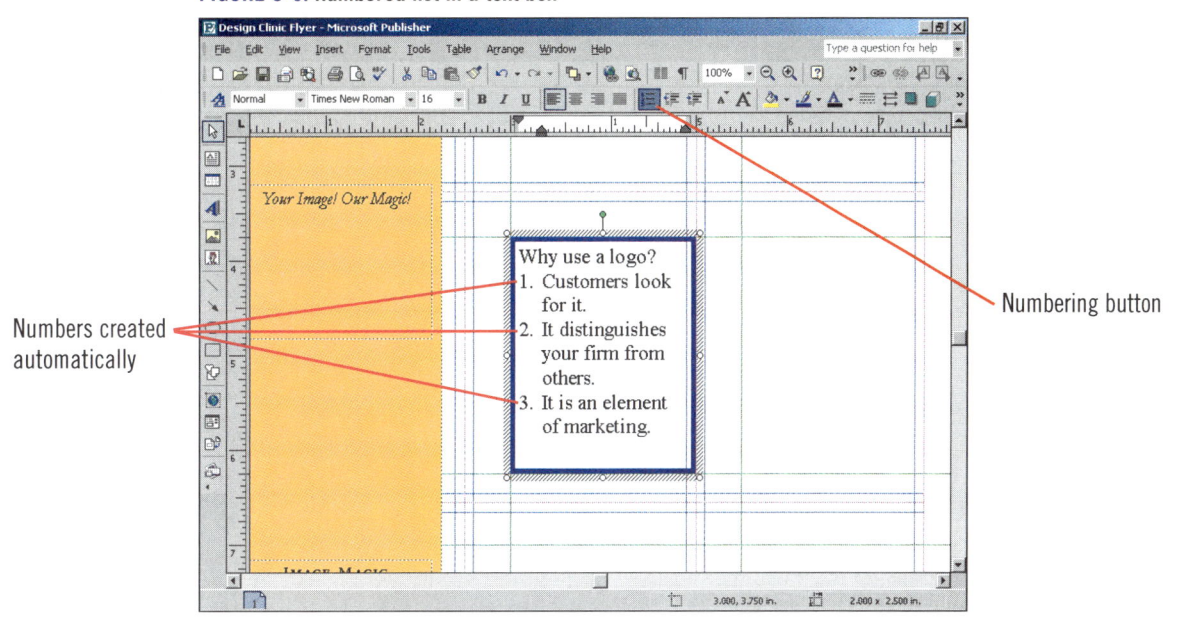

Numbers created automatically

Numbering button

FIGURE C-9: Indents and Lists dialog box

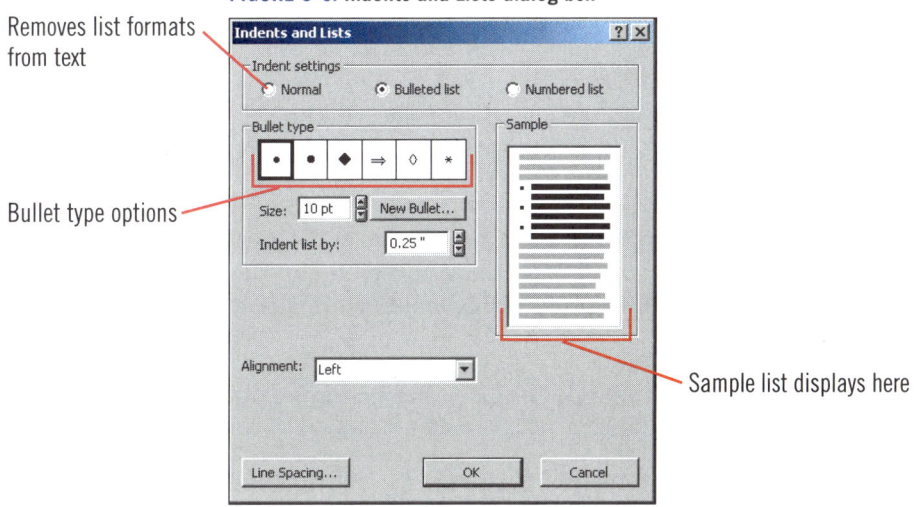

Removes list formats from text

Bullet type options

Sample list displays here

FIGURE C-10: Numbered list changed to a bulleted list

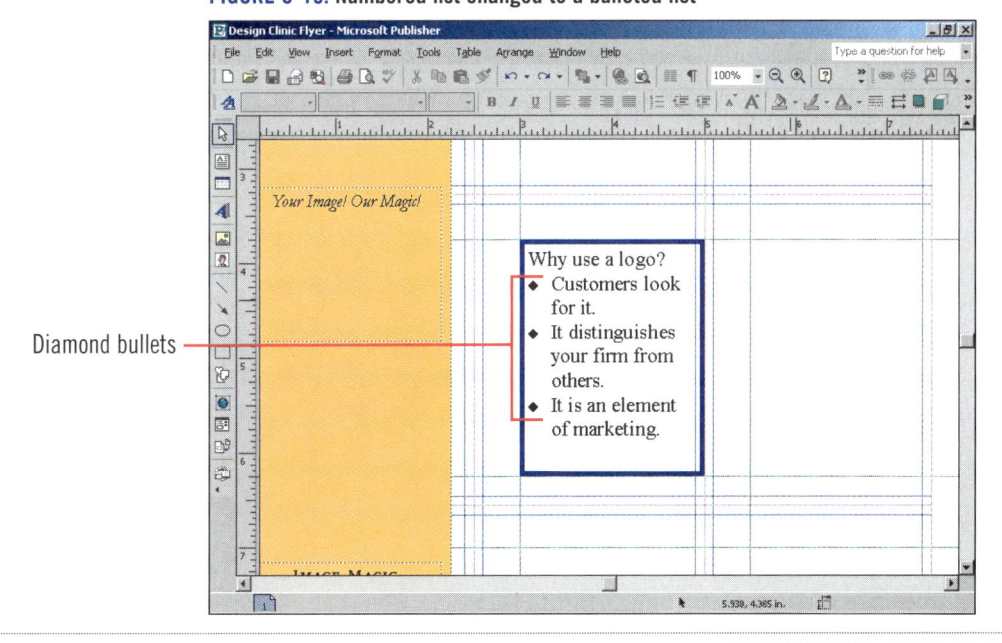

Diamond bullets

WORKING WITH TEXT

Checking Spelling

Publisher 2002 — Unit C

Spelling errors can ruin the most beautifully designed and well-written publication by distracting the reader from the message. Fortunately, using the **Spelling Checker** prevents embarrassment over misspelled words. The Spelling Checker is available only if a text box is selected. You can then check spelling using the Tools menu, or by right-clicking text, pointing to Proofing Tools, then clicking Spelling. Spelling errors are shown immediately as you type, indicated by a wavy red underline. You can add correctly spelled personal or industry-specific words not already in the dictionary as you work. ➤ Mike adds a text box and then imports text into the publication. Once the text is inserted, he checks for spelling errors.

Steps

1. Click the **Text Box button** on the Objects toolbar, drag + from **5½" H / 3¾" V** to the margin guide at **7⅜" H / 6¼" V**, then press **[F9]**
   The text box appears on the page. Text placed in a text box is sometimes referred to as a story. You want to insert a story into the text box.

2. Click **Insert** on the menu bar, click **Text File**, locate the drive and folder where your Project Files are stored, click the file **Pub C-1**, then click **OK**
   The text stored in the document file Pub C-1 is inserted into the text box, as shown in Figure C-11. This text contains misspelled words that you want to correct.

   Trouble? If you receive an error message saying that you do not have the correct converter installed, see your instructor or technical support person.

3. Click **Tools** on the menu bar, point to **Spelling**, then click **Spelling**
   The Check Spelling dialog box opens, as shown in Figure C-12. The first incorrect word found is "prievious." Publisher checks its dictionary to determine a word's spelling and places a suggestion in the Change to text box, so you don't have to click a suggestion. You can just replace the incorrect word with the word already in the Change to text box.

4. Click **Change**
   The Spelling feature advances to the next misspelled word, "ebent." This word is incorrect and should be "event."

   QuickTip To check the spelling of an individual word, click anywhere within the word, then press [F7].

5. Click **event** in the Suggestions list, then click **Change**

6. Accept the suggestions for the remaining misspelled words: **gaols**, **Leeder**, **prestigous**, and **Desing**
   The Spelling feature finished checking the text box. You do not want to check the other text boxes in your publication.

   QuickTip To choose not to accept the suggestion, click Ignore. You can also add words Publisher identifies as misspellings, such as proper names, to the dictionary by clicking Add.

7. Click **No** in the warning dialog box, click **OK**, then press **[Esc]** twice
   Compare your corrected text to Figure C-13.

8. Press **[F9]**, then click the **Save button** on the Standard toolbar
   You can examine the flyer and correct any errors in your work before continuing.

PUBLISHER 58   WORKING WITH TEXT

FIGURE C-11: Spelling errors in text

Misspelled words underlined in red

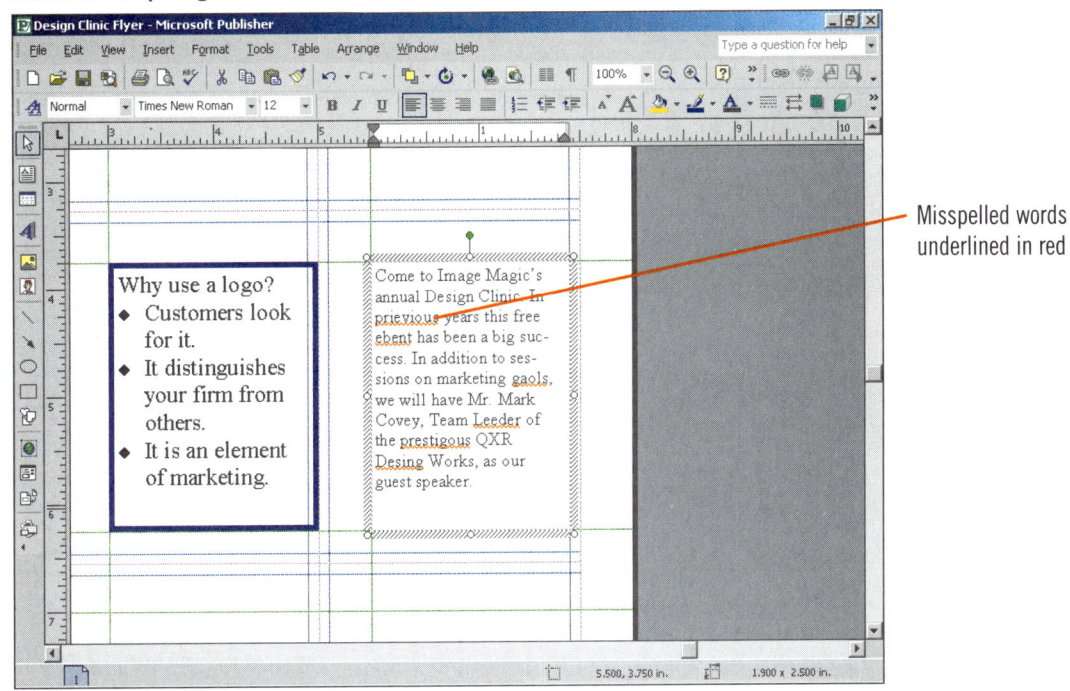

FIGURE C-12: Check Spelling dialog box

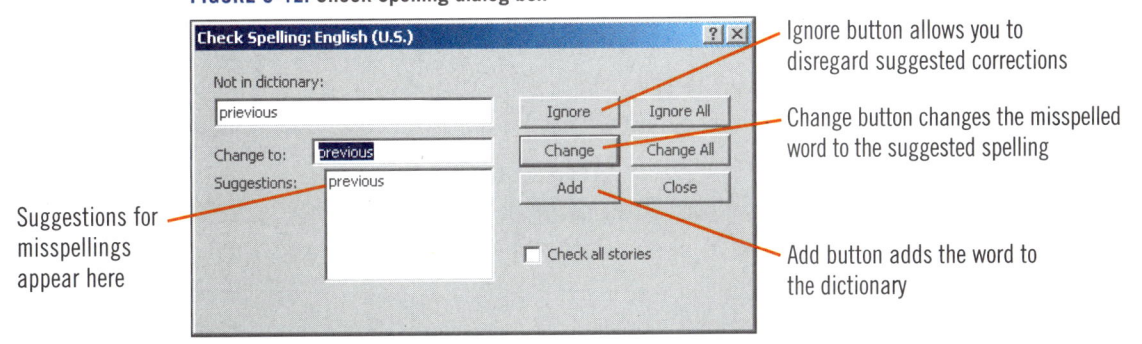

Suggestions for misspellings appear here

Ignore button allows you to disregard suggested corrections

Change button changes the misspelled word to the suggested spelling

Add button adds the word to the dictionary

FIGURE C-13: Corrected spelling

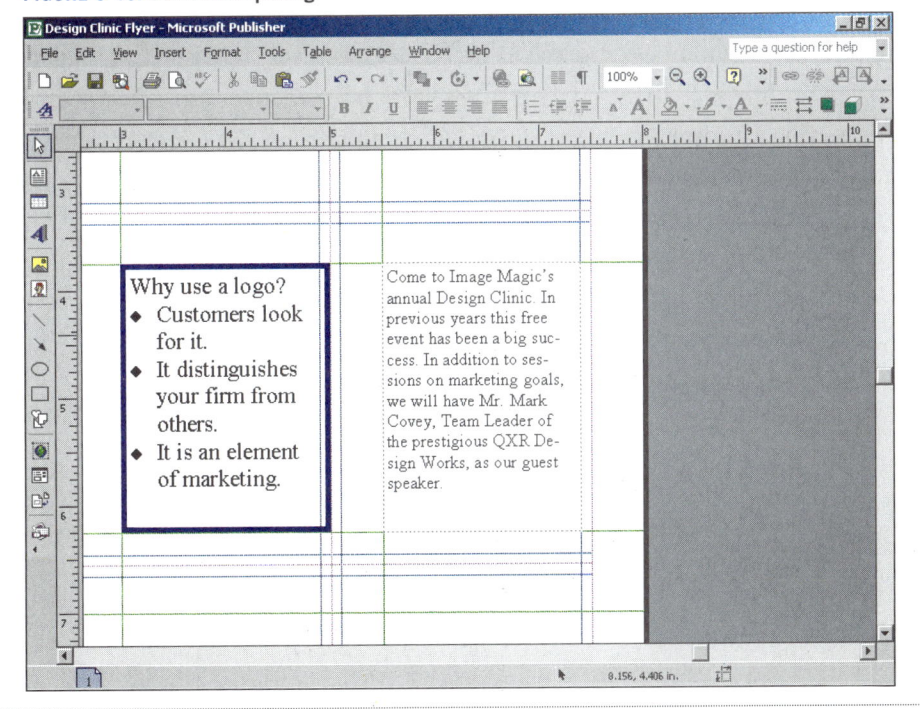

WORKING WITH TEXT   PUBLISHER 59

Modifying a Smart Object

Unit C — Publisher 2002

When you use the Publication Gallery to create a publication, you may find objects within that publication that contain a Wizard button. These **Smart Objects** contain text or graphic images from a Personal Information Set or from the Design Gallery. This feature is an easy way to change the content of a publication while ensuring accuracy and consistency. Mike wants to add an Attention Getter from the Design Gallery. First, he adds a ruler guide to help place the object.

Steps

1. **Press and hold [Shift], position ▷ over the horizontal ruler, drag ↕ to 3" on the vertical ruler, release [Shift], then release the mouse button**
   You can add ruler guides at any time during the design process to make positioning objects easier.

2. **Click the Design Gallery Object button on the Objects toolbar, click Attention Getters in the Categories list, click the Arrowhead Attention Getter, then click Insert Object**
   You will use the ruler guides to help you position the new object.

3. **Place ▷ over the Attention Getter object, use 🚚 to drag the object to 5½" H / 3" V, then press [F9]**
   Text within a Smart Object can be modified, and you can use the AutoFit Text feature to fill the text box.

4. **Select the text Free Offer in the Smart Object text box, type Special, press [Enter], type Guest, press [Enter], type Speaker, press [Ctrl][A], then click the Bold button B on the Formatting toolbar**
   Compare your work with Figure C-14. You can change which Smart Object is inserted by clicking the Wizard button and making another selection.

5. **Click the Wizard button**
   The Attention Getter Designs task pane opens. You can use this task pane to apply a different design to the selected Smart Object.

6. **Click Corner Starburst in the Attention Getter Designs task pane**
   The Corner Starburst is substituted for the Arrowhead and the text you typed is inserted in the new object. You want the Attention Getter to be wider for consistency with the width of the text.

7. **Place ▷ over the selected object's right-center handle, drag ⇔ to 7½" H, close the task pane, press [Esc], then press [F9]**
   Compare your work with Figure C-15.

8. **Click the Save button on the Standard toolbar**

FIGURE C-14: Smart Object positioned and new text inserted

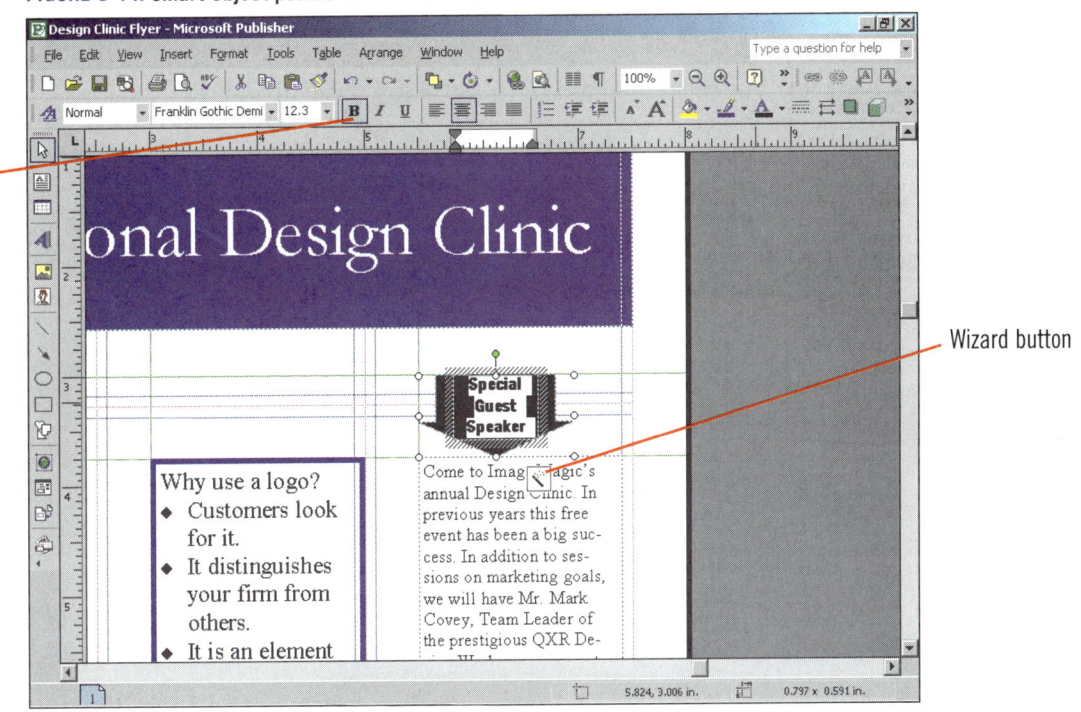

FIGURE C-15: Smart Object replaced and resized

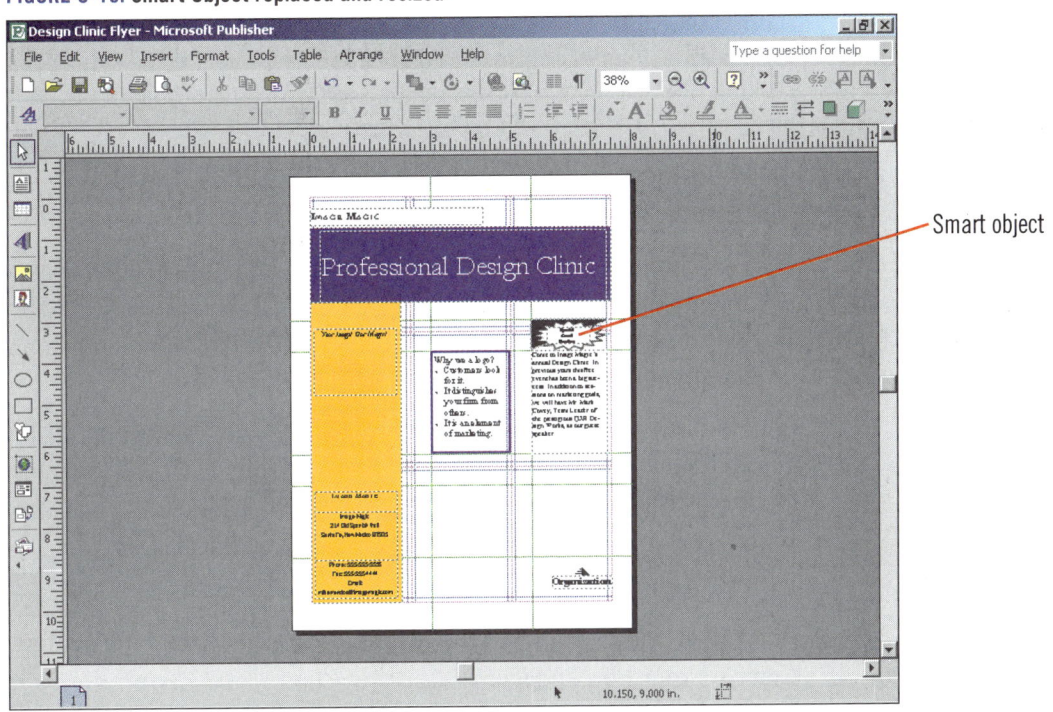

Clues to Use

Nudging an object

You can use the keyboard arrow keys to move a selected object, a technique called **nudging**. This is helpful for moving an object a relatively small distance because the object only moves in the direction of the key you are pressing. Each time you press an arrow key, the object moves a fraction of an inch (0.13") in the direction of the key you pressed. You can change the distance an object is nudged by clicking Tools on the menu bar, clicking Options, clicking the Edit tab, clicking the Arrow keys nudge object by text box to edit the default nudging distance, then clicking OK.

WORKING WITH TEXT PUBLISHER 61

Painting Formats

Publisher 2002 — Unit C

Toolbar buttons can be used to apply object formatting or text attributes such as bold, italics, and underlining, as well as to increase or decrease font size. If you are applying the same formatting combinations to text in different locations in your publication, this process can get repetitive. To help you apply formats with consistency and without difficulty, you can use the Format Painter button on the Standard toolbar, or you can select the text and use the Font dialog box to change the formatting. Once Mike applies formats to text, he uses the commands available to apply the same formatting to other text.

Steps

1. **Click anywhere within the text box with the blue border, then press [F9]**
   To draw attention to certain words in each sentence, you want to apply specific formats. One method of formatting is to use buttons on the Formatting toolbar.

2. **Select the text Why use a logo?, then click the Bold button on the Formatting toolbar**
   You also want this bolded text to be in small capital letters and a different color so it will stand out. You use the Font dialog box to apply different text attributes.

3. **Click Format on the menu bar, click Font, click the Color list arrow, click the Accent 3 (blue) color box, then click the Small caps check box**
   Compare the Font dialog box to Figure C-16. You can add as many attributes as you want by clicking the check boxes in this dialog box, but some are mutually exclusive. For example, Small caps and All caps can not be selected at the same time.

4. **Click the Shadow check box, then click OK**
   Now that the formatting attributes have been applied, you can apply them to other text.

5. **Click the Format Painter button on the Standard toolbar, position in the text box, then click and drag over Customers**
   You can double-click to apply the same formatting to more than one location. To turn off the feature, press [Esc].

6. **Double-click, drag over firm, drag over marketing, then press [Esc]**
   You think the blue color of the newly formatted bulleted text and small caps are too distracting, so you decide to change back to the original format.

   > **Trouble?**
   > Once you save your work, you cannot undo the steps you performed.

7. **Click the Undo button three times, then press [Esc] twice**
   Your formatting of the text box is now complete.

8. **Press [F9], then click the Save button on the Standard toolbar**
   Compare your work to Figure C-17.

WORKING WITH TEXT

FIGURE C-16: Font dialog box

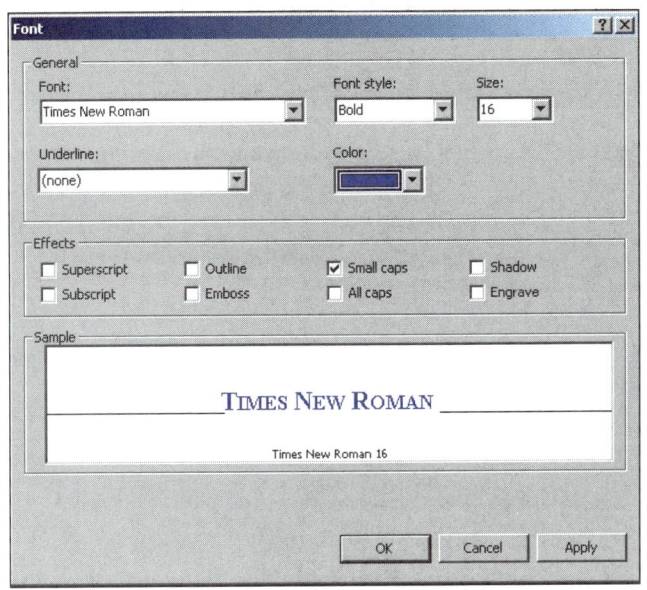

FIGURE C-17: Formatting applied

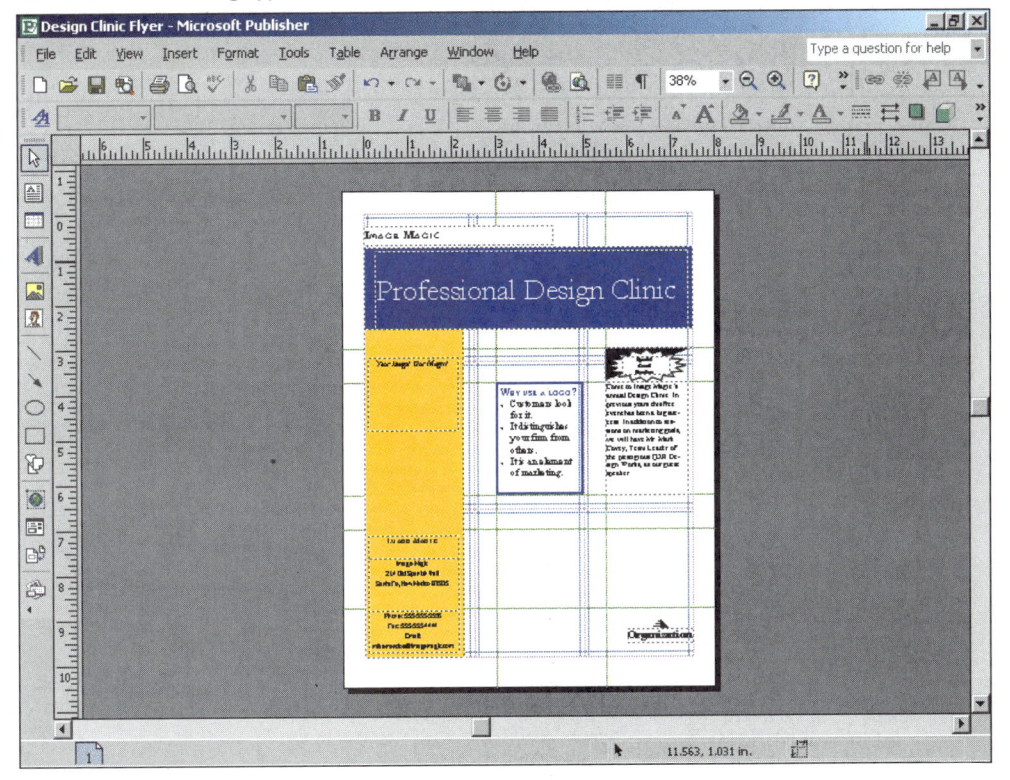

Creative deletion

Identifying poor design is an important skill, but mere recognition is not enough. Once a design flaw is identified, you have to either fix it or delete it. Not only is there nothing wrong with deleting flawed design elements, creative deletion is actually one of the most important skills a designer can learn. It is particularly important to be able to edit your own work. Look for elements that either detract from or fail to support the publication's message. If the element detracts or is unnecessary, it should be changed or deleted in favor of a constructive design element or more white space.

Adding a Table

Publisher 2002 — Unit C

Some information is more easily communicated in a table because its organization allows for quick reference. A **table** is a collection of information formatted in a grid of columns and rows. To create a table, you first need to determine the number of columns and rows required. The size of the frame and the number of columns and rows can be changed, if necessary. Publisher comes with 23 different table formats from which you can choose. Mike wants to include a table that contains six rows and three columns. The table will contain a preliminary agenda for the design clinic.

Steps

1. Click the **Insert Table button** on the Objects toolbar, then drag + from **3" H / 7" V** to **7½" H / 8¾" V**

   The Create Table dialog box opens, as shown in Figure C-18. The available table formats contain combinations of formatting attributes, borders, and shading. Regardless of the table format you choose, you are free to change the numbers of columns and rows to fit your needs.

2. Scroll down the Table format list, click **List with Title 2**, click the **Number of rows down arrow** until **6** appears in the text box if necessary, click the **Number of columns down arrow** until **3** appears in the text box, then click **OK**

   > **QuickTip**: You can also navigate the cells in a table using the arrow keys.

   The table appears in the table frame. You can type directly in the cells of the table, pressing [Tab] to move from cell to cell. You enter the column headings in the first row.

3. Press **[F9]**, type **Session Title**, press **[Tab]**, type **Description**, press **[Tab]**, then type **Speaker**

   When first created, table columns are all the same width. The second column will contain the most information, so you want to widen that column and make column 3 narrower. When you place the pointer between column boundaries of a selected table, it changes to ↔. Dragging the boundary with ↔ will change the size of the table. You change the width of a column but retain the same table size by holding [Shift] while dragging ↔ to the new width.

4. Place I between the Description and Speaker columns until the pointer changes to ↔, press and hold **[Shift]**, drag ↔ to **6½" H**, release the mouse button, then release [Shift]

   > **QuickTip**: Use ↕ to change row height.

   With the column width resized, you can now enter information in the table.

5. Enter the table data using Figure C-19 as a guide

6. Replace **Wilson** with **your name**, click outside the table to deselect it, then press **[F9]** to zoom out

   > **QuickTip**: Press [Tab] at the end of the last cell in a table to insert a new row in the table. Press [Enter] in any cell to insert lines within the row.

   You are pleased with the progress of the flyer and want to print it. You save, print, and exit Publisher.

7. Click the **Save button** on the Standard toolbar, click the **Print button** on the Standard toolbar, then exit Publisher

► PUBLISHER 64   **WORKING WITH TEXT**

FIGURE C-18: Create Table dialog box

Available table formats are listed here

Sample of selected table

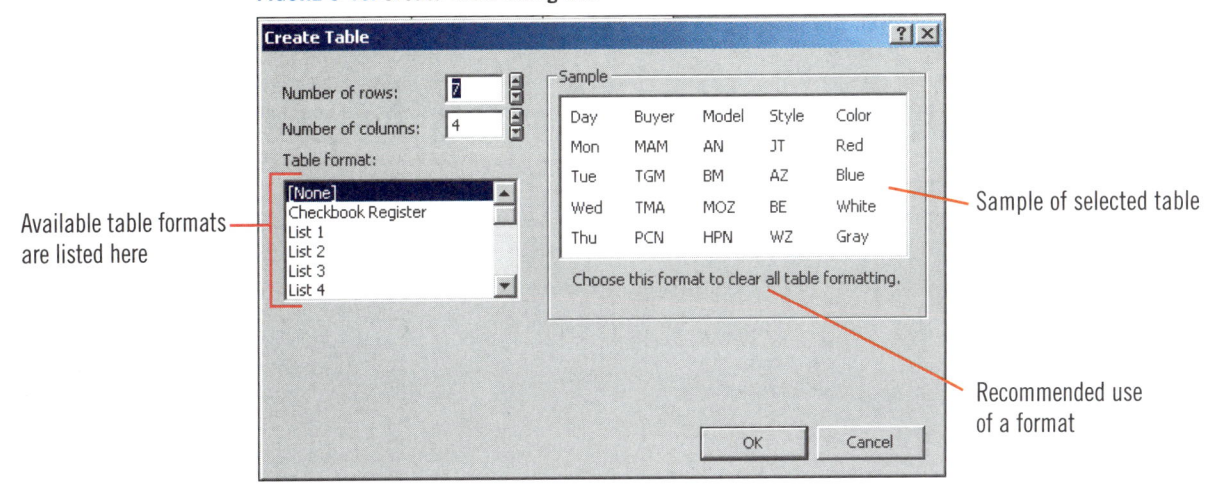

Recommended use of a format

FIGURE C-19: Completed table

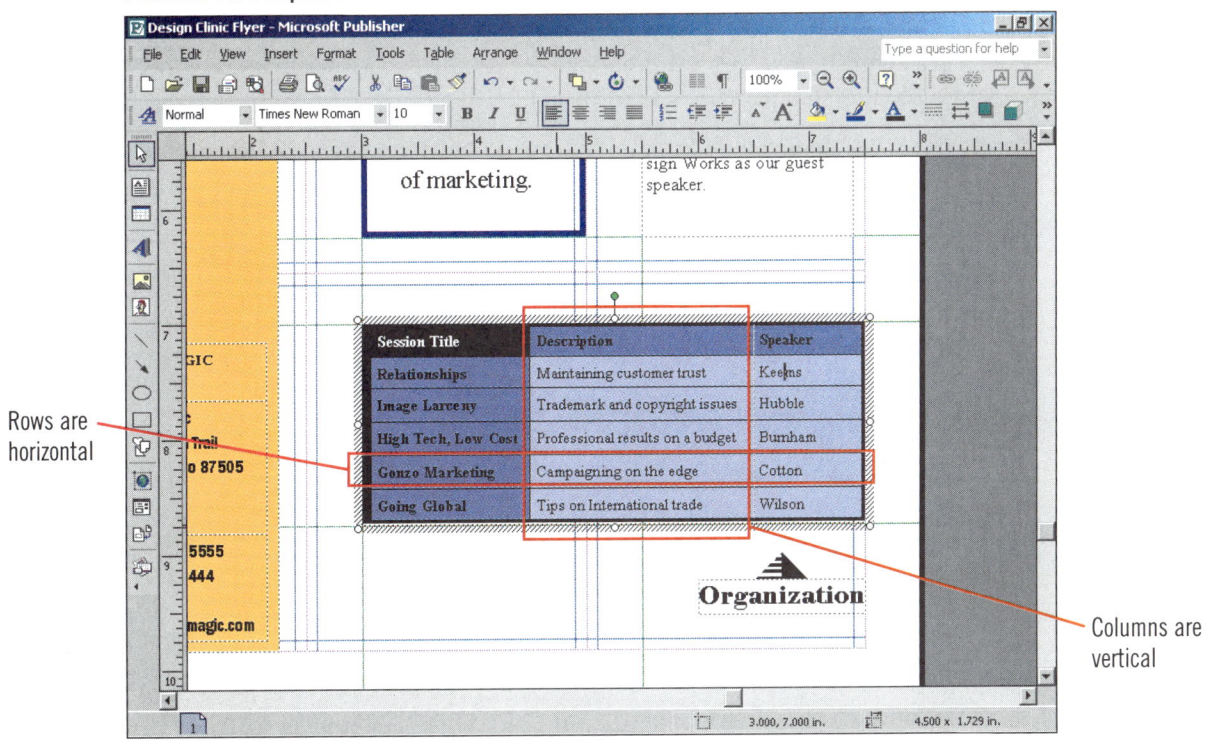

Rows are horizontal

Columns are vertical

Using AutoFormat

An existing table's design can be changed using the AutoFormat feature. The **Table AutoFormat** feature looks similar to the Create Table dialog box, except that it contains only table formats. Open the Auto Format dialog box by clicking Table on the menu bar, then clicking Table AutoFormat. Choose a new Table format, then click OK, and the new table format will replace the old. In order to use AutoFormat, you must select a table.

FIGURE C-20: Auto Format dialog box

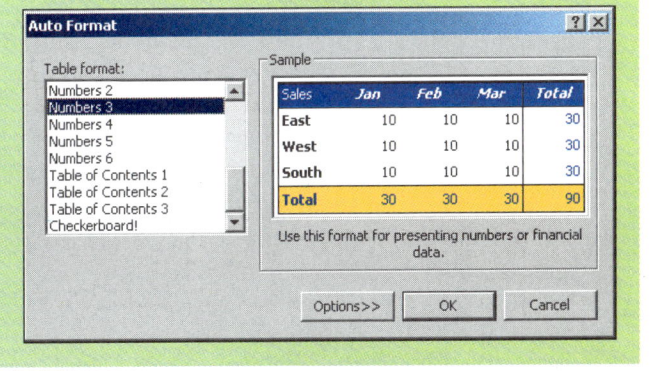

WORKING WITH TEXT   PUBLISHER 65

Capstone Project: College Brochure

Unit C — Publisher 2002

You have learned how to change layout and margin guides and how to use ruler guides. You have also learned to format a text box, and add and modify bullets, numbering, and Smart Objects. Additionally, you now know how to paint formats, add a table, and check spelling. Mike needs to create a flyer promoting the Camelback Community College Library Book Sale. The flyer needs some focal points to emphasize key information.

Steps

1. Start **Publisher**, click **Flyers** in the By Publication Type list in the New Publication task pane, click **Sale**, click **Book Sale Flyer** in the Publication Gallery, then save it to the drive and folder where your Project Files are stored as **Book Sale Flyer**
   The template you selected from the Publication Gallery has the right tone for the flyer. The publication has placeholder text that you will modify to fit your message.

2. Click the **Book Sale placeholder**, then change it to read **Library Book Sale**
   You will add a design element so you want to add some guides to make placing the objects easier.

3. Click **Arrange** on the menu bar, click **Layout Guides**, change all the margin guides to **0.4"**, change the grid guides to **3 Columns** and **3 Rows**, then click **OK**
   The publication looks good, but you think a design element might make it more eye-catching. The Design Gallery object that most resembles a book is the Brick Attention Getter.

4. Click the **Design Gallery Object button** on the Objects toolbar, click **Attention Getters**, click **Brick Attention Getter**, click **Insert Object**, drag the object to ½" H, ½" V, then close the task pane
   Making the Attention Getter larger and changing the text will help the reader decide immediately if he or she is interested in reading further.

5. Press **[F9]**, resize the selected object to **2¾" H × 1" V** by dragging the lower-right handle, click the **Free Offer text**, type **Great Books**, press **[Ctrl][A]**, click **Format** on the menu bar, click **Font**, click the **All caps check box**, click **OK**, press **[F9]**, then press **[Esc]** three times
   Compare your work to Figure C-21. You like the formatting and placement of the Attention Getter.

6. Click the text box at **7" H / 5" V**, click **Format** on the menu bar, click **Indents and Lists**, click the **diamond bullet**, increase the bullet point size to **15 pt**, then click **OK**
   You think the diamond bullets fit the design of the publication better, and they help to emphasize the items on your list.

7. Click the text box at **7" H / 8" V**, replace the text with the name of your school, click the text box at **7" H / 9" V**, replace the text with your school's address, type **Attention:**, then type **your name**
   You like the formatting changes you made to the publication.

8. Save the publication, print the first page, compare your work to Figure C-22, then exit Publisher

FIGURE C-21: Inserted Smart Object with text replaced and formatted

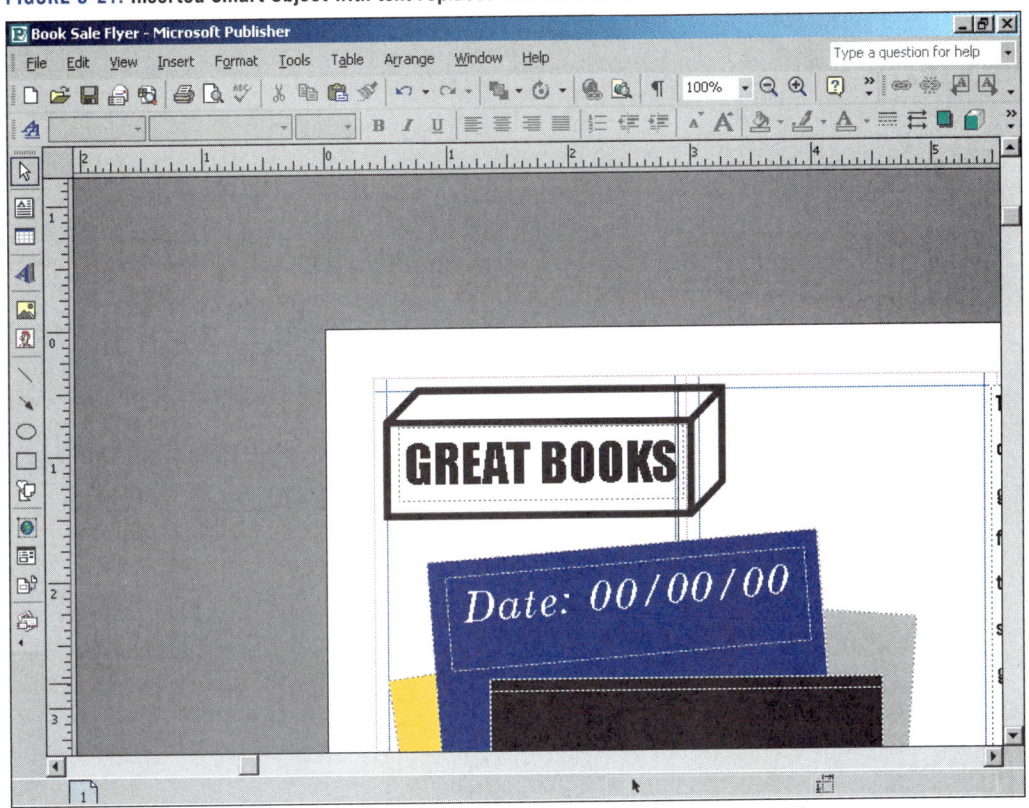

FIGURE C-22: Completed publication

WORKING WITH TEXT PUBLISHER 67

Publisher 2002 Practice

▶ Concepts Review

Label each of the elements of the Publisher window shown in **Figure C-23**.

FIGURE C-23

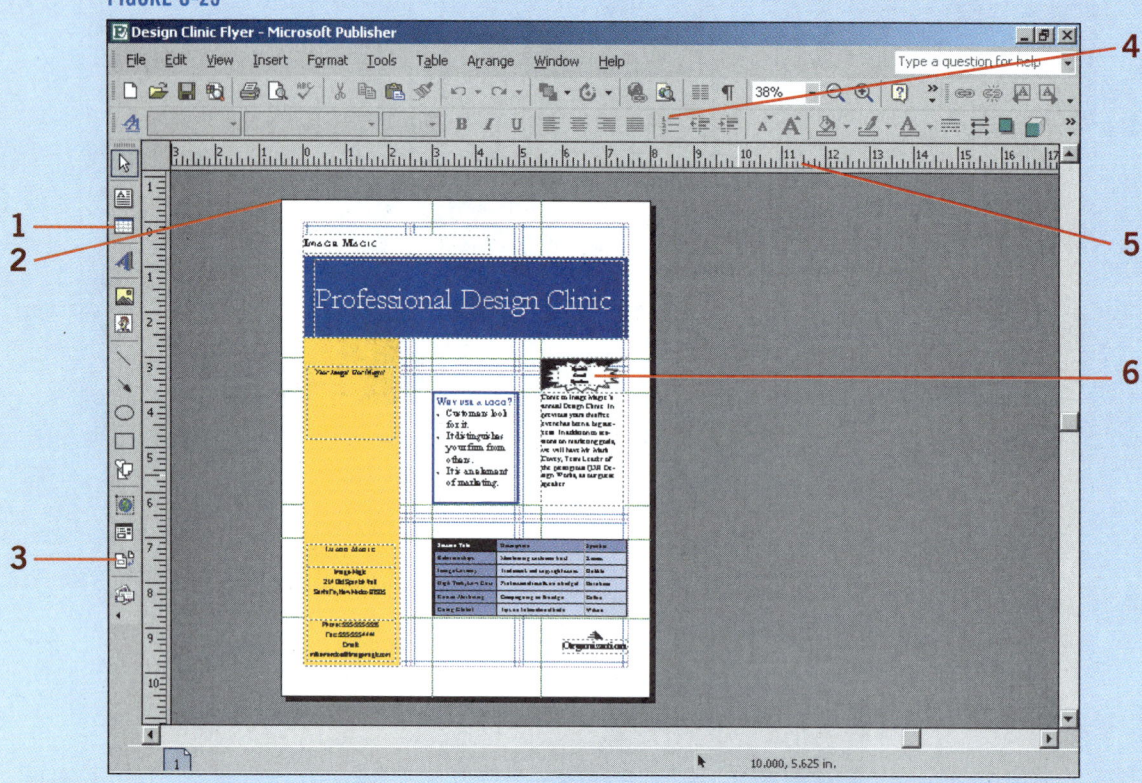

Match each of the buttons with the statement that describes its function.

7. ↔
8.
9.
10.
11.
12. **B**

a. Inserts a table
b. Smart Object Wizard
c. Paints formatting attributes
d. Opens the Design Gallery
e. Makes text bold
f. Changes a column's width

Select the best answer from the list of choices.

13. To maintain a table's size, resize a column while holding the _____ key.
   a. [Shift]
   b. [Alt]
   c. [Ctrl]
   d. [Esc]

▶ PUBLISHER 68 **WORKING WITH TEXT**

Practice

14. You can draw a table frame when the pointer turns to _____.
    a. ↘
    b. ↔
    c. +
    d. I

15. Ruler guides are:
    a. Blue.
    b. Green.
    c. Pink.
    d. Red.

16. Each of the following is true about layout guides, except:
    a. Objects can snap to them.
    b. They occur on every page in a publication.
    c. They appear on the Master Page.
    d. They appear in the foreground.

17. Which of the following is not a font attribute?
    a. Bold
    b. Snap
    c. Italics
    d. Shadow

18. Each of the following buttons is used for formatting text, except _____.
    a. *I*
    b.
    c.
    d. **B**

19. Modify a smart object by:
    a. Clicking any element within it.
    b. Using a command on the Edit menu.
    c. Clicking Arrange on the menu bar.
    d. Clicking the Smart Object Wizard button.

20. The Spelling feature in Publisher:
    a. Identifies misspelled words.
    b. Finds all spelling and grammatical errors.
    c. Gets rid of the blue wavy lines.
    d. Can't check words in a table.

▶ Skills Review

1. **Use layout guides.**
   a. Start Publisher, click Flyers on the New Publication task pane, then click Event.
   b. Use the Company Picnic Flyer and the Bluebird color scheme, close the task pane, then save the file to the drive and folder where your Project Files are located as **Company Picnic Flyer**.
   c. Use the Arrange menu to open the Layout Guides dialog box.
   d. Change the margin guides if necessary to 0.5 left, 0.5 right, 0.5 top, and 0.66 bottom.
   e. Use the Layout Guides dialog box to create three columns and three rows of grid guides in this publication.
   f. Save your work.

2. **Use ruler guides.**
   a. Move the vertical ruler closer to the page.
   b. Create horizontal ruler guides at ¼", 1", 7⅞", and 9½". Create vertical ruler guides at ½", 4", 5¾", and 7".
   c. Save your work.

3. **Format a text box.**
   a. Move the vertical ruler back to the left side of the screen.
   b. Click the text box at 2" H / 5" V, then zoom in to view the text box.
   c. Create a 4 pt blue border around the text box, zoom out so you can see the full page, then deselect the text box.
   d. Save your work.

4. **Add bullets and numbering.**
   a. Select the text box at 5" H / 5" V, then zoom in to view the text box.
   b. Replace the text under the Highlights heading with the following information, pressing [Enter] after each activity to create a bulleted list: **Volleyball**, **Live music**, **Sack race**, **Softball**, **Pie-eating contest**.
   c. Change the bullet style to a 12 pt open arrow, zoom out, then save the publication.

WORKING WITH TEXT PUBLISHER 69

Publisher 2002 *Practice*

5. **Check spelling.**
   a. Select and zoom in to the text box at 2" H / 5" V, then replace the existing text in the box with the file **PUB C-2** from the drive and folder where your Project Files are stored.
   b. Correct the spelling of the selected text. (*Hint*: You should find four spelling errors.) Do not check the spelling in the rest of the publication.
   c. Zoom out so that you can see the entire publication, deselect the highlighted text if necessary, then save the publication.

6. **Modify a Smart Object.**
   a. Click the Design Gallery Object button on the Objects toolbar, click the Attention Getters category, then insert the Chevron Attention Getter.
   b. Move and resize the object so that the upper-left edge has the coordinates 5 ¾" H / ¼" V and the dimensions are 1¼" H x 1" V, then zoom in to the object.
   c. Change the text to **Too Much Fun!**
   d. Click the Wizard button, change the design to Double Slant, then close the Attention Getter Designs task pane.
   e. Zoom out, then save the publication.

7. **Paint formats.**
   a. Select the bulleted list and zoom in.
   b. Select the text "Volleyball" and format it using the Engrave effect and Accent 3 (orange) color.
   c. Use the Format Painter to paint "Live music" with the same formatting.
   d. Double-click the Format Painter button on the Standard toolbar.
   e. Apply the formatting to the following text: Sack race, Softball, and Pie-eating contest.
   f. Zoom out so that you can see the entire page, then save your work.

8. **Add a table.**
   a. Resize the three text boxes above the Time text box so that their right edges end at 4" H. Delete the border element between the text boxes.
   b. Create a table frame from 4" H / 7⅞" V to 7¾" H / 9½" V, using the List 3 format.
   c. Create six rows and three columns. Click Yes to create a table larger than the selected area.
   d. Zoom in, then enter the following text for the three column headings: **Activity**, **Contact**, and **Extension**.
   e. Enter the information in Table C-1, then resize the columns so the left edge of the Extension column begins at 6¾" H.
   f. Replace Greta Tolkmann's name with your name.
   g. Zoom out so that you can see the full page.
   h. Deselect the table, then save your work.
   i. Print the publication, then exit Publisher.

TABLE C-1

Activity	Contact	Extension
Volleyball	Lucy Evans	4828
Live music	Frank Etherton	4689
Sack race	Roger Hubbard	5220
Softball	Gail Farnsworth	1096
Pie-eating contest	Greta Tolkmann	3117

▶ Independent Challenge 1

The firm of Eisner, Biheller, and Harpur has hired you to design a postcard that invites people to a promotion party.
   a. Start Publisher if necessary, use the New Publication task pane and the Publication Gallery to select the Blends Informational Postcard, use the color scheme of your choice, save it as **Promotion Announcement** to the drive and folder where your Project Files are stored, then close the task pane.
   b. Delete the text box that is just under the upper margin.
   c. Move the zero points to the top-left margin, then add a vertical ruler guide at 1" and a horizontal ruler guide at ⅛".

Practice

d. Move the Product/Service Information text box so that the upper-left corner is at ⅛" V / 1" H, create a two pt Accent 1 red border around it, then type **Eisner, Biheller and Harpur Announce**.
e. Align all of the text boxes so their left sides are on the vertical ruler guide.
f. Select the text box that starts "Place text here" and insert the text found in Pub C-3.
g. Use the Spelling Checker to correct any errors in the text.
h. Type the firm's name in the text box found at 1" H / 2 ¼" V, then modify text and formatting to create a meaningful invitation.
i. Create text that has bold and italic formatting, then use the Format Painter to copy formats for the text.
j. Add a text box that includes your name, save and print the publication, then exit Publisher.

▶ Independent Challenge 2

The seminar you are teaching in London on International Business Leadership is about to end. At the conclusion, you would like to present each attendee with a certificate of completion.

a. Start Publisher, if necessary, use the New Publication task pane to select Award Certificates, choose the Plain Paper option, the Celtic Knotwork Certificate, and the color scheme of your choice.
b. Save the publication as **International Leadership Certificate** to the drive and folder where your Project Files are stored, then close the task pane.
c. Move the zero points to the top-left margin.
d. Replace the Name of Recipient with your name, then change the words "Certificate of Appreciation" to **Certificate of Completion**.
e. Format the Certificate of Completion text box border so it is a 5 pt, red solid line.
f. Format the "Name of Recipient" text using the formatting of your choice.
g. Modify any existing text to create a meaningful certificate of completion.
h. Save and print the publication, then exit Publisher.

Publisher 2002 *Practice*

▶ Independent Challenge 3

The local music appreciation society asks you to design a program for its upcoming festival.

- **a.** Start Publisher if necessary, then use the New Publication task pane to create a Music Program. Save the publication as **Music Program** to the drive and folder where your Project Files are stored, then close the task pane.
- **b.** On page 2, delete the existing table (for The Singers) and replace it with a 3-column, 8-row table with the format of your choice.
- **c.** Make up the names of the singers, the songs they will sing, and the type of music (for example, opera, folk, or jazz).
- **d.** Enter your name on page two under "Conductor's Name."
- **e.** Replace any existing text on pages two and three with information that creates a meaningful music program.
- **f.** Format text using at least two attributes, then use the Format Painter to copy the formatting to other text.
- **g.** Use the Spelling Checker to correct any errors in the text.
- **h.** Save and print pages two and three of the publication, then exit Publisher.

Practice

Independent Challenge 4

Your keen mind, artistic tastes, and desire to make money are leading you to pursue business opportunities that involve designing publications. To become more credible, you decide to learn more about different fonts.

   a. Connect to the Internet, then using your favorite search engine or Web site (such as google.com or about.com), search for information on choosing fonts and typefaces.
   b. Use the New Publication task pane and the Publication Gallery to create any style of flyer, then save it as **Different Font Flyer** to the drive and folder where your Project Files are stored.
   c. Create a heading that uses and names your favorite font.
   d. Add a text box that contains a bulleted list that uses and names five other fonts that you find easy to read.
   e. Add a text box that discusses the differences between serif and sans serif fonts.
   f. Format the text to illustrate both sans serif and serif fonts.
   g. Add a prominently placed text box with your name in a clearly readable font and point size.
   h. Use your judgment to delete any objects that do not contribute to the design of your publication.
   i. Add a colorful border to the text boxes.
   j. Use the Spelling Checker to correct any errors in the text, save and print the publication, then exit Publisher.

Publisher 2002 Practice

▶ Visual Workshop

Use the Publication Gallery to create an Estate Sale Flyer. Save this publication as **Estate Sale Flyer** to the drive and folder where your Project Files are stored. Use Figure C-24 as a guide. Use the Bluebird color scheme and replace all text as shown in the figure. Include your name on the flyer. Save and print the flyer.

FIGURE C-24

11/10/03
Time: 10:00-4:00 PM

ESTATE SALE

- **Jewelry**
- **Furniture**
- **Tools**
- **Paintings**
- **Sculpture**

American folk art dating to post Civil War, pre-Impressionist European paintings and representational sculpture, 8 Persian rugs, an extensive collection of woodworking and ship building tools.

The sale will be held rain or shine at the Hibb House (23 Garden Street) adjacent to the Public Gardens.

▶ PUBLISHER 74 **WORKING WITH TEXT**

Publisher 2002

Unit D

Working
with Art

Objectives

- ▶ Insert and resize clip art
- ▶ Copy and move an object
- ▶ Crop an image
- ▶ Align and group images
- ▶ Layer objects
- ▶ Rotate art
- ▶ Use drawing tools
- ▶ Fill drawn shapes
- ▶ Capstone Project: Flower Show Web Page

Artwork is much more than decoration. At its best, art expresses ideas and feelings that words cannot. At minimum, artwork can grab a reader's attention and enhance the understanding of a publication. Proper positioning of graphic images can relieve the monotony of text, add emphasis to the written word, and separate subjects. Mike Mendoza is working on the artwork for a flyer for a veterinary hospital fundraiser. His first task is to lay out the artwork; the text will be added later. The client wants the fundraiser flyer to be inviting and friendly, with lots of graphics.

Inserting and Resizing Clip Art

Publisher 2002 — Unit D

The Insert Clip Art task pane, makes it easy to dress up any publication. There is so much clip art available, online and from commercial sources, that you can always find an image to represent a topic or round out a theme. With the Insert Clip Art task pane, you can use the Search feature to locate specific artwork by keyword or topic. The Clip Organizer contains pictures, motion clips, and sounds, and is not limited to the artwork that comes with Publisher. You can customize the Clip Organizer by adding any electronic image you wish. Mike is ready to search for artwork to resize and add to the flyer.

Steps

1. Start Publisher, open the file **Pub D-1** from the drive and folder where your Project Files are stored, click **File** on the menu bar, click **Save As**, then save the file as **Fundraiser Flyer**
   You want to look for clip art that can be added to support the text of the flyer.

2. Click the **Clip Organizer Frame button** on the Objects toolbar
   The Insert Clip Art task pane opens. It contains options that allow you to limit your search to specific collections, and search for different types of media, such as clip art, photographs, movies, and sounds, arranged by content. You want to find art representative of a veterinary hospital setting.

3. Click the **Search text text box**, type **animal**, click the **Results should be list arrow**, click **Clip Art** to select it if necessary, click the **Search in list arrow**, click the **My Collections** and **Office Collections check boxes** to select them if necessary, then click **Search**
   The results of the search appear, as shown in Figure D-1.

4. Position over the **second image from the left in the first row**, click the **down arrow** on the right side of the clip art, click **Preview/Properties**, verify that j0216724.wmf is the filename, click **Close**, right-click the **image**, click **Insert**, then click the **Close button** on the Insert Clip Art task pane

5. Press **[F9]**, place over the **clip art** until the pointer changes to , click the **clip art**, drag so that the upper-left corner is at **2¾" H / 3¾" V**, then release the mouse button
   Compare the repositioned clip art to Figure D-2.

6. Place over the lower-right corner frame handle until the pointer changes to , press and hold **[Shift]**, then drag to **5¼" H / 6⅞" V**
   The inserted ruler guides made it easy to resize the object.

7. Click the **Save button** on the Standard toolbar

> **Trouble?**
> If you do not have the images used in this unit, choose similar ones from the Microsoft Clip Organizer.

▶ PUBLISHER 76 **WORKING WITH ART**

FIGURE D-1: Insert Clip Art task pane after search

Image j0216724.wmf

Pictures found in the search. Your results may differ

Clicking this will connect you to the Internet for additional clips

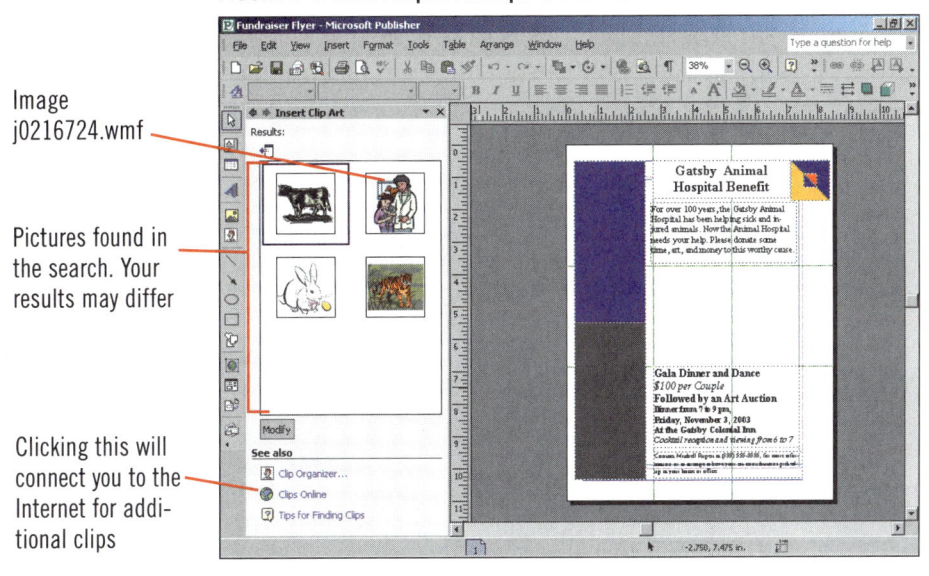

FIGURE D-2: Clip art picture inserted and resized

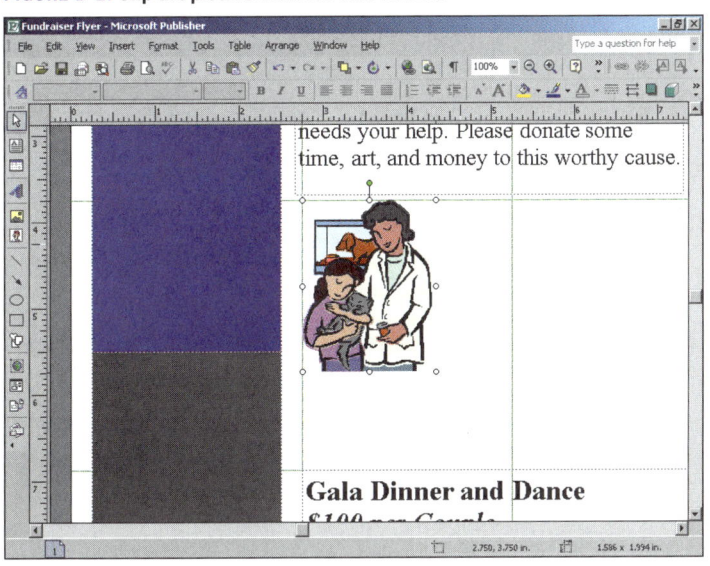

Browsing the Design Gallery Live

If you have access to the Internet, you can add to the Microsoft Clip Organizer from the Microsoft Design Gallery Live Web site. This site, located at the URL http://dgl.microsoft.com, offers a constantly changing selection of artwork. Figure D-3 shows some of the choices offered at this Web site, although it will look different when you view it, as it changes constantly. This site lets you constantly update your clip art so you always have new, exciting types of artwork to include in your publications. You can download clip art, photographs, sounds, and video clips from this Web site.

FIGURE D-3: Microsoft Design Gallery Live Web site

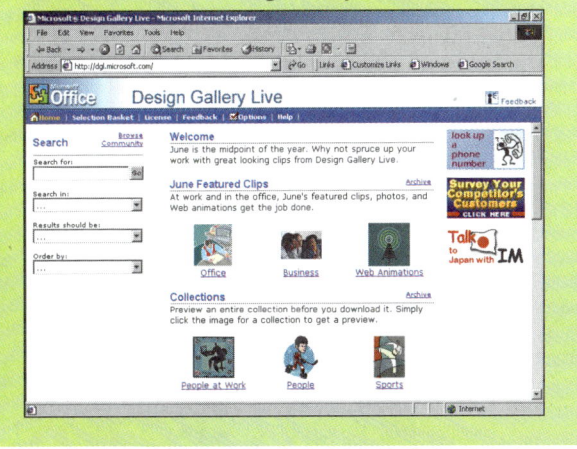

WORKING WITH ART   PUBLISHER 77

Unit D — Publisher 2002

Copying and Moving an Object

Images can be inserted into a publication, then copied and moved to get just the right results. By copying artwork, you can create interesting effects with duplicated images. You can also use copied images for experimentation in manipulating their colors, contours, cropping, dimensions, and orientations, without changing the design of your original publication. A copied image is held temporarily in the Windows **Clipboard**, a temporary storage area for copied or cut items. ➤ Mike wants to copy a Microsoft Clip Organizer image and move the copy to a new location.

Steps

QuickTip
You can also copy a selected object by clicking the Copy button on the Standard toolbar, then paste it by clicking the Paste button.

1. **Right-click the selected object, then click Copy**
   Although it looks as though nothing happened, the clip art object was copied to the Clipboard. Once an image is on the Clipboard, you can paste it repeatedly, using any pasting method. Next, you paste a copy of the object into the publication.

2. **Right-click again, then click Paste**
   A copy of the object appears overlapping the original object, as shown in Figure D-4. The newly copied image is selected and is on top of the original image. This copy appears slightly offset from the original image's location. You can now move the copy within the publication.

QuickTip
Once it's on the Clipboard, you can repeatedly paste an object using any pasting method.

3. **Position over the selected copy until it changes to , then drag the selected object so the upper-left corner is at 5¼" H / 3¾" V**
   The scratch area is a convenient place to store and alter design elements while working on the overall design of a publication.

4. **Press [F9], position the pointer over the selected object until it changes to , press and hold [Ctrl], press and hold [Shift], then drag so that the upper-left corner is on the scratch area at 9" H / 3¾" V, release the mouse button, release [Shift], then release [Ctrl]**
   The second copy of the clip art is placed in a direct line to the right of the original object, but off the page. You now have three images, two below the text box, and one on the scratch area. You can easily delete any selected object.

5. **Right-click the object, then click Cut**
   The second copy is no longer visible. You can flip an image to create mirror images and creative displays. A **mirrored image** is reversed so that what was on the left side is now on the right side, as though you are viewing the object in a mirror.

6. **Click the image whose upper-left corner is at 5¼" H / 3¾" V, click Arrange on the menu bar, point to Rotate or Flip, then click Flip Horizontal**
   The copy is flipped, as shown in Figure D-5, and you can see the original image next to the flipped copy. You decide you do not like its appearance.

7. **Right-click the copy, click Delete Object, then press [F1]**
   The mirrored image is no longer visible. Deleted items are not sent to the Office Clipboard.

8. **Click the Save button on the Standard toolbar**

PUBLISHER 78 WORKING WITH ART

FIGURE D-4: Pasted object overlapping original object

Copy appears on top of the original clip art

FIGURE D-5: Flipped image

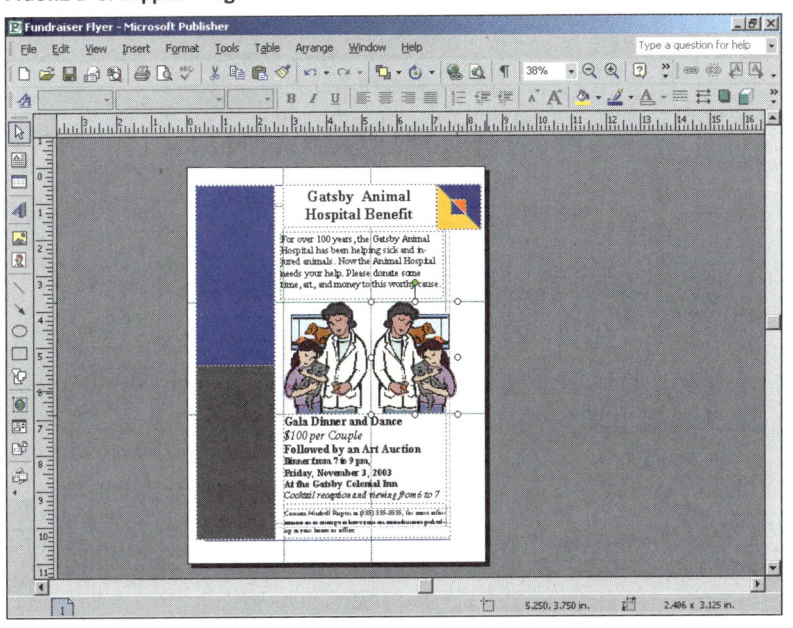

Using the Office Clipboard

The Office Clipboard lets you copy and paste multiple items, such as text, images, or tables, within or between Microsoft Office applications. The Office Clipboard can hold up to 24 items copied or cut from any Office program. You choose whether to delete the first item from the Clipboard when you copy the 25th item. The collected items remain in the Office Clipboard and are available to you until you close all open Office programs. You can specify when and where to show the Office Clipboard task pane by clicking the Options list arrow at the bottom of the Clipboard task pane.

FIGURE D-6: Clipboard task pane

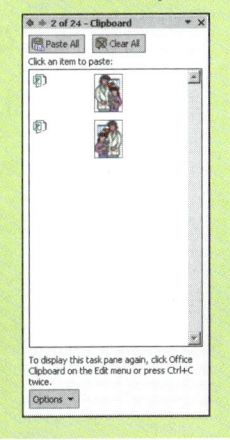

WORKING WITH ART PUBLISHER 79

Publisher 2002

Cropping an Image

Even though Publisher comes with thousands of images from which you can choose, you may find that the art you've chosen needs some modification. Perhaps a part of a picture's contents is not to your liking because it interferes with the publication's message or contains too much white space. In any case, you can trim, or **crop**, portions of the artwork to modify it to fit your needs. A graphic image can be cropped vertically, horizontally, or both at the same time. Even though they are not visible, the cropped portions of an image are still there—they are just concealed and can be made visible again. Mike will add a photographic image and crop unwanted portions.

Steps

1. Click **Insert** on the menu bar, point to **Picture**, click **From File**, locate the drive and folder where your Project Files are stored, click the file **Pub D-2**, click **Insert**, then move the image so that the upper-left corner is at **9" H / 1" V** on the scratch area
   A photograph of two puppies is placed on the scratch area. You can use the Picture toolbar to modify an image.

   QuickTip
   You can move the toolbar by clicking and dragging its title bar.

2. Click **View** on the menu bar, point to **Toolbars**, then click **Picture** to select it if necessary
   The Picture toolbar appears, as shown in Figure D-7. In this image, you can improve its appearance by hiding the excess white space.

3. Click the **Crop button** on the Picture toolbar, use the scroll bars if necessary so that you can see the entire image, position over the upper-left handle, when the pointer changes to click the **upper-left handle**, then drag to approximately **10" H x 3" V**
   The Crop button stays selected until you turn it off, so you can continue cropping until you are finished. The surplus white space on the left edge will be concealed later. The remaining white space can be cropped using the same technique.

   QuickTip
   To crop both edges simultaneously and equally, click the Crop button, press and hold [Ctrl], then drag.

4. Click the **lower-right handle**, drag to approximately **14" H x 6½" V**, press **[Esc]** to deselect the cropping tool, then click the **Close button** on the Picture toolbar if necessary
   The cropped image now has approximate dimensions of 4⅛" H x 3½" V. It still needs to be resized so that it will fit next to the existing artwork on the page.

5. Click the **photo image** to select it, place over the lower-right handle, when it changes to press **[Shift]**, then drag until the right border of the image is at **12½"** on the horizontal ruler
   The resized image now has a width of 2½" and can be placed on the page.

6. Click the cropped and resized **image**, then drag it using so that the upper-left corner is at **2¾" H x 4½" V**
   The cropped image is directly on top of the clip art for now, but you will move it later. Compare your image to Figure D-8.

7. Click the Save button on the Standard toolbar

WORKING WITH ART

FIGURE D-7: Image before cropping

Picture toolbar. Yours may be in a different location

Crop to the image of the puppies

Crop button

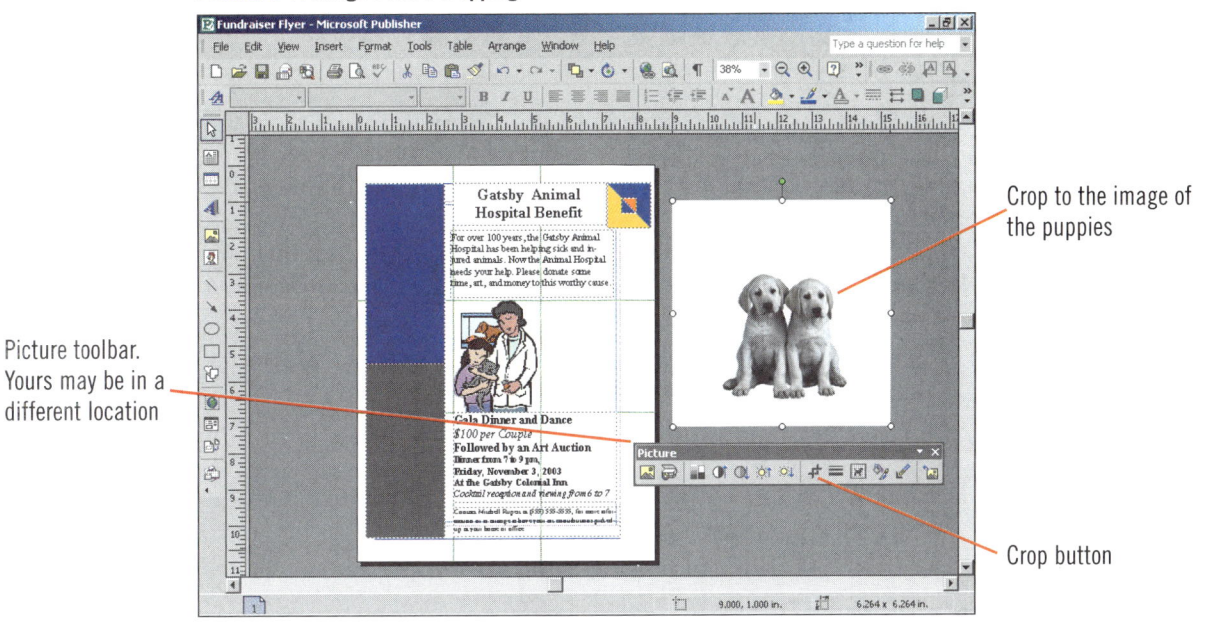

FIGURE D-8: Image cropped, resized, and placed on page

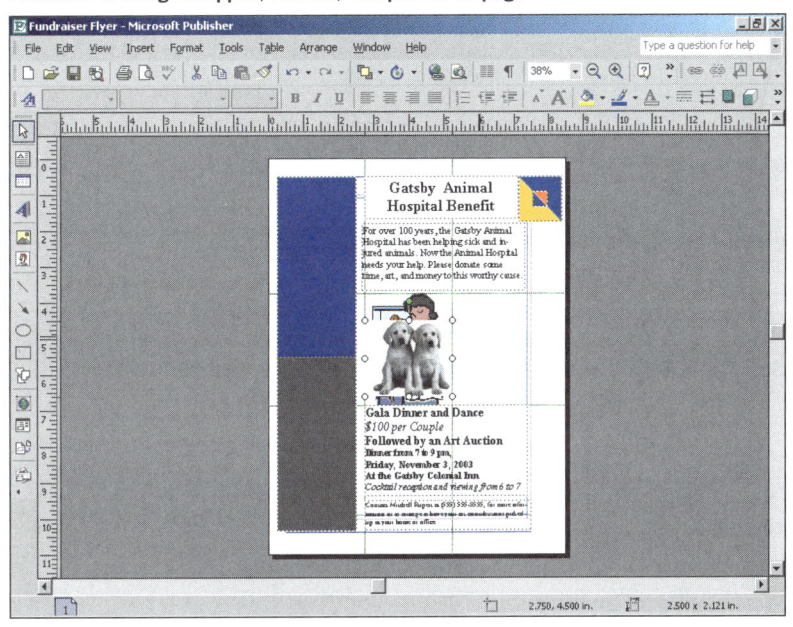

Cropping as creative deletion

Cropping is used to remove portions of an image that do not support the publication's design. How do you decide what images should be cropped and how they should be cropped? Look for elements that either interfere with or fail to carry the publication's message. Just as with text or other objects, if a part of the image is distracting or unnecessary, it should be changed or deleted in favor of a beneficial design element. Often, it is white space in a photo or in clip art that should be cropped. If white space is needed, it can be added with a margin around the art.

WORKING WITH ART PUBLISHER 81

Unit D
Publisher 2002

Aligning and Grouping Images

Once you insert clip art, you can align multiple images so that the layout of the publication looks professionally designed. The alignment helps guide the reader's eye across the page by avoiding isolated patches of white space that might be distracting. Artwork can be aligned from left to right or from top to bottom. Images can also be arranged in groups. A group makes it easy to move several pieces of art as one unit. Mike wants to make sure the three images on the page are lined up precisely, then he will maneuver them as a group.

Steps

1. With the cropped image still selected, press and hold **[Shift]**, click the **text boxes** at **6" H / 3" V** and **6" H / 8" V**, then release [Shift]
   All three images should be selected, as shown in Figure D-9.

2. Click **Arrange** on the menu bar, then point to **Align or Distribute**
   The Align or Distribute menu appears. You want the objects lined up along their right edges.

3. Click **Align Right**, then press **[Esc]** to deselect the objects
   The text boxes and the photo image are lined up on the right edge, as shown in Figure D-10. You want to align the bottom of the photo image with the bottom of the clip art. The easiest way to accomplish alignment is by just dragging the photo image. Holding [Shift] while you move an object moves it in a straight line, either vertically or horizontally.

4. Press **[Shift]**, click the cropped **photo image**, then using drag the photo image until its top-left corner is at **5" H / 4¾" V**
   The images are aligned along their bottom edges, and the text boxes are perfectly aligned with the photo image along their right edges. You want to preserve the alignment of the clip art and the photo image.

5. With the photo image still selected, press and hold **[Shift]**, click the **clip art image** to select it, then click the **Group Objects button**
   The two selected objects are transformed into a single selected object. Since the photo image is in black and white and the clip art image is in color, you want to see how the images would look if flipped horizontally. Flipping the grouped object would add color to the right side of the publication.

6. Click **Arrange** on the menu bar, point to **Rotate or Flip**, then click **Flip Horizontal**
   Compare your work with Figure D-11. You don't like this change. The space above the puppies' heads is unusable white space, and the publication seems unbalanced with the objects reversed. You decide to undo your changes and try a different design idea later.

7. Click the **Undo button**
   You don't want to retain the grouping; you can always regroup later if needed.

8. Click the **Ungroup Objects button**, then press **[Esc]**
   The objects are deselected and the Picture toolbar is no longer visible.

9. Click the **Save button** on the Standard toolbar

▶ PUBLISHER 82 WORKING WITH ART

FIGURE D-9: All three objects selected

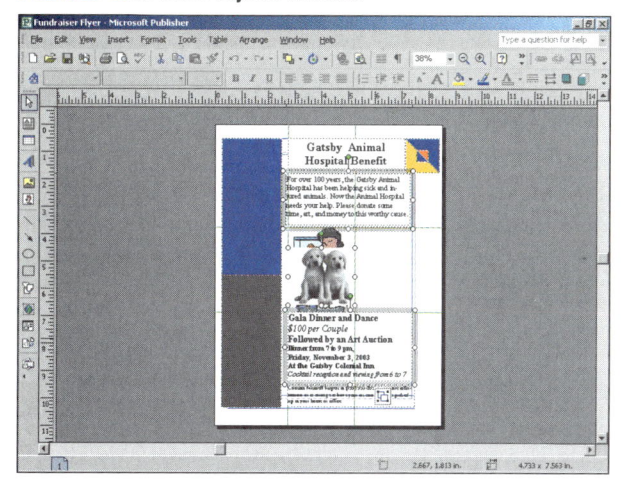

FIGURE D-10: Objects aligned right

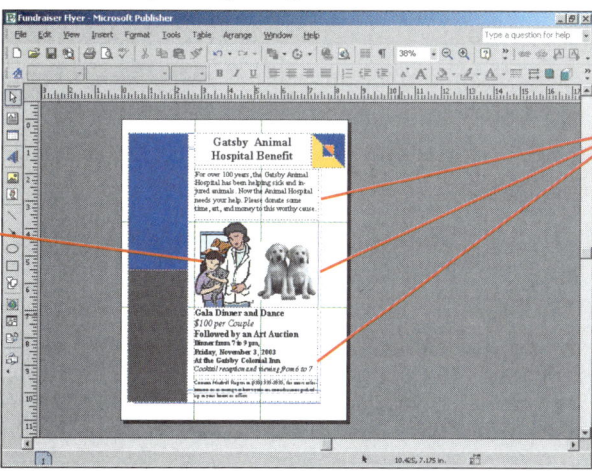

Selected objects right-aligned

Overlap from the photo image covers part of the clip art

FIGURE D-11: Grouped objects flipped horizontally

Objects flip horizontally along the vertical axis

Ungroup button

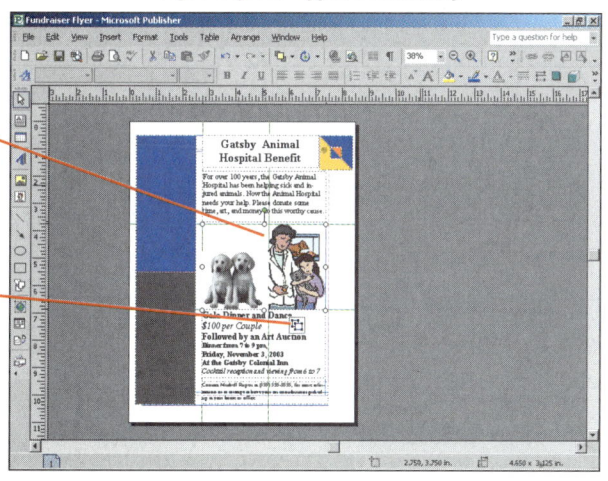

Scanning artwork

If you have a favorite photo or piece of artwork that does not exist in electronic form, you can convert it to a digital computer file with a scanner. A variety of scanners is available in either hand-held, sheetfed, or flatbed format. You can scan text, line art, or full-color images with amazing accuracy, enabling you to use virtually any image in publications. Every scanner comes with its own imaging software. With the camera or scanner in place and the software installed, Publisher lets you scan directly into a publication by clicking Insert on the menu bar, pointing to Picture, then clicking From Scanner or Camera.

WORKING WITH ART

Publisher 2002

Layering Objects

When positioning objects, you might want some images to appear in front of others. This layering effect can be used with any type of object. Sometimes you will want text to display on top of a shape, or an object to overlap another object to conceal a part of an image. You might want to superimpose a text box in front of one object or a collection of objects. You can send an image to the back so that it appears to be underneath an object, or bring it to the front so it appears to be on top of an object. Mike experiments with layering objects to improve the look of the flyer.

Steps

1. Click the image at **4" H / 5" V**, press **[F9]**, then click the **Bring to Front button** on the Standard toolbar

   The clip art image of the Animal Hospital now overlaps the photograph, as shown in Figure D-12. You think the images look better with this amount of overlap since it reduces the white space separating the two images. You think the design might be improved by reversing the clip art image.

2. Make sure that the image at **4" H / 5" V** is still selected, click **Arrange** on the menu bar, point to **Rotate or Flip**, then click **Flip Horizontal**

   The overlap is maintained when the image is flipped. Flipping the clip art image lines up the subjects of the image in a strong diagonal that guides the eye from the upper-left to the lower-right. It also changes the apparent view of the veterinarian from one animal to all the animals and the little girl. You want to add some humor to the flyer with a callout.

   Trouble?
   You may have to use the vertical scroll bar to see 3 ¼" V.

3. Click the **AutoShapes button** on the Objects toolbar, point to **Callouts**, click the **Oval Callout** (third shape from the left in the first row), then drag + from **5¼" H / 3¼" V** to **8" H / 4½" V**

   The image of the puppy on the left now has a cartoon balloon to which you will add a caption note indicating that one of the effects of inserting the callout is movement of some text in the text box above to accommodate the object.

4. Type **They are even nice to cats!**, press **[Ctrl][A]**, click **Format** on the menu bar, point to **AutoFit text**, then click **Best Fit**

   Now you will adjust the position of the cartoon balloon so that it appears to originate from the puppy's mouth.

5. Click the **AutoShape** to select it, position the pointer over the **yellow guide**, then drag to approximately **6¼" H / 5¼" V**

   The callout is positioned over the picture of the puppies, as shown in Figure D-13.

6. Click the **Save button** on the Standard toolbar

WORKING WITH ART

FIGURE D-12: Image after it is brought to front

- Bring to Front button
- List arrow has more layering options
- All of an image is visible when brought to front

FIGURE D-13: Clip art flipped, callout added to photo

- Oval callout

Using the Bring Forward and Send Backward commands

By creatively using the Format AutoShape and Format Text dialog box commands and the Bring to Front and Send to Back buttons, you can superimpose text boxes on all kinds of objects and shapes. Without these features, the shapes could be distracting and easily obscure the text, making it unreadable. Figure D-15 shows a text box on top of several geometric shapes. This effect is achieved using the Bring Forward and Send Backward commands on the Arrange menu. Unlike Bring to Front and Send to Back, these commands move an image forward or back one layer at a time.

FIGURE D-14: Layered text box and shapes

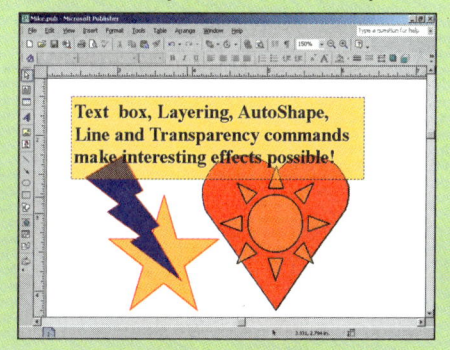

WORKING WITH ART   PUBLISHER 85

Publisher 2002

Publisher 2002

Rotating Art

The **rotation** of an image—measured in degrees from a vertical plane—can be changed using the green rotation handle on a selected object, or using menu commands. The rotation of art and other objects can change and guide the reader's focus and create visual interest. You can rotate a selected object in 90-degree increments by using the Rotate commands found on the Arrange menu, or in specific degree increments by using the Format *item* (where item stands for AutoShape, Text box, Table, etc.) dialog boxes found on the short cut menus. Objects can even be rotated around a point on its base by pressing [Ctrl] while dragging the green rotation handle. Mike wants to rotate the cartoon balloon to catch the reader's attention and make the tone of the publication lighter and good-natured.

Steps

1. Make sure the callout is still selected, click the **green rotation handle** on the callout, then drag until it is at **6¾" H / 3" V**

   The AutoShape is rotated to the right, as shown in Figure D-15. You think a more precise placement would make it look better.

   QuickTip
   You could also use the Measurement toolbar to adjust the rotation of the callout in addition to the spacing of the text.

2. Right-click the **callout**, click **Format AutoShape**, then click the **Size tab**

   The Size tab in the Format AutoShape dialog box is shown in Figure D-16. You can rotate an image a specific number of degrees.

3. Select the contents of the Rotation text box, type **4**, then click **OK**

   The AutoShape is rotated four degrees clockwise. Compare your image with Figure D-17.

4. Press **[F9]**, then click the **Save button** on the Standard toolbar

▶ PUBLISHER 86   **WORKING WITH ART**

FIGURE D-15: Object rotated with handle

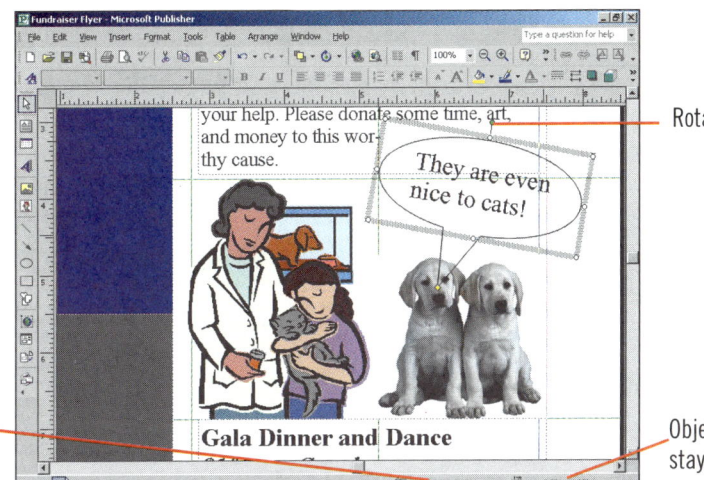

Rotation handle

Object coordinates remain unchanged after the object's rotation

Object dimensions stay the same

FIGURE D-16: Size tab of Format AutoShape dialog box

Precise degree of rotation shown to two decimal places (yours may differ)

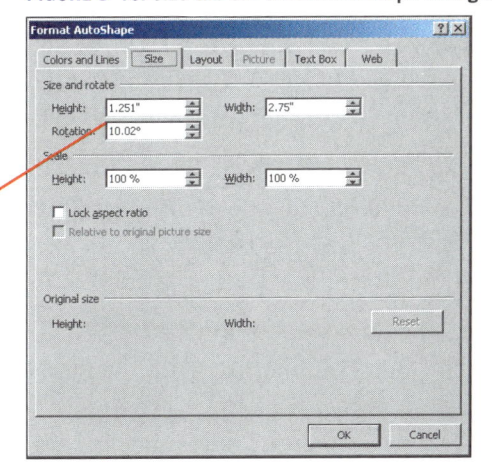

FIGURE D-17: Precisely rotated object

Clues to Use

Using the Measurement toolbar

The Measurement toolbar lets you precisely move and resize graphic images or text boxes, and fine-tune text. To display the Measurement toolbar, click View on the menu bar, click Toolbars, then click Measurement. Text point size, distance between characters, and line spacing can be adjusted using this toolbar, as can an object's height, width, length, and rotation. The available options of the toolbar depend on the type of object that is selected.

WORKING WITH ART PUBLISHER 87

Using Drawing Tools

Publisher 2002

Publisher has a variety of drawing tools that you can use to create your own geometric designs. The Objects toolbar contains five drawing tools that let you draw lines, arrows, ovals, rectangles, and add AutoShapes. Any shape drawn on a page can be moved, resized, or formatted to meet your design specifications. Similar to objects, shapes created with drawing tools can be flipped as well as rotated. Mike wants to add a geometric design to the gray rectangle at the lower-left corner of the page. He begins by drawing a border to frame the design and make it easier to resize.

Steps

1. **Click the Rectangle button on the Objects toolbar**
   You can create a shape by dragging the pointer to create the size you need.

2. **Drag + from ½" H / 8¼" V to 2¼" H / 10" V, then press [F9]**
   The box is layered on the gray rectangle and has the dimensions 1¾" × 1¾". You can add an interesting shape, such as a heart, using the AutoShapes button.

3. **Click the AutoShapes button on the Objects toolbar, point to Basic Shapes, the Basic Shapes menu appears as shown in Figure D-18, click the heart, then drag + from ½" H / 8¼" V to 2½" H / 10" V**
   The heart is inside the rectangle you just created. You want to layer another heart on top of the first.

   > **QuickTip**
   > If you want to repeat a designed shape with the identical dimensions, create one with all the formatting attributes you want, then copy and paste it.

4. **Click, point to Basic Shapes, click the heart, then drag + from ¾" H / 8½" V to 2" H / 9¾" V**
   You see how easy it is to create interesting and professional-looking design elements in a publication.

5. **Right-click the selected heart, click Format AutoShape, click the Line Color list arrow, click Gold color box (third from the left), then click OK**
   The heart shape is now outlined with a yellow line. You used the rectangle as a guide to place the hearts. It is no longer needed.

6. **Click the rectangle, then click [Delete]**
   Compare your work to Figure D-19.

7. **Click the Save button on the Standard toolbar**

▶ PUBLISHER 88 WORKING WITH ART

FIGURE D-18: Basic Shapes menu

Heart shape

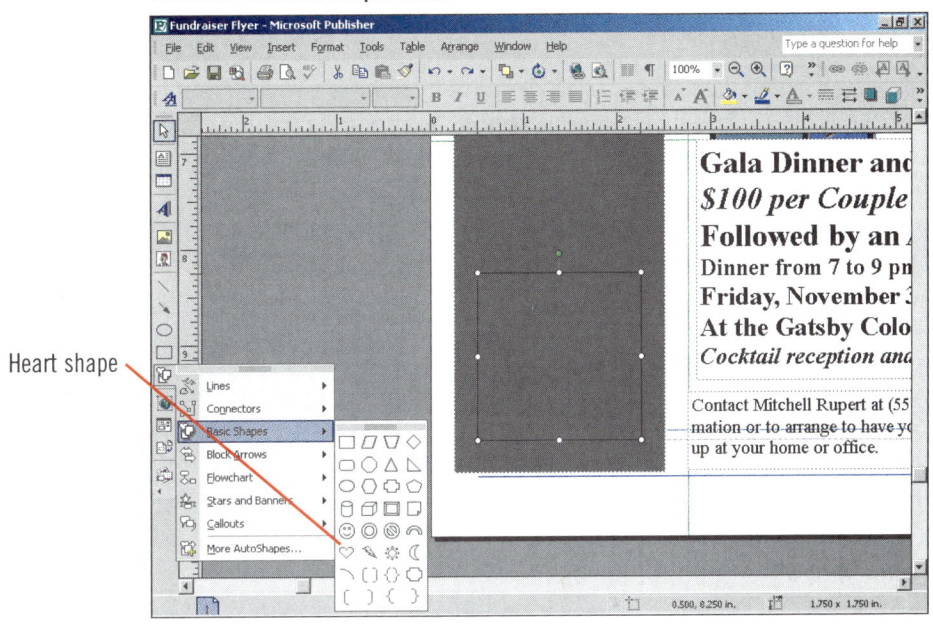

FIGURE D-19: Design created with drawing tools

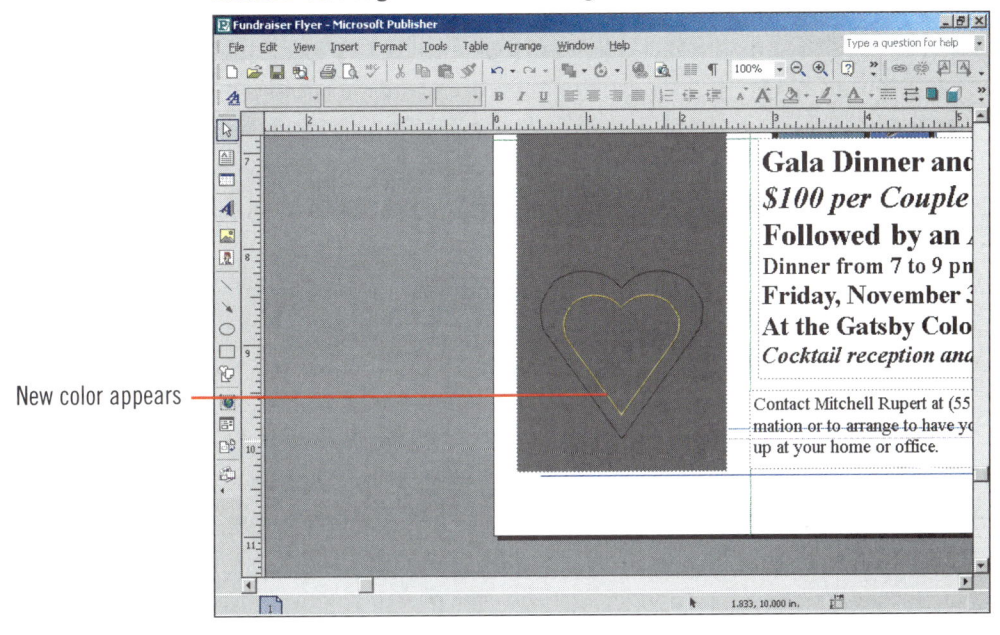

New color appears

Drawing perfect shapes and lines

Sometimes you want to draw an exact shape or line. To draw a square, click the Rectangle button then press and hold [Shift] as you drag. Press and hold [Shift] to create a circle using the Oval button. Press and hold [Shift] to create a horizontal, vertical, or 45-degree angle straight line using the Line button. To center an object at a specific location, click the tool to create the object, place the pointer where you want the center of the object to be, then hold [Ctrl] as you drag the mouse. Remember to always release the mouse button before you release [Ctrl] or [Shift].

WORKING WITH ART

Fill Drawn Shapes

Publisher 2002

Colors and patterns enhance overall design and help you create elegant original graphics. Drawn shapes can be left with their default attributes—displaying whatever background exists—or you can fill them using a variety of colors and patterns. Dialog boxes for colors and patterns can be accessed from the menu bar, or from buttons on the Formatting toolbar. Mike wants to add color and patterns to the shapes in his design. He begins by adding color to the callout and one of the hearts.

Steps

> **QuickTip**
> As you drag the mouse over each color displayed by the Fill Color list arrow, its name appears in a ScreenTip.

1. Select the **small heart**, press **[F9]**, press **[Shift]**, click the **Oval callout** at **7" H / 4" V**, release **[Shift]**, click the **Fill Color list arrow** on the Formatting toolbar, then click the **Accent 2 (gold) color box**

   Gold is added to the small heart and the callout to make them stand out.

> **QuickTip**
> No ScreenTip giving the name of the color appears when you display the colors from the Format AutoShape dialog box.

2. Press **[Esc]**, right-click the **large heart**, click **Format AutoShape**, click the **Fill Color list arrow**, click the **blue color box** (second from the left), then click **OK**

   On examination, you think a red fill would be a more appropriate color for the small heart.

3. Right-click the **small heart**, click **Format AutoShape**, click the **Fill Color list arrow**, click **More Colors**, the Colors dialog box opens as shown in Figure D-20, click the **red color box** (third box from the left in the next-to-the-bottom row), click **OK** to close the Colors dialog box, then click **OK** to close the Format AutoShape dialog box

   A yellow outline still surrounds the small heart. You decide to reduce the contrast by changing to the red you just selected.

4. Press **[F9]**, click the **Line Color list arrow** on the Formatting toolbar, then click the **red color box** (beneath the gray line)

   The red was added to your palette for this publication. It will not be added to the palette in subsequent publications even if you choose the same color scheme. The publication still doesn't appeal to you. You think perhaps the red heart is too bright and decide to dull it by making it transparent to some of the blue underneath.

5. Right-click the selected **red heart**, click **Format AutoShape**, select the text in the **Transparency text box**, type **15**, click **OK**, then press **[Esc]**

   The smaller heart is now darker. You think the overall design is nice. Compare your work to Figure D-21.

6. Click the **text box** at **4" H / 10" V**, select **Mitchell Rupert**, type **your name**, press **[F9]**, then press **[Esc]** twice

   Compare your work with the completed flyer in Figure D-22. The art is well placed, all the text is readable, and the colors are complementary.

7. Click the **Save button** on the Standard toolbar, then click the **Print button** on the Standard toolbar

8. Exit Publisher

WORKING WITH ART

FIGURE D-20: Colors dialog box

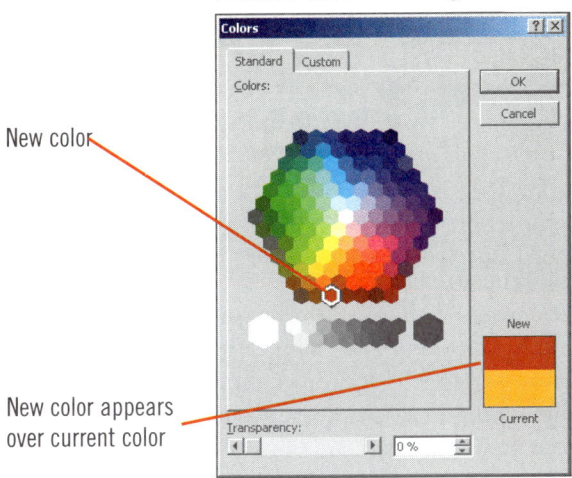

FIGURE D-21: Re-colored objects

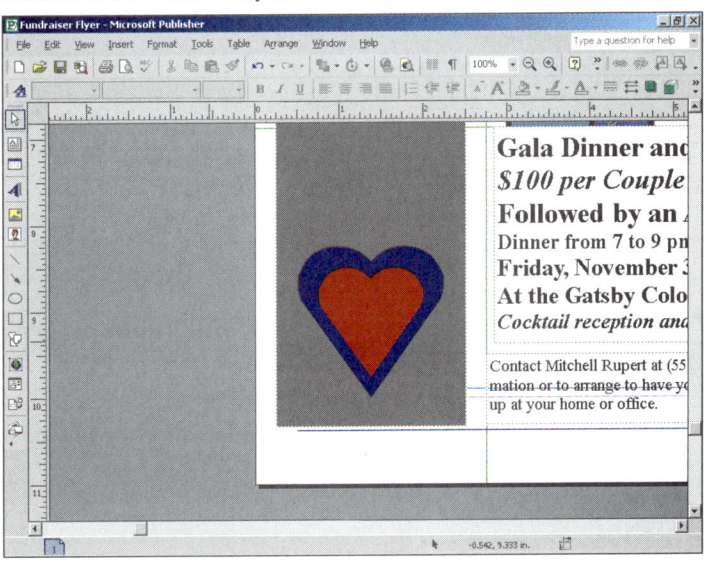

FIGURE D-22: Completed flyer

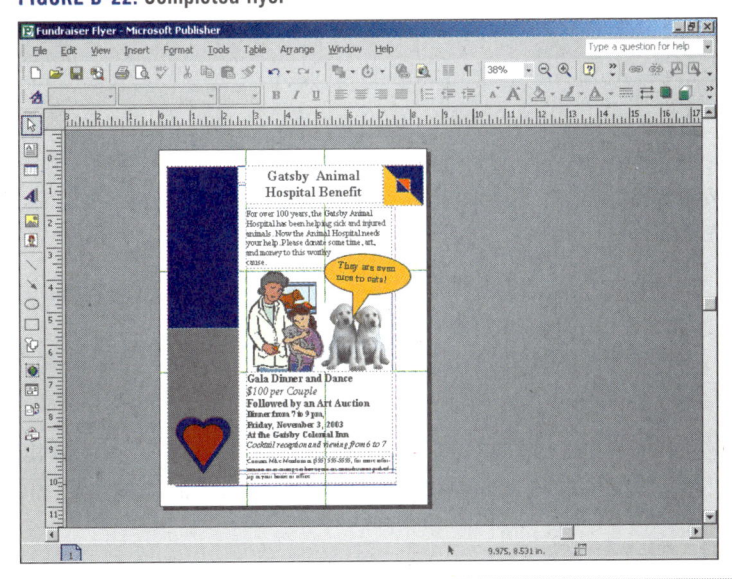

WORKING WITH ART PUBLISHER 91

Capstone Project: Flower Show Web Page

Publisher 2002 — Unit D

You have learned the skills necessary to insert, resize, and rotate clip art. You can copy and move objects, and crop, align, and group objects. You have used drawing tools and filled drawn shapes. Now you will use these skills to add and manipulate artwork on a Web site. Image Magic was contracted to create a Web Page for an annual flower show. Mike was assigned to head the project. He did some preliminary work and wants to improve upon it with some artwork. Throughout this project, he will zoom in and out, as necessary.

Steps

1. Start Publisher, open the file **Pub D-3** from the drive and folder where your Project Files are stored, then save it as **Flower Show Web Page**
   Since the Web page is advertising a flower show, you decide to start your search by looking for photos and clip art related to flowers.

2. Click the **Clip Organizer Frame button** on the Objects toolbar
   Use the Search Option boxes that allow you to search for: Pictures, Sounds, and Motion Clips arranged by content. For simplicity sake, you decide to limit your search to artwork that is on your computer.

3. Click the **Search text text box**, type **flowers**, click the **Search in list arrow**, click **My Collections** and **Office Collections** if necessary to select them, click the **Results should be list arrow**, click **Clip Art** and **Photographs** to select them if necessary, then click **Search**
   Your search finds two objects, as shown in Figure D-23. You think that the white flowers surrounded by the green leaves will create an interesting look against a white background.

4. Insert the picture of the **white roses** (*Hint:* The filename is j0281904.wmf), then close the Insert Clip Art task pane
   You want to move the art to a better position on the page.

5. Move the picture so that the upper-left corner is at **1½" H / 6" V**
   You are pleased with the art, so you decide to make a copy of it.

6. With the object still selected click the **Copy button**, click the **Paste button**, then position the pasted image so that its upper-left corner is at **3½" H / 6" V**
   You wonder if flipping the copy would improve the appearance of the artwork.

7. Click **Arrange** on the menu bar, point to **Rotate or Flip**, then click **Flip Horizontal**
   You think that the mirrored images of the white roses surrounded by the green foliage are interesting.

8. Create a text box at **¼" H / 3" V**, type **your name**, then modify the font and point size so that the text is readable
   Your changes are limited to the upper portion of the Web page, so there is no point in printing both pages of the publication. Compare your work to Figure D-24.

9. Click the **Save button** on the Standard toolbar, click **File** on the menu bar, click **Print**, select the **Current page button**, click **OK**, then exit Publisher

▶ PUBLISHER 92   WORKING WITH ART

FIGURE D-23: Results of clip art search

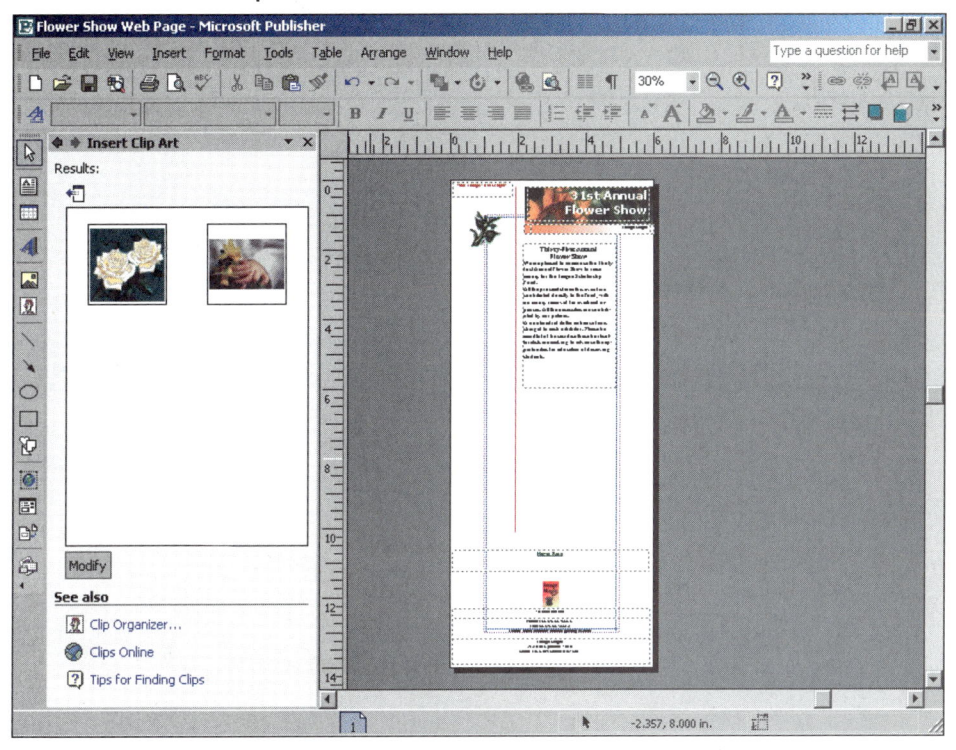

FIGURE D-24: Completed Web Page

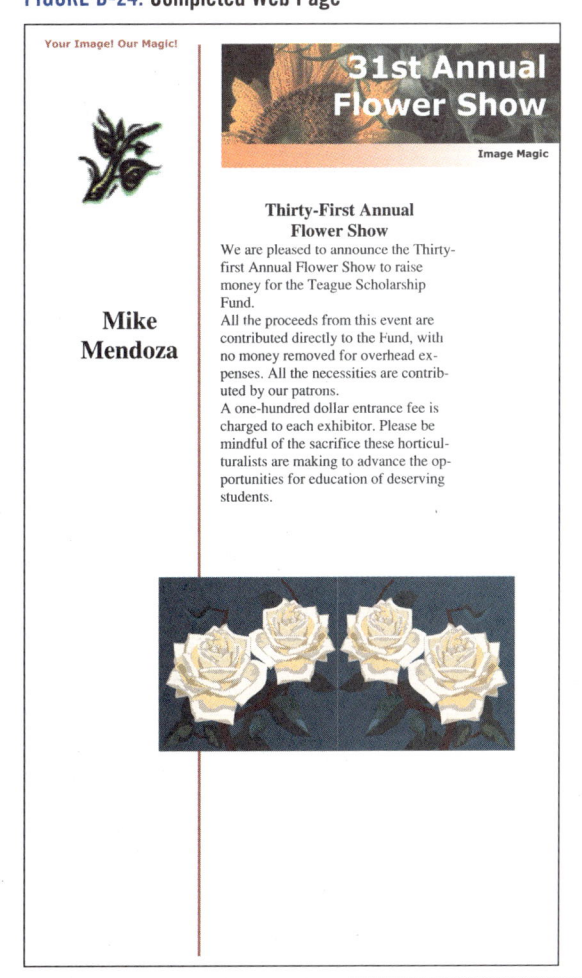

WORKING WITH ART

Publisher 2002

Practice

▶ Concepts Review

Label each of the elements of the Publisher window shown in Figure D-25.

FIGURE D-25

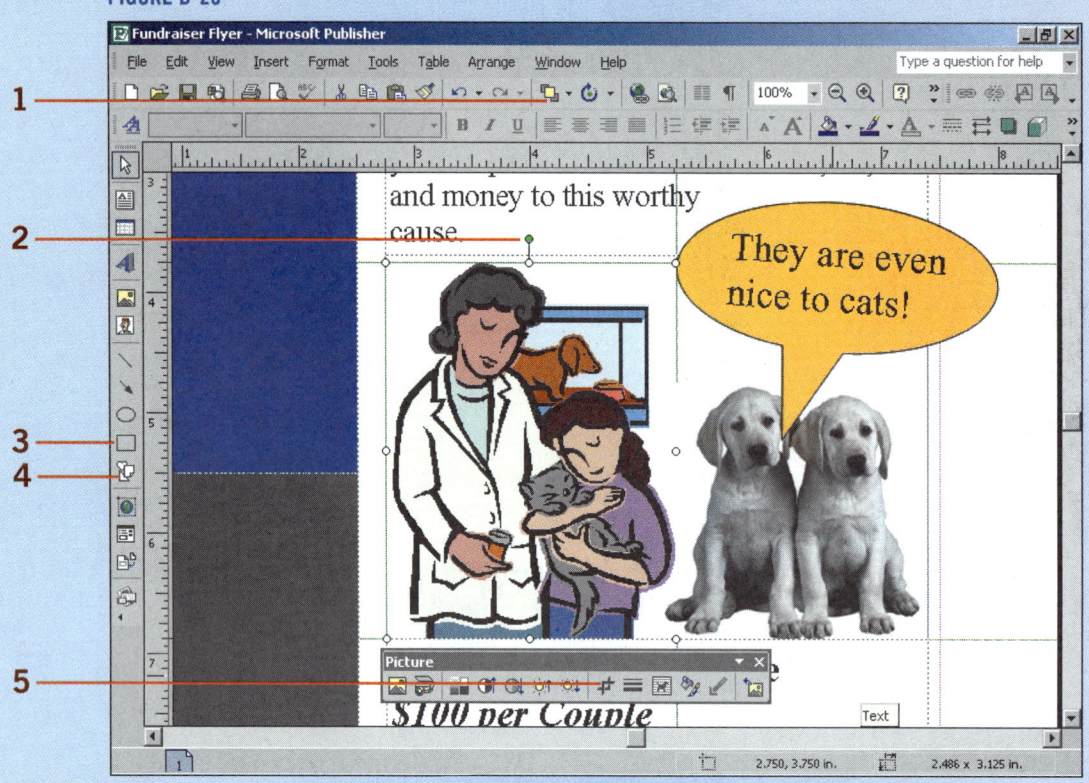

Match each of the terms with the statement that describes its function.

6.
7.
8.
9.
10.
11.

a. Contains clip art
b. Flips an object horizontally
c. Conceals part of an image
d. Colors a line or border
e. Fills an object with color
f. Creates a custom shape

Select the best answer from the list of choices.

12. Create a square using the Rectangle button by holding _____ while dragging +.
    a. [Ctrl]
    b. [Alt]
    c. [Shift]
    d. [Esc]
13. You can do each of the following with clip art, except:
    a. Rotate.
    b. Italicize.
    c. Flip.
    d. Crop.

▶ PUBLISHER 94 **WORKING WITH ART**

Practice

14. Which button cannot be used with clip art?
    a.
    b.
    c.
    d.
15. Rotate an object clockwise in 90-degree increments by clicking:
    a. Flip Horizontal.
    b. Free Rotate.
    c. Rotate Left.
    d. Rotate Right.
16. To resize an object, maintaining its scale while dragging, press and hold _____.
    a. [Shift]
    b. [Alt][Shift]
    c. [Ctrl]
    d. [Alt]
17. Which pointer is used to insert an AutoShape?
    a.
    b.
    c.
    d.
18. To create a circle, click _____, then press and hold [Shift] while dragging the pointer.
    a.
    b.
    c.
    d.
19. Which pointer is used to copy an object without placing a copy on the Clipboard?
    a.
    b.
    c.
    d.
20. Which button is used to add colors and patterns to objects?
    a.
    b.
    c.
    d.

▶ Skills Review

Throughout this exercise, zoom in and out whenever necessary.

1. **Insert and resize clip art.**
    a. Start Publisher.
    b. Open the file Pub D-4 from the drive and folder where your Project Files are located, then close the task pane.
    c. Save the file as **Family Reunion Postcard**.
    d. Use the Microsoft Clip Organizer to search My Collections and Office Collections for clip art and photographs using the word "home." Locate the image of a house that appears on the top row of the task pane, second from the right (filename: j0185604.wmf).
    e. Insert the image so that the upper-left corner is at ½" H / 3" V (the clip art's dimensions should be approximately 1" H × 1" V), then close the task pane.
    f. Press and hold [Shift], then resize the image by placing the pointer over the lower-right handle, then drag until the lower-right corner is at 1¼" H / 3¾" V. The image should now be approximately ¾" H × ¾" V.
    g. Save the publication.
2. **Copy and move an object.**
    a. Copy the selected image, then paste the image on the publication.
    b. Move the newly pasted copy so that the upper-left corner is at 4¼" H / 3" V.
    c. Flip the copy horizontally, then deselect it. (*Hint*: The image's chimneys will be on opposite sides.)
    d. Save the publication.
3. **Crop an image.**
    a. Move the image of the flowers from the upper-right corner of the publication so that the upper-left corner is at 2" H / 2" V.
    b. If the Picture toolbar is not visible, click View on the menu bar, click Toolbars, then click Picture.

WORKING WITH ART

Publisher 2002 — Practice

    c. Click the Crop button on the Picture toolbar. Crop the top edge of the image using the center cropping handle, hiding ⅛" of the image so that the top-left corner is now at 2" H / 2 ⅛" V, then press [Esc].
    d. Save the publication.

4. Align and group images.
    a. Press and hold [Shift], select the two clip art images of the house, then select the image of the flowers.
    b. Right-click, point to Align or Distribute, then click Align Bottom.
    c. Right-click, point to Align or Distribute, then click Distribute Horizontally.
    d. Save the publication.

5. Layer objects.
    a. Copy the object at 1" H / 3½" V, then paste and drag the copy so that its upper-left corner is at 1" H / 2¾" V.
    b. Send the copied object behind the original object.
    c. Copy the object at 4¼" H / 3½" V, paste it, then drag the copy so that its upper-left corner is at 3¾" H / 2¾" V.
    d. Send the copied object behind the original object.
    e. Save the publication.

6. Rotate art.
    a. Flip the image of the flowers horizontally.
    b. Right-click the image of the flowers, click Format Picture, use the dialog box to change the rotation to 300 degrees (*Hint*: Use the Size tab in the Format Picture dialog box.), then deselect the image.
    c. Save the publication.

7. Use drawing tools.
    a. Click the AutoShapes button, point to Basic Shapes, then click the heart (sixth row down on the left).
    b. Draw the heart so that its upper-left corner is at 4½" H / ¼" V and it has the dimensions ¾" H x ¾" V.
    c. Create a copy of this shape, paste the copy, then drag it so that the upper-left corner is at 4 ¼" H / ¼" V (the two hearts should overlap).
    d. Save the publication.

8. Fill drawn shapes.
    a. Add red fill color to both heart shapes. (*Hint:* Click the More Colors button on the Fill Color drop-down list.)
    b. Select the right heart, then change the transparency to 30%.
    c. Create a text box with the upper-left corner at ½" H / 2¼" V with the dimensions 2" H × ½" V, then insert your name using AutoFit Text to adjust the point size as necessary.
    d. Save and print the publication, then exit Publisher.

▶ Independent Challenge 1

You are considering new layouts for your business cards, and decided to come up with a design.
    a. Start Publisher, if necessary, use the Scallops Business Card (Plain Paper) from the Publication Gallery, with Landscape orientation, include a logo placeholder, one card in the center of the page, then close the task pane.
    b. Save the publication as **New Business Card Design** to the drive and folder where your Project Files are stored.
    c. Enter and use any appropriate information about yourself in the Primary Business Personal Information Set, then change the color scheme to Parrot.
    d. Use at least three drawing tools to create an interesting series of shapes in the upper-right corner of the business card. Change the fill color and fill effects of at least two shapes.
    e. If desired, rotate and layer the artwork.
    f. Save and print the publication, then exit Publisher.

Practice

▶ Independent Challenge 2

A local clothing store asks you to use your design skills to create a gift certificate for a new sales promotion.
  a. Start Publisher, then use the Mobile Special Gift Certificate found in the Publication Gallery.
  b. Save the publication as **Gift Certificate** to the drive and folder where your Project Files are stored.
  c. Enter appropriate information in the Secondary Business Personal Information Set, then change the color scheme to Monarch.
  d. Use the Microsoft Clip Organizer to search My Collections and Office Collections for clip art and photographs using the word "maps," then insert the globe (filename: j0335112.wmf) at approximately 0" H / 2" V.
  e. Add an AutoShape of your own choosing.
  f. Make at least two copies of the AutoShape, resize them, then place them according to your own sense of design.
  g. Add different fill colors to the AutoShapes.
  h. Type your name in the Authorized by text box.
  i. Save and print the publication, then exit Publisher.

▶ Independent Challenge 3

You decide to spruce up your work area, and a customized calendar is just what you need.
  a. Start Publisher, if necessary, then use the Full Page Blends Calendar from the Publication Gallery for the next month of this year.
  b. Save the publication as **Next Month's Calendar** to the drive and folder where your Project Files are located.
  c. Enter appropriate information about yourself in the Primary Business Personal Information Set.
  d. Change the color scheme to one of your own choosing.
  e. Click Change date range on the task pane and change the range to start and end next month, then close the task pane.
  f. Add clip art of your choosing to the calendar.
  g. Add objects created with drawing tools, and add color and patterns, if appropriate. If necessary, resize any drawn objects.
  h. Save and print the publication, then exit Publisher.

ⓔ Independent Challenge 4

There are many sources on the Web for clip art. Some require payment to use an image, while other images are free to download. You need to find some free clip art that relates to your favorite hobby.
  a. Connect to the Internet, then use your browser and favorite search engine to find free clip art sites. Some possible free clip art sites are: www.free-clip-art.com, www.absolutely-free-clipart.com, and free-clipart.net.
  b. Print out the home page from at least two of the sites you found. Take note of any restrictions regarding use of graphic images.
  c. Right-click any of the free clip art images that appeals to you, then download it by choosing "Save image as." Save it to the drive and folder where your Project Files are stored using the artwork's default name, then disconnect from the Internet.
  d. Start Publisher, use the Publication Gallery to create a single-page Quick Publication using any design you choose, then save the publication to the drive and folder where your Project Files are located as **"your name's" hobby**.
  e. Replace a placeholder with downloaded file, add appropriate text (if necessary) to describe the artwork, then add your name somewhere on the page.
  f. Format the artwork by cropping any undesirable elements, then copy and align images to enhance the publication.
  g. Save and print the publication, then exit Publisher.

Publisher 2002 | Practice

▶ Visual Workshop

Use the elements found in Pub D-5 to create the party invitation seen in Figure D-26, using it as a guide. Save this publication as **Party Invitation** to the drive and folder where your Project Files are located. Substitute your name for Pat Dyson, then save and print the flyer.

FIGURE D-26

Promotion Party

The pleasure of your company is requested in celebration of the promotion of Pat Dyson to Campaign Manager.

28 November 2003
7:30 PM

Seurat's Pointilist Restaurant
214 River View Road
Santa Fe, NM 87504

▶ PUBLISHER 98 **WORKING WITH ART**

Publisher 2002

Unit E

Enhancing
a Publication

Objectives

- Define styles
- Modify and apply a style
- Change a format into a style
- Create columns
- Adjust text overflows
- Add Continued on/from notices
- Add drop caps
- Create reversed text
- Capstone Project: Solar System Newsletter

Text in a publication should be easy to read. Professionals advise you not to use more than two fonts per page because too many fonts make a page look busy and detract from the message. Experts recommend formatting fonts in different sizes, with bold, italics, or other effects to add visual interest without distraction. To further enhance readability, story text can be formatted in one or more columns, depending on the desired layout. Story text that does not fit within a single text box on a page can be continued elsewhere in a publication. Publisher has tools to help map and link the text boxes to create a cohesive publication. Mike Mendoza is the new account executive for Image Magic's client, *Route 66 Traveler*, a quarterly newsletter. He is revising styles and formatting for upcoming issues. The client wants to make sure that its newsletter has a strong, consistent style, and that it is enjoyable to read.

Defining Styles

The appearance of text in a publication contributes to its readability. Text that is too large looks awkward; text that is too small or too fancy is distracting and hard to read. You can create consistently readable text by using styles. A **style** is a defined set of text and formatting attributes, such as font, font size, and paragraph alignment. As a reader goes from page to page, it will be clear what is an article headline, what is pull-quote text, etc. This is especially important in multi-page documents. The Styles and Formatting task pane contains all of the styles specific to a particular publication, and displays each style exactly as it will look. You can create your own styles and modify those that already exist. These new styles apply only to the publication for which they are created, but they can also be imported into other publications. By naming a style, you can make it available for further use. When naming a style, it is important to make it descriptive to distinguish it from other styles that exist, or that you will create for a publication. Mike wants to define a new style that he will use throughout the newsletter.

Steps

1. **Start Publisher, open the file Pub E-1 from the drive and folder where your Project Files are stored, then save it as Route 66 Traveler**
   You want to make sure that text within the newsletter is easily readable and focuses the reader on the message, rather than the style of the publication.

2. **Click the Styles and Formatting button on the Formatting toolbar**
   The Styles and Formatting task pane opens, as shown in Figure E-1. Publisher comes with many text styles, but also allows you to create your own.

   > **QuickTip**
   > You can also open the Styles and Formatting task pane by clicking the list arrow on any open task pane, then clicking Styles and Formatting.

3. **Click the Create new style button on the task pane**
   The Create New Style dialog box opens, as shown in Figure E-2. You can change the font and font size, modify the alignment of indents and lists, change the line and character spacing, adjust the tabs, and even modify the appearance of the horizontal rules.

4. **Type 66 Traveler in the Enter new style name text box, click the Font and size button, click the Font list arrow, click Times New Roman, click the Size list arrow, click 14, then click OK**
   The 66 Traveler style will be Times New Roman font, which is a very common type style for the body text of documents because it is easy to read.

5. **Click the Indents and lists button, click the Alignment list arrow, click Right, then click OK**
   The sample in the Create New Style dialog box indicates how the new style will look, as shown in Figure E-3.

6. **Click OK**
   The Create New Style dialog box closes and the new style appears in the list of existing styles in the task pane.

7. **Click the Save button on the Standard toolbar**
   Now the style can be applied to text in the publication.

PUBLISHER 100   ENHANCING A PUBLICATION

FIGURE E-1: Styles and Formatting task pane

- Styles and Formatting button
- Available styles are listed alphabetically
- Create new style button

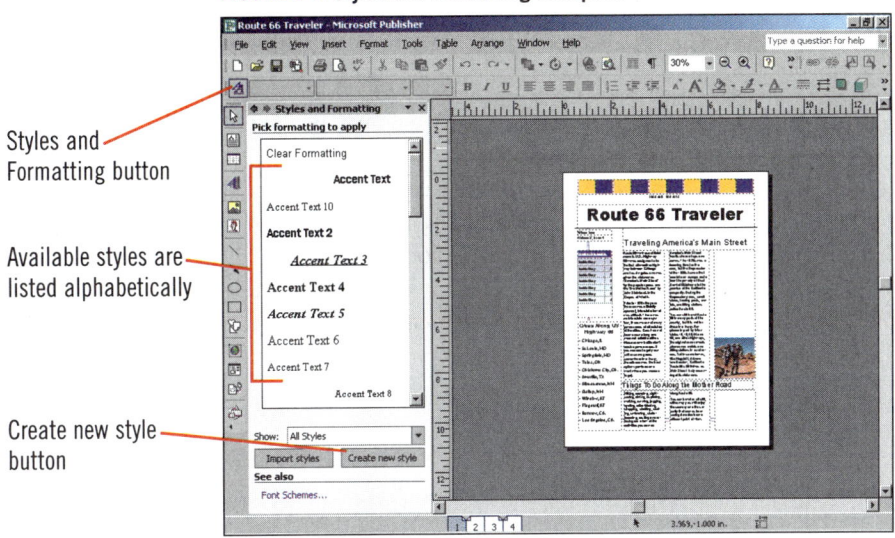

FIGURE E-2: Create New Style dialog box

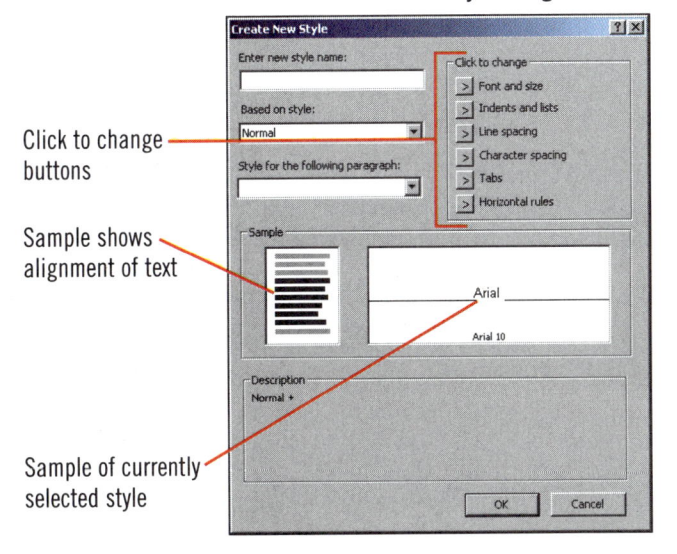

- Click to change buttons
- Sample shows alignment of text
- Sample of currently selected style

FIGURE E-3: New style shown in Create New Style dialog box

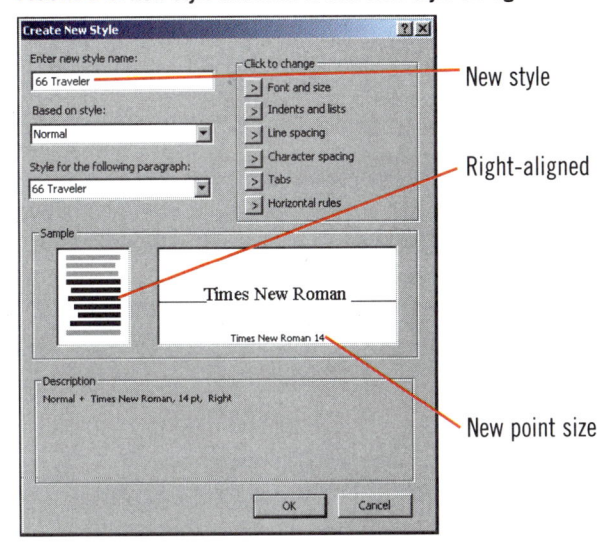

- New style
- Right-aligned
- New point size

Design Matters

Choosing fonts

Serifs are small decorative strokes added to the end of a letter's main strokes. Serif, or roman, types are useful for long passages of text because the serifs help distinguish individual letters and provide continuity for the reader's eye. **Sans serif** fonts are typefaces that do not have serifs. Generally these are a low-contrast design, such as Arial. Sans serif faces lend a clean, simple appearance to headlines and titles but are avoided for long passages of unbroken text because they are more difficult to read than serif fonts.

ENHANCING A PUBLICATION PUBLISHER 101

Modifying and Applying a Style

Publisher 2002 — Unit E

Since any style can be modified, you have the freedom to change the appearance of all the text assigned to a specific style within a publication. Once you define a style, you can apply it to text so that your publication develops a consistent look with similar attributes, or you can change the style, and the newly modified style will be applied automatically. ➤ Mike modifies the style he just created, then inserts a Word document and applies the defined style.

Steps

1. **Position** the pointer over **66 Traveler** in the Pick formatting to apply area of the task pane, click the **66 Traveler list arrow**, then click **Modify**
   The Change Style dialog box opens.

2. Click the **Font and size button**, click the **Size list arrow**, click **12**, then click **OK**
   The font size for 66 Traveler changes from 14 point to 12 point, and the change appears in the sample.

3. Click the **Indents and lists button**, click the **Alignment list arrow**, click **Left**, then click **OK**
   The Indents and Lists dialog box closes. The modified text size and alignment should appear in the Change Style dialog box, as shown in Figure E-4.

   > **QuickTip**
   > You can determine the attributes of any style in the Pick formatting to apply list by placing the pointer over the style name.

4. Click **OK** to close the Change Style dialog box
   The Change Style dialog box closes. Any new and existing text that has the 66 Traveler style applied to it will look consistent with text already in the publication.

5. Click the text box at **3" H / 5" V**, press **[Ctrl][A]**, then click the **Zoom In button** until **50%** appears in the Zoom box on the Standard toolbar
   You can see the task pane and the top and bottom of the text box.

6. Click **66 Traveler** in the Pick formatting to apply list in the task pane, then press **[Esc]** twice
   The selected text was converted to the 66 Traveler style, as shown in Figure E-5.

7. Click the **Save button** on the Standard toolbar

► PUBLISHER 102   ENHANCING A PUBLICATION

FIGURE E-4: Change Style dialog box

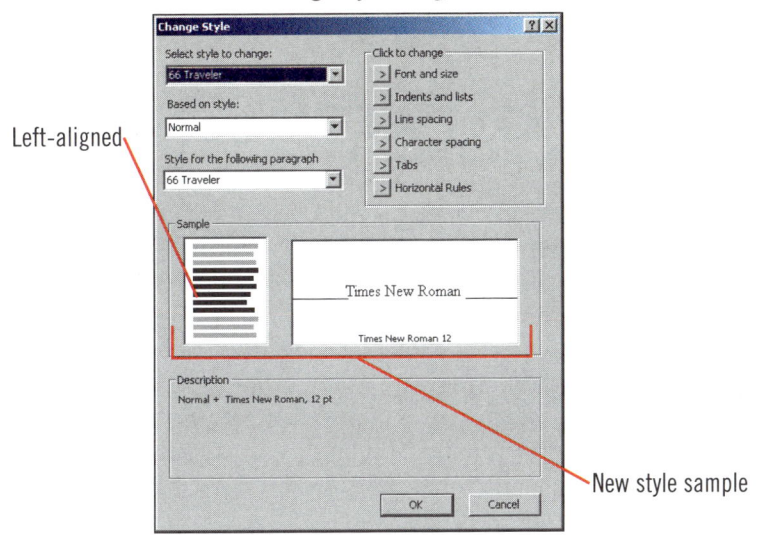

Left-aligned

New style sample

FIGURE E-5: New style applied

Modified style appears in task pane

Design Matters

Adjusting spaces between characters

Sometimes characters don't look quite right: they may seem packed too close together or spread too far apart. This is particularly true of typefaces at 14 points and larger. Adjusting the spacing between specific character pairs, or kerning, can make large text look better. Publisher automatically kerns characters with point sizes of 14 and larger, but you can kern any characters you choose by selecting the character pair(s) to be adjusted, clicking Format on the menu bar, then clicking Character Spacing. Using the Character Spacing dialog box, you can change scaling, the width of the text characters, and tracking, the distance between text characters, in addition to kerning, and the point size where automatic kerning begins, as shown in Figure E-6.

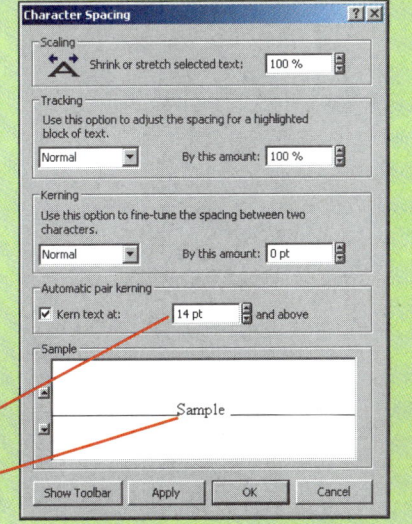

FIGURE E-6: Character Spacing dialog box

Automatic kerning setting

Spacing options sample box

ENHANCING A PUBLICATION PUBLISHER 103

Changing a Format into a Style

A style can be created from formatted text even without knowing all the attributes that make up a text's appearance. This process is called creating a **style by example**. Formatted text can be used to create a style by selecting the text, then typing a name in the Style text box on the Formatting toolbar. Creating a style by example makes the style available for use over and over again in the publication. It is important to note that there is a real difference between using a style and using the Format Painter. The Format Painter button reformats selected characters according to the style of currently selected characters, but does not store or name the style, or update similarly formatted text automatically. Mike likes the style of the story title and wants to create a style from this format that he can use throughout the publication.

Steps

Trouble?
Scroll up to see the text box, if necessary.

1. **Click the text box at 3" H / 2¾" V**
   The text box containing the headline is selected.

2. **Click Heading 2 in the Style box on the Formatting toolbar**
   The current style is selected. You want to be consistent in naming styles so that you can easily identify their particular uses and pairings with other styles.

3. **Type 66 Heading, then press [Enter]**
   The Create Style By Example dialog box opens, as shown in Figure E-7. You entered a new name in the Style box to create a style based on the formatting of the selected text in the lead story headline. The Sample box shows you the current style's font and size, as well as its alignment setting.

4. **Click OK, then press [Esc]**
   The Create Style By Example dialog box closes. Notice that the new name, 66 Heading, appears in the Style box on the Formatting toolbar. You can now apply this style anywhere in the publication.

5. **Click the text box at 5" H / 1½" V, click the Style box on the Formatting toolbar, type 66 Masthead, press [Enter], then click OK in the Create Style By Example dialog box**
   The new style is listed in the Pick formatting to apply list, and you can apply it to any text in the publication. Compare your publication to Figure E-8.

6. **Click the Save button on the Standard toolbar**

▶ PUBLISHER 104   ENHANCING A PUBLICATION

FIGURE E-7: Create Style By Example dialog box

New style name is entered from Style box

Current alignment

Current font and size

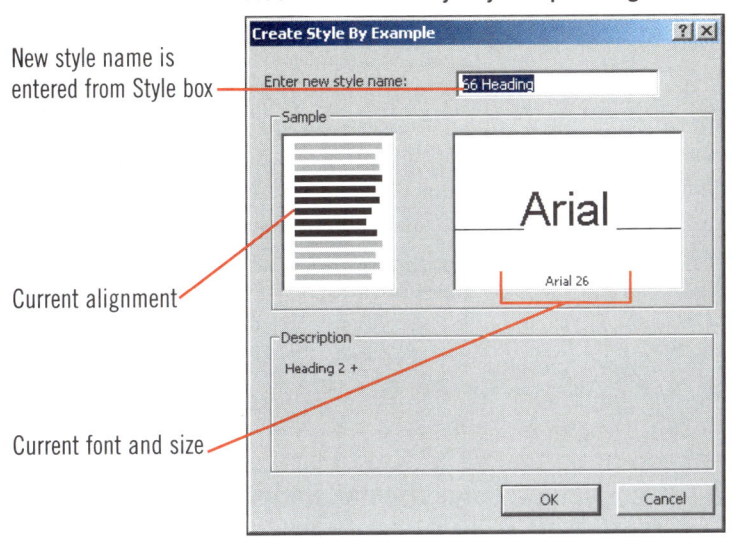

FIGURE E-8: New style name appears in Style box and task pane

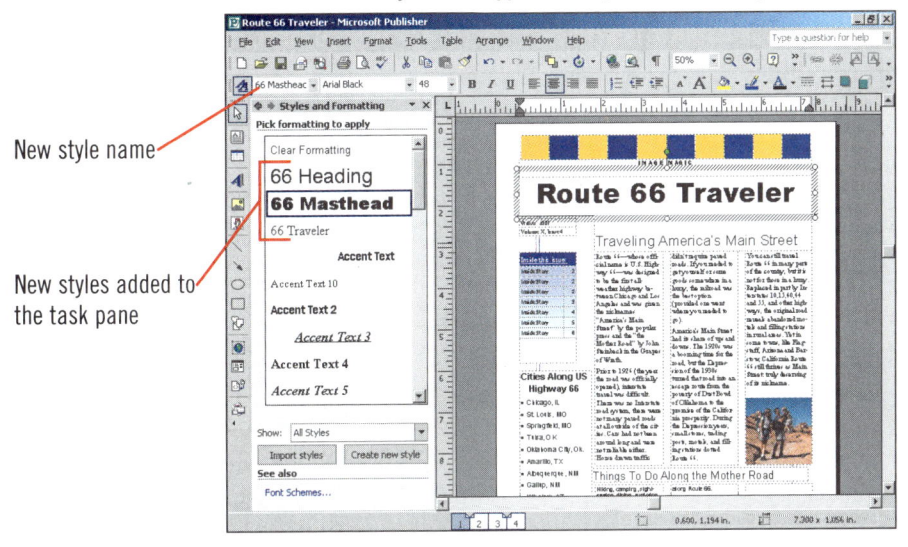

New style name

New styles added to the task pane

Design Matters

Horizontal text alignment

Text can be horizontally aligned in four ways: left-aligned so that each new line begins on the left margin; right-aligned so that each line ends on the right margin; centered so that each line is equally spaced between the margins; and justified so that lines of text begin and end on the margins. Justified and left-aligned text are the most common settings for ordinary text. In most publications, text is left-aligned because the ragged right edge adds an element of white space, making it easier for the reader to move between lines. Some people are attracted to the neatness of text that lines up perfectly on the left and right when justified. While justified text may lend an air of formality to a publication, it requires extra attention to hyphenation and careful proofing to avoid awkward looking gaps of white space. It does offer the advantage of letting you pack more text in the same amount of space as left-aligned.

ENHANCING A PUBLICATION PUBLISHER 105

Publisher 2002

Creating Columns

Most newsletter stories are formatted in multiple columns to make them easier to read and to improve their appearance. When you create a publication using the Publication Gallery, a page may have a three-column layout, but you can use the Page Content task pane to change the layout to fewer columns, or a mixed number of columns, on the same page. These easily applied design techniques can add visual interest and separate stories. Mike wants to see different ways the columns can be arranged on page three to evaluate how the arrangement of the columns affects the overall design of the publication.

Steps

1. **Click the 2-3 page icon** on the horizontal status bar, click the **Zoom box**, type **30**, press **[Enter]**, then use the scroll bars so that both pages are visible, if necessary

   The Page Content task pane lets you select the number of columns for specific pages.

2. Click the **Styles and Formatting task pane list arrow**, click **Page Content**, click the **Select a page to modify list arrow**, then click **Right inside page**

   Your screen should look like Figure E-9. You want to see how the right inside page looks with a mixed number of columns.

3. Click the **Mixed button** under Columns on Right Page

   You think this is an improvement because the three-column story is positioned above two columns on the lower half of the page, and is more consistent with the three-column design of the rest of the publication. You decide to experiment further to see how the page would look with just two columns.

4. Position over **2** under Columns on Right Page, click the **2 list arrow**, then click **Apply to the Page**

   The layout of page three, the right inside page, changes to two columns. This provides some visual interest, but is less attractive than the mixed columns, and is not consistent with the rest of the publication. You think three columns on the right page would be best.

5. Position over **3** under Columns on Right Page, click the **3 list arrow**, then click **Apply to the Page**

   The layout changes to three columns, as shown in Figure E-10. The design is consistent with the rest of the publication and seems balanced. You decide you prefer this layout.

6. Close the task pane, then click the **Save button** on the Standard toolbar

▶ PUBLISHER 106 ENHANCING A PUBLICATION

FIGURE E-9: Page Content task pane

Select a page to modify box

One Column on Right Page box

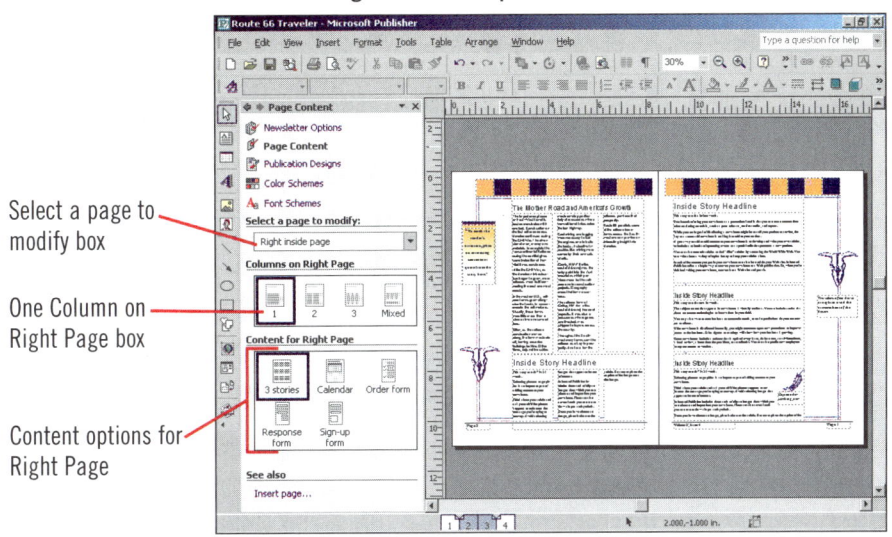

Content options for Right Page

FIGURE E-10: Layout of page with three columns

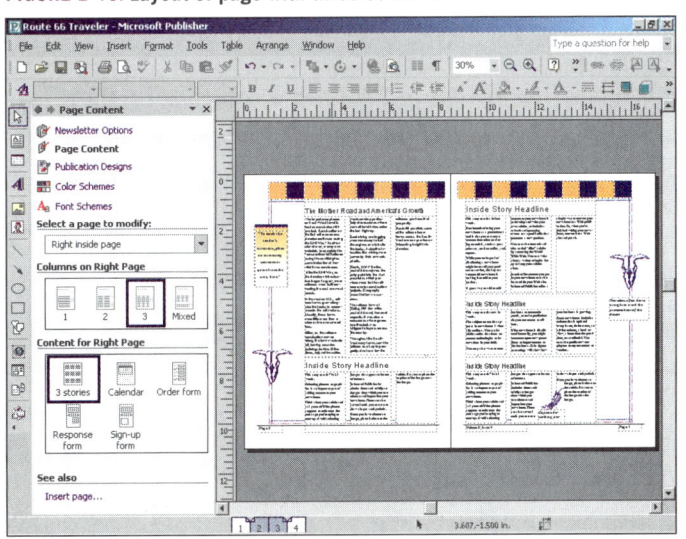

Clues to Use

Manually creating multiple columns

Using the Text Box button creates a text box with a single column. You can add multiple columns to a text box by clicking the Columns button on the Formatting toolbar and selecting the number of columns you want. The text box is then divided into multiple columns of equal width with equal space between them. The number of columns and the spacing between them can be changed using the Columns dialog box. In the Format Text Box dialog box, select the Text Box tab, then click the Columns button. The Columns dialog box appears, as shown in Figure E-11.

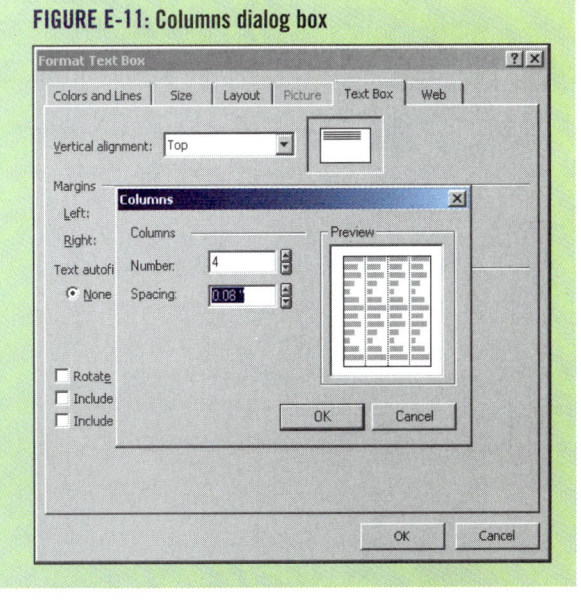

FIGURE E-11: Columns dialog box

ENHANCING A PUBLICATION PUBLISHER 107

Adjusting Text Overflows

Publisher 2002

Text does not always fit neatly within text boxes on a page. In some situations, such as the creation of a newsletter, you may want a story to begin on one page and continue on others. Publisher makes it easy to take the overflow from one text box and pour it into another text box, using the Connect button at the bottom of the text box. Text boxes that have text poured into them are linked to the previous text box. You can ask Publisher to automatically pour the text into an available text box, called **autoflow**, or you can pour the text manually. Pouring the text manually gives you greater control over where the text is placed. Various buttons and pointers help identify and navigate connected text boxes. Mike will import a large text file and pour the overflow text from a story on page two into a text box on page three.

Steps

1. Close the Styles and Formatting task pane, click the **Zoom list arrow**, click **Whole Page**, click the text box at **10" H / 2" V**, press **[Ctrl][A]**, right-click, then click **Delete Text**

   You have a long Word document that will continue into this text box from the text box at the bottom of page two.

   Trouble?
   If you get a warning saying that you need to install a converter, contact your instructor or technical support person.

2. Right-click the text box at **3" H / 9" V**, point to **Change Text**, click **Text File**, select the file **PUB E-2** from the drive and folder where your Project Files are stored, click **OK**, then click **No** when asked if you want to use autoflow

   The Text in Overflow button at the bottom of the text box indicates that there is overflow text. Text that does not fit in this text box can be continued in other text boxes, using and. You want to pour this text into the text box on page three.

   Trouble?
   If you do not see, click View on the menu bar, click Toolbars, then click Connect Frames.

3. Click the **Create Text Box Link button** on the Standard toolbar

   The pointer changes to when placed on objects on the page. When you place this pitcher over an empty text box, it changes to a pouring pitcher, as shown in Figure E-12, indicating that you can pour the text into the text box. You want the overflow to begin pouring in the upper-left text box on page three.

4. Position at **10" H / 3" V**, then click the left mouse button

   The remaining text fills the text boxes. If additional overflow remained (indicated by the appearance of), you would repeat this process until no overflow text remained. Compare your page to Figure E-13.

   QuickTip
   To break a link between connected frames, click.

5. Click the **Save button** on the Standard toolbar

PUBLISHER 108 ENHANCING A PUBLICATION

FIGURE E-12: Preparing to pour overflow text

Indicates overflow text

Create Text Box Link button

Pouring pitcher helps to place overflow text

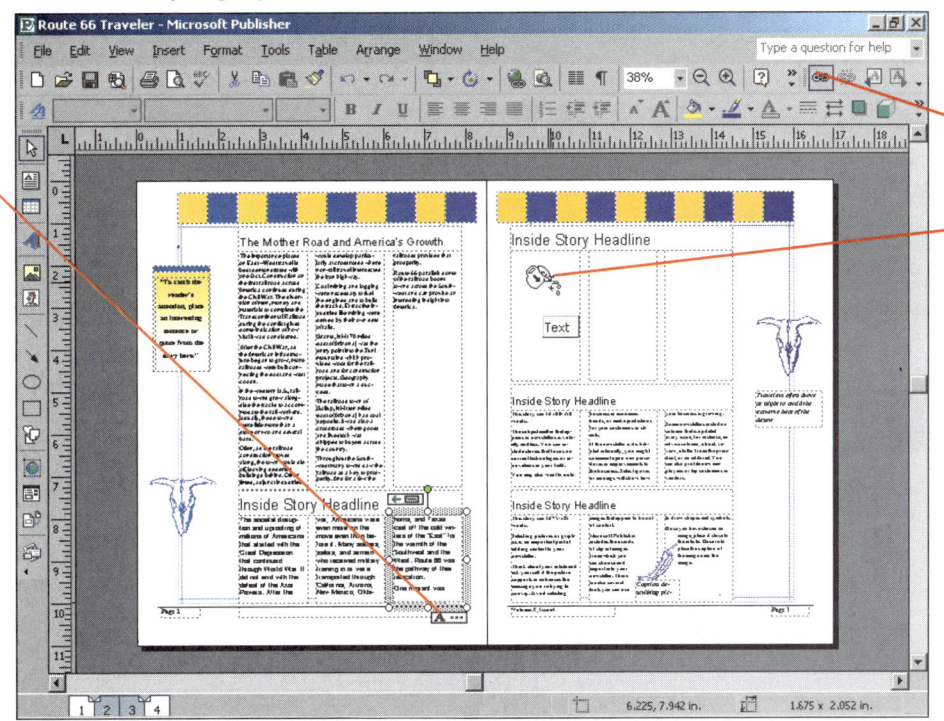

FIGURE E-13: Overflow text poured into text box

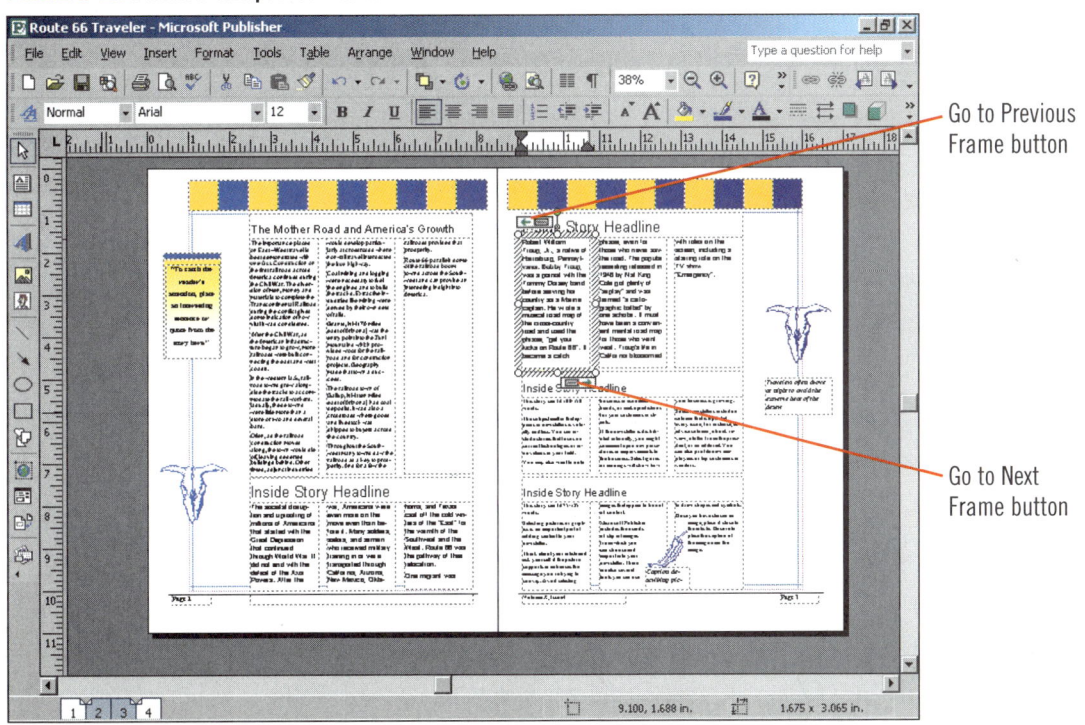

Go to Previous Frame button

Go to Next Frame button

ENHANCING A PUBLICATION PUBLISHER 109

Publisher 2002

Adding Continued on/from Notices

Publisher 2002 — Unit E

When it is not possible to start and finish a story on the same page, continued notices can be added. Sometimes publications are specifically designed with stories spanning several pages to encourage readers to see all the pages in the publication. To make it as easy as possible to find and read all segments of a story, you can create **Continued on** and **Continued from** notices. These notices automatically insert text with the correct page reference, and they update automatically if you move the text box. Continued on/from notices make a story take up more space on a page, adding several lines to its length. Mike inserts Continued on and Continued from notices in the story that spans two pages.

Steps

1. **Click the text box at 7" H / 9" V, then press [F9]**
   You want the first Continued on notice to appear at the bottom of this text box since the text continues on page three. You create a Continued on notice by modifying the text box's properties.

2. **Click Format on the menu bar, click Text Box, then click the Text Box tab**
   The Text Box tab appears, as shown in Figure E-14.

   > **Trouble?**
   > Continued on/from notices appear only if they refer to text on pages other than the current page.

3. **Click the Include "Continued on page" check box, then click OK**
   Compare your page to Figure E-15. You want to insert a Continued from notice in the text box on page three. If a single text box continues on another page, you can insert the Continued on and Continued from notices at the same time.

4. **Click the Go to Next Frame button at the bottom of the text box**
   The insertion point is on page three at the continuation of the story. The story needs a Continued from notice on page three.

   > **QuickTip**
   > Continued on/from notices can be turned on or off for each text box. This can help you adjust the quantity of text in a text box to enhance its appearance.

5. **Press [F9] twice to center the selected text box on the screen, right-click the selected text box, click Format Text Box, click the Text Box tab, click the Include "Continued from page" check box, click OK, press [Esc], then press [F9]**
   The Continued from notice appears at the beginning of the text box, as shown in Figure E-16.

6. **Click the Save button on the Standard toolbar**

Design Matters: Changing the style of continued notices

If the appearance of a Continued on or Continued from notice does not appeal to you, it can be changed. Each type of continued notice has a defined style—you can see the style name of a selected continued notice in the Style box on the Formatting toolbar. Change the style of a continued notice by selecting the notice you want to change, making formatting modifications, clicking the Style box, changing the name of the style, pressing [Enter], then clicking OK in the Create Style By Example dialog box.

PUBLISHER 110 ENHANCING A PUBLICATION

FIGURE E-14: Format Text Box dialog box

Include "Continued on page" check box

Include "Continued from page" check box

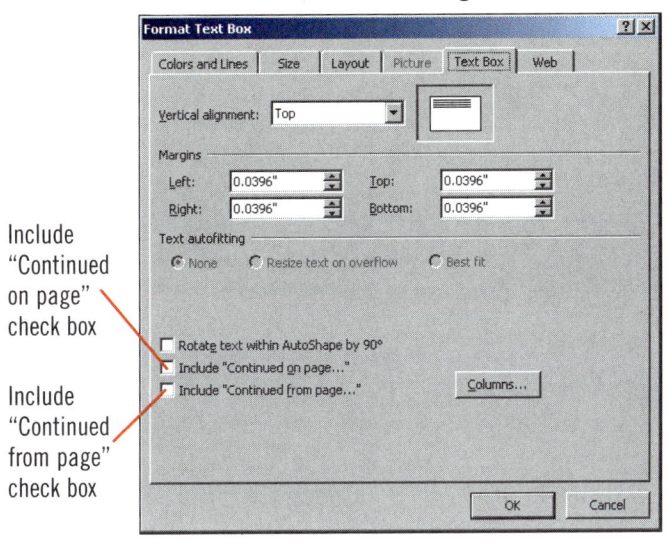

FIGURE E-15: Continued on notice

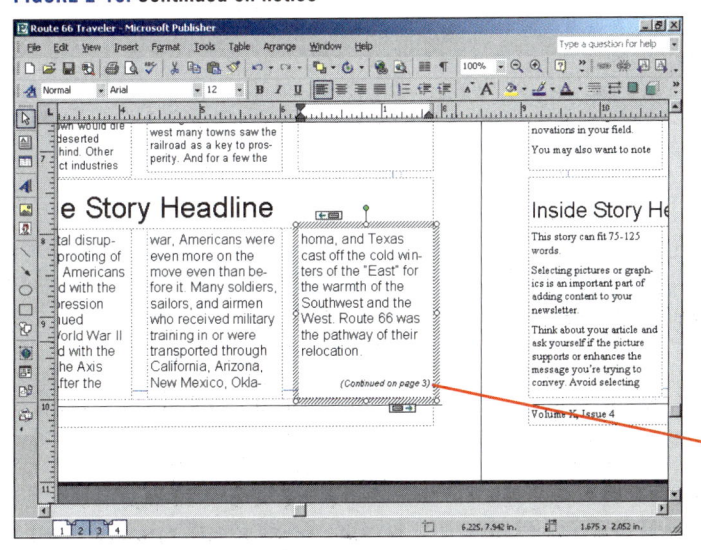

Notice automatically cites the correct page

FIGURE E-16: Continued notices

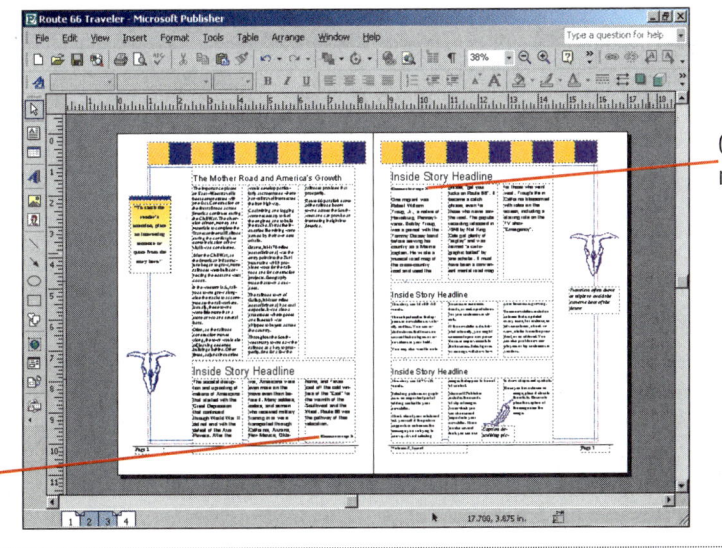

Continued from notice

Continued on notice

ENHANCING A PUBLICATION PUBLISHER 111

Publisher 2002

Adding Drop Caps

In addition to using defined styles to give stories a consistent look, you can also add a **drop cap**, a large fancy first letter at the beginning of text. A drop cap can occur wherever you choose: at the beginning of each paragraph in a story, or only at the beginning of the story. Publisher lets you choose from defined character types that use different fonts and line heights, or you can create your own. Because the addition of drop caps adds to the length of a story, they may cause the story to overflow. Mike wants to dress up several stories using drop caps. He starts by applying a pre-defined drop cap to the story he just worked on.

Steps

1. **Click the text box at 3" H / 8" V on page two**
   You want to apply a drop cap in the first paragraph of a story to make it stand out.

2. **Click Format on the menu bar, then click Drop Cap**
   The Drop Cap dialog box opens, as shown in Figure E-17.

3. **Click the Custom Drop Cap tab**
   You can change the default drop cap height to make the story fit its frame. You want a drop cap that is two lines high.

4. **Click Dropped, select the contents of the Size of letters text box, type 2, compare your dialog box to Figure E-18, click OK, then press [F9]**
   Compare your work to Figure E-19.

5. **Press [Esc], then click the Save button on the Standard toolbar**
   Your work is saved with the modifications.

> **QuickTip**
> The default font for the drop cap is the same as the font in the selected story.

Design Matters

Font schemes

A font scheme is a defined set of two or more fonts associated with a publication. For example, a font scheme might be made up of one font for headings, one for body text, and another for captions. Font schemes facilitate changing all the fonts in a publication to give it a new look. Within each font scheme, both a major font and a minor font are specified. Generally, a major font is used for titles and headings, and a minor font is used for body text.

▶ PUBLISHER 112   ENHANCING A PUBLICATION

FIGURE E-17: Drop Cap dialog box

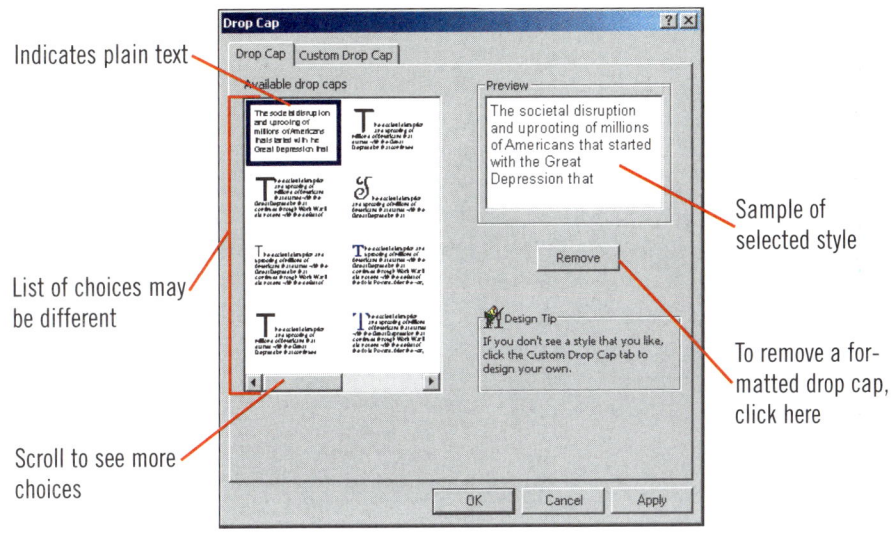

- Indicates plain text
- List of choices may be different
- Scroll to see more choices
- Sample of selected style
- To remove a formatted drop cap, click here

FIGURE E-18: Creating a Custom Drop Cap

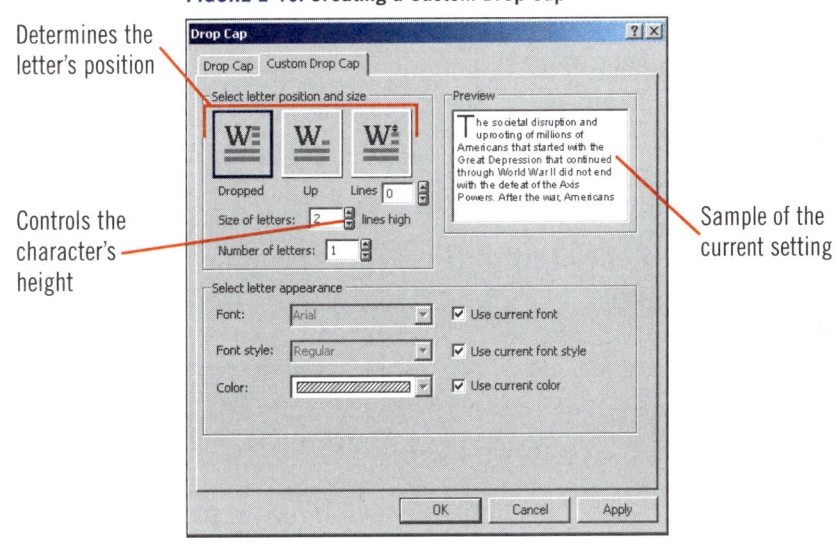

- Determines the letter's position
- Controls the character's height
- Sample of the current setting

FIGURE E-19: Drop cap added

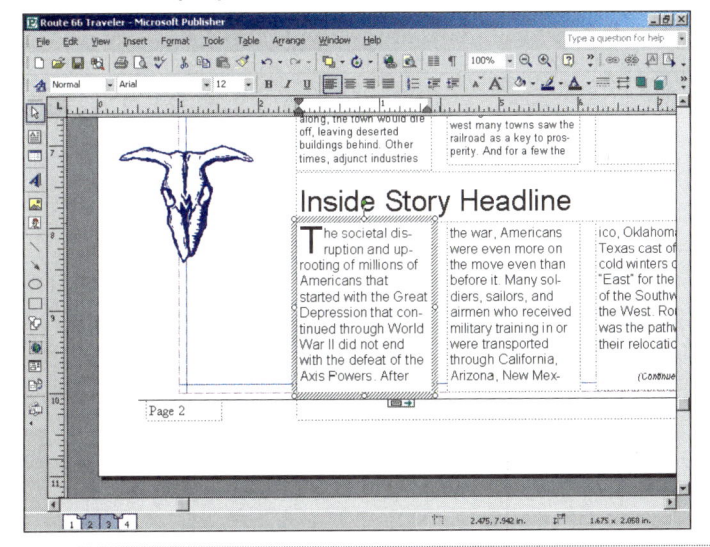

ENHANCING A PUBLICATION   PUBLISHER 113

Publisher 2002

Unit E
Publisher 2002

Creating Reversed Text

Another way to add emphasis to text is to create reversed text. **Reversed text** is light characters on a dark background. Although any color combination can be used, it is best to use contrasting colors to ensure readability. This effect makes the text look as though it was cut out of the background. Reversed text is often used on titles in newsletters or other publications because it is eye-catching, readable, and distinguishable from text used in an article. Mike wants to create the effect of reversed text in the inside story headline at the bottom of page two.

Steps

1. Click the **Inside Story Headline text** at **3" H / 7½" V**
   You will replace the headline with your own text.

2. Type **The Musical Map of Route 66**
   The headline text is replaced. Changing the font color is just one step in creating reversed text.

3. Press **[Ctrl][A]**, click the **Font Color list arrow** on the Formatting toolbar, then click the **Accent 5 (white) option**
   The text in the text box seems to disappear. When creating reverse text, the order in which you change the font color or object color doesn't matter. Regardless of the order, when you create black and white reverse text, at some point, they will both be the same color. Now you can change the fill color of the text box.

4. Click the **Fill Color list arrow** on the Formatting toolbar, then click the **Main (black) option**
   The background changes to black. In order to see the reversed text effect, you must deselect the text box.

5. Press **[Esc]** twice
   Compare your work to Figure E-20.

6. Press **[F9]**, click the **pull quote** at **1" H / 3" V**, press **[F9]**, then replace the existing text with the sample shown in Figure E-21, substituting your name for Mike Mendoza
   You've made good progress on the newsletter, applying many enhancements to the text.

7. Click the **Save button** on the Standard toolbar, click **File** on the menu bar, click **Print**, then print page two of the newsletter

8. Click **File** on the menu bar, then click **Exit**

▶ PUBLISHER 114　ENHANCING A PUBLICATION

FIGURE E-20: Reversed text

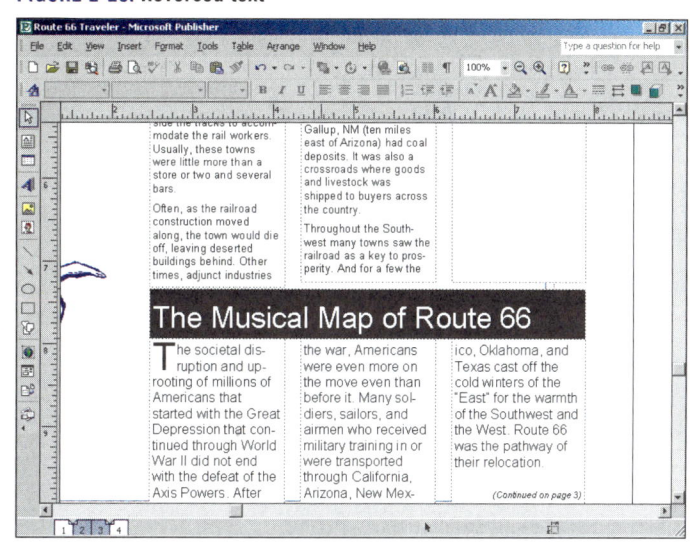

FIGURE E-21: Pull quote text

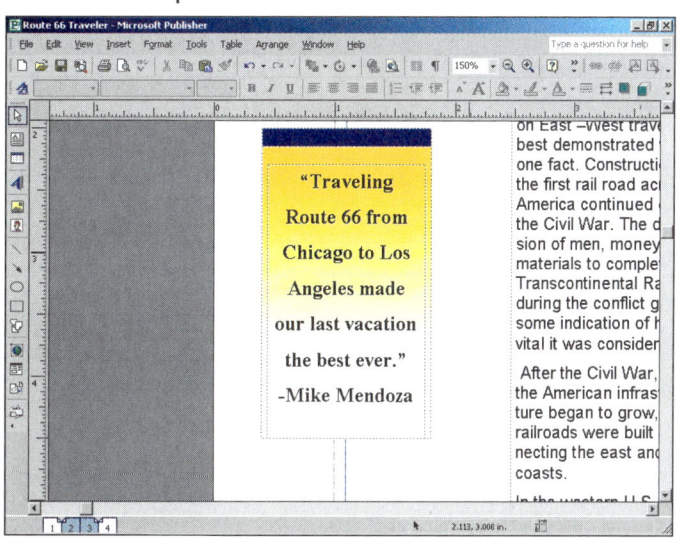

Design Matters

Attracting a reader's attention

Experts recommend that you never use more than three different fonts on a page, and usually suggest that two are enough. So, how do you make your publications look jazzy and attract a reader's attention? Instead of using more fonts, make full use of a limited palette. Use bold and italic versions of your fonts for prominence, and reverse text for a stylized headline. Never underline type, and don't use full capitalization in ordinary text. This was done on typewriters for emphasis when there were no alternatives, but is considered outdated now. With a desktop publishing program, you have the ability to attract readers with a wide variety of tools.

ENHANCING A PUBLICATION   PUBLISHER 115

Publisher 2002

Capstone Project: Solar System Newsletter

You have learned the skills necessary to enhance a publication. You can modify and apply text styles, change a format into a style, create columns, and adjust text overflows. You added Continued on and from text, added drop caps, and created reversed text. Now you will use these skills to add and manipulate text in a newsletter. Image Magic was asked to produce a sample copy of a newsletter for a group of astronomers. Mike will keep the client's objectives in mind: clarity, color, and elegance.

Steps

1. Start Publisher, open the file **Pub E-3** from the drive and folder where your Project Files are stored, then save it as **Solar System Newsletter**
   Creating a style for the headline will allow you to apply the same formatting consistently to all headlines in the newsletter.

2. Create a style based on the headline at **3" H / 3½" V**, name it **Space Headline**, apply it to the headline at **3" H / 8½" V**, then press **[Esc]**
   You will now add text to the newsletter. Your story is too long for one text box, so you must continue it onto another page.

3. Click the text box at **3" H / 9" V**, insert the text file **Pub E-4**, click **No** when asked if you want to use autoflow, then adjust the text overflow to fill the two empty columns on page two
   To make the story easy to read as it jumps to another page, you must add notices that alert the reader that the story continues elsewhere, and where to find it. This action also links the text boxes together. If one is moved to another location, the page reference automatically changes.

4. Add **Continued on** and **Continued from** text to the inserted story
   A drop cap will make each paragraph in the story stand out.

5. Add **custom drop caps** to the first paragraphs of both stories on **page one** with two-line high letters
   Reversed text makes a headline stand out and sets it apart from other text in the publication.

6. Reverse the text in the headline at **3" H / 2" V** using **Accent 5 (white)** for the text and **Accent 1 (blue)** for the fill
   You like the way the newsletter looks. You made it easy to read, consistent, and emphasized certain text.

7. Replace the **pull quote** at **1" H / 4½" V** on page one with your name, save your work, then print page one
   Compare your work to Figure E-22.

▶ PUBLISHER 116   ENHANCING A PUBLICATION

The Society of Solar and Planetary Observers

Summer 2003

Volume XII, Issue 2

Solar System Times

No Money Has Ever Been Spent in Space!

Mike Mendoza

Inside this issue:

Inside Story	2
Inside Story	2
Inside Story	2
Inside Story	3
Inside Story	4
Inside Story	5
Inside Story	6

By Stuben Waterford, III

It is no secret that space exploration is expensive. It costs billions of dollars globally to support space programs internationally. But have you ever considered where the money is spent?

All the money is spent right here on the third planet from old Sol. Not one penny has ever been spent off the earth. No Martian or Venusian has ever made a dime off us earthlings.

Who does profit? Well, everyone benefits. The jobs provided by the space programs worldwide result in paychecks here on earth. Some portion of those paychecks go to taxes, another portion goes for housing, another goes for terrestrial travel.

But the story doesn't end there. All those dollars that are spent by employees on housing, gas, food, clothing, vacations, books and electrical appliances goes right back into the economy.

Where does it end? Well, it doesn't end. It doesn't end any more than ocean currents end. It doesn't end any more than air currents end. That is why we call it currency. It ebbs and flows but is in constant motion. It circulates all across the earth, into your pocket and mine. It provides jobs and dreams.

Mars, the Salmon Planet

Mars, (Greek: Ares), the planet named for the god of War, is tough to observe. Mars is only half the diameter of the Earth and it never approaches closer than 140 times the distance of the Moon from the Earth. Most of the time Mars is much further away, so even though it is one of our closest neighbors and has been known since prehistoric time, it is pretty hard to appreciate

(Continued on page 2)

Publisher 2002 Practice

▶ Concepts Review

Label each of the elements in the Publisher window shown in Figure E-23.

FIGURE E-23

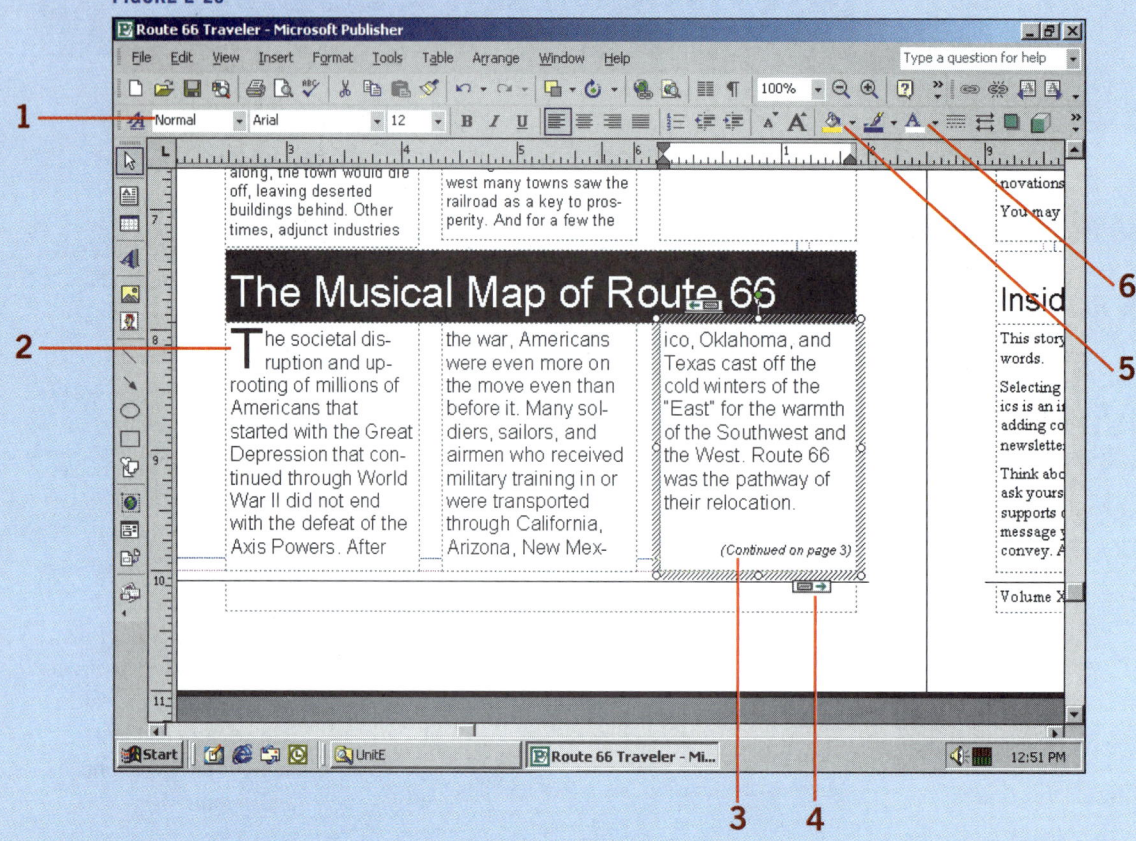

Match each of the buttons or pointers with the statement that describes its function.

7.
8.
9.
10.
11.
12.

a. Pouring pointer
b. Pitcher pointer
c. Go to Next Frame button
d. Text in Overflow button
e. Go to Previous Frame button
f. Create Text Box Link button

▶ PUBLISHER 118 ENHANCING A PUBLICATION

Practice

Select the best answer from the list of choices.

13. Select the entire contents of a text box by pressing _____.
    a. [Shift][A]
    b. [Alt][A]
    c. [Ctrl][A]
    d. [Esc][A]
14. Once you click the Connect Frame button, the pointer looks like:
    a. (arrow icon)
    b. (pointing hand icon)
    c. (text box icon)
    d. (frame icon)
15. Which button takes you to the next text box?
    a. (icon)
    b. (icon)
    c. (icon)
    d. (icon)
16. Which button indicates the existence of overflow text?
    a. (icon)
    b. (icon)
    c. (icon)
    d. (icon)
17. Which dialog box is used to create Continued on/from notices?
    a. Continued Notices
    b. Notices
    c. Frame Formatting
    d. Format Text Box
18. Changing a format into a style is called:
    a. Format stylization.
    b. Creating a style by example.
    c. Styling a format.
    d. Creating a format master.
19. Which pointer is used to pour overflow text into a text box?
    a. (icon)
    b. (icon)
    c. (icon)
    d. (icon)
20. Adjusting the spacing between a pair of characters is called:
    a. Spacing.
    b. Kerning.
    c. Fonting.
    d. Adjusting.
21. In which dialog box can you change the spacing of columns in a text box?
    a. Text Box Characteristics
    b. Columns in Text box
    c. Columns
    d. Text Box Formatting
22. In which dialog box can you add, modify, or remove a drop cap?
    a. Drop Cap
    b. Format Text box
    c. Fancy First Letter
    d. Spacing Between Characters

▶ Skills Review

1. Define styles.
    a. Start Publisher.
    b. Use the Publication Gallery to create a newsletter for Guanajuato, Mexico. Select the Southwest Newsletter, then use the Personal Information set of your choosing.
    c. Save the file as **Guanajuato Newsletter** to the drive and folder where your Project Files are stored.
    d. Create a new text style that is 18 point Franklin Gothic Demi, left-aligned.
    e. Name the new style **Southwest Headline**.
    f. Click the 2-3 page icon, then apply the Southwest Headline style to the inside story headline at 3" H / 7¾" V.
    g. Return to page one of the newsletter.
    h. Save your work.

ENHANCING A PUBLICATION   PUBLISHER 119 ◀

Publisher 2002 Practice

2. **Modify and apply a style.**
   a. Change the font size of the Southwest Headline style to 20 point.
   b. Change the effect of the Southwest Headline style to Shadow.
   c. Apply the Southwest Headline style to the Secondary Story Headline on page one.
   d. Save your work.
3. **Change a format into a style.**
   a. Click the Lead Story Headline on page one. Use the Style box to create a style called Amigos Headline that uses the same formatting.
   b. Apply the **Amigos Headline** style to the Inside Story Headline on page three at 10" H / 7¾" V.
   c. Save your work.
4. **Create columns.**
   a. Show the Page Content task pane.
   b. Change the number of columns on the left inside page to a mixed-column layout, then close the task pane.
   c. Save the publication.
5. **Adjust text overflows.**
   a. Select the text box on page two at 3" H / 2" V, then delete the text.
   b. Above the empty text box, select the Inside Story Headline on page two and change it to **Guanajuato Rocks**.
   c. Select the text box on page three at 10" H / 6" V, then delete the text.
   d. Select the Inside Story Headline on page three at 10" H / 5" V, then change it to **Guanajuato Rocks**.
   e. Select the Lead Story Headline text on page one at 2½" H / 3" V, then change it to **Guanajuato Rocks**.
   f. Delete the text from the text box on page one at 3" H / 4" V and insert the text file PUB E-5. Do not use autoflow.
   g. Click the Create Text Box Link button, then pour the text into the empty text box on page two.
   h. Click the Create Text Box Link button, then pour the remaining text into the empty text box on page three.
   i. Save the publication.
6. **Add Continued on/from notices.**
   a. Add a Continued on notice in the third column text box in the "Guanajuato Rocks" story on page one.
   b. Click the Go to Next Frame button, then add a Continued from notice and a Continued on notice in the single column of the "Guanajuato Rocks" story on page two.
   c. Click the Go to Next Frame button, then add a Continued from notice in the first column of the "Guanajuato Rocks" story on page three.
   d. Save the publication.
7. **Add drop caps.**
   a. Click anywhere in the first paragraph of the Guanajuato Rocks story on page one.
   b. Create a dropped custom first letter three lines high, using the default font.
   c. Save your work.
8. **Create reversed text.**
   a. Select the contents of the Newsletter Title on page one at 1" H / 1½" V and replace it with the name **Guanajuato**.
   b. Change the font color to the color of your choosing.
   c. Change the fill color to the color of your choosing.
   d. Replace the Special Points of Interest text on page one at 1" H / 6¾" V with your name.
   e. Print pages one through three of the publication.
   f. Save your work.
   g. Exit Publisher.

Practice

▶ Independent Challenge 1

A local investment company, Finance Wizardry, wants to hold monthly seminars to make people feel more comfortable with financial instruments. They hire you to create a brochure that announces these free seminars. You will use the Publication Gallery to create the brochure and start planning some of the brochure style elements.

a. Start Publisher, if necessary, then create a new publication using the Slant Event Brochure from the Publication Gallery. Use Personal Information sets to enter placeholder information of your choosing.
b. Change the color scheme to Island.
c. Save the publication as **Finance Wizardry Brochure** to the drive and folder where your Project Files are stored.
d. Create a style called **Main Heading** that uses a 14 point Arial italic font and is center-aligned.
e. Apply the Main Heading style to the Main Inside Heading at 1" H / ¾" V on page two.
f. Select the story at 1" H / 4½" V and add a two-line custom drop cap.
g. On page one, replace the text in the text box at 9" H / 4" V with the name **Finance Wizardry**.
h. Create a reversed text effect in the text box at 9" H / 1¾" V. Change the text to the Accent 5 (white) color. Change the fill to the Main (black) color.
i. Substitute your name for the business name at 5" H / 6½" V.
j. Save and print both pages of the publication.
k. Exit Publisher.

▶ Independent Challenge 2

To attract new homebuyers and businesses, the Chamber of Commerce hires you to create an informational Web site about your community. This Web site will be available to anyone seeking information about your community.

a. Start Publisher, if necessary, then open the file Pub E-6 from the drive and folder where your Project Files are stored.
b. Change the color scheme to Lilac.
c. Save the publication as **Community Promotion Web Site** to the drive and folder where your Project Files are stored.
d. Create a style by example called **Homepage Headline** based on the Our Home Town Home Page Headline.
e. Apply the new style to the "A Great Place To Live" headline.
f. Use your word processor to write a four- to six-paragraph story about what you like about your community. Save this story as **A Great Place**.
g. Delete the text in the text boxes at 2" H / 5½" V and 2" H / 2" V.
h. Insert the "A Great Place" text file into the text box at 2" H / 2" V. Do not use autoflow.
i. Pour the overflow text from the first text box into the second text box at 2" H / 5½" V.
j. Add a two-line-high drop cap to the first paragraph of your story.
k. Substitute your name for the e-mail address at the bottom of the page.
l. Save and print the publication.
m. Exit Publisher.

ENHANCING A PUBLICATION

Publisher 2002 *Practice*

▶ Independent Challenge 3

Your school wants to hold a fund-raiser for the local homeless shelter. You volunteered to create this flyer and choose the type of fund-raising activity.

   a. Start Publisher if necessary, use the Mobile Fund-raiser Flyer from the Publisher Gallery to create a new publication. Use Personal Information sets to enter placeholder information of your choosing.
   b. Change the color scheme to Parrot.
   c. Save the publication as **Homeless Shelter Flyer** to the drive and folder where your Project Files are stored.
   d. Decide on a title for your fund-raiser, then type it into the text box at 2" H / 2" V.
   e. Make up your own text describing the event for the text box at 5" H / 5" V.
   f. Create a new style called **Fundraiser Text** using 14 point Times New Roman, right-aligned.
   g. Apply this style to the text box at 5" H / 5" V.
   h. Substitute your name for the e-mail address at 1" H / 8½" V.
   i. Save and print the publication.
   j. Exit Publisher.

Practice

e Independent Challenge 4

BBB Road Club asks you to design a brochure for a bus trip to see the leaves change in New England during late September and October. Before you design this brochure, you plan to use the Internet to find out more about the New England countryside and its foliage.

a. Connect to the Internet, then use your browser and favorite search engine to find information about the New England countryside and its foliage. Find out what towns and attractions might be of interest when the leaves are changing.
b. Start Publisher if necessary, use the Profile Informational Brochure from the Publisher Gallery. Use the Personal Information set of your choice.
c. Change to the Monarch color scheme.
d. Save the publication as **New England Foliage Brochure** to the drive and folder where your Project Files are stored.
e. Use the information you obtained from the Internet to write a four to six-paragraph document about what to see and do in New England using your word processor. Save this document as **New England Attractions**.
f. Replace any default text with text about New England.
g. Choose two locations on different pages for the New England Attractions document. Create additional text boxes if necessary.
h. Delete any placeholder text from the text boxes, then pour the story into the text boxes.
i. Add drop caps and continued notices.
j. Substitute your name for the e-mail address on page two of the publication.
k. Print the publication.
l. Save the publication.
m. Exit Publisher.

ENHANCING A PUBLICATION   PUBLISHER 123

Publisher 2002 Practice

▶ Visual Workshop

Open the file Pub E-7 from the drive and folder where your Project Files are stored. Save this publication as **SW Brochure**. Using Figure E-24 as a guide, change all the Canyon style text to Times New Roman and resize it to fit the text boxes. Rename the style with a name of your choosing. Change the headline text from Canyon Heading to Arial and reverse the text, then rename the style with a name of your choosing. Replace the Image Magic text in the text box at 9" H / 6½" V with your name. Save the publication, then print it.

FIGURE E-24

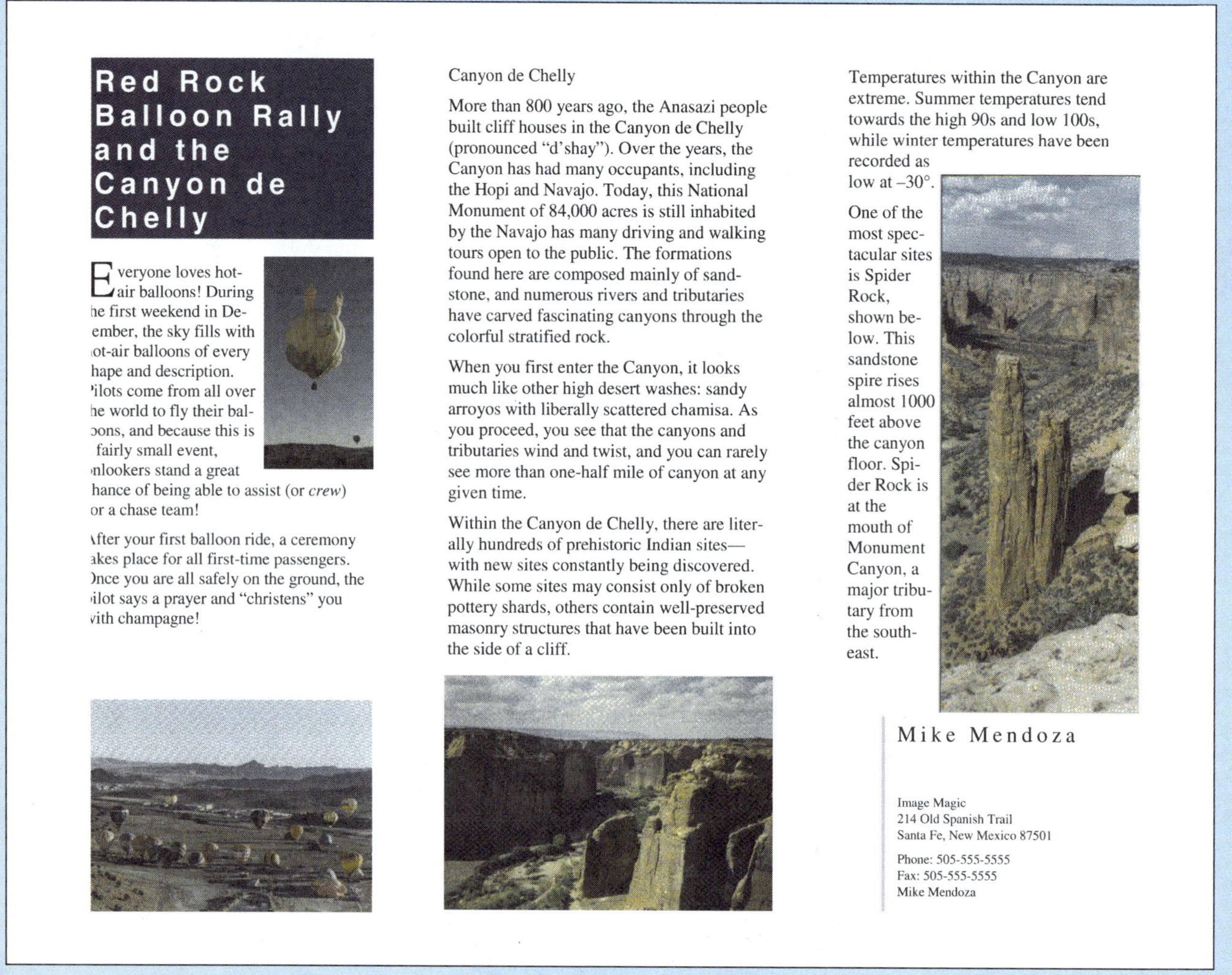

Publisher 2002

Unit F

Improving
a Publication

Objectives

- ▶ Critique a publication
- ▶ Strengthen a masthead
- ▶ Rearrange elements
- ▶ Modify objects
- ▶ Refine a page
- ▶ Experiment with design elements
- ▶ Capstone Project: Flower Shop Flyer

It takes more than adding text boxes and clicking buttons to produce an effective publication. Although you can be proficient at using Publisher, focusing on the design is necessary to create an attractive, professional publication. **Design** focuses on the selection, formatting, and placement of the elements on each page. You can resize and reposition elements to make them more effective and better convey the message of your publication. In making such modifications, your publication becomes more striking and more successful. The non-profit organization, Global Parenting, is an Image Magic client. They asked Pat Dyson to review their in-house monthly newsletter and give them suggestions to improve its design.

Publisher 2002
Unit F
Critiquing a Publication

Details

Casting a critical eye towards someone's work is difficult, challenging, and maybe even enjoyable to some. Others feel uncomfortable criticizing someone else's work. You can be critical of a person's work without being critical of that person. Many of us learn best by having our mistakes pointed out, and then making corrections. Being critical of one's own work is even more difficult, and not remotely enjoyable. While the design of any publication is highly subjective, there are some fundamental principles that can be used during the critiquing process. When done constructively, the critiquing process can be a positive learning experience for everyone involved. Examining the strengths and weaknesses of another person's work can be a helpful method of refining a publication so that it looks professional and achieves your goals. It can also help you develop a more constructive eye towards your own designs. As you learn to critique designs, you may find that the most effective designs are the simplest. Pat reviews the client's in-house monthly newsletter: Concerned Parent. Pat opens the publication shown in Figure F-1 and thinks about the critiquing process:

▶ Take in all the elements
At first glance, everything on the cover seems pleasing. Once you take in the visual elements, ask yourself a series of questions that determines the purpose of a particular page, and the arrangement of elements that helps you achieve that goal. Such questions might be: To which elements are your eyes drawn? Where is the text? Is the text legible? Are any/all of the elements on the page necessary? Are any elements distracting? In Figure F-1, your eyes may be drawn to the central graphic and the blue text box because they are colorful, and because of their size and position. Unfortunately, the text in the blue box is illegible, and the caption above and below the central graphic is broken up, which makes it difficult to read and comprehend the safety message. Also, the elongated table of contents distracts the eye from the image of the children and the crossing guard.

▶ Decide what is important
While every publication has a goal, each page's goal is a subset of the overall goal of the publication. A goal can be as simple as making you look at an image, or enticing you to read a compelling story. While the goal of this issue of Concerned Parent is children and safety, the goal of a particular page may be reading the executive director's article on the topic. The job of the design is to reflect that goal throughout the entire publication. Before a good design can be created, you must know the goal. During the critiquing process, you should continually ask yourself if the design achieves the goal.

▶ Share the message with the reader
As the designer, your focus is on assembling various visual elements—graphic images, text, or tables—that share the message with the reader. Figure F-2 shows a preliminary rearrangement of the cover elements. In this design, the central element is the children and the crossing guard. This graphic has been cropped to eliminate unnecessary imagery. By rearranging the elements on the page, the message of children and safety is featured more prominently. The use of white space and elimination or refining of distracting elements, such as the blue text box and the table of contents, force the reader's eye to focus on the central image.

▶ Keep it simple
Microsoft Publisher offers so many exciting and interesting design elements that it's often tempting to use as many graphics, Word Art, borders, etc., as possible. Such overindulgence can lead to a cluttered, ineffective design that will not help readers see the whole message, and they may miss the point entirely. It's usually best to choose a few key elements that convey the message, then feature those items prominently. In the redesigned cover, there is only one central object. The reader is free to read the enlarged text beneath the image, but it is not necessary to understanding the safety message.

▶ PUBLISHER 126   IMPROVING A PUBLICATION

FIGURE F-1: Initial cover art

Title text is separated by image

Blue background draws attention

FIGURE F-2: Revised cover art

Redesigned masthead

Shortened title

Central design element

Enlarged text

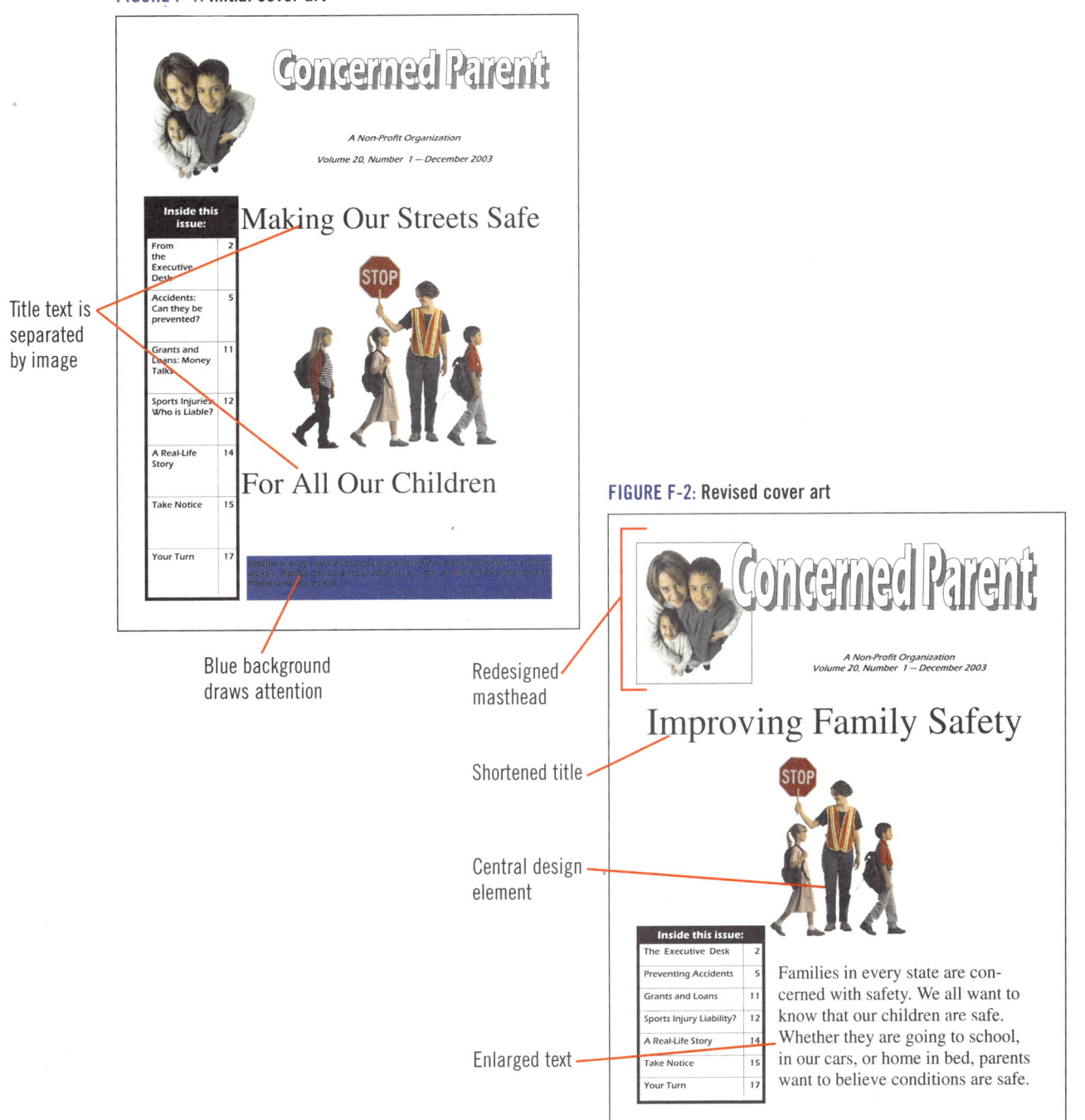

Using diplomacy

How do you tell people that their work could use some improvement? People's designs are a reflection of their own opinions about what makes an effective and attractive publication. Therefore, it isn't easy to tell people why and how their publications could be improved, and you must be sensitive to their feelings when delivering feedback. You may be able to minimize hurting someone's feelings by involving the person whose work you're critiquing in the solution phase. If you make the changes yourself, or instruct someone else to, not only will you create friction in the workplace, but the original author may be offended, and will have learned nothing in the process. By working with people to help them revise their work, they will benefit from maintaining control over it, and will learn some important design concepts in the process.

IMPROVING A PUBLICATION PUBLISHER 127

Strengthening a Masthead

Publisher 2002 — Unit F

Most newsletters feature a **masthead**, an arrangement of text and graphic elements that provide important information about the publication. A masthead contains important information that rarely changes, such as the newsletter's title. The only changing information in a masthead is the issue information, such as the publication month, or the number and volume. The masthead is generally featured prominently, and provides a first impression of the publication. Pat examines the existing masthead and applies her design techniques to improve this area of the publication.

Steps

1. **Start Publisher, open the file PUB F-1 from the drive and folder where your Project Files are stored, then save it as Concerned Parent Newsletter**
   It will be easier to manipulate the masthead elements if you zoom in on it.

   QuickTip: Use the horizontal and vertical scroll bars to center the masthead on the screen if necessary.

2. **Click the newsletter at 4" H / 2½" V, press [F9], then close the task pane**
   The selected text box contains important information, but its size is out of proportion.

3. **Position over the upper-center handle, click and drag to 2½" V, press [Delete], click the blank line beneath the A Non-Profit Organization text, press [Delete], then press [Esc] twice**
   The text box containing the issue information was resized, as shown in Figure F-3. The publication title can be more prominent, and can overlap slightly onto the existing image.

   Trouble? If the WordArt toolbar opens, close it by clicking the Close button.

4. **Click the object at 4" H / 1" V, position over the lower-center handle, click and drag to 1¾" V, position over the left-center handle, then click and drag to 2¼" H**
   The title is larger and partially obscured by the graphic image, as shown in Figure F-4. You can move the selected object on top of the image by changing the layering.

5. **Click the Bring to Front button**
   The newsletter title appears to overlap part of the image. The image is an important element within the masthead and can be strengthened by the addition of an outline.

6. **Right-click the image at 2" H / 2" V, click Format Picture, click the Colors and Lines tab, click the Line Color list arrow, click the black color box (the first box from the left), then click OK**
   The masthead image is surrounded by a black outline. The black outline visible between the "C" and the "o" in the title can be hidden using a mask. A **mask** is an object designed to hide a specific area. You create a long skinny rectangle that can hide a portion of the outline.

7. **Click the Rectangle button on the Objects toolbar, drag + from 2 9/16" H / 5/8" V to 2¾" H / 1¾" V (Hint: Use the position coordinates 2.563" H / 0.600" V to start the mask)**
   The rectangle can be formatted to blend into the background, then layered to hide the outline.

8. **Right-click the rectangle, click Format AutoShape, click the Line Color list arrow, click No Line, click the Fill Color list arrow, click the white color box (the first box from the right), click OK, click the Bring to Front list arrow, then click Send Backward**
   The rectangle was formatted to blend into the background, and is positioned between the text and the graphic image.

9. **Press [Esc] to deselect the rectangle, then click the Save button on the Standard toolbar**
   Compare your masthead to Figure F-5.

PUBLISHER 128 IMPROVING A PUBLICATION

FIGURE F-3: Resized text box

Smaller text box reflects decreased importance

FIGURE F-4: Enlarged title

Masthead text partially hidden

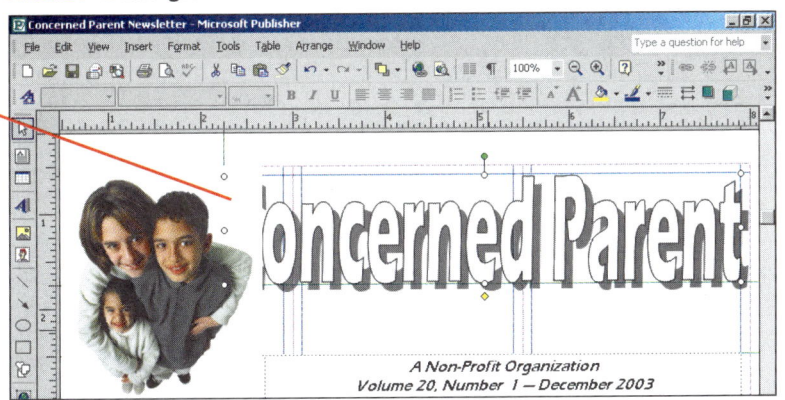

FIGURE F-5: Redesigned masthead

Design Matters

Examine the components

As it can be overwhelming to critique an entire publication, you may find it helpful to examine its individual components. In the case of a newsletter cover, the components include the masthead, the artwork and text, and the table of contents. Within the masthead, you can consider the size, appearance, and placement of the newsletter title, and artwork, and the size and placement of other text boxes. On inside pages, the elements can include the number of stories, related artwork, and the surrounding white space. Breaking down these elements to their components can make it easier to locate and refine problem areas. When viewed in their entirety, these elements create a single cohesive unit.

Publisher 2002

Rearranging Elements

The type of elements used within a page is important, but of equal importance is the way in which the elements are arranged. The components of any page should form a cohesive unit so that the reader is unaware of all the different parts, yet is influenced by all the elements. For example, if a large image is used, it should be easy for the reader to connect the image with any descriptive text. There should be a flow between the text and the artwork, and the reader should be able to seamlessly connect them. Pat begins by fixing the title that describes the central graphic image. She likes the image, but wants the remove the distracting text beneath it.

Steps

1. Press **[F9]**, click the table at **1" H / 3½" V**, then drag at the top of the table to the ruler guide at **7⅜" V**

   The table is reduced in size, which opens up the left side of the page. You can modify the title text by deleting the text box beneath the graphic image.

2. Right-click the text box at **4" H / 8½" V**, then click **Delete Object**

   Compare your screen to Figure F-6. With the table reduced and out of the way, you can improve the appearance of the title text.

3. Click the text box at **3" H / 3½" V**, then use to drag the left-center handle to **½" H**

   You want a single line of text that is large enough to see and easy to read. The location of this text is the optical center of the page. The **optical center** occurs approximately ⅜" from the top of the page and is the point around which objects on the page are balanced. Because this text is the focal point, it should be large enough to be read easily.

4. Press **[Ctrl][A]** to select the text, click the **Font Size list arrow** on the Formatting toolbar, then click **48**

   The text is selected and enlarged. Cover text should be descriptive, yet short and to the point. The previous text was too long and was difficult to read because it was split by the image. You replace the selected text.

5. Type **Improving Family Safety**, click the **Center button** on the Formatting toolbar, then press **[Esc]** twice

   The title is larger, centered, and better expresses the message of the cover. Compare your work to Figure F-7.

6. Click the **Save button** on the Standard toolbar

► PUBLISHER 130 IMPROVING A PUBLICATION

FIGURE F-6: Text box deleted

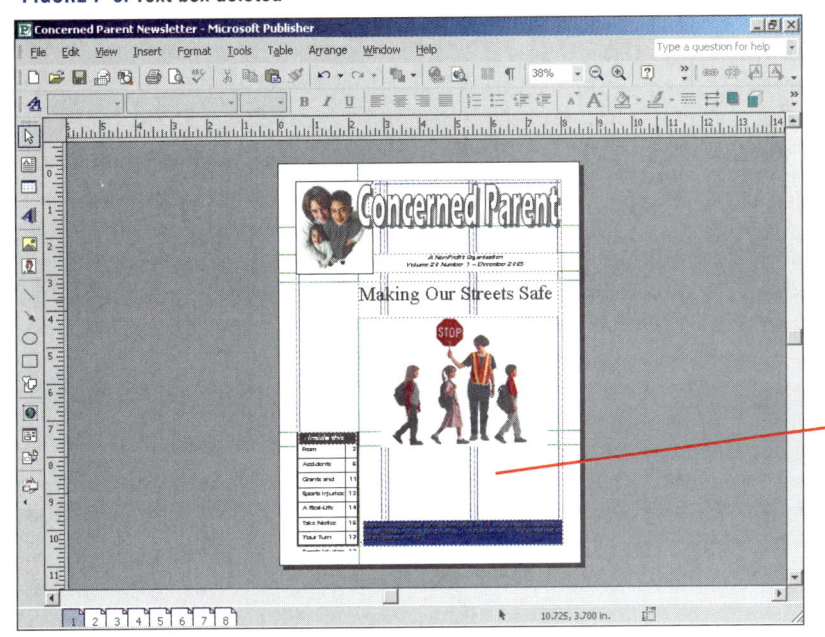

Text box removed from beneath image

FIGURE F-7: Title text completed

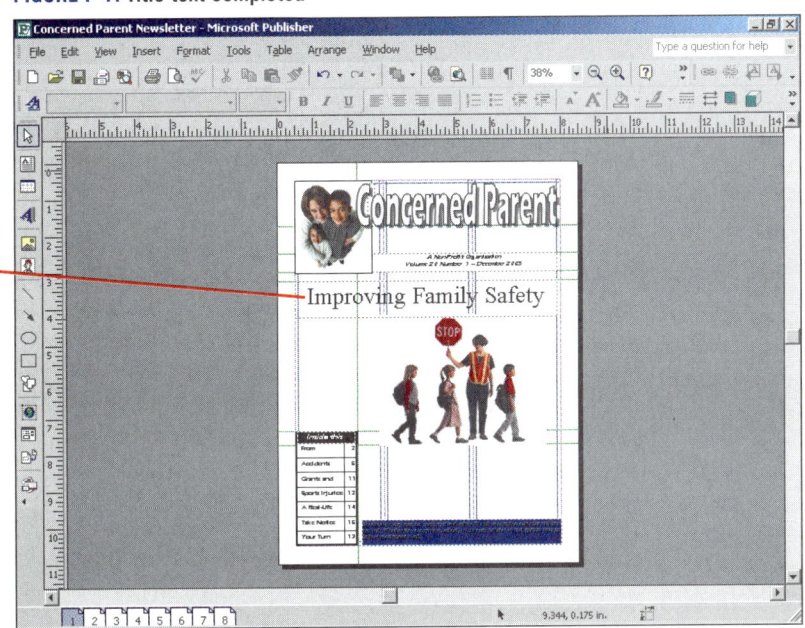

Optical center containing centered text

Overcoming the fear of white space

What is the difference between the file open now and the one opened at the beginning of this unit? White space. The best example of the use of white space is margins surrounding a page. This white space acts as a visual barrier—a resting place for the eyes. Without white space, the words on a page would be bumping into each other, and the effect would be a cluttered, ugly page. This technique makes it possible for you to guide the reader's eye from one location on the page to another. One of the first design hurdles that must be overcome is the irresistible urge to put too much *stuff* on a page. When you are new to design, you may want to fill each page completely. Remember, less is more. Think of white space as a beautiful frame surrounding an equally beautiful image.

IMPROVING A PUBLICATION PUBLISHER 131

Publisher 2002

Modifying Objects

The position and size of objects on a page determine what a reader sees, and the order in which they see things. Once the optical center is located, objects can be positioned around it. A page can have a symmetrical or asymmetrical balance relative to an imaginary vertical line in the center of the page. In a **symmetrical balance**, objects are placed equally on either side of the vertical line. This type of layout tends toward a restful, formal design. In an **asymmetrical balance**, objects are placed unequally relative to the vertical line. Asymmetrical balance uses white space to balance the positioned objects, and is more dynamic and informal. A page with objects arranged asymmetrically tends to provide more visual interest and is more startling in its appearance. Pat wants to make use of white space to balance the few objects on the page using an asymmetrical layout. She begins by zooming into the image on the page.

Steps

QuickTip
If the Picture toolbar does not appear, click View on the menu bar, click Toolbars, then click Picture. You can click the Picture toolbar's title bar and drag it to a new location if it obscures your view.

Trouble?
If the Picture toolbar is still visible, click the Close button on the toolbar.

1. Click the object at **5" H / 5" V**, then click the **Zoom In button** on the Formatting toolbar until the Zoom factor is **66%**
   The image containing the crossing guard is selected, and the Picture toolbar appears. While this is a nice image, it can be cropped to show less information, then centered.

2. Click the **Crop button** on the Picture toolbar, position over the left-center handle, drag to 4⅛" H as shown in Figure F-8, release the mouse button, then click
   The little girl on the left is no longer visible. The object handles reappeared when the cropping tool was turned off.

3. Position over the selected object, press and hold **[Shift]**, drag the selected object so its left edge is at **3" H**, release **[Shift]**, click the **Send Backward list arrow** on the Standard toolbar, click **Send to Back**, then press **[Esc]**
   The object is centered on the page, and the Picture toolbar is no longer visible. Holding [Shift] while you moved the object maintained the vertical measurement as you changed the horizontal position. You can modify the blue text box to make it easier to read and a more effective element.

4. Click the **Zoom Out button** on the Formatting toolbar until the Zoom factor is **50%**, click the text box at **5" H / 10" V**, position over the upper-left handle, then drag to 3⅛" H / 7¾" V
   You can enlarge the existing text to make it readable.

5. Press **[Ctrl][A]**, click the **Font Size list arrow** on the Formatting toolbar, then click **24**
   The text is readable. The blue background serves no useful purpose here, and is a distraction.

6. Click the **Fill Color list arrow** on the Formatting toolbar, then click **No Fill**
   The background was removed, making the text box less prominent and easier to read.

7. Click the **Zoom list arrow** on the Formatting toolbar, click **Whole Page**, then click **[Esc]** twice
   Compare your publication to Figure F-9. You decide to widen the table so it takes up more space.

8. Click the table at **2" H / 9" V**, use to drag the right-center handle to **3" H**, then press **[Esc]**
   Your screen should look like Figure F-10.

9. Click the **Save button** on the Standard toolbar

▶ PUBLISHER 132   IMPROVING A PUBLICATION

FIGURE F-8: Image cropped

New image outline

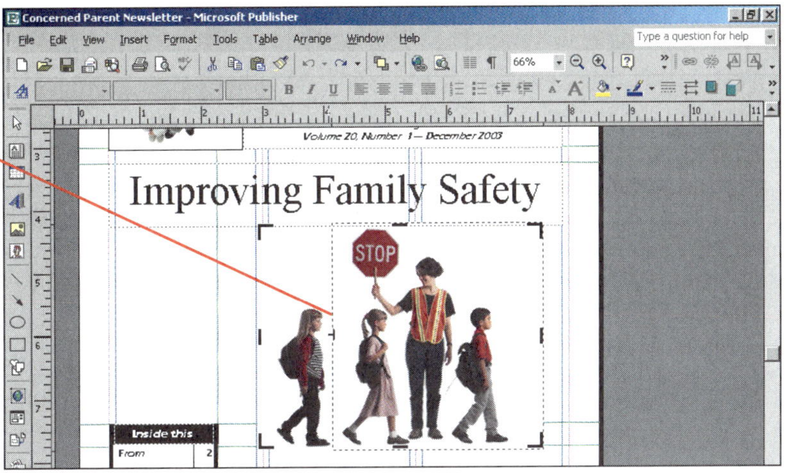
Concerned Parent Newsletter - Microsoft Publisher
Type a question for help
Volume 20, Number 1— December 2003
Improving Family Safety
STOP
Inside this
From

FIGURE F-9: Text box improved

Text enlarged and blue background removed

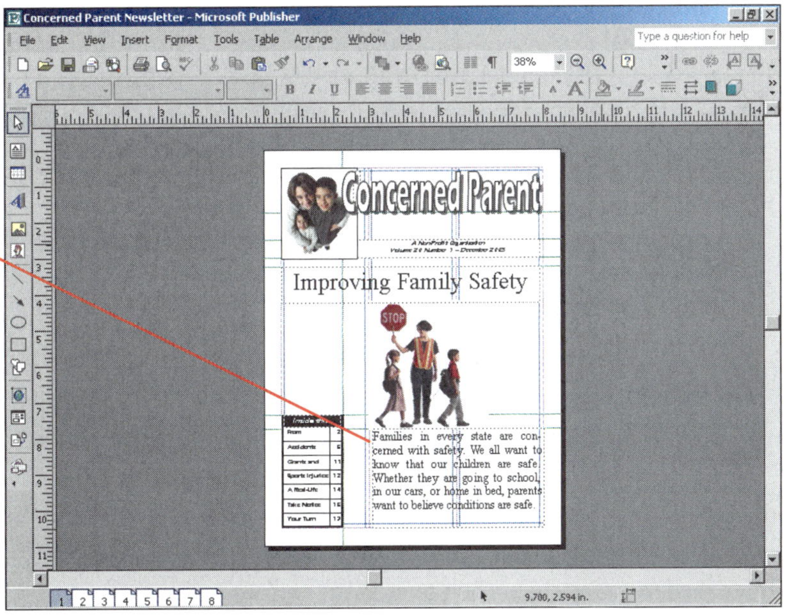
Concerned Parent Newsletter - Microsoft Publisher
Type a question for help
Concerned Parent
Improving Family Safety
STOP
Families in every state are concerned with safety. We all want to know that our children are safe. Whether they are going to school, in our cars, or home in bed, parents want to believe conditions are safe.
9.700, 2.594 in.

FIGURE F-10: Objects moved and resized

Title reworded and centered

Image cropped and moved

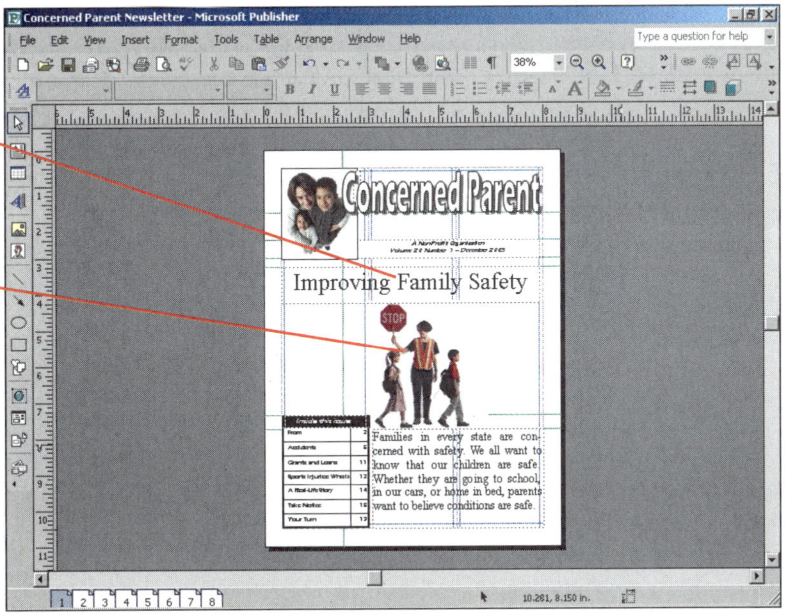
Concerned Parent Newsletter - Microsoft Publisher
Type a question for help
Concerned Parent
Improving Family Safety
STOP
Families in every state are concerned with safety. We all want to know that our children are safe. Whether they are going to school, in our cars, or home in bed, parents want to believe conditions are safe.
10.281, 8.150 in.

Publisher 2002 Unit F

Refining a Page

When reading a magazine or newsletter, articles are often continued on several pages. This strategy gives the reader an opportunity to see the beginning of a featured story, and then read the rest of the article on various pages throughout the publication. Pages that have nothing but text on them can overwhelm the reader, so text boxes are broken up by art and other elements to add visual interest, and provide a mental break for the reader. The goal of every story is to be read, and the goal of page design is to encourage readers to read the stories. The Executive Director of Concerned Parent wrote an important article that will be featured in this issue. The current layout has this story occupying the entire page, which seems overwhelming. Pat has some advice that will make this article more inviting and effective. She begins by adding vertical lines between the columns.

Steps

1. **Click the page 2 icon**, click the **Line button** on the Objects toolbar, press and hold **[Shift]**, drag ✛ from **3" H / 1½" V** to **3" H / 10" V**, then release **[Shift]**

   The [Shift] key assures that the line is straight. The vertical line between the two columns provides a visual boundary. Without this line, the columns run together, making it difficult to read the story. You want to copy this line and place the copy between columns 2 and 3.

   > **Trouble?**
   > Reposition the pointer until ▹⁺ displays before dragging the selected object or it will not be copied.

2. Press and hold **[Ctrl]**, position ▹⁺ over the selected object, click the **left mouse button**, drag ▹⁺ to **5½" H / 1½" V**, then release **[Ctrl]**

   Compare your page to Figure F-11. Currently, this page contains a single story. You feel that this is not a good practice, and you recommend splitting the story between this page and another, although you have not yet decided on a new location. For now, you want to shorten the text box containing the current story, and you will place the remainder of the text later.

   > **QuickTip**
   > Opening up a page by distributing story text can provide visual relief from too much text.

3. Click the text box at **7" H / 9" V**, position ▹ over the bottom-center handle, then drag ↕ to **3" V**

   The majority of column 3 is now available, as shown in Figure F-12. At a later date, you may want to include another story, an advertisement, or a graphic image in this space.

4. Click the text box at **2" H / 2" V**, click **Format** on the menu bar, then click **Drop Cap**

   The Drop Cap dialog box opens. Adding a drop cap to the beginning of this story will add emphasis and make the page look nicer.

5. Click the first choice below the current selection, then click **OK**

   The drop cap appears in the first paragraph of the story. The addition of this feature caused the text to be slightly rearranged, but since there are no other elements on this page, the effect on the current layout is inconsequential.

6. Press **[Esc]** twice to deselect the text box, then click the **Save button** on the Standard toolbar

   Compare your publication to Figure F-13.

▶ PUBLISHER 134 **IMPROVING A PUBLICATION**

FIGURE F-11: Vertical lines between columns

Lines provide visual boundaries between columns

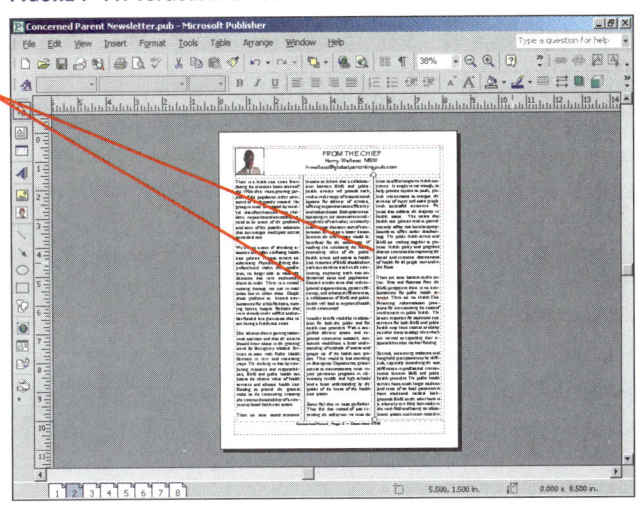

FIGURE F-12: Text box shortened

Additional elements can be placed here

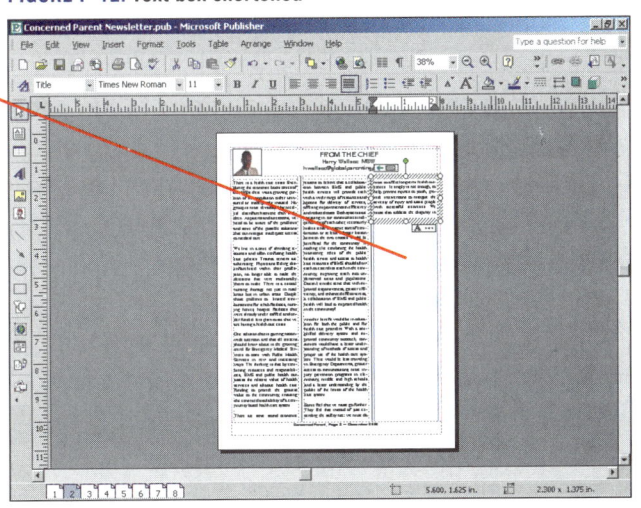

FIGURE F-13: Drop cap added

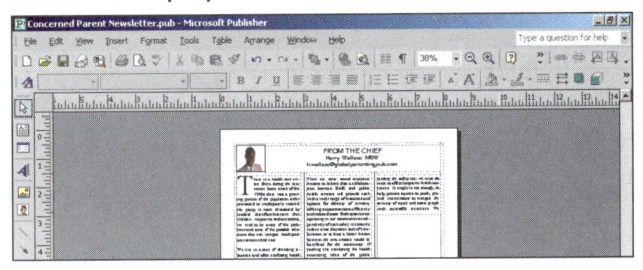

Design Matters

Working with advertisements

Publications often depend on advertising dollars to defray their costs. When stories are continued on various pages, advertisements are more likely to be seen by readers than if one or more pages is devoted to ads. This means that advertising artwork can become an integral part of page layout. Your advertisers and your readers want clever, attractive ads that potential clients will remember. In many cases, your advertisers will give you camera-ready artwork. This artwork is complete and only needs to be included in the layout. The good news is that your artwork doesn't have to satisfy the advertiser. The bad news is that you have no say in terms of the ad's appearance or design values. In most publications, the cost of running an advertisement is determined by size, color, and placement on the page.

IMPROVING A PUBLICATION PUBLISHER 135

Experimenting With Design Elements

Publisher 2002 — Unit F

Layout often requires experimentation. Design elements should guide the reader from story to story, without providing unnecessary distractions. Some design elements, such as a relevant graphic image, or an interesting advertisement, can provide a nice break from reading a particularly intense story. Among the elements you can use to enhance the layout of a page are pictures, drop caps, and pull quotes. It's hard to say which element will best improve a particular page; sometimes you must experiment with a variety of elements and configurations until you find the layout that works. Pat wants to experiment with several design elements to see which ones look the most effective in the new space in column 3. Unsure if she'll like this layout, she starts by creating a pull quote on this page.

Steps

1. Click the **Design Gallery Object button** on the Objects toolbar, click **Pull Quotes** in the categories list, click the **Bars Pull Quote**, then click **Insert Object**

   The pull quote is inserted on the page. You want to place it between columns 1 and 2.

2. Using move the selected **pull quote** until the upper-left corner of the object is at **2" H / 3" V**, then press **[F9]**

   In order to generate the reader's interest, you want to extract a compelling sentence from the story, modify it slightly, then use it as a pull quote.

3. Click the **center of the pull quote**, type **No group is more devastated by the lack of medical attention than children.**, press **[F9]**, then press **[Esc]**

   Compare your page to Figure F-14. The text box is still selected, but you're not sure you like the effect of this element on the page since the page still looks busy. You want to save this pull quote in case you decide to use it by dragging the object to the scratch area.

4. Use to drag the pull quote to **10" H / 3" V** on the scratch area

   The object can be used later, if necessary. This page seems to need some color so you decide to look for health-related graphic images. The previous designer placed a piece of clip art on page 5 that you think will complement the article.

5. Click the **page 5 icon**, click the image at **7" H / 9" V**, click the **Copy button** on the Standard toolbar, then click the **page 2 icon**

   The clip art is on the Clipboard, and can be placed onto page two. Pat thinks that the image will look nice there since the artwork shows a doctor examining a child. The additional color will make the page look friendlier and more attractive.

6. Click the **Paste button** on the Standard toolbar, then use to drag the image so that its upper-left corner is at **2" H / 4" V**

   The image is placed in a slightly lower location occupied by the pull quote, as shown in Figure F-15. You feel that the graphic image adds a splash of color to the page and looks more inviting than the pull quote. You also realize that this page is far from finished, but you are done working on it for now.

7. Click the **Text Box button** on the Objects toolbar, then create a text box from **½" H / 10¼" V** to **2" H / 10½" V**, press **[F9]**, type **your name**, press **[Esc]** twice, then press **[F9]**

> **Trouble?**
> Click No if asked if you want to save items on the Clipboard.

8. Click the **Save button** on the Standard toolbar, print pages one and two, then exit Publisher

▶ PUBLISHER 136   IMPROVING A PUBLICATION

FIGURE F-14: Pull quote in story

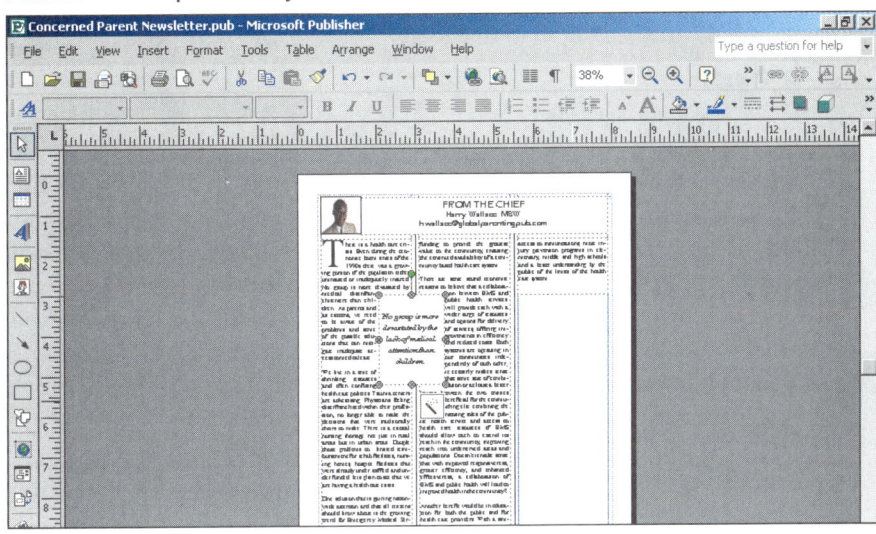

FIGURE F-15: Clip art in story

Pull quote is available on the scratch area

Artwork in story

Design Matters

Using contrast to add emphasis

Contrast is an important design principle that provides variety in the physical layout of a page and publication. Just as you can use contrasting fonts to emphasize text, you can use contrasting elements to add emphasis to objects on a page. Contrast can be achieved in many ways: by changing the sizes of objects; by varying object weights, such as making a line heavier surrounding an image; by altering the position of an object, such as changing the location on the page, or rotating the image so it is positioned on an angle; by drawing attention-getting shapes or a colorful box behind an object that makes it stand out (called a **matte**); or by adding carefully selected colors that emphasize an object.

IMPROVING A PUBLICATION PUBLISHER 137

Capstone Project: Flower Shop Flyer

Publisher 2002 — Unit F

You have learned how to critique a publication, strengthen a masthead to make a good first impression, rearrange elements to make the best effect, and work with objects and page layouts to create a professional publication. Pat is asked by the owner of a flower shop to critique a problematic flyer. The owner is under tremendous pressure to get the store open, and doesn't know or care about design issues. The flyer is for a newly opened flower shop, and the owner wants to offer a 40% discount on perennials during the grand opening celebration. The initial publication is colorful but it is disorganized and fails to promote the discount.

Steps

1. Start Publisher, open the file **PUB F-2** from the drive and folder where your Project Files are stored, then save it as **Flower Shop Flyer**
   Compare your screen to Figure F-16. The border of roses distracts from the text and central object in the flyer.

2. Click the object at **7" H / 4" V**, then press **[Delete]**
   The bunch of tulips can be enlarged. Instead of having many images of flowers, you decide it will be more dramatic to make one image the focal point of the flyer.

3. Click the tulips at **5" H / 5" V**, press and hold **[Ctrl]**, then drag at the upper-left corner until the object snaps to the ruler guides at **1½" H / 2½" V**
   With the tulips enlarged, you can begin rearranging the other elements on the page.

4. Click the text box at **4" H / 7" V**, use to drag the object so that its upper-left corner is at the guides at **1½" H / 8" V**, select the date and time text, click the **Bold button** on the Formatting toolbar, then change the font size of the selected text to **20**
   The repositioned text box and the contrasting text are more attractive. The text at the top of the flyer is too long and poorly aligned.

5. Click the text box at **2" H / 2" V**, press **[Ctrl][A]** to select the text, type **Faye's Flowers**, press **[Enter]**, then type **Grand Opening and Sale**
   You can make the text look balanced by centering it within the text box, and add emphasis to the name of the shop by enlarging the font size.

6. Press **[Ctrl][A]**, click the **Center button** on the Formatting toolbar, select the text **Faye's Flowers**, click the **Font Size list arrow** on the Formatting toolbar, then click **48**
   A matte that frames the object and makes it stand out can be added.

7. Click the **Rectangle button** on the Objects toolbar, create a shape from **1" H / 1" V** to **7½" H / 8¾" V**, click the **Dash Style button** on the Formatting toolbar, click **No Line**, click the **Fill Color list arrow** on the Formatting toolbar, click the **third color box from the left**, click the **Send to Back button** on the Formatting toolbar, then press **[Esc]**
   You can format the AutoShape to make it look more attractive.

8. Click the **Design Gallery Object button** on the Objects toolbar, click **Coupons**, click **Open Background Coupon** if necessary, click **Insert Object**, then modify the object so it looks like the coupon in Figure F-17
   Compare your publication to Figure F-17. The elements in the publication were modified, resulting in an improved appearance.

9. Select the text **Faye**, type **your name**, resize the text box if necessary, save your work, print, then exit Publisher

IMPROVING A PUBLICATION

FIGURE F-16: Existing flyer design

FIGURE F-17: Modified flyer

IMPROVING A PUBLICATION

Publisher 2002

Practice

▶ Concepts Review

Identify the design flaw in each element in **Figure F-18**.

FIGURE F-18

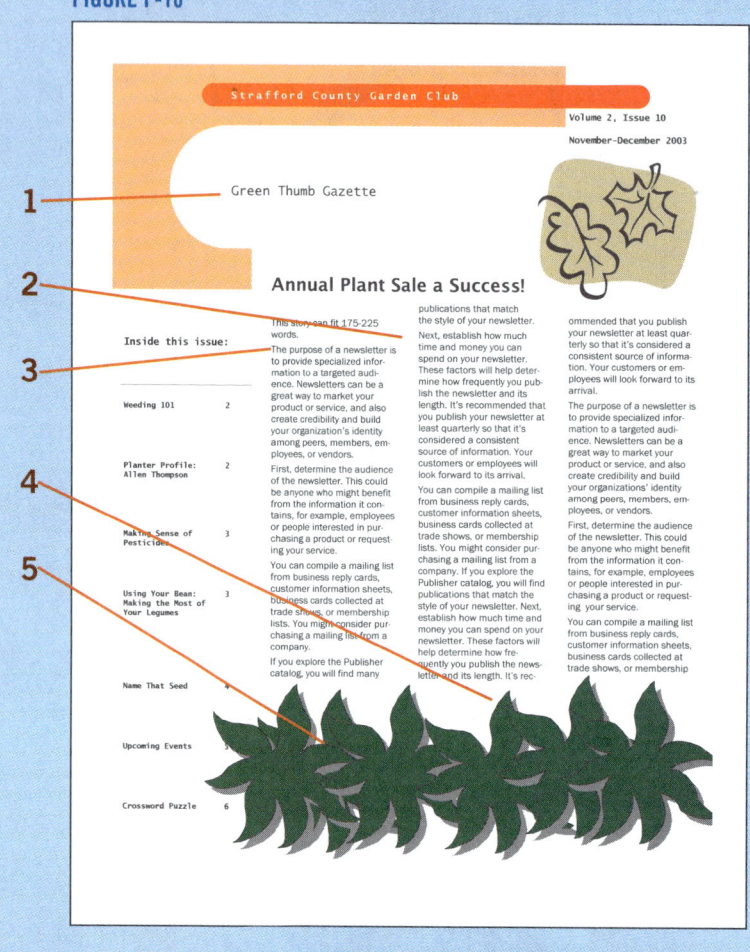

Match each of the design flaws with a solution.

6. Text is too small
7. Too many design elements on the page
8. Columns of text run together
9. There is no color and all of the fonts are the same

a. Add contrast, such as a matte, to the publication
b. Increase the amount of white space
c. Increase the font size
d. Add a visual boundary

Select the best answer from the list of choices.

10. When critiquing people's work, how do you avoid hurting their feelings, and help them to learn better design techniques?
    a. Make the changes yourself.
    b. Involve them in the solution phase.
    c. Instruct someone else to make the changes.
    d. Ignore the problems with their work — design is only one element of an effective publication.

▶ PUBLISHER 140   IMPROVING A PUBLICATION

Practice

11. A consistent arrangement of text and graphic elements that appears at the top of each issue of a publication is called a:
    a. Mask.
    b. Matte.
    c. Masthead.
    d. Mark.
12. The optical center occurs where on the page?
    a. ⅜" from the top
    b. In the center of the publication
    c. ⅜" from the bottom
    d. Upper-right corner
13. Which is not an example of white space?
    a. Margins
    b. Space between lines of text
    c. Space around a graphic
    d. Lines separating columns of text
14. In asymmetrical balance, the elements on a page are _____.
    a. Placed equally on either side of the vertical line
    b. Grouped near the center of the page
    c. Placed unequally on either side of the vertical line
    d. Placed in the white space
15. Which of the following is NOT true about working with advertisers?
    a. They may give you camera-ready artwork to place.
    b. They help support your publication financially.
    c. The cost of running an advertisement is determined by its size, amount of colors, and placement in the publication.
    d. Ads are most likely to be read when grouped together on a single page.
16. _____ is an important design principle that provides variety in physical layout.
    a. Contrast
    b. Symmetrical balance
    c. White space
    d. Diplomacy

▶ Skills Review

1. **Critique a publication**.
   a. Start Publisher, open the file PUB F-3 from the drive and folder where your Project Files are stored, then save it as **Daily Specials Menu**. Throughout this exercise, zoom in and out as necessary.
   b. Take a look at each visual element on the page, and determine where the focal points are, and whether there are any unnecessary or distracting elements on the page. Find three things you would change to improve the publication.
   c. Create a text box on page 2, type **Critiquing the publication**, then write your three improvements and how you would implement them.
   d. Create a second text box on page 2 that includes your thoughts on what the goals of the publication are, and how well you think the publication meets the goals.
2. **Strengthen a masthead**.
   a. The Daily Specials Menu is similar to a newsletter in that it has consistent text and graphics at the top of each menu that indicate the name of the restaurant and other important information.

IMPROVING A PUBLICATION

Publisher 2002 Practice

    b. Delete the graphic in the upper-right corner of page one, then increase the size of the graphic in the upper-left corner of the page to 2¾" H x 2¾" V.
    c. Move the text boxes for the name of the restaurant, the text "Daily Specials," and the text box that includes the date up (in this order). Leave a 2" margin between the top of the page and the restaurant name text box. Leave a 3½" margin between the left edge of the page and the three text boxes.
    d. Change the font size of the restaurant name to 17 point, left-align the text in the text box, then change the font color from black to something more colorful. Adjust the size of the text box, as necessary.
    e. Increase the font size of the "Daily Specials" text to 14 point, left-align the text in the text box, then make it the same font and font color as the restaurant name.
    f. Increase the font size of the date text to 12 point, and make it the same font but a different font color than the restaurant name. Adjust the size of the text box, as necessary.
    g. Save your work.

3. Rearrange elements.
    a. Move the table so that its upper-left corner is 1" H / 4¼" V.
    b. Delete the graphics in the lower-left and right corners.
    c. Move the text box that has the payment information to the bottom of the page at ¾" H / 8¼" V.
    d. Move the text box that has the address, phone number, and Web site so that its upper-left corner is ¾" H / 9½" V.
    e. Save your work.

4. Modify objects.
    a. Click the table.
    b. Press [Ctrl][A] twice, then increase the font size by pressing [Ctrl] []] (right bracket) five times.
    c. Resize the table so that its dimensions are 6½" H x 3½" V.
    d. Use the fill color of your choice on the table to provide contrast between the background and the table. Make sure that the fill color complements the font colors you used in the masthead.
    e. Save your work.

5. Experiment with design elements.
    a. Click the Design Gallery Object button on the Objects toolbar, click Coupons, click Top Oval Coupon, then click Insert Object.
    b. Drag the coupon to the scratch area.
    c. Click the "2 for 1" text box, then type **Dessert Special**.
    d. Click the "Name of Item or Service" text box," then type **Free dessert with lunch entrée**.
    e. Click the "Describe your location by landmark or area of town" text box, then type **12 Kimball Street**.
    f. Enter your name in the phone number text box, and an expiration date of September 1, 2003 in the remaining text box.
    g. Move the coupon to 4¼" H / 8¼" V.
    h. Save the publication, print it, then exit Publisher.

▶ Independent Challenge 1

You are asked to use your design and layout skills to redesign an existing business card for a corporate executive. Start Publisher, open the file PUB F-4 from the drive and folder where your Project Files are stored, then save it as **Corporate Business Card**. Use Figure F-19 as a guide to make changes to the business card. Once you make all the corrections, replace the existing name in the business card with your name. Save the changes, print the publication, then exit Publisher.

FIGURE F-19

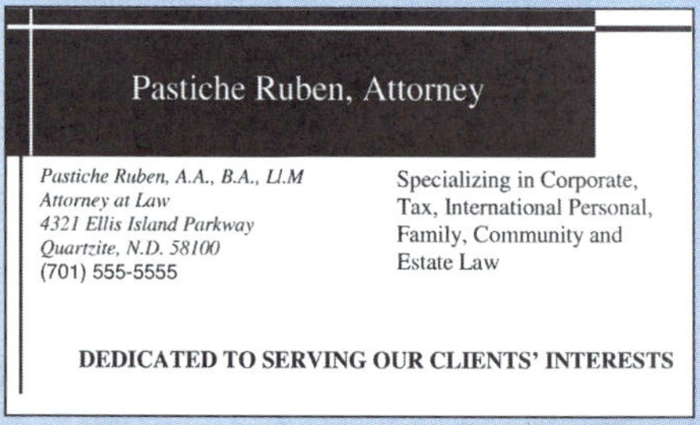

Pastiche Ruben, Attorney

Pastiche Ruben, A.A., B.A., LL.M
Attorney at Law
4321 Ellis Island Parkway
Quartzite, N.D. 58100
(701) 555-5555

Specializing in Corporate, Tax, International Personal, Family, Community and Estate Law

DEDICATED TO SERVING OUR CLIENTS' INTERESTS

▶ PUBLISHER 142   IMPROVING A PUBLICATION

Practice

▶ Independent Challenge 2

Your design services consulting firm is really taking off. You are asked to suggest ways of improving a certificate that was laid out by someone with no design experience. To start you off, one element was already corrected in Figure F-20. What other elements do you think need correcting?

FIGURE F-20

a. Start Publisher, open the file PUB F-5, then save it as **Certificate of Appreciation** to the drive and folder where your Project Files are stored.
b. Change the name in the existing publication to your name.
c. Print the publication before any other changes are made, then mark at least five areas that need improvement.
d. Make the changes you noted in the previous step.
e. Save and print the publication.
f. Exit Publisher.

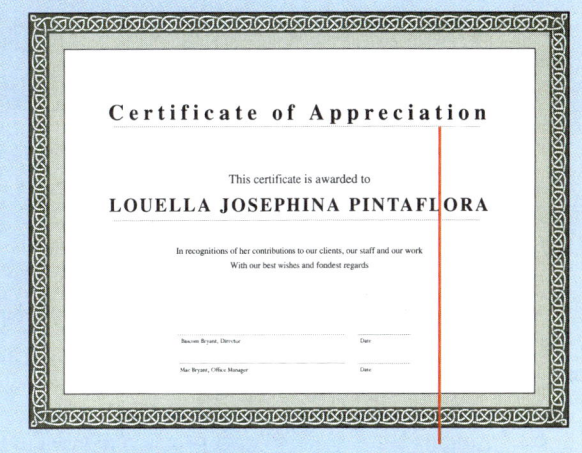

e Independent Challenge 3

As the Design Coordinator at Super Design and Layout, you want to find convincing examples of good and bad design in print and on Web sites. Seeing both types of examples will be helpful to your students. You can use the Web to find examples of good and bad design.

a. Connect to the Internet, then use your browser and search engine to locate information on design concepts. (*Hint:* One possible site where you can determine design tips and techniques is the DTP/HTML Tutorials Plus Web site at www.dtp-aus.com/.)
b. Find one site that offers design tips, then print out the home page.
c. Find one example of a site you consider to have bad design, then print the home page. Mark on the printed page the elements you think exhibit bad design, and how you would fix these elements.
d. Write your name on each printed page.

▶ Independent Challenge 4

You are asked to be the guest speaker at the next Publisher class, and the topic is design techniques. As part of the class, you want to be able to open a publication that has elements of poor design. During the class, you plan an active discussion, in which you fix this problematic publication. You also want to have the same publication with all the design flaws fixed.

a. Start Publisher, create a newsletter using your choice of design, then save it as **Design Techniques-Bad** to the drive and folder where your Project Files are stored.
b. Using the first page in the publication, incorporate improper techniques, such as a page that has too little white space, text that is too small, or a story that has no visual boundaries. Use as many incorrect elements as possible. (*Hint:* You can use any graphic elements and text stories available on your computer.)
c. Add your name to the masthead at the top of the first page.
d. Save the publication, then print page 1 of the publication.
e. Save this publication as **Design Techniques-Good** to the drive and folder where your Project Files are stored.
f. Fix all the areas you consciously created using poor design techniques.
g. Save the publication, then print the first page.
h. Exit Publisher.

IMPROVING A PUBLICATION

Publisher 2002 Practice

▶ Visual Workshop

Open the file PUB F-6 and save it as Tour Guide Flyer to the drive and folder where your Project Files are stored. Use your knowledge of design techniques and your Publisher skills to make the Project File look like the flyer in Figure F-21. Print the publication.

FIGURE F-21

Suzanna Demona's Vacation Nation Hospitality Enterprises – Invites YOU

Apply for Tour Guide Training. The hospitality industry is booming and you can capitalize on its growth. Become a Certified Tour Guide.

- Retirement benefits
- 401 K plans
- Interesting people
- Exotic locales
- Unlimited growth
- Subsidized shelter
- Good pay
- Rapid promotions

Call 555 555-5555 today for an application packet and complete information

▶ PUBLISHER 144   IMPROVING A PUBLICATION

Publisher 2002

Unit G

Working
with Multiple Pages

Objectives

- ▶ Add pages
- ▶ Delete pages
- ▶ Work with a Master Page
- ▶ Create a header and footer
- ▶ Add page numbers
- ▶ Edit a story
- ▶ Modify a table of contents
- ▶ Create labels
- ▶ Capstone Project: Jewelry Tools Catalog

Many publications, such as flyers, business cards, or signs, are on a single page. However, catalogs, newsletters, and some other publications have multiple pages. Using Publisher, it is easy to add, copy, and delete pages. For a more professional and compelling design, descriptive text, such as a motto, page numbers, or a date, can be repeated at the top or bottom of each page. A table of contents and page numbers can be added to organize the publication and help readers find specific stories. Mike Mendoza is designing a catalog of Navajo rugs for a Native American trading company. The client asked for a subdued catalog that will educate potential customers, but let the colorful rug designs speak for themselves. When finished, this catalog will be quite large and will require elements common to multi-page documents.

Adding Pages

Pages can be added to a publication one at a time or in batches. Depending on the type of publication you are creating and how your publication is laid out, you may want to add pages in multiples of two or four. A catalog, for example, prints pages in groups of four, so adding pages in multiples other than four can make printing difficult. Background items, for example, layout guides, and objects, such as headers and footers, can be added automatically to new pages using the Master Page feature. **Master Pages** are the background of a publication page, where repeated information, such as a pattern, header, or footer, can be viewed and edited. You also have the option to copy text or graphic objects from any page to a newly inserted page. Mike starts a new publication for the catalog. He decides to try adding and deleting pages to and from the publication.

Steps

1. Start Publisher, open the file **Pub G-1** from the drive and folder where your Project Files are located, then save it as **Rug Catalog**

   The catalog appears on the screen, and the Catalog Options task pane opens.

2. Click the **Close button** on the Catalog Options task pane, click the **Zoom list arrow** [44%], then click **Whole Page**

   The catalog has eight pages. You can add pages either before or after the current page. To retain a consistent design, you can insert whole pages with objects, such as text boxes or picture frames, on any page. You want to insert four new pages after page three.

   > **QuickTip**
   > Each of the nineteen layout choices is designed to be used in catalogs.

3. Click the **page 2–3 icon** on the status bar, click **Insert** on the menu bar, click **Page**, then use the list arrows and scroll bars to select **4 items, offset pictures** on the left-hand page, and **4 items, squared pictures** on the right-hand page

   List arrows and scroll bars for the left- and right-hand pages allow you to select the type of layout on each new catalog page, as shown in Figure G-1.

4. Click **More Options**

   The Insert Page dialog box opens, as shown in Figure G-2. You can use this dialog box to control the number of new pages added, as well as options, such as inserting blank pages, duplicating all of the objects on a specific page, or adding a hyperlink to a Web navigation bar.

   > **QuickTip**
   > To move a page, insert a new page, duplicate the objects from the page you want moved, then delete the original page.

5. Click **Cancel** in the Insert Page dialog box, click **OK** in the Insert Pages dialog box, then click **Yes** to automatically insert four pages

   Compare your work to Figure G-3. The page 4–5 icon button is selected on the status bar, and the presence of the other icon buttons indicates that the publication now has 12 pages. The newly inserted pages (4–7) have the same layout on both pages.

6. Click the **Save button** on the Standard toolbar

FIGURE G-1: Insert Pages dialog box

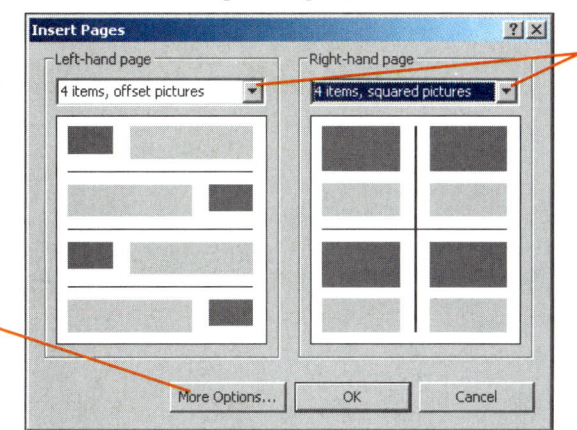

Nineteen page layout options are available from either list arrow

More Options button opens the Insert Page dialog box

FIGURE G-2: Insert Page dialog box

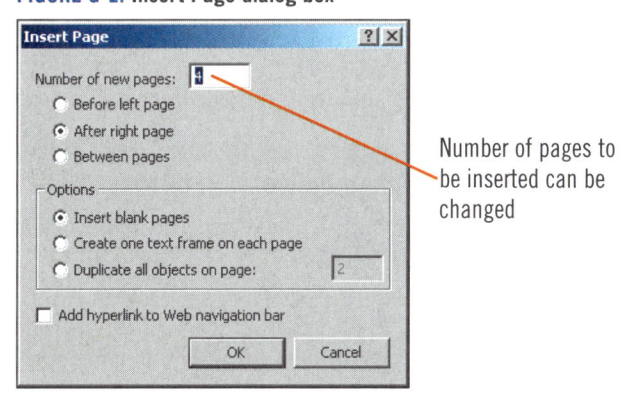

Number of pages to be inserted can be changed

FIGURE G-3: Publication with added pages

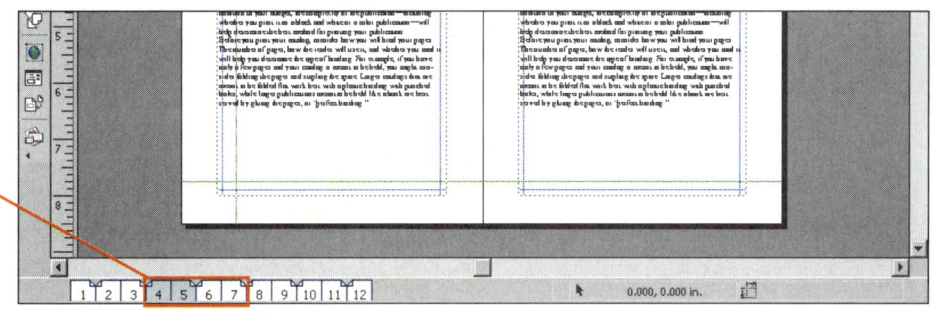

Pages added to publication

Design Matters

Printing multi-page documents

When you think of a page, you probably think of an 8½" × 11" sheet of paper; publications can contain several "pages," but more than one page can be on a sheet of paper. A four-page brochure can be printed front and back on one sheet of paper and folded in half so that there are four pages. Commercial printing of publications larger than four pages prints pages this way, then the folded pages are bound together. This is why catalogs print in multiples of four, because they are printed on the front and back of a single piece of paper. When printing books or other large publications, paper is printed in multiples of eight, called **signatures**. Blank pages at the end of a novel indicate there was not enough text to fill the last signature.

WORKING WITH MULTIPLE PAGES

Unit G
Publisher 2002

Deleting Pages

Unnecessary pages should be deleted to streamline your publication and keep file sizes down. You should always view the pages that you are deleting to ensure that you are deleting the correct pages, and that there aren't any elements you want saved, such as clip art or a pull quote. When you delete a page, any objects on that page are deleted from the publication, Continued on/Continued from notices are automatically recalculated, and text in a connected text box is moved to the closest available text box on the next page. Mike wants to keep the file size small so he eliminates any unnecessary pages. He wants to delete the four new pages as well as four additional pages.

Steps

1. Click the **page 4–5 icon** on the status bar if necessary, click **Edit** on the menu bar, then click **Delete Page**

   The Delete Page dialog box opens, as shown in Figure G-4. The Both pages option button is selected, although you could just delete the left or right page. Since you know that a catalog adds and deletes an even number of pages, you want to see what happens if you try to delete a single page.

2. Click the **Left page only option button**, then click **OK**

   The warning dialog box shown in Figure G-5 opens. This tells you that you can delete a single page, but your layout may be negatively affected, or you can cancel the single page deletion.

> **QuickTip**
> If you delete a page in error, immediately click the Undo button on the Standard toolbar.

3. Click **Cancel**, click **Edit** on the menu bar, click **Delete Page**, verify that the **Both pages option button** is selected, click **OK**, click **OK** in the multiple page spread warning box, then click **OK** in the Delete this page warning box

   The Multiple page spread warning box appears because you were deleting only two pages, not a multiple of four. You can see that your publication now has 10 pages. Pages 6–7 now are pages 4–5. You want to delete these pages as well.

4. With **pages 4–5** still active, click **Edit** on the menu bar, click **Delete Page**, verify that the **Both pages option button** is selected, click **OK**, then click **OK** in the Delete this page warning box

   The Multiple-page spread warning box does not appear because the total number of remaining pages is a multiple of four. There are now eight pages in the publication. You want to delete four more pages from this publication.

5. With **pages 4–5** still active, click **Edit** on the menu bar, click **Delete Page**, verify that the **Both pages option button** is selected, click **OK**, click **OK** in the Multiple page spread warning box, then click **OK** in the Delete this page warning box

   The Multiple-page spread warning box was active again. There are now six pages in the catalog.

6. With **pages 4–5** still active, click **Edit** on the menu bar, click **Delete Page**, verify that the **Both pages option button** is selected, click **OK**, click **OK**, then click the **page 2–3 icon**

   Compare your catalog to Figure G-6. There are now four pages in the publication.

7. Click the **Save button** on the Standard toolbar

FIGURE G-4: Delete Page dialog box

FIGURE G-5: Multiple page spread warning box

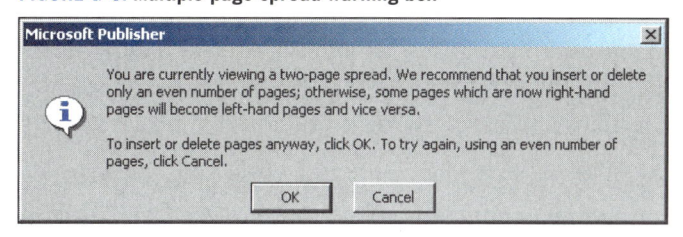

FIGURE G-6: Two-page spread

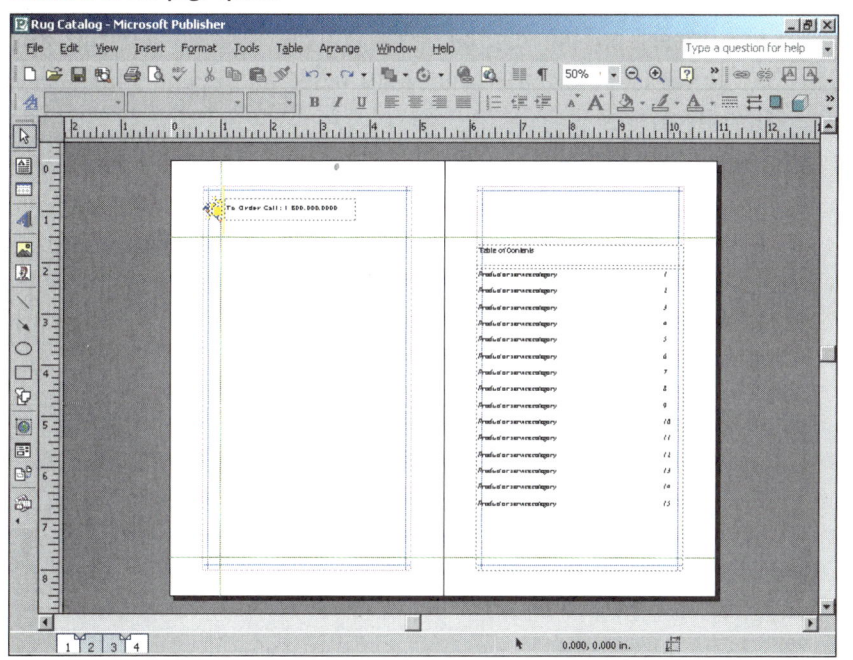

Saving objects on a page

When a page is deleted, all the objects on that page are also deleted. What if you want to save some of those objects for later use? Any object can be dragged onto the scratch area. Objects in the scratch area are saved along with the publication, and can be viewed and accessed from all pages in the publication. When you decide where you want an object from the scratch area to be used, move it to its new location using any copying or pasting technique. Alternately, you can cut an object before deleting the page so it will automatically be stored on the Clipboard, where it can easily be retrieved until the publication is closed.

WORKING WITH MULTIPLE PAGES

Publisher 2002 Unit G

Working with a Master Page

Every publication has a Master Page that can be used to add text or objects that you want on every page. A publication without **mirrored guides** has a single Master Page, while a publication with mirrored guides has both left and right Master Pages. You can use the Master Page to add an object, such as a logo, to each page, or to only one page. **Washouts**, faded images that appear behind text and objects on a page, also known as watermarks, can be added to the Master Page. Mike wants descriptive text about Navajo rugs on page 2. Once he inserts this text, he adds a muted image of a rug to the background page.

Steps

1. Click the **Text Box button** on the Objects toolbar, then drag + from **1" H / 1½" V** to **4¾" H / 7¾" V**

   The text box appears on the page. You insert prepared text in the text box.

2. Right-click the **text box**, point to **Change Text**, click **Text File**, locate the file **PUB G-2** from the drive and folder where your Project Files are located, then click **OK**

   All of the text fits within the text box, as shown in Figure G-7.

3. Click **View** on the menu bar, then click **Master Page**

   The blank mirrored background pages appear. Master Pages can accommodate both text and graphics. The catalog will look very elegant with recolored rug images in the background.

   > **QuickTip**
   > Modify an existing Master Page by switching to the Master Page view and editing objects.

4. Click **Insert** on the toolbar, point to **Picture**, click **From File**, click the image **NavajoRug1.tif** from the drive and folder where your Project Files are stored, then click **Insert**

   The picture is placed on the master pages.

5. Position the picture so that its top-left corner is at **1" H / 1½" V**

   The picture is inserted into the picture frame. Using the Washout feature on the picture will give it a nice effect.

6. Right-click the **picture**, click **Format Picture**, click the **Color list arrow**, click **Washout**, then click **OK**

   The rug image has a brown and gray appearance, as shown in Figure G-8.

7. Click **View** on the menu bar, then click **Master Page** to deselect it

   The washout image appears behind the text in the frame. Compare your publication to Figure G-9.

   > **QuickTip**
   > You can toggle between the regular and Master Page views by pressing [Ctrl][M].

8. Click the **Save button** on the Standard toolbar

Design Matters

Changing from double to single Master Pages

If you have mirrored layout guides, you also have left and right Master Pages. Having both a left and right Master Page increases your design flexibility. For example, you might want to have an image appear in the bottom-left corner on the left master page, and the bottom-right corner on the right Master Page. To change from double to single Master Pages, click Arrange on the menu bar, click Layout Guides, then deselect the Create Two Master Pages With Mirrored Guides check box in the Layout Guides dialog box. When this check box is not selected, you have only one Master Page. What was previously the right Master Page is now used as the publication's background page and is applied to all the pages.

▶ PUBLISHER 150 **WORKING WITH MULTIPLE PAGES**

FIGURE G-7: Text file added to publication

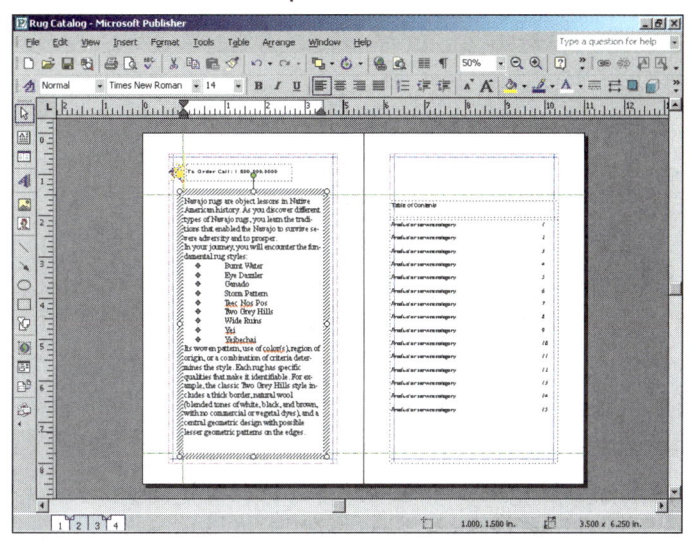

FIGURE G-8: Washout image added to Master Page

Image in left Master Page

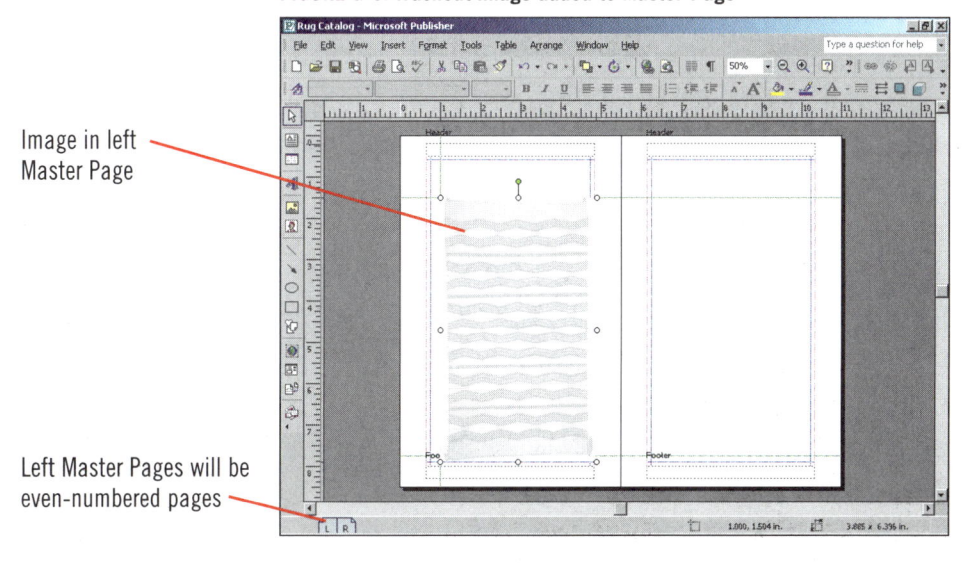

Left Master Pages will be even-numbered pages

FIGURE G-9: Text in foreground, image in background

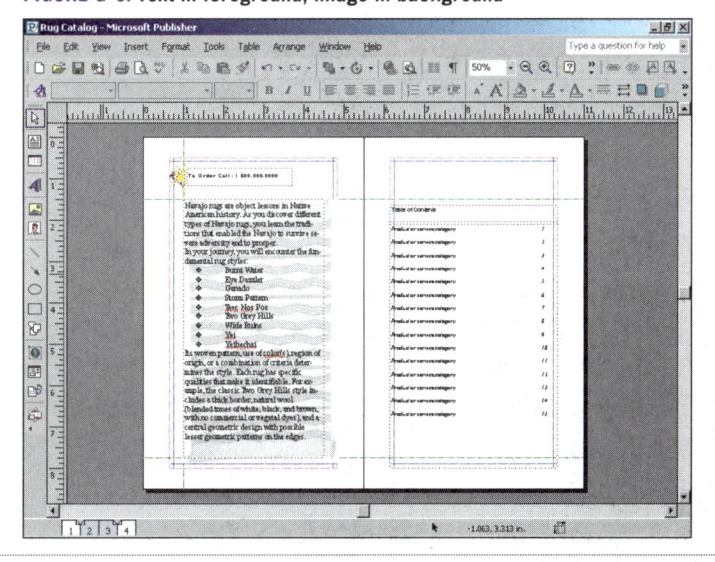

WORKING WITH MULTIPLE PAGES PUBLISHER 151

Creating a Header and Footer

Text that appears on the top of each page is called a **header**, and text that appears on the bottom of each page is a **footer**. Special text boxes for the header or footer text are created and positioned on the right and left master page. Images can also be included in headers or footers to enhance the publication. Usually, the headers and footers are not shown on the first page of a publication. Table G-1 describes the buttons on the Header and Footer toolbar and how they are used. Mike wants to add descriptive headers to emphasize the themes of the catalog.

Steps

1. Click **View** on the menu bar, then click **Header and Footer**
   The view changes to the Master Page, the Header and Footer toolbar is open, and header and footer text boxes appear on pages 2 and 3. The header text box at the top of page 2 is selected.

2. Type **Navajo Rugs: Cultural Expressions** in the header text box on the left master page
   This text will appear on all left-hand pages. Now you will add a header for the right-hand pages.

3. Click the header text box at **6¼" H / ¼" V**, type **Navajo Rugs: Strong Visual Statements**, then click the **Align Right button**
   Compare your page to Figure G-10.

4. Click **Close** on the Header and Footer toolbar, click the **Zoom list arrow**, then click **Whole Page**
   The headers appear on pages 2 and 3, as shown in Figure G-11.

5. Click the **page 1 icon** on the status bar
   The header is visible on page 1. Catalogs, like other multi-page publications, typically don't display headers on the first page.

6. Click **View** on the menu bar, then click **Ignore Master Page**
   Because you chose to ignore the background on this first page, any objects on the right master page are not visible on this page.

7. Click the **Save button** on the Standard toolbar

TABLE G-1: Header and footer toolbar buttons

button	name	description
	Insert Page Number	Inserts a page number automatically into a header or footer
	Insert Date	Inserts current date into a header or footer
	Insert Time	Inserts current time into a header or footer
	Show Header/Footer	Used to toggle between the header and footer

▶ PUBLISHER 152 **WORKING WITH MULTIPLE PAGES**

FIGURE G-10: Header text box on right Master Page

Header and Footer toolbar

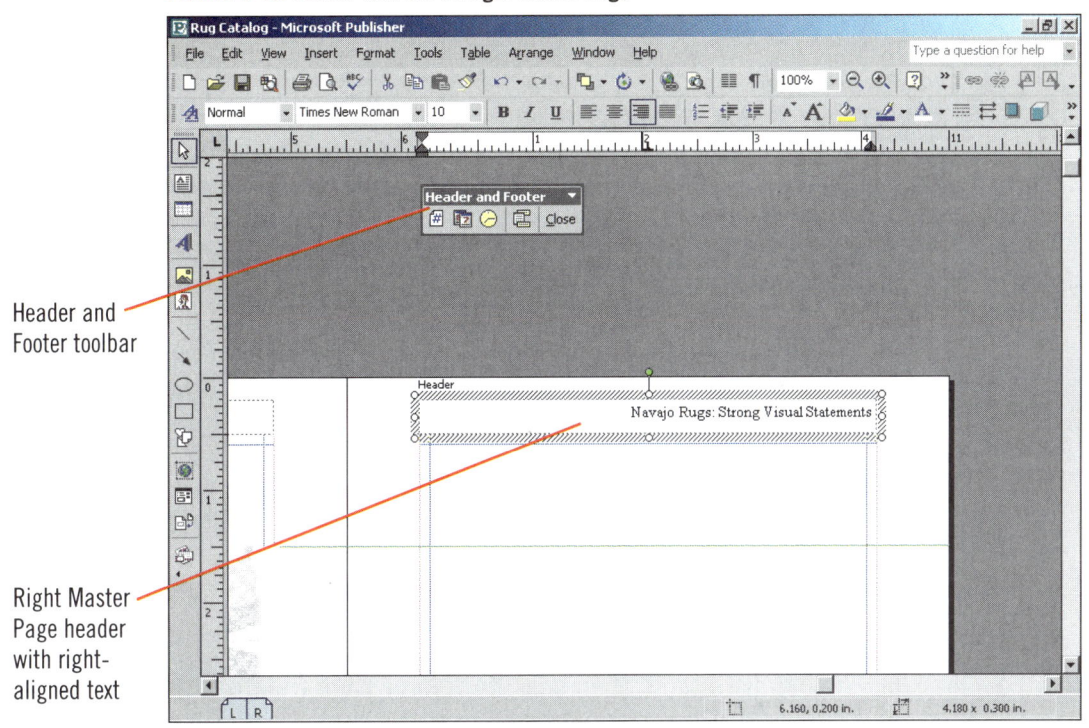

Right Master Page header with right-aligned text

FIGURE G-11: Headers visible on left and right pages

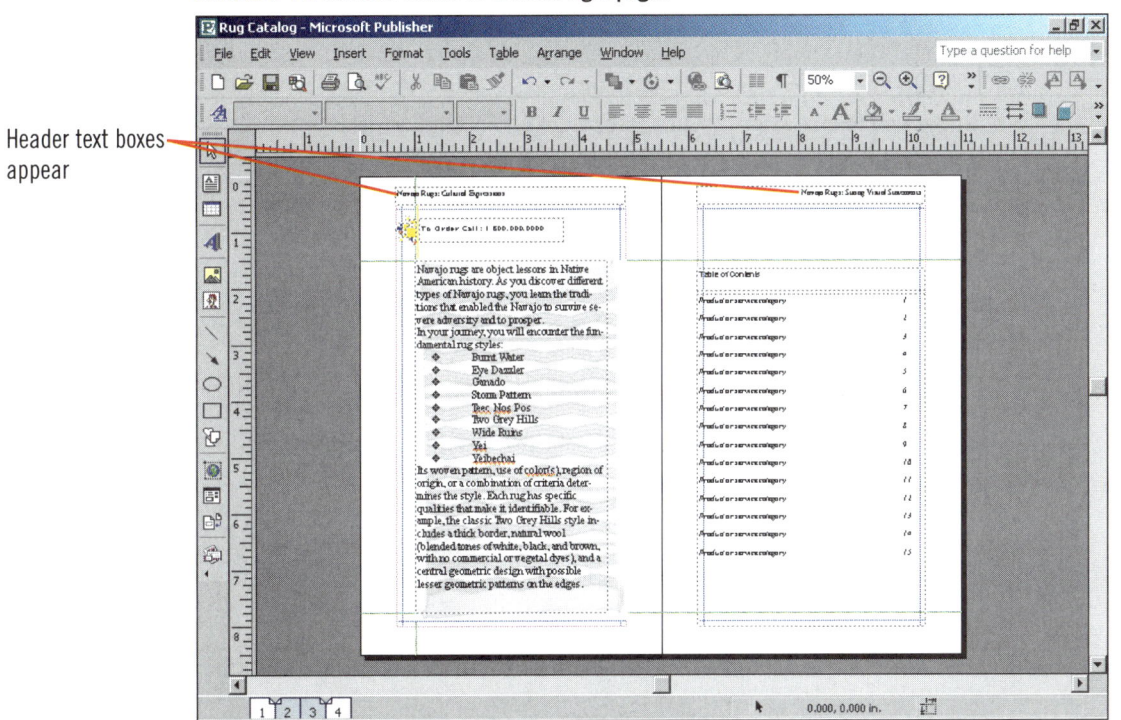

Header text boxes appear

WORKING WITH MULTIPLE PAGES PUBLISHER 153

Adding Page Numbers

Publisher 2002 — Unit G

You will probably want to add page numbers to publications that have more than two pages. **Page numbers** help readers find specific stories, and find the continued parts of stories that appear in multiple text boxes on different pages. You can insert page numbers either by using the Page Number button on the Header and Footer toolbar, or by using the Insert Page Number dialog box. With either method, the pound sign (#) is inserted into the publication as a placeholder. Publisher then automatically substitutes the correct page number for the placeholder. As pages are added and deleted, your page numbers remain accurate. Like headers and footers, page numbers are added to the Master Pages. Mike wants automatic page numbers in the footers at the bottom of each page, except the first page.

Steps

1. Click the **page 2–3 icon** on the status bar, click **Insert** on the menu bar, then click **Page Numbers**
   The Page Numbers dialog box opens, as shown in Figure G-12. You want the page numbers to appear on the bottoms of the pages.

2. Click the **Position list arrow**, then click **Bottom of page (Footer)**
   You want the page numbers to appear in the bottom-left corner of the left pages and the bottom-right corner of the right pages. This appeals to your design sense because it balances the headers appearing on the outsides of the pages.

3. Click the **Alignment list arrow**, then click **Outside**
   Most often the first page of a publication does not display a page number.

4. Deselect the **Show page number on first page check box**
   The page numbering feature will count the first page, but the number will not appear.

5. Click **OK**
   Compare the placement of your page numbers with Figure G-13. You want to see how the page number feature appears on the master page.

6. Press **[Ctrl][M]**, click the footer at **7" H / 8" V**, then press **[F9]**
   The master page shows the page number feature as "#" inside the footer.

7. Press **[F9]**, then press **[Ctrl][M]**
   The publication is shown in foreground page view.

8. Click the **Save button** on the Standard toolbar

PUBLISHER 154 WORKING WITH MULTIPLE PAGES

FIGURE G-12: Page Numbers dialog box

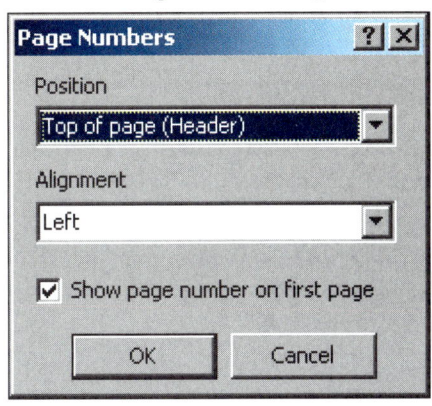

FIGURE G-13: Page numbers on both pages

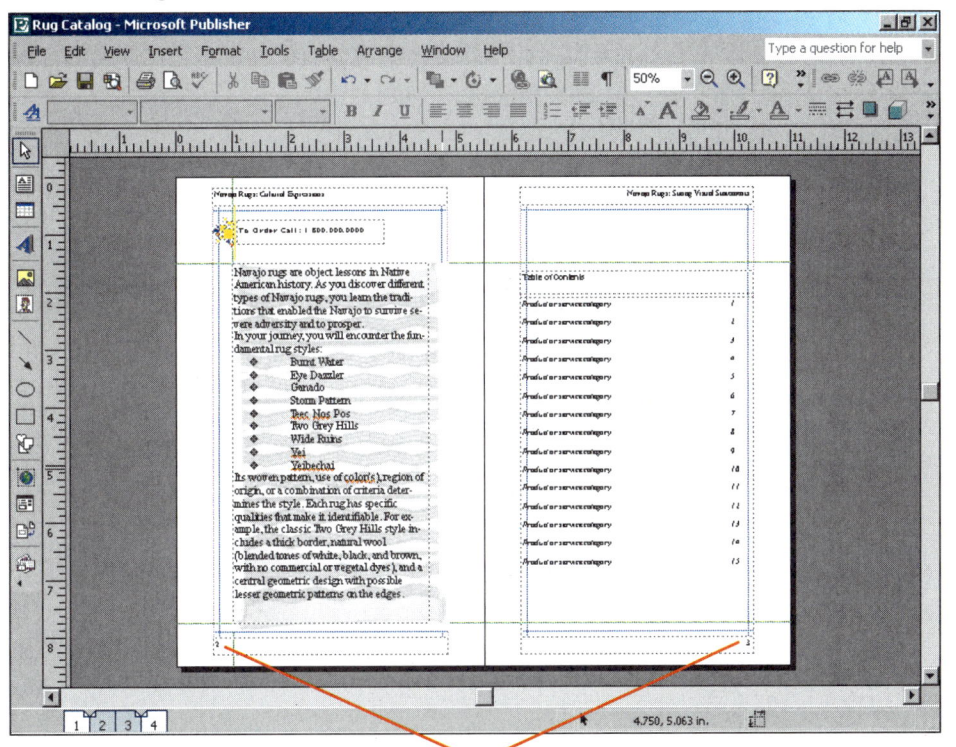

Page numbers appear in footers

WORKING WITH MULTIPLE PAGES

Unit G
Publisher 2002

Editing a Story

Stories can be typed directly into a text box, or prepared beforehand and inserted as a text file. Editing directly in Word lets you take advantage of the features of a powerful word processor from within Publisher. If you don't require those features, you might choose to edit a story while working in Publisher. But editing in Publisher means that your changes cannot be saved to the original text file. If a version of Microsoft Word 6.0 or later is installed on your computer, you can edit the story directly in Word. After reading the publication, Mike wants to make changes to the descriptive text on page 2.

Steps

Trouble?
If Word isn't installed on your computer, edit the story directly in Publisher. If you edit the story in Publisher, skip Steps 1 and 4.

1. Right-click the text box at **3" H / 3" V**, point to **Change Text**, click **Edit Story in Microsoft Word**, then click the **Maximize button** in the upper-right corner of the Document in Rug Catalog window if necessary
   Microsoft Word opens, displaying the story's text, as shown in Figure G-14. Any edits you make to this text in Word will be applied to the selected story in the Publisher text box.

2. Select the text **discover different types of**, then type **explore**
   You changed the phrase "discover different types of" to "explore" in the first paragraph to make it more succinct. To save space, you will combine the headings for two related types of rugs.

QuickTip
Some text formatting, such as drop caps, are lost when moving from Word to Publisher.

3. Click to the right of **Yei** (the eighth bullet), press **[Spacebar]**, type **and**, press **[Spacebar]**, then press **[Delete]** twice
   You combined the two related bulleted items into one bullet. When your edits are complete, you can exit Word and return to the story in Publisher.

4. Click **File** on the menu bar, then click **Close & Return to Rug Catalog**
   Word closes and you see your edits applied to the text in the Publisher story.

5. Click anywhere within the **first paragraph**, click **Format** on the menu bar, click **Drop Cap**, click the **drop cap** directly under the current selection, then click **OK**
   The drop cap is added to make the story stand out. Compare your work to Figure G-15.

6. Click the **Save button** on the Standard toolbar

Design Matters

Copyfitting text

As you create a publication, you may find that you have either too much or too little text. **Copyfitting** is a term used to describe the process of making the text fit the available space within a publication. If you have too much text, you can narrow the margins, decrease the point size of the font, enlarge the text box, flow text into a text box on another page, or delete some text by editing. You can solve the problem of too little text by inserting a graphic image or pull quote, making margins wider, increasing the point size of the font, or adding some text. The AutoFit Text command found on the Format menu works by increasing or decreasing the point size of the fonts.

▶ PUBLISHER 156 **WORKING WITH MULTIPLE PAGES**

FIGURE G-14: Editing a story in Word

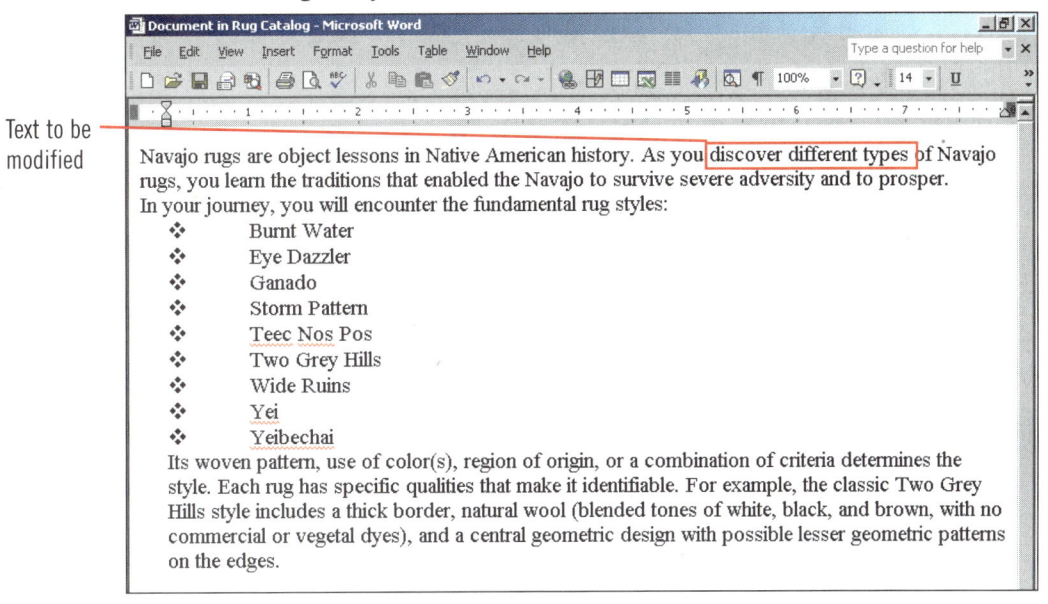

Text to be modified — Navajo rugs are object lessons in Native American history. As you discover different types of Navajo rugs, you learn the traditions that enabled the Navajo to survive severe adversity and to prosper.
In your journey, you will encounter the fundamental rug styles:
- Burnt Water
- Eye Dazzler
- Ganado
- Storm Pattern
- Teec Nos Pos
- Two Grey Hills
- Wide Ruins
- Yei
- Yeibechai

Its woven pattern, use of color(s), region of origin, or a combination of criteria determines the style. Each rug has specific qualities that make it identifiable. For example, the classic Two Grey Hills style includes a thick border, natural wool (blended tones of white, black, and brown, with no commercial or vegetal dyes), and a central geometric design with possible lesser geometric patterns on the edges.

FIGURE G-15: Edited story

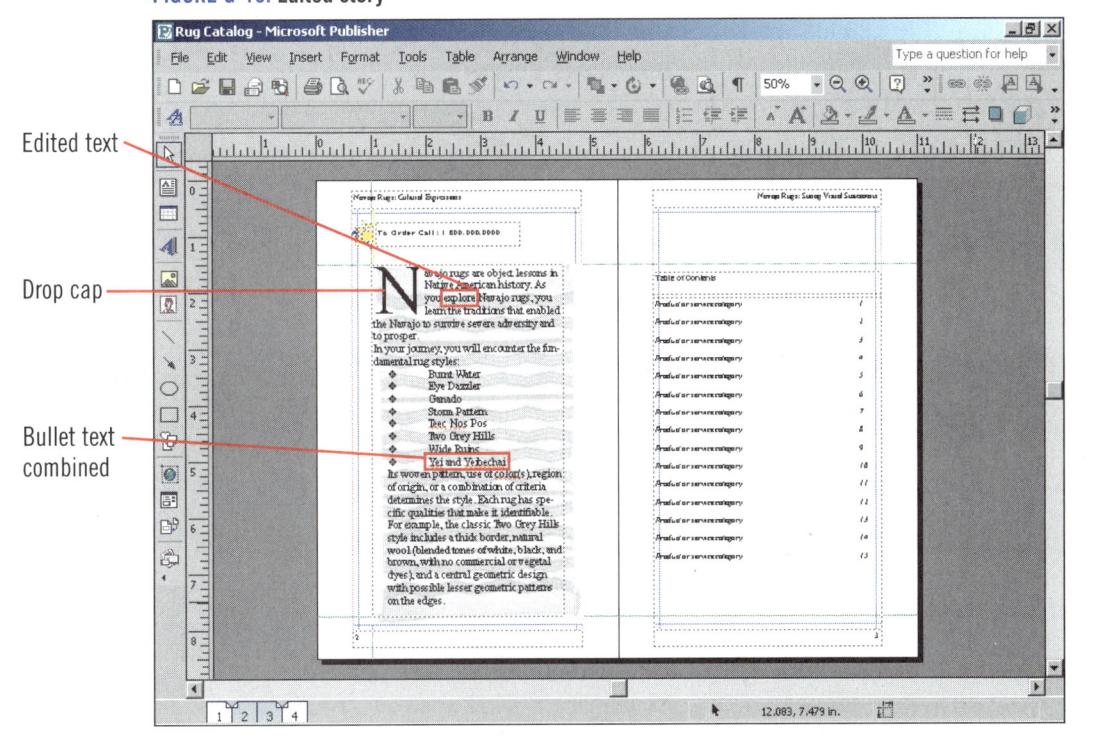

- Edited text
- Drop cap
- Bullet text combined

WORKING WITH MULTIPLE PAGES PUBLISHER 157

Publisher 2002

Modifying a Table of Contents

Unit G — Publisher 2002

A **table of contents** helps readers locate specific information they want to read. A table of contents in Publisher uses tabs to align columns of information concerning content and the page numbers of the content. To make a table of contents, type text into a text box, then add tabs and leaders to connect the text and page numbers. A **tab**, or tab stop, is a defined location to which the insertion point advances when you press [Tab]. **Leaders** are a series of dots, dashes, or lines that lead up to a tab, and automatically adjust to fit the space between the columns. ✒ Mike wants to modify the table of contents in the catalog by adding dot leaders to make reading easier. Although he still has a lot of work to do, he'll also make entries to approximate where information will be found in his catalog.

Steps

1. **Click the text box at 7" H / 2½" V, then press [F9]**
   The first item in the table of contents is for page 1. The reference to this page is not necessary, as the reader can easily see everything that's on page 1. Rather than adjust each of the subsequent entries, you delete this line.

2. **Select the first line of text, then press [Delete]**
   The first line is deleted, and the second line begins with page 2.

3. **Press [Ctrl][A], right-click the text, point to Change Text, then click Tabs**
   The Tabs dialog box opens, as shown in Figure G-16. You want each tab to be preceded by a dot leader.

4. **In the Leader section of the Tabs dialog box, click the Dot option button, click OK, then click outside of the text box to deselect the text**
   Each of the entries in the text box has a dot leader preceding the page number.

5. **Select the text Product or service category in the first line, then type Introduction to Navajo Rugs**
   The first entry in the table of contents is complete.

6. **Delete the entry for page 3, then delete the entries for pages 13–15**
   Now you will add the remaining table of contents entries.

7. **Type the table of contents information as shown in Figure G-17 using the techniques described in Step 5, then type your name as a final entry to the table of contents**
   The table of contents looks good and is a tool that will help clients locate information about the rugs when the catalog is complete.

8. **Press [F9], click the Save button 🖫 on the Standard toolbar, then click the Print button 🖨 on the Standard toolbar**
   Review the four printed pages of the catalog.

9. **Click File on the menu bar, then click Close**
   The publication is closed and Publisher is still open and available for additional work.

▶ PUBLISHER 158   **WORKING WITH MULTIPLE PAGES**

FIGURE G-16: Tabs dialog box

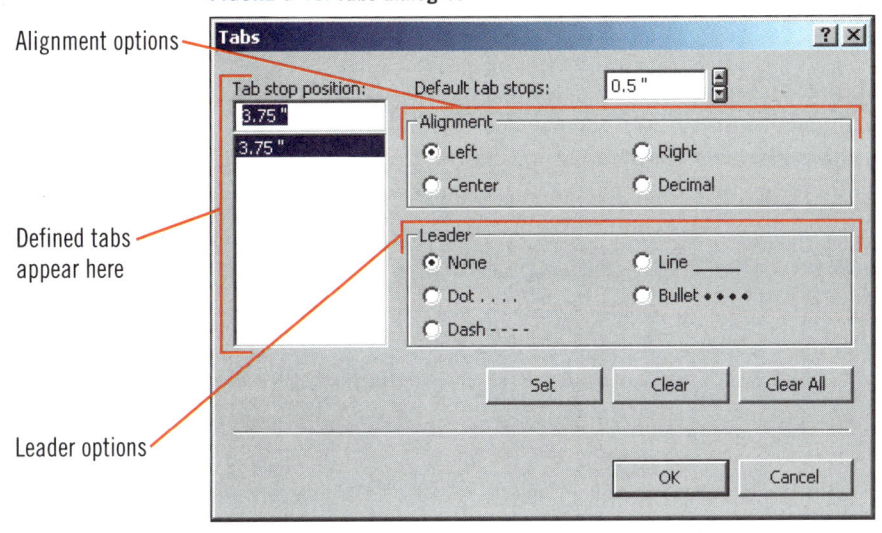

Alignment options

Defined tabs appear here

Leader options

FIGURE G-17: Completed Table of Contents

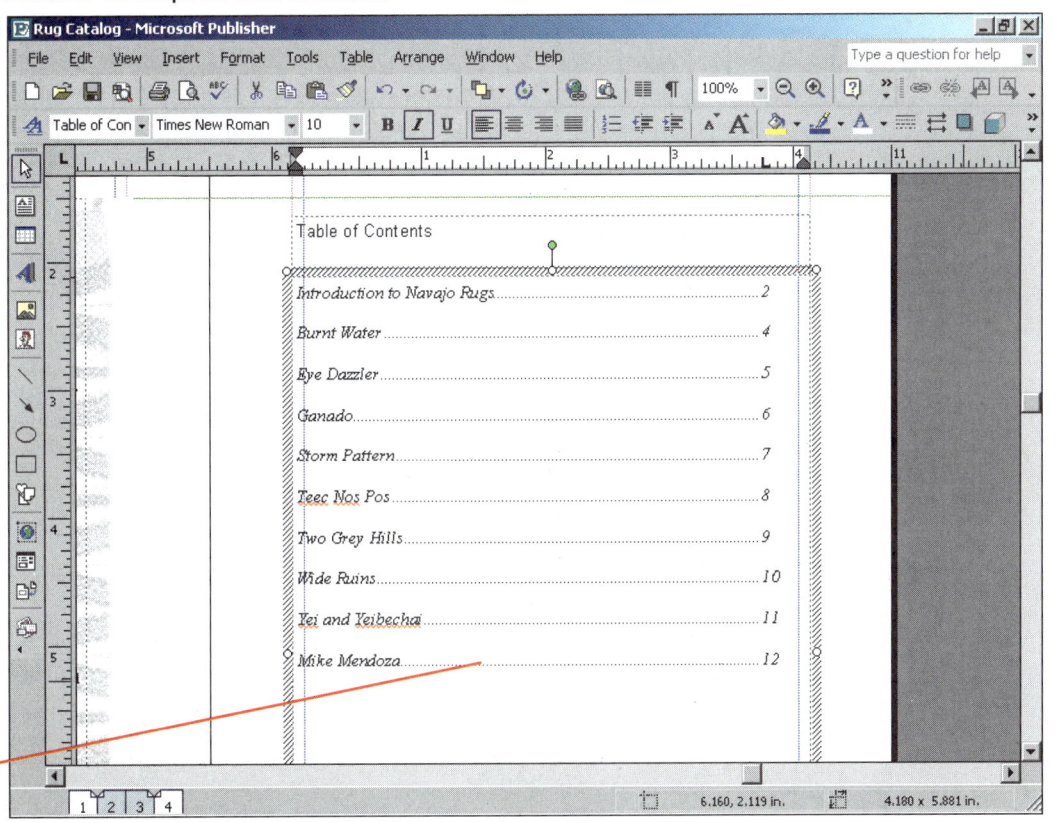

Table of Contents

Introduction to Navajo Rugs 2
Burnt Water 4
Eye Dazzler 5
Ganado 6
Storm Pattern 7
Teec Nos Pos 8
Two Grey Hills 9
Wide Ruins 10
Yei and Yeibechai 11
Mike Mendoza 12

Dot leaders inserted

WORKING WITH MULTIPLE PAGES   PUBLISHER 159

Publisher 2002

Creating Labels

You can use Publisher to create professional-looking labels for a variety of items, such as retail products, CDs, or notebooks. These labels are designed to print directly on a page of commercially available labels in a wide range of sizes and styles. Mike uses the New Publication task pane and the Publication Gallery to create a sheet of 30 labels that can be attached to rugs made by one of the rug makers, Rose Begay.

Steps

QuickTip
Different sheets of labels will have a different number of labels per sheet.

1. Click **File** on the menu bar, click **New**, click **Labels** on the New Publication task pane, click **Identification**, then click the **Made By Tag** in the Publication Gallery
   The label appears on the screen. It is ready to print on Avery Label #5160, as indicated on the screen; this information will not show up when printing the labels.

2. Click **Color Schemes** on the Publication Designs task pane, click **Desert**, then save the publication as **Rug Label** to the drive and folder where your Project Files are located
   Any publication, even a label, has a foreground and background. You decide that an image of a rug would be a nice addition to the label.

3. Click the **Close button** on the Color Schemes task pane, press **[Ctrl][M]**, click **Insert** on the menu bar, point to **Picture**, click **From File**, click the file **NavajoRug2.tif** from the drive and folder where your Project Files are located, then click **Insert**
   Compare your label to Figure G-18. You want to recolor the image, but this time you want to increase the contrast between the background and the text.

4. Use to position the picture so that the left edge is at ½" H and it is centered within the vertical margin guides, right-click the **object**, click **Format Picture**, select the contents of the **Brightness control box**, type **75%**, click the **Contrast control box**, type **25%**, then click **OK**
   The image is now a much lighter shade than before. You need to change the text and make the text box transparent.

5. Press **[Ctrl][M]**, select the text **Made especially for you by:**, type **Authentic Navajo Rug made by:**, then press **[Ctrl][T]**
   You can now see the image of the rug very clearly behind the text.

6. Click the text box at **1" H / ¾" V**, type your name, press **[Ctrl][A]**, click the **Bold button** on the Formatting toolbar, click the **Font Size list arrow** on the Formatting toolbar to change the point size to **16**, press **[Ctrl][T]**, then press **[Esc]** twice
   Compare your label to Figure G-19.

7. Click the **Save button** on the Standard toolbar, click **File** on the menu bar, click **Print**, then exit Publisher

▶ PUBLISHER 160 **WORKING WITH MULTIPLE PAGES**

FIGURE G-18: Label master page with image inserted

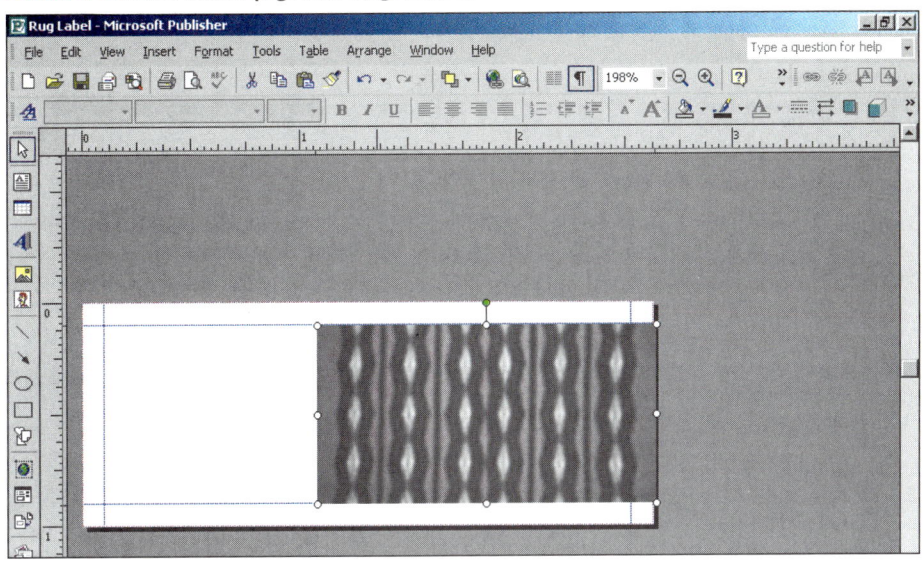

FIGURE G-19: Completed label with recolored image

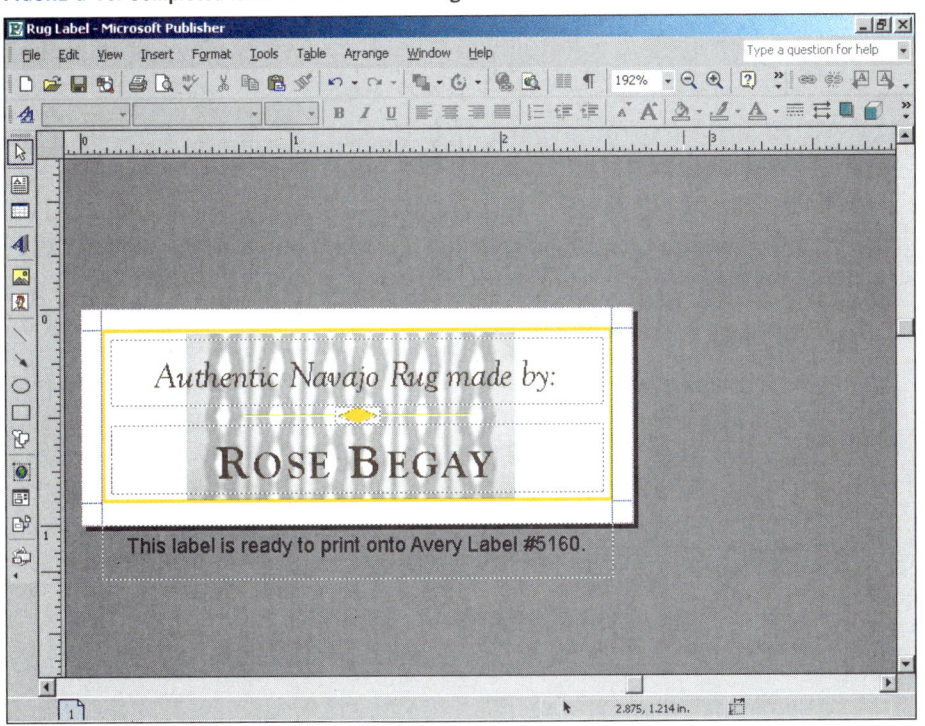

WORKING WITH MULTIPLE PAGES PUBLISHER 161

Unit G
Publisher 2002

Capstone Project: Jewelry Tools Catalog

You have inserted and deleted pages, worked with Master Pages, created headers and footers, added page numbers, modified a table of contents, and edited a story in Word. You will use these skills to work on a new catalog. Mike is designing a metal workers' catalog. The customers want a simple, uncluttered design. They will add pictures and text later.

Steps

1. Start Publisher, open the file **Pub G-3** from the drive and folder where your Project Files are located, then save it as **Jewelry Tools Catalog**
   Most of the elements of design in the first three pages will be carried throughout the catalog. You delete four pages knowing that they will be replaced when the client adds content.

2. Close the task pane, click the **page 4-5 icon** on the status bar, click **Edit** on the menu bar, click **Delete Page** to delete pages 4-5, click **OK** at each warning or dialog box, then repeat the process to delete the next two pages, which are now pages 4 and 5
   The publication now has four pages. The catalog should appeal to jewelers. You think a pair of gold earrings in the background of page 2 will look elegant and add interest to the page.

3. Click the **page 2-3 icon** on the status bar, click **View** on the menu bar, click **Master Page**, click **Insert** on the menu bar, point to **Picture**, click **From File**, then double-click the file **Pub G-4** from the drive and folder where your Project Files are located
   You want the image to be centered, the brightness increased, and the contrast decreased.

4. Position the image so that its top-left corner is at **1¼" H / 3" V**, right-click the **image**, click **Format Picture**, click the **Color list arrow**, click **Washout**, then click **OK**
   The image looks subdued and will be elegant with black text imposed over the gold color. You decide to add headers and footers while still in the Master Page view.

5. Click **View** on the menu bar, click **Header and Footer**, type **The Best Jewelry Tools Gathered from Around the World!** in the header text box on the left master page, click the **Show Header/Footer button**, type **Page**, press **[Spacebar]**, click the **Insert Page Number button**, copy all the entries in the left footer to the right footer, click the **Align Right button** to right-align the right footer, then press **[Ctrl][M]**
   Page numbers will help customers navigate to specific items. To make it easier to use the table of contents, you add tabs and line leaders.

6. Press **[F9]**, click the text box at **6½" H / 2" V**, click **Format** on the menu bar, click **Tabs**, click the **Line option button**, then click **OK**
   There is still an entry for page 1 that must be deleted.

7. Right-click the **text box**, point to **Change Text**, click **Edit Story in Microsoft Word**, delete the entry for page 1, click **File** on the menu bar, then click **Close & Return to Jewelry Tools Catalog**

8. Click the text box at **2" H / ¾" V**, substitute your name for the phone number, press **[Esc]** twice, then compare your work to Figure G-20

9. Click the **Save button** on the Standard toolbar, print pages 2 and 3, then exit Publisher

▶ PUBLISHER 162   **WORKING WITH MULTIPLE PAGES**

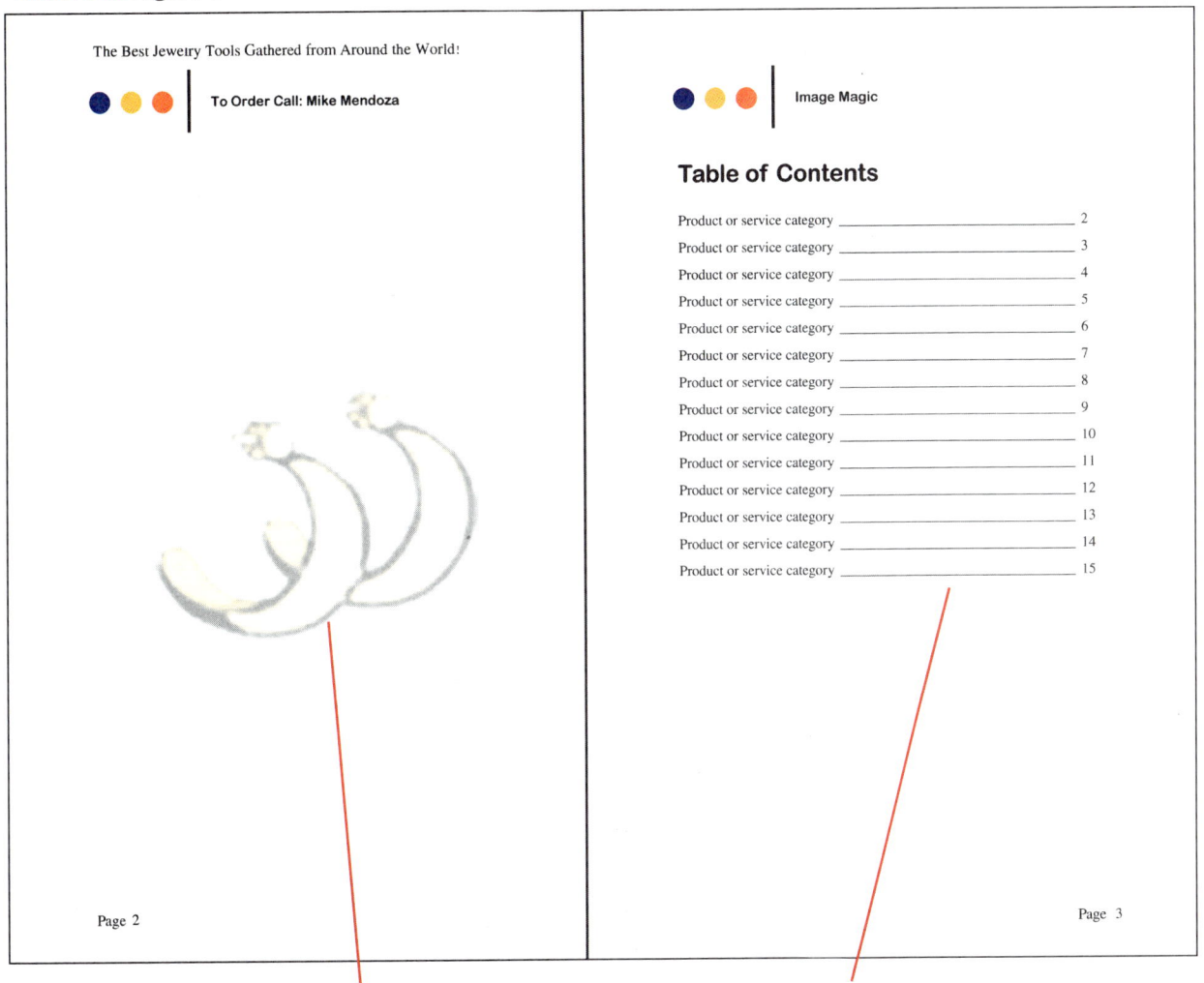

FIGURE G-20: Pages 2-3

The Best Jewelry Tools Gathered from Around the World!

● ● ●　To Order Call: Mike Mendoza

● ● ●　Image Magic

Table of Contents

Product or service category _____ 2
Product or service category _____ 3
Product or service category _____ 4
Product or service category _____ 5
Product or service category _____ 6
Product or service category _____ 7
Product or service category _____ 8
Product or service category _____ 9
Product or service category _____ 10
Product or service category _____ 11
Product or service category _____ 12
Product or service category _____ 13
Product or service category _____ 14
Product or service category _____ 15

Page 2

Page 3

Washout image inserted and formatted

Line leaders inserted

Publisher 2002 Practice

▶ Concepts Review

Label each of the elements in the Publisher window shown in **Figure G-21**.

FIGURE G-21

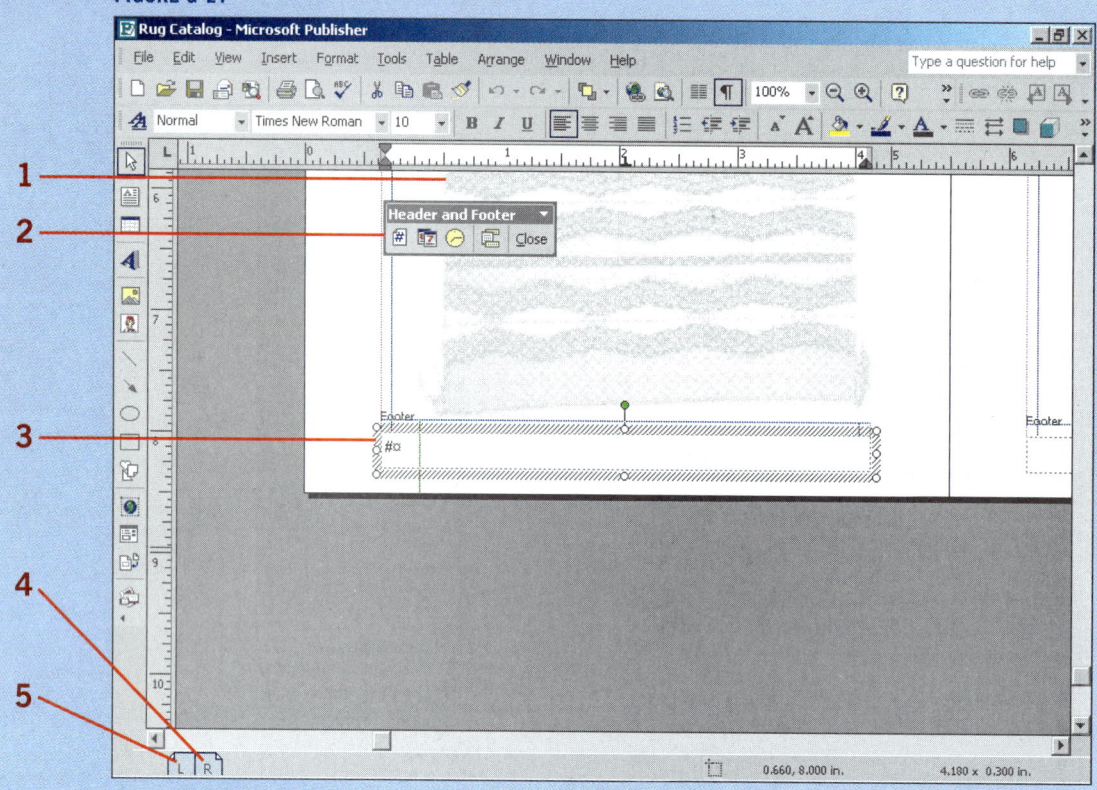

Match each of the features with the correct term, menu, dialog box, or command.

6. Footer
7. Format menu
8. Header
9. [Ctrl][M]
10. Tabs dialog box
11. Edit menu

a. Changes between Master Page and foreground page view
b. Text that repeats on the bottom of each page
c. Text that repeats at the top of each page
d. From here you can access the command that deletes a page
e. From here you can access the command that adds dot leaders
f. From here you can access the command that adds a drop cap

Select the best answer from the list of choices.

12. Each of the following is true about adding a page, except:
    a. Pages can be added before or after the current page.
    b. You can only add one page at a time.
    c. Existing layout guides are added to the new page(s).
    d. You can duplicate objects found on other pages in the publication.

Practice

13. Which command is used to toggle between Master Page and foreground page views?
    a. [Ctrl][M]
    b. [Ctrl][Y]
    c. [Ctrl][N]
    d. [Ctrl][B]
14. Where in a publication are headers and footers usually placed?
    a. AutoShapes
    b. Picture frame
    c. On the Clipboard
    d. On the Master Page(s)
15. Which character symbolizes automatic page numbers?
    a. @
    b. #
    c. !
    d. &

▶ Skills Review

1. **Add pages.**
   a. Start Publisher, then create a catalog for a video store. Use the Marquee Catalog. Use Personal Information sets. Close the task pane.
   b. Save the file as **Video Store Catalog** to the drive and folder where your Project Files are located.
   c. Display pages 2-3 in foreground view.
   d. Insert four pages after page 3 (each with two columns, text and pictures layout). You now have 12 pages.
   e. Save your work.

2. **Delete pages.**
   a. Display pages 8 and 9, then delete pages 8-11. (*Hint:* First delete pages 8 and 9, then repeat.)
   b. Display pages 6 and 7, then delete pages 6 and 7, then delete pages 4 and 5. You now have four pages.
   c. Display pages 2 and 3, then save your work.

3. **Work with a Master Page.**
   a. Change to Master Page view.
   b. Open the Insert Clip Art task pane, search My Collections and Office Collections for the text "TVs.", select the image j0229385.WMF, then close the Insert Clip Art task pane.
   c. Position the image so that its top-left corner is at ¾" H / 3" V.
   d. Press and hold [Shift], then drag the lower-right handle until the image is approximately 4" H x 2¾" V.
   e. Save your work.

4. **Create a header and footer.**
   a. Open the header on the left master page, type **Classic Videos**, then make the text bold.
   b. Type **Classic Videos** in the header on the right master page.
   c. Right-align the text in the right header text box, make the text bold, then save the publication.

5. **Add page numbers.**
   a. View the footer on the right page, then add page numbers to the footers on both pages with outside alignment.
   b. Close the Header and Footer toolbar, then return to foreground view.
   c. Delete the Page Number text boxes at the bottom of the left and right foreground pages (at 1" H / 17¾" V, and 9½" H / 17¾" V), then return to page 1.
   d. Prevent the page number from appearing on the first page, then save the publication.

WORKING WITH MULTIPLE PAGES

Publisher 2002   Practice

6. **Edit a story.**
   a. Use the page icon button on the status bar to return to page 2.
   b. Draw a text box at 1¼" H / 2½" V to 4¼" H / 6½" V.
   c. Insert the text file PUB G-5 into the text box, then open Word to edit the story.
   d. Add the following text in a matching font and text size as a new paragraph at the end of the story: **If we don't have what you're looking for, we can get it for you.** Close Word and return to the catalog, then verify that the text was added to the story.
   e. Add a three-line custom drop cap character to the first paragraph, then save the publication.

7. **Modify a table of contents.**
   a. Select the text box at 6½" H / 2" V on page 3 (the table of contents text), then open it in Word.
   b. Delete the entries for pages 1-3, then close Word and return to the catalog.
   c. Select the table of contents text, then change the tabs for the remaining entries to dot leaders.
   d. Change the remaining entries, using Table G-2 below. Delete any unnecessary text.
   e. Add a final entry to the Table of Contents that contains your name.
   f. Save your work, then print pages 2 and 3. Close the publication, but do not exit Publisher.

8. **Create a label.**
   a. Create a Video Face Label.
   b. Save the label as **Video Label** to the drive and folder where your Project Files are located.
   c. Change the Video Title text to **Sunset Boulevard**.
   d. Change the date text to the current date.
   e. Change the company name text to your name.
   f. Save your work, print the publication, then exit Publisher.

TABLE G-2

page headings	page #
1930s	4
1940s	6
1950s	8
1960s	10
Award Winners	12
Independent Films	14

▶ Independent Challenge 1

You are a member of a small theater group. You are asked to create the program for the next production.
   a. Start Publisher, then use the New Publication task pane and the Publication Gallery to select the Theater Program.
   b. Use Personal Information sets to enter appropriate information, then close the Publication Designs task pane.
   c. Save the publication as **Play Program** to the drive and folder where your Project Files are located.
   d. Use the View menu to add headers with the name of the play to each page. Choose any play with which you are familiar, such as *Rent*, *A Chorus Line*, or *Man of La Mancha*. Right-align the header on the right page.
   e. Insert page numbers at the bottoms of the pages. If necessary, move any information so that your header and footer fit correctly and are visible.
   f. Add any appropriate clip art to the master page, recoloring the clip art if necessary.
   g. Return to the foreground view, then make sure the page number, header, and footer do not appear on the first page.
   h. Delete the table containing the cast on page 2, then create a text box that will contain the names of cast members. Use friends and family members for cast members.
   i. Use Word to create and edit a paragraph describing the play in the existing text box on page 3.
   j. Replace any placeholders so that all of the text in the program pertains to the play you chose.
   k. Add your name as the director on page 1.
   l. Check the spelling in the publication, save and print the publication, then exit Publisher.

Practice

▶ Independent Challenge 2

You decide to use the Label Wizard in Publisher to create a shipping label you can use to send items to other people.
  a. Start Publisher, then select the Borders Shipping Label (Avery 5164).
  b. Use Personal Information sets to enter appropriate information, change to any color scheme you choose, then close the Publication Designs task pane.
  c. Save the publication as **Personal Shipping Label** to the drive and folder where your Project Files are located.
  d. Edit the return address information at 1" H / 1" V, using your name and address.
  e. Save and print the publication, then exit Publisher.

▶ Independent Challenge 3

A local elementary school asks you to design a newsletter for its staff and students. The staff and students will provide all of the stories except for one that you will write.
  a. Start Publisher, use the New Publication task pane and the Publication Gallery to select the Kid Stuff Newsletter.
  b. Use Personal Information sets to enter appropriate information.
  c. Change the color scheme to Orchid, then close the Color Schemes task pane.
  d. Save the publication as **School Newsletter** to the drive and folder where your Project Files are located.
  e. Delete pages 2 and 3. Open the Insert Pages dialog box. Click the Left-hand page list arrow, then click Calendar. Click the Right-hand page list arrow, click Response Form, then click OK.
  f. Replace the newsletter title with your elementary school's name, followed by the word **News**.
  g. Make up your own headings and replace at least one story with your own original story.
  h. Edit the story in Word if you have this program available to you, then check the spelling in the publication.
  i. Add your name in the Table of Contents on the first page of the newsletter.
  j. Save and print the publication, then exit Publisher.

▶ Independent Challenge 4

Your employer asks you to teach a one-day course on how to use Publisher. You decide to create a newsletter to inform the students about the features of Publisher, and show them an example of a great publication.
  a. Connect to the Internet and use your browser to go to www.microsoft.com. Find the home page for Publisher 2002.
  b. Find information about Publisher's highlights and capabilities, then print out any necessary information.
  c. Start Publisher if necessary, then select the newsletter of your choice.
  d. Save the publication as Publisher Newsletter to the drive and folder where your Project Files are located.
  e. Use Personal Information sets to enter appropriate information, then delete pages so that only two pages remain.
  f. Create a title, then create a lead and secondary story. Use information from the Publisher Web site.
  g. Add any clip art you feel is appropriate, then check the spelling in the publication.
  h. Create a text box on page 1, type your name, save and print the publication, then exit Publisher.

WORKING WITH MULTIPLE PAGES

Publisher 2002 Practice

▶ Visual Workshop

Open the file Pub G-6 from the drive and folder where your Project Files are stored. Save the publication as **Rug Collection Binder**. Use Figure G-22 as a guide. Replace all text as shown, and add the image NavajoRug3.tif to the master page, from the drive and folder where your Project Files are located. At the bottom of page 1, substitute your name. Save and print the page.

FIGURE G-22

NAVAJO RUGS

A Living History

Navajo Rug Association
Mike Mendoza, Manager

Publisher 2002

Unit H

Using
Special Features

Objectives

- ▶ Add BorderArt
- ▶ Design WordArt
- ▶ Wrap text around an object
- ▶ Rotate a text box
- ▶ Understand mail merge
- ▶ Create a mail merge
- ▶ Prepare for commercial printing
- ▶ Use the Pack and Go Wizard
- ▶ Capstone Project: Automotive Gift Certificate

Now that you have a real grasp of Publisher basics, you are ready to explore adding interesting elements to your work, and how to get your message in the mail. You can add fancy borders to text boxes, create curved text designs, wrap text around a frame, rotate text boxes, make your work portable, and get it into the hands of your audience. Emma Rose is a manager for Piano Forte, a company that sells and services pianos. Emma is reviewing and enhancing a draft of the design work done by Image Magic on a brochure. Emma wants the publication to be polished and include detailed text and graphics. She will use a customer database to address each brochure.

Unit H
Publisher 2002

Adding BorderArt

Attractive borders can add pizzazz to a publication. Borders can be added to any frame or text box. As with any design element, judicious use creates a smart, professional look; overuse distracts from the message. **BorderArt** allows you to use fancy decorative borders that come with Publisher, or develop your own unique borders. A border is added to a text box using the BorderArt dialog box. ✍ Emma wants to add an eye-catching, imaginative border design to the first page of the brochure.

Steps

1. Start Publisher, open the file **Pub H-1** from the drive and folder where your Project Files are located, then save it as **Piano Brochure**
   The brochure appears on the screen.

2. Click the text box at **8" H / 1" V**
   Compare your screen to Figure H-1. Once a frame or object is selected, you can modify its border.

3. Press **[F9]**, right-click the **text box**, click **Format Text Box**, then click the **BorderArt button**
   The BorderArt dialog box opens. Borders can be simple lines of varying thickness or color, or they can be graphic images that will help reinforce the theme of your document. You want a border that suggests a musical theme.

4. Scroll through the **Available Borders list**, then click **Music Notes**
   Figure H-2 shows the BorderArt dialog box with the Music Notes border selected. Available borders are listed in alphabetical order. When you click a border, the sample appears around the perimeter of the Preview box. You can change the size of the individual images in BorderArt to modify the border's appearance.

5. Click the **Always apply at default size check box** to deselect it, click **OK**, select the contents of the **Weight text box**, type **14**, then click **OK**
   The BorderArt pattern appears on the edge of the text box, as shown in Figure H-3. Now that the BorderArt has been added to the object, you are on your way to creating a brochure that has the style you want.

6. Press **[F9]**, then click the **Save button** 🖫 on the Standard toolbar

> **QuickTip**
> To remove existing BorderArt from a selected text box, open the Format Text Box dialog box, select the Color and Lines tab, click the Preset that represents the configuration you want, then click OK.

Design Matters

Creating custom BorderArt
Almost any simple clip art or graphic image can be turned into BorderArt. Once the BorderArt dialog box is open, click the Create Custom button. You can choose from images in the Clip Gallery, or elsewhere on your computer. You can even create BorderArt from images you created. Click the Choose Picture button, locate the image, click the image, click OK, choose a name for your border, then click OK.

FIGURE H-1: Text box selected

BorderArt will be applied to text box

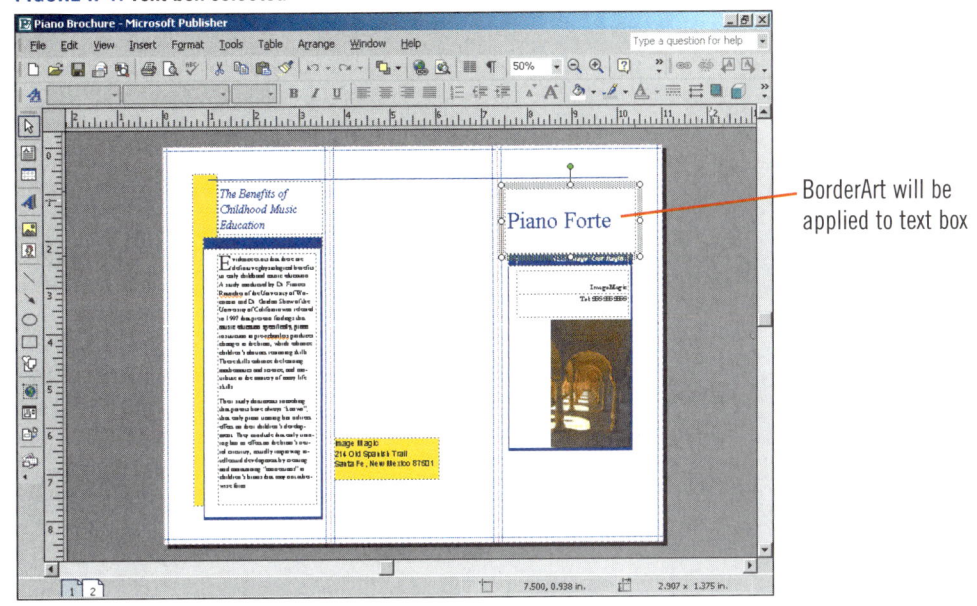

FIGURE H-2: BorderArt dialog box

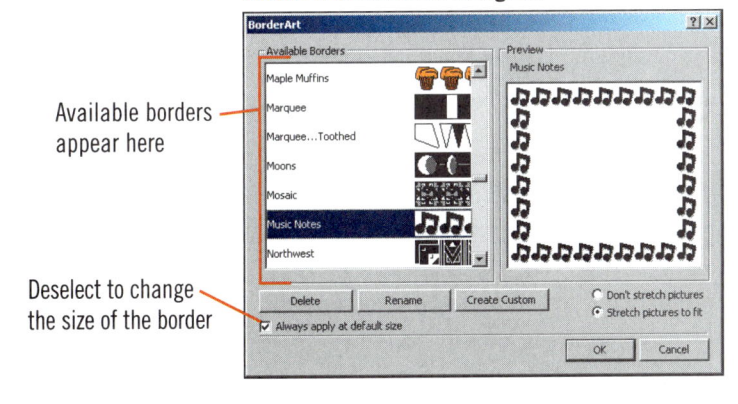

Available borders appear here

Deselect to change the size of the border

FIGURE H-3: BorderArt added to text box

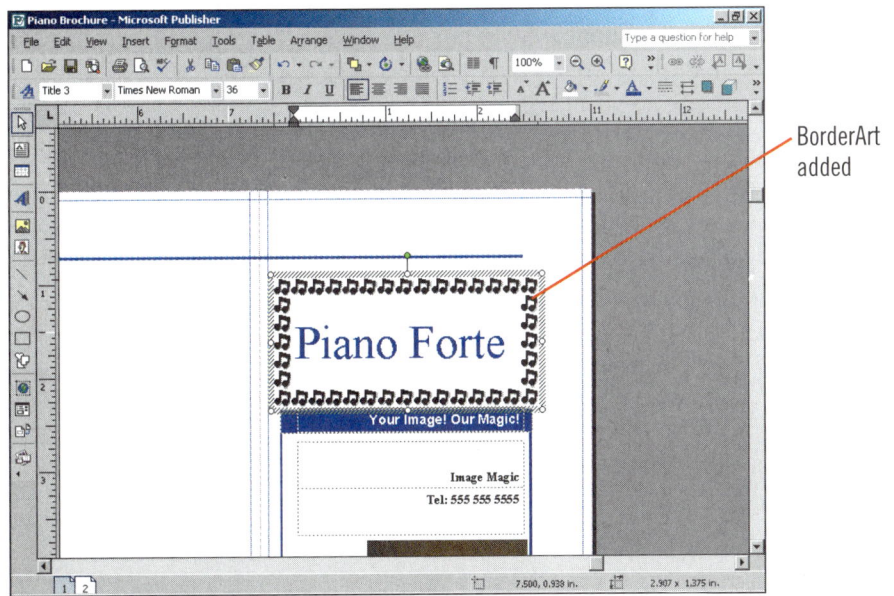

BorderArt added

USING SPECIAL FEATURES   PUBLISHER 171

Publisher 2002

Publisher 2002

Designing WordArt

You have probably seen text in publications that is curved, or in a specific shape, such as a circle or semi-circle. This effect can be created using **WordArt**. WordArt gives you a wide variety of text styles and effects from which to choose. Text can be transformed into many shapes, shadows and patterns can be added, and text color can be changed. Emma wants to add WordArt to the right panel of page 2 to identify the store on what will be the back cover of the flyer. As a design goal, Emma wants to emphasize the curve of the piano in the image at the bottom of the panel by curving the WordArt.

Steps

1. Click the **page 2 icon** on the status bar, click the **Insert WordArt button** on the Objects toolbar, then click the **first box in the second row** of the WordArt Gallery
   The WordArt Gallery displays 30 WordArt styles, as shown in Figure H-4.

2. Click **OK**, type **Piano Forte** in the Edit WordArt Text dialog box, click the **Size list arrow**, click **28**, then click **OK**
   The Piano Forte WordArt object and the WordArt toolbar appear on the screen. You want to place the text in the upper-right corner.

3. Using , drag the WordArt object so that its upper-left corner is at **8¼" H / ½" V**
   You can change the shape of the WordArt so that the text curves in a way to complement the curves of the piano.

4. Click the **WordArt Shape button** on the WordArt toolbar, then click **Wave 2** (the sixth shape from the left in the third row)
   The text takes on a "wavy" shape. You think that the color of the WordArt should be the blue accent color to match the color already in use and create a focal point that draws the reader's eye across the page.

5. Click the **Format WordArt button** on the WordArt toolbar, click the **Fill Color list arrow**, click the **Accent 1 (blue) color box**, then click **OK**
   The text looks good. You think that the addition of shadows to the text would improve your design by adding an illusion of depth to the panel.

6. Click the **Shadow Style button** on the Formatting toolbar, then click **Shadow Style 6** (the second from the left in the second row)
   The shadows appear in the text design.

7. Click anywhere on the **scratch area**
   The WordArt is deselected and the WordArt toolbar closes. Compare your page to Figure H-5.

8. Click the **Save button** on the Standard toolbar

▶ PUBLISHER 172 USING SPECIAL FEATURES

FIGURE H-4: WordArt Gallery

FIGURE H-5: WordArt design in publication

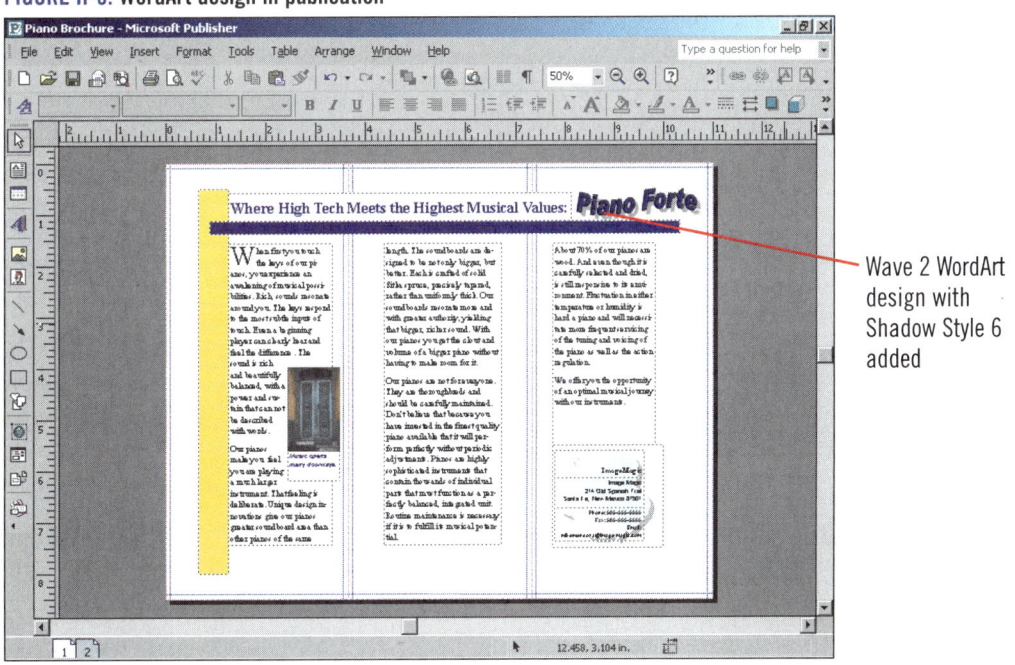

Wave 2 WordArt design with Shadow Style 6 added

TABLE H-1: WordArt toolbar buttons

button	name	description
	Insert WordArt	Opens WordArt Gallery
Edit Text...	Edit Text	Opens Edit WordArt Text dialog box
	WordArt Gallery	Contains WordArt style samples
	Format WordArt	Allows application of formatting attributes
Abc	WordArt Shape	Allows you to change the current WordArt shape
	Text Wrapping	Determines how text wraps with the WordArt object
Aa	WordArt Same Letter Heights	Makes all letter heights equal
	WordArt Vertical Text	Places text on the vertical axis
	WordArt Alignment	Allows you to change text alignment
AV	WordArt Character Spacing	Allows you to change the character spacing within the WordArt object

USING SPECIAL FEATURES   PUBLISHER 173

Publisher 2002

Publisher 2002 — Unit H

Wrapping Text Around an Object

You can enhance the appeal of a story by **wrapping** text around an image or other object. The careful integration of an image with text creates a polished look, and can contribute to the design. Depending on an object's width, a story can appear at the top and bottom, or along the sides, of a frame surrounding an image. For added effect, you can make the text flow around the image within the frame, and even control how the text wraps around the image by using the Edit Wrap Points feature. Emma likes what she has done so far, but wants to experiment with adding another image of a piano to page 2. She thinks that adding an object to the lower-left of the publication would create a new focal point, and wrapping text around an image could guide the reader's eyes across the page. The image of a piano will reinforce the subject matter of the brochure and direct the reader's eyes up and to the right.

Steps

1. Right-click the **photograph** at **3" H / 4½" V**, then click **Delete Object**
   The placeholder image disappears, and the text fills that space. You will need the additional space to insert another image of a piano.

2. Click **Insert** on the menu bar, point to **Picture**, click **From File**, click **Piano1.tif** from the drive and folder where your Project Files are located, then click **Insert**
   The piano image is attractive. Now you will place it in the publication.

3. Right-click the **picture**, click **Format Picture**, click the **Layout tab**, select the contents of the **Horizontal text box** in the Position on page section, type **1.25**, select the contents of the **Vertical text box** in the Position on page section, type **5.5**, then click **OK**
   The picture frame is inserted into the text box and Publisher's default text wrapping style, square, has been applied, as shown in Figure H-7. The image takes up so much space inside the connected text boxes that some text in the third text box doesn't fit. To make space for this text and enhance the appeal of the design, you choose a different wrapping style.

> **QuickTip**
> Text wrapping can create awkward-looking hyphenations and isolated gaps of white space.

4. Right-click the **picture**, click **Format Picture**, click the **Layout tab**, click the **Tight Wrapping Style button**, then click **OK**
   Text is tightly wrapped around the image and slants upward along the lines of the image, as shown in Figure H-8. You don't see any problems with hyphenation, and the text that was in overflow is now inside the text box.

5. Click the **Save button** on the Standard toolbar

Design Matters

Editing shapes for text wrapping

Publisher lets you display and edit the handles surrounding any object to modify text wrapping. To edit shapes, select the image, click Arrange on the menu bar, click Text Wrapping, then click Edit Wrap Points. Each of the handles will appear around the image. You can add or delete handles by pressing and holding [Ctrl]. Figure H-6 shows the handles on an irregularly shaped picture with some of the handles moved to illustrate how that affects text wrapping. You can click and drag any handle to create interesting effects.

FIGURE H-6: Text wrapped around points surrounding image

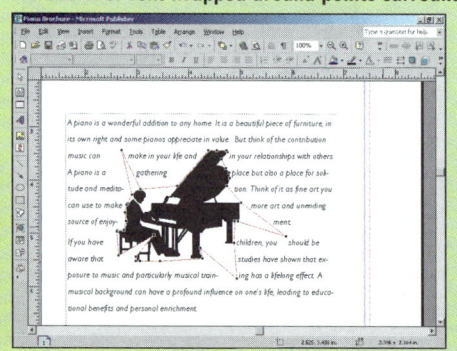

PUBLISHER 174   USING SPECIAL FEATURES

FIGURE H-7: Image inserted in text box

Square text wrapping style is the default

FIGURE H-8: Text wrapped to image

Tight text wrapping style applied

Slant of the wrapped text complements the image

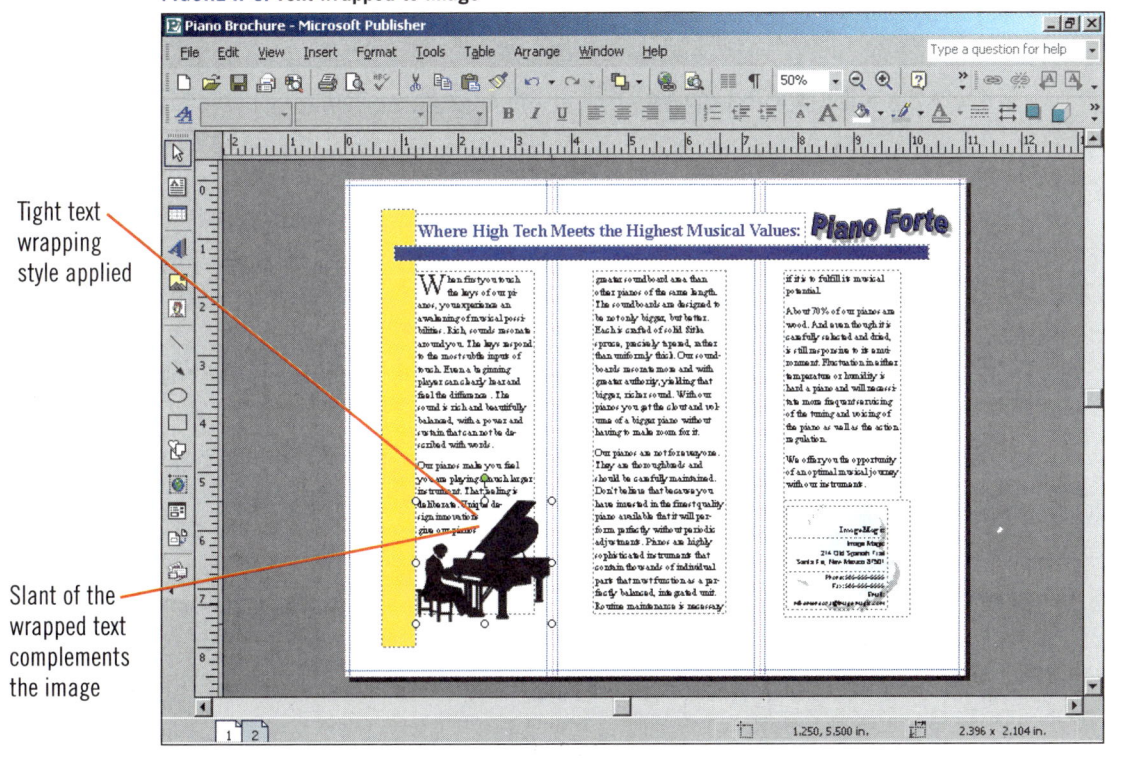

USING SPECIAL FEATURES   PUBLISHER 175

Rotating a Text Box

Publisher 2002

You can rotate a text box to create interesting effects. Enhancing a design is just one reason for rotating a text box—you may need to reorient text for a specific purpose, such as when a publication will be folded and mailed. By carefully arranging the design of the publication, you can include the recipient's address and your return address in the layout so that it can be folded and mailed with minimal effort and maximum attractiveness. Emma wants to use a rotated text box on the bottom of the first panel to add important text. She also needs to prepare the brochure for mailing. She will create a text box, enter her message, then rotate it into position on the page. Then she will rotate a text box that contains the store's return address on the second panel, and create a text box to hold the recipient's address.

Steps

1. Click the **page 1 icon**, click the **Text Box button** on the Objects toolbar, then drag ✛ from **7¾" H / 7¼" V** to **10¼" H / 7¾" V**
   Once the text box is drawn, you can add your text.

2. Type **In-Store Piano Lessons**
   The text appears in the text box, but it is too small to be legible.

   > **QuickTip**
   > The promotional text should be brief but prominent; it is a visual analogy to a sound bite.

3. Press **[Ctrl][A]**, click the **Font list arrow** [Times New Roman] on the Formatting toolbar, click **Arial Narrow**, click the **Font size list arrow** [12.2] on the Formatting toolbar, click **18**, click the **Bold button**, then press **[Esc]**
   Compare your screen to Figure H-9. You can rotate the text box to any angle.

4. Right-click the **text box**, click **Format Text Box**, click the **Size tab**, make sure that the height of the box is **0.5"** and the width is **2.5"**, select the contents of the **Rotation text box**, type **20**, then click **OK**
   The text box is rotated 20 degrees. Since the text indicates a promotional offer, it should be made more noticeable by adding an attractive fill color.

   > **QuickTip**
   > You can drag the text box into different positions and use the green rotation handle to fine-tune the positioning.

5. Click the **Fill Color list arrow** on the Formatting toolbar, then click the **Accent 2 (yellow) color box**
   You want to prepare the brochure for mailing. The center panel will contain the customer's address, the return address, and postage. You start by rotating the return address to the proper orientation.

6. Click the text box at **5" H / 6½" V**, click **Arrange** on the menu bar, point to **Rotate or Flip**, then click **Rotate Left**
   With the return address placed and oriented, you must insert a text box to hold the recipient's address, and rotate it to the proper position.

7. Click, then drag ✛ from **4½" H / 3" V** to **7" H / 4½" V**, click **Arrange** on the menu bar, point to **Rotate or Flip**, then click **Rotate Left**
   Compare your work to Figure H-10.

8. Click the **Save button** on the Standard toolbar

PUBLISHER 176 USING SPECIAL FEATURES

FIGURE H-9: Completed text in text box

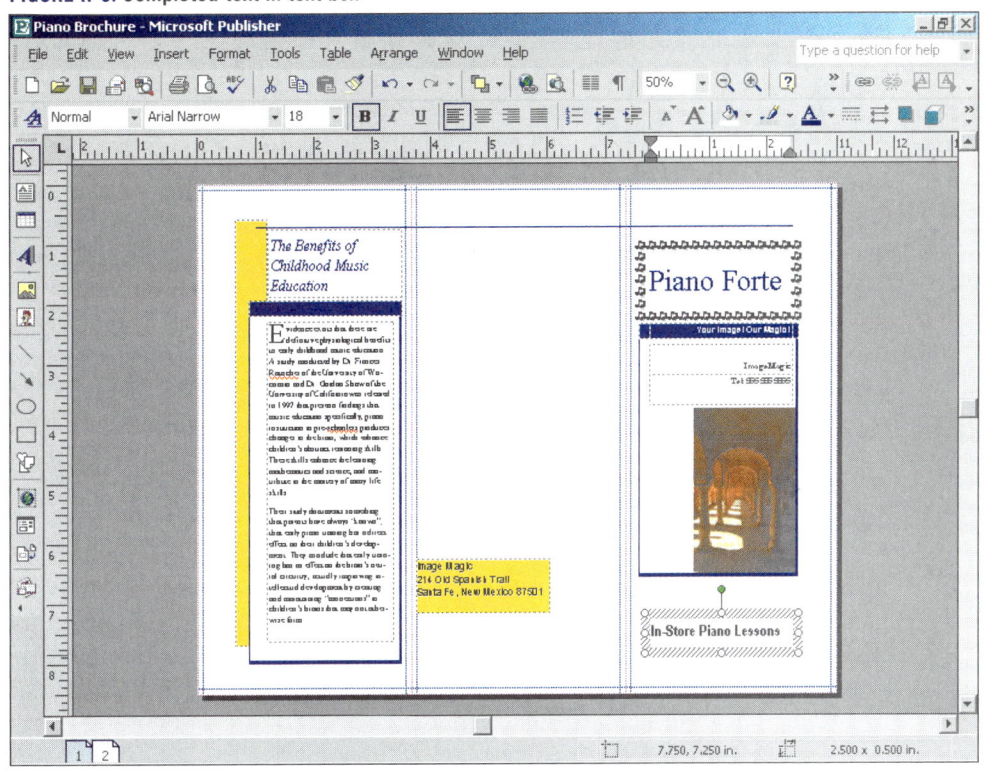

FIGURE H-10: Rotated text boxes

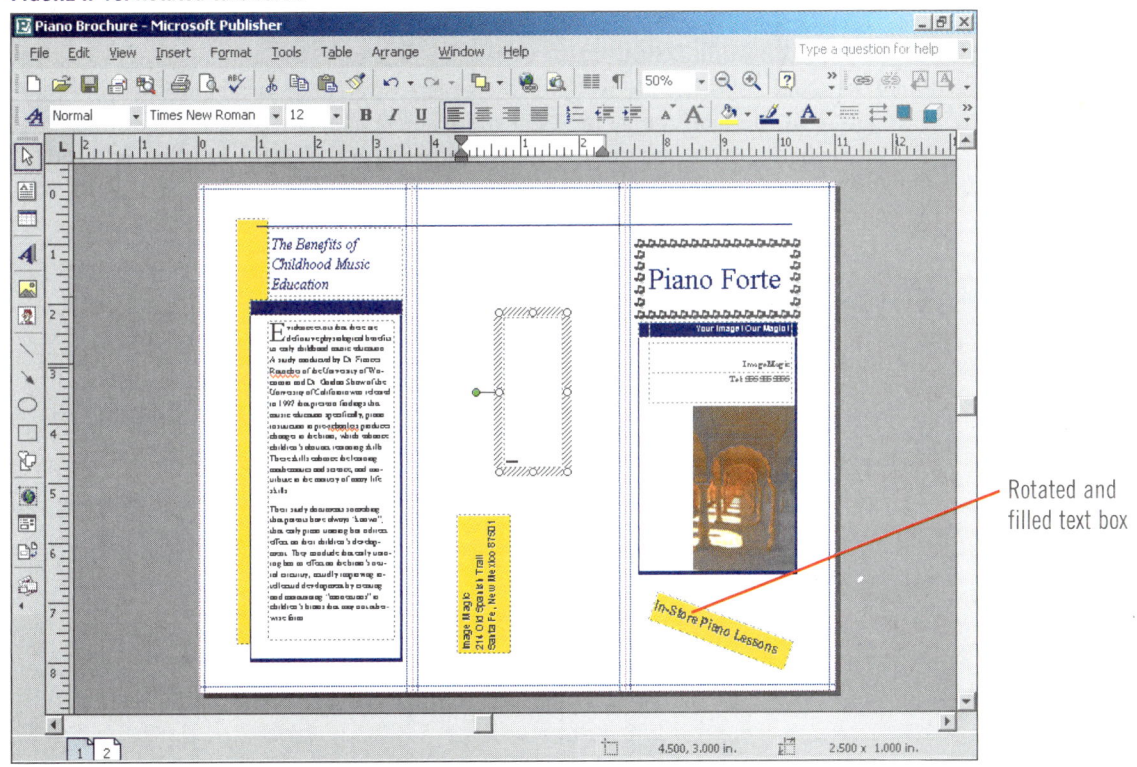

Rotated and filled text box

USING SPECIAL FEATURES   PUBLISHER 177

Publisher 2002

Understanding Mail Merge

A **mail merge** blends a publication that contains generic information with a data source that contains unique pieces of information. For example, a Publisher-generated gift certificate could contain the store's location and details about the gift, but the first and last names of each of the recipients would have to come from a data source. Combining the two documents results in many customized versions of the publication. Figure H-11 shows an overview of a mail merge. Types of publications that can be customized include sales literature, postcards, greeting and invitation cards, catalogs, award certificates, gift certificates, and labels. Emma knows that once the publication is complete, Piano Forte will want the brochure personalized with information it has collected about potential customers. Before she begins the mail merge process, she considers all the necessary steps.

▶ Select the recipients

A **data source** is the file that contains information about the recipients. A data source is made up of fields organized into records. A **field** is a category of information—such as last name, first name, address, state, or zip code. A **record** is a set of information about an individual or an item—for example, a person's complete address. **Data source files** can come from several programs, but you will most likely use a database, a spreadsheet, a Microsoft Outlook contact list, or a table from a word processing program.

If you don't have a data source file from another program, or prefer to create a new one, you can create one using Publisher. The creation and entry of information is easy because the Mail Merge Wizard guides you through building the file, entering information, and saving it. The Mail Merge Wizard offers choices as to the type of information you can collect for the data source file, and even lets you add your own fields. Some commonly used mail merge information fields are address, city, zip code, country, e-mail address, and home phone.

▶ Create the publication

The actual Publisher file contains the generic information that appears in every merged publication. In the mail merge process, you insert a text box or a table frame that will contain the merge fields, where the unique information about the recipient is placed inside the publication. For example, you can insert the person's name in the Greeting line so that it will read "Dear John Smith". With the Mail Merge Wizard, it is easy to go back and edit the fields until you get exactly the publication you want.

▶ Preview the publications

This feature allows you to look over the merged output before it is printed to catch any mistakes without wasting paper. This is particularly important since printing and mailing publications is so expensive. Paper, inks, envelopes, and even bulk postal rates are costly.

▶ Print the publication

Publisher's Mail Merge Wizard uses dialog boxes to guide you through printing your publications.

FIGURE H-11: Mail merge process

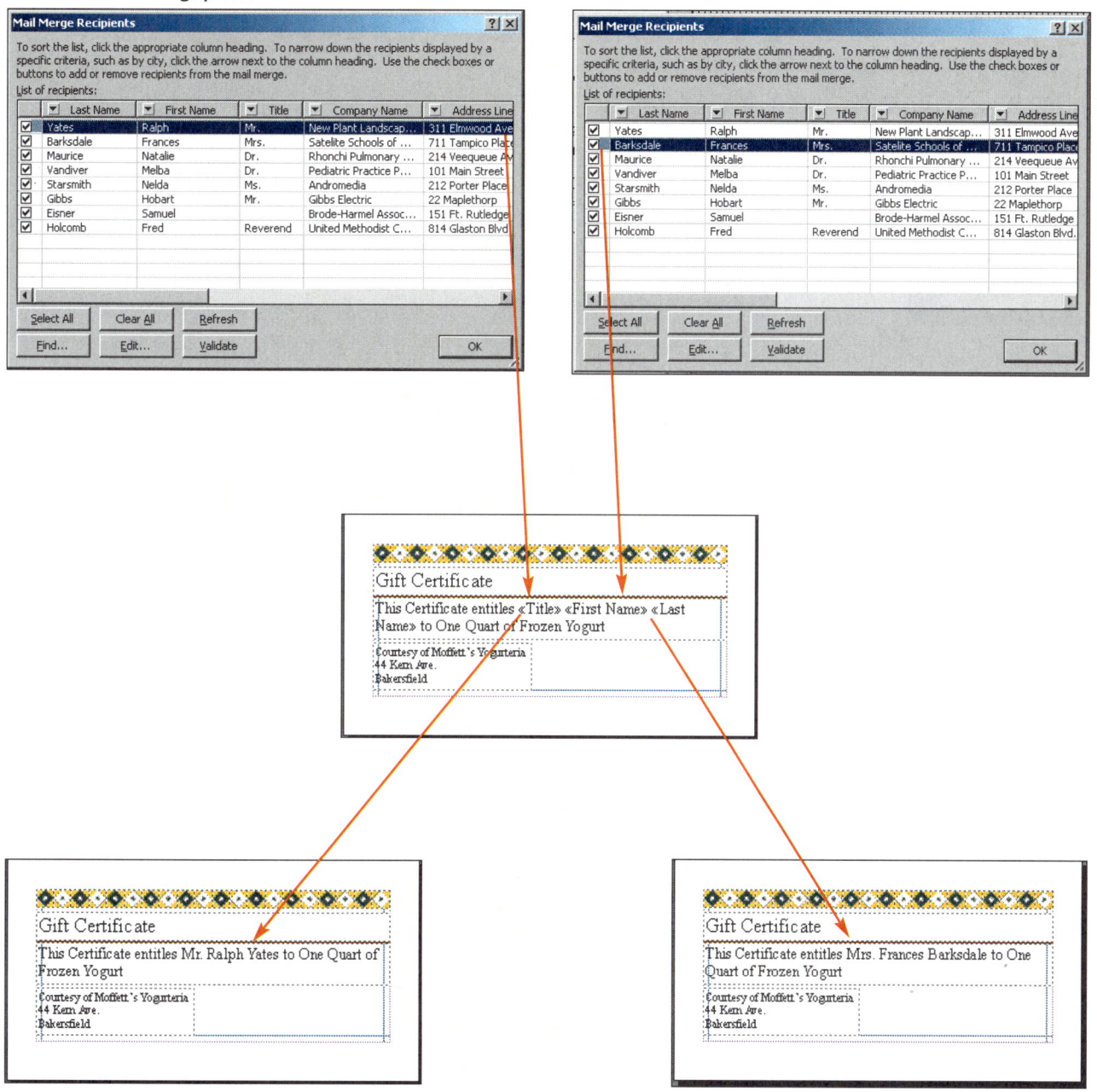

Design Matters

Catching costly errors

There are several types of spelling errors that demand your attention. The most obvious is the danger of misspelled words in a publication. Such errors make your company seem unprofessional. Another important spelling error is the misspelling of a person's name. Errors in people's names and titles are offensive to them. A simple misspelling or a misuse of Mrs. or Ms. may annoy potential clients to the point that they will not do business with your company. When in doubt, find a way to verify a potential misspelling: it pays off. Bulk mailings are often a one-way communication and you may never know that a recipient was offended.

USING SPECIAL FEATURES   PUBLISHER 179

Publisher 2002

Creating a Mail Merge

The **Mail Merge Wizard** is an effective way of creating personalized publications. The wizard consists of four task panes that guide you though the process and allow you to customize your document. It unites the power of the database and the functionality of the desktop publishing program. To test the effectiveness of the brochure, Emma wants to personalize the brochure to send to a small group of potential customers that have children. She wants to add their addresses to the middle panel of the second page.

Steps

1. Click **Tools** on the menu bar, point to **Mail Merge**, then click **Mail Merge Wizard**
   The Mail Merge task pane opens, displaying the first of four pages. This page lets you select the recipients from existing lists or Outlook contacts, or create a new list.

2. Click **Browse** in the Use an existing list section, open the file **Pub H-2** from the drive and folder where your Project Files are located, then click **OK** in the Mail Merge Recipients dialog box
   Once the data source file is selected, you can move on to the next task pane page.

3. Click **Next: Create the publication** at the bottom of the Mail Merge task pane, if necessary click the text box at **5½" H / 4" V** to select it, click **Address block** on the Mail Merge task pane, then click **OK** to accept all the defaults in the Insert Address Block dialog box shown in Figure H-12
   The Insert Address Block dialog box provides a wide variety of ways to insert the recipient's name in the address block, and shows a preview of how it will look. On your screen, the address block field appears in the text box. It is difficult to read on the screen since it is rotated 90 degrees, but when the publications are printed and folded the recipient's address will be in just the right spot for mailing.

4. Click **Next: Preview the publications** at the bottom of the Mail Merge task pane
   The third task pane opens and the address of the first recipient is inserted in the text box.

> **Trouble?**
> If you added extra spaces to either the Title or Name fields, the spaces will appear in the text box, and your name and title will be shown with the extra spaces.

5. Click **Edit recipient list**, click the first entry in the Mail Merge Recipients dialog box, then click the **Edit button**
   Compare your screen to Figure H-13.

6. Replace the first three entries with your preferred title and your first and last names, click **Close**, then click **OK**
   Your name and title should appear in the text box on the brochure. Compare your screen to Figure H-14.

7. Click **Next: Complete the merge** at the bottom of the Mail Merge task pane, click **Print**, make sure that the correct printer is selected, then click the **Test button** in the Print Merge dialog box
   Examine your publication. If you find any mistakes in the mail merge, use the Previous Wizard Step commands at the bottom of the task pane to go back and correct the mistakes. If necessary, print the pages again using the Test button.

8. Click the **Cancel button** to close the Print Merge dialog box, then click the **Close button** on the Mail Merge task pane

9. Click the **Save button** on the Standard toolbar

▶ PUBLISHER 180   USING SPECIAL FEATURES

FIGURE H-12: Insert Address Block dialog box

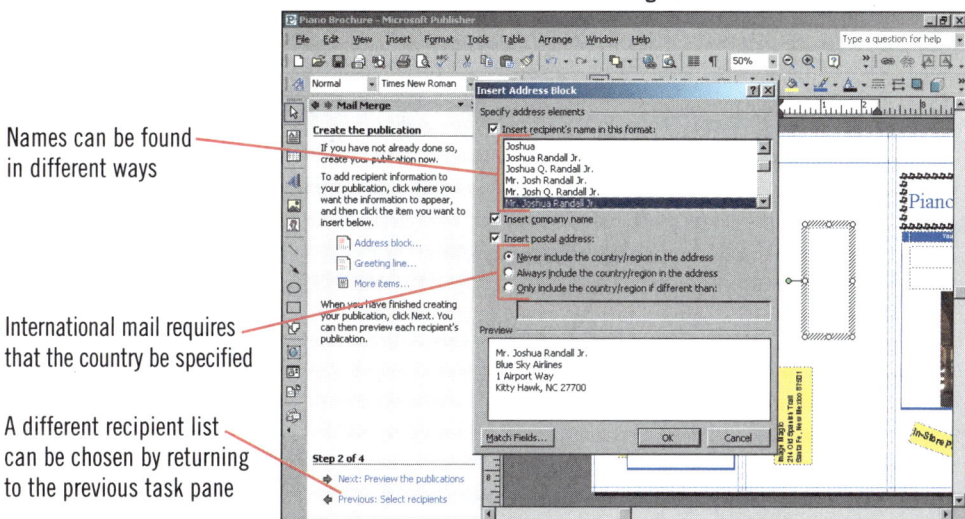

- Names can be found in different ways
- International mail requires that the country be specified
- A different recipient list can be chosen by returning to the previous task pane

FIGURE H-13: Mail Merge Recipients dialog box

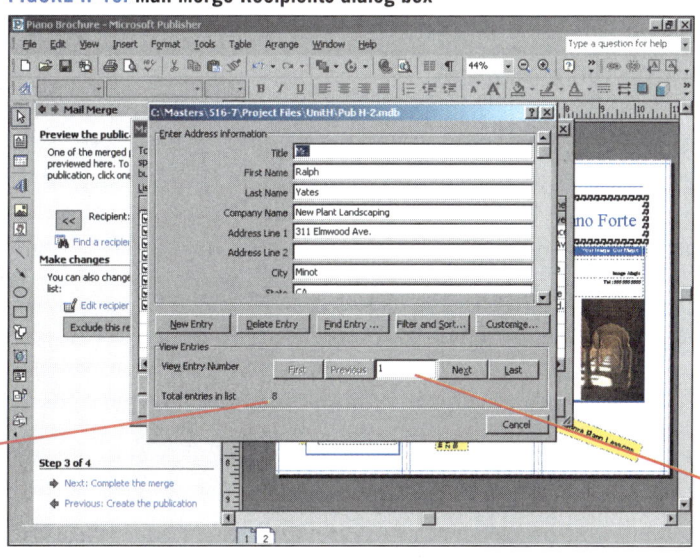

- Number of recipients on list
- View is of first entry

FIGURE H-14: Preview of the mail merge

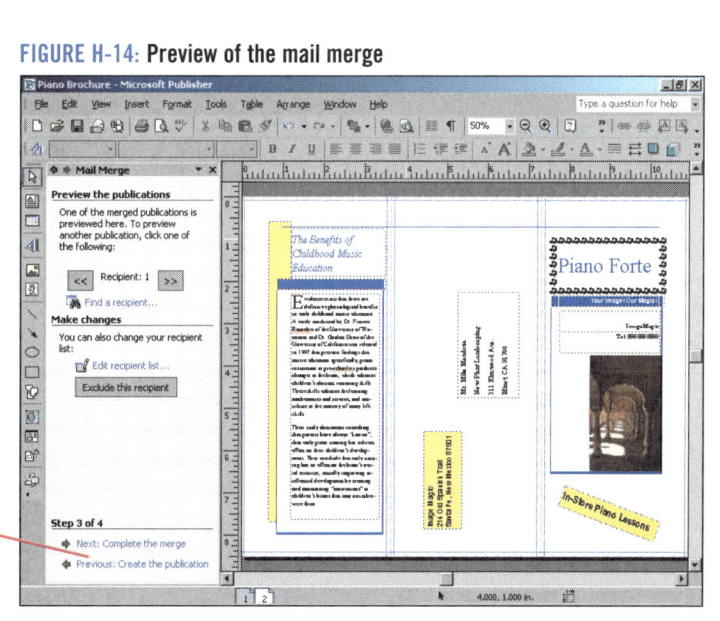

- Corrections and modifications can still be made in the previous task panes

USING SPECIAL FEATURES   PUBLISHER 181

Preparing for Commercial Printing

Once your publication is completed, you can print it yourself, or send the files to a commercial printer for bulk printing with high-quality options and results. For professional output, it is important to consult with the printer during the design process to save time and expense. Emma knows that once the project is complete and successfully tested, Piano Forte will want the brochure professionally printed. She examines the commercial printing options so she can start making arrangements.

Details

▶ Consult the commercial printing professionals early

Cost is important. You will need to know about quantity, quality, paper stock, binding, folding, trimming, and deadlines so that you can determine a budget and schedule. Ask your printer for recommendations on ways to reduce costs. For example, updating your own graphics by doing your own scanning, or creating your own art files instead of relying on the printer's art services may reduce expenses.

▶ Determine the file format

Once the printer is selected, find out the required hand-off format. The **hand-off format** is the final format the printer receives. Publisher can create files in the PostScript or Publisher formats. There are advantages to using the Publisher format, but your options may be limited depending on the commercial printing service you choose. You also need to know if your printer prefers to accept transferred files on disks, or electronically, such as by e-mail.

▶ Explore the PostScript file format

If your commercial printer doesn't accept Publisher files, or uses only Macintosh computers, you can use the **PostScript** file format. To do this, you can use Publisher's Help feature to install a PostScript printer driver on your computer, then follow the steps to use this driver. Figure H-15 shows the Save As PostScript File dialog box.

Ask your commercial printing service if it wants you to apply any specific print settings, then save the publication in the PostScript format. Be aware that due to its large size, you may not be able to save a PostScript file directly to a floppy disk. Try saving to your hard drive, then copying to a floppy disk, or transferring the file to the commercial printer via the Internet.

▶ Learn about the Publisher format and the Pack and Go Wizard

If your commercial printing service accepts Publisher format hand-off files, you can take advantage of several important features. The Publisher format is accessible with the Pack and Go Wizard, and verifies linked graphics, embeds TrueType fonts, and will pack all the files your printing service might need.

The printing service can use Publisher format to do **pre-press work**. As part of this process, the printer can verify the availability of fonts and linked graphics, make color corrections or separations, and set the final printing options. Figure H-16 shows the Fonts dialog box, and Figure H-17 shows the Graphics Manager dialog box. Each of these dialog boxes gives your printing service important information about elements that make up your publication. If any of these elements is missing, the printer will be able to tell you exactly where the trouble lies.

QuickTip

Once the file is saved as a PostScript, you cannot make any changes to it, so be sure to ask your commercial printer if it wants you to apply specific print settings.

FIGURE H-15: Save As PostScript File dialog box

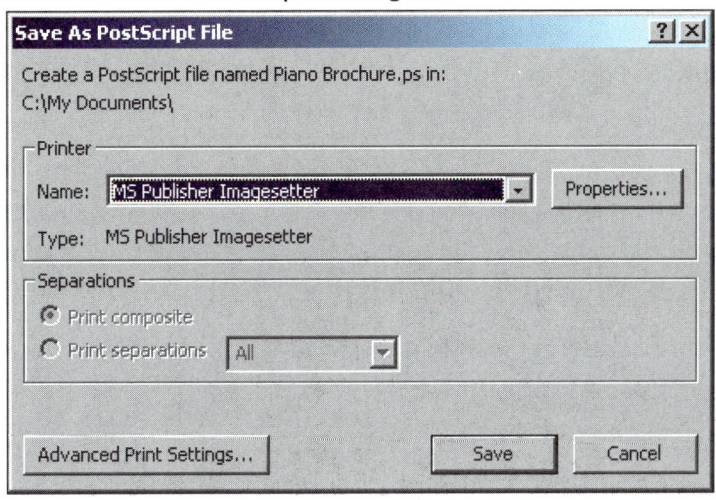

FIGURE H-16: Fonts dialog box

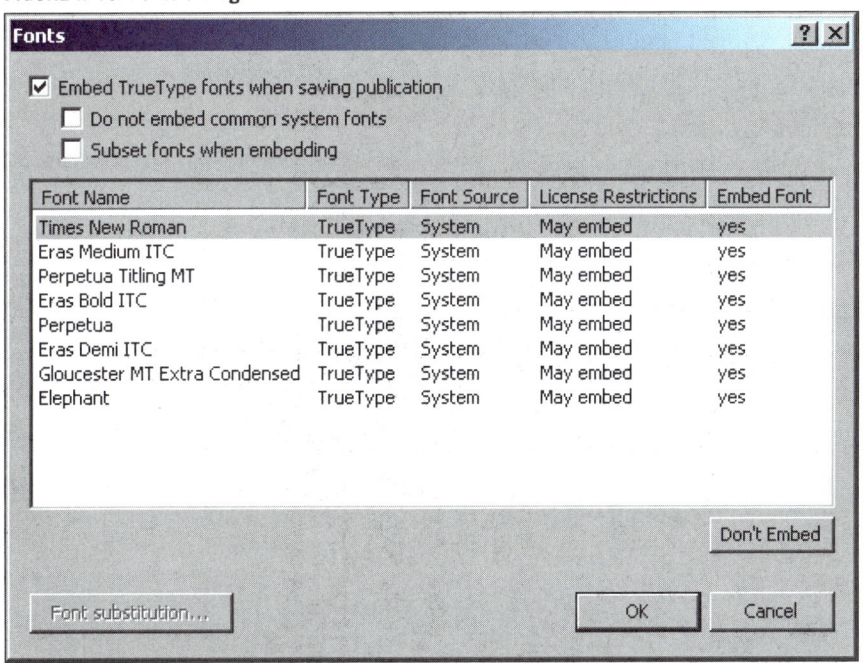

FIGURE H-17: Graphics Manager dialog box

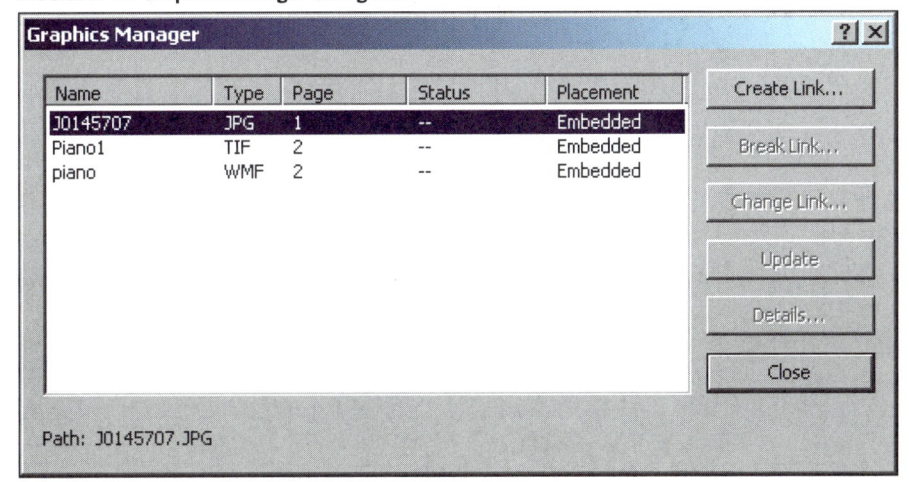

USING SPECIAL FEATURES   PUBLISHER 183

Publisher 2002

Using the Pack and Go Wizard

For this lesson, you will need a blank, formatted disk. You may need to put a publication on a disk to take to a commercial printing service, or to use at another computer. The **Pack and Go Wizard** lets you package all the fonts and graphic images needed to work with your publication elsewhere. Emma arranged to have the Piano Forte brochure printed by a commercial printing service. Since she has never used the Pack and Go Wizard, she wants to become familiar with it so she can use it easily, when necessary.

Steps

QuickTip
If you are using a floppy disk for your Project Files, save the Publisher file to a new blank formatted floppy disk before beginning this lesson.

1. Click **File** on the menu bar, point to **Pack and Go**, then click **Take to a Commercial Printing Service**
   The Pack and Go Wizard dialog box opens, as shown in Figure H-18. The first Pack and Go Wizard dialog box explains the advantages of using the wizard. The items included in the packaged publication file include embedded TrueType fonts and linked graphics. As part of the packing process, the wizard also prints the publication.

2. Click **Next**
   The second Pack and Go Wizard dialog box lets you determine where you want the packaged files.

3. Make sure the **A:\ option button** is selected, place a blank formatted floppy disk in drive A, then click **Next**
   The third Pack and Go Wizard dialog box lets you decide what attributes to include. You can embed TrueType fonts, include linked graphics, and create links for embedded graphics, or you can deselect any of these options, if necessary. By default, all three check boxes are selected.

4. Click **Next**
   The fourth Pack and Go Wizard dialog box is shown in Figure H-19. It lets you know the options you've selected, the file-naming scheme it will use, and how to unpack the files.

5. Click **Finish**
   As the Pack and Go Wizard works, you'll see that as the files are completed, several processes take place. The files are compressed and your publication (Piano Brochure.pub) is saved as packed01.puz. Once the publication has been successfully packed, the final Pack and Go Wizard dialog box appears, as shown in Figure H-20.

6. Click **OK**
   As part of the packaging process, the Wizard prints the publication.

7. Click **File** on the menu bar, then click **Exit**

Taking files to another computer

Using the Pack and Go Wizard to take a publication to another computer is similar to using it to take a publication to a commercial printing service. To use the Pack and Go Wizard to package files for another computer, click File on the menu bar, point to Pack and Go, then click Take to Another Computer. Click Next to advance through the dialog boxes, click Finish, then click OK.

▶ PUBLISHER 184   USING SPECIAL FEATURES

FIGURE H-18: First Pack and Go Wizard dialog box

Pack and Go Wizard

Prepare your files for commercial printing

The wizard will prepare your publication to take to a commercial printing service.

You can use the wizard to:

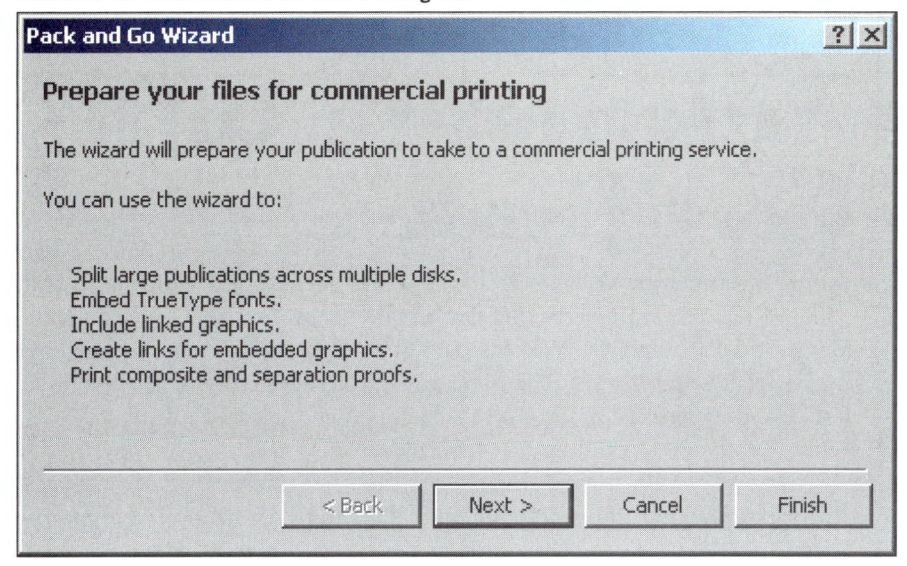

- Split large publications across multiple disks.
- Embed TrueType fonts.
- Include linked graphics.
- Create links for embedded graphics.
- Print composite and separation proofs.

[< Back] [Next >] [Cancel] [Finish]

Figure H-19: Fourth Pack and Go Wizard dialog box

Pack and Go Wizard

Pack my publication

When you click Finish, the wizard will:

- Compress your publication into a file named "packed01.puz" and save it on drive A:\.
- Embed TrueType fonts used in your publication.
- Include linked graphics.
- Create links for embedded graphics.

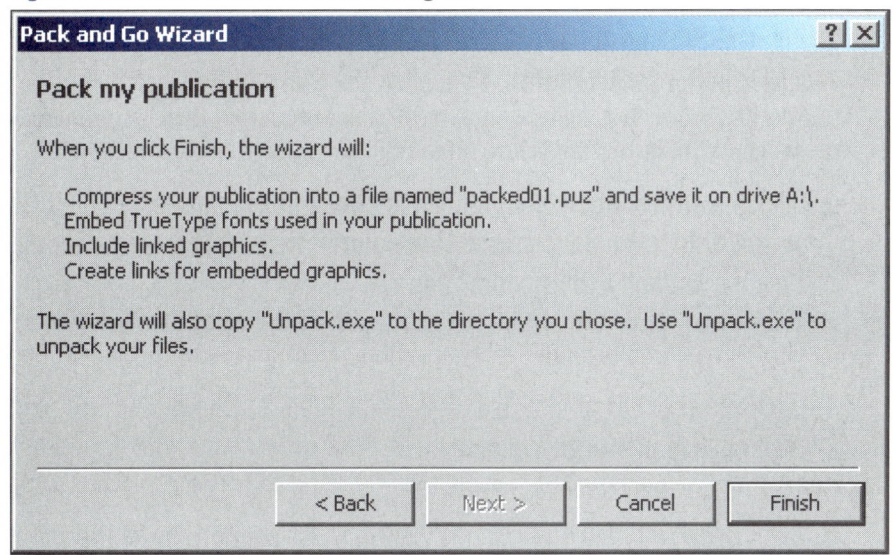

The wizard will also copy "Unpack.exe" to the directory you chose. Use "Unpack.exe" to unpack your files.

[< Back] [Next >] [Cancel] [Finish]

Figure H-20: Final Pack and Go Wizard dialog box

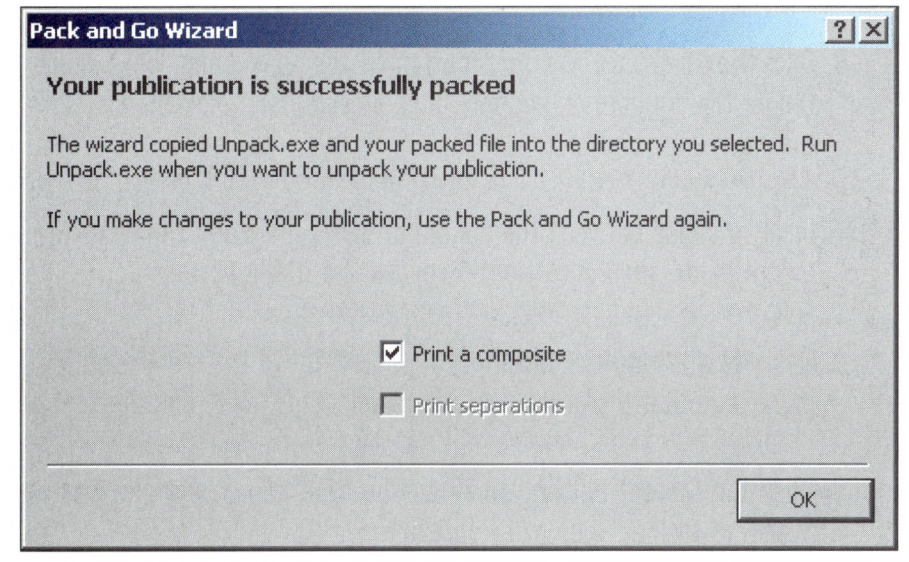

Pack and Go Wizard

Your publication is successfully packed

The wizard copied Unpack.exe and your packed file into the directory you selected. Run Unpack.exe when you want to unpack your publication.

If you make changes to your publication, use the Pack and Go Wizard again.

☑ Print a composite
☐ Print separations

[OK]

Capstone Project: Automotive Gift Certificate

Publisher 2002 — Unit H

You have learned the skills necessary to add BorderArt and WordArt to publications. You have wrapped text around objects and rotated text boxes. You have learned about and used the Mail Merge and Pack and Go Wizards, and steps you should take for having your work printed commercially. Pat Dyson was asked to create a colorful gift certificate for an automotive service and to personalize the gift certificates to send to some customers.

Steps

1. Start Publisher, open the file **Pub H-3** from the drive and folder where your Project Files are located, then save it as **Automotive Gift Certificate**

   You want to continue the theme of stars on the certificate and call attention to the gift, so you will add BorderArt around a text box.

2. Right-click the text box whose top-left corner is at **4½" H / 1½" V**, click **Format Text Box**, click the **BorderArt button**, then click the **Stars option**

   You need to adjust the size and color of the border so that it complements the publication design. With the mass of yellow on the left, you think that blue might add balance to the design.

3. Click the **Always apply at default size check box** to deselect it, click **OK**, change the Line weight to **11**, click **OK**, click the **Line color list arrow** on the Formatting toolbar, then click the **Accent 1 (blue) color box**

   The BorderArt pattern appears on the edge of the text box, as shown in Figure H-21. You think it meets your design goals of calling attention to the text box and adding some color.

4. Click the text box at **2½" H / 2" V**, click **Tools** on the menu bar, point to **Mail Merge**, then click **Mail Merge Wizard**

   The Mail Merge task pane opens. You will select the recipients from your existing list.

5. Click **Browse** under the Use an Existing List section, open the file **Pub H-2** from the drive and folder where your Project Files are located, click **Open**, substitute your first and last names in the first record if necessary, then click **OK**

   Once the data source file is selected, you can move on to the next task pane page.

6. Click **Next: Create the publication** in the task pane, click **More items** under the Create the publication section, click **First Name**, click **Insert**, click **Last Name**, click **Insert**, then click **Close**

   The First and Last Name fields appear in the text box, but there is no spacing between them.

   Trouble?
   If your work needs editing, click Edit recipient list or Previous: Create the publication on the task pane to make corrections.

7. Insert a space between the double arrows separating the First Name and Last Name merge fields, then click **Next: Preview the publications**

   Your first and last names appear in the text box.

8. Click **Next: Complete the merge**, click **Print** in the Merge section of the task pane, make sure that the correct printer is selected, then click the **Test button**

   Compare your publication to Figure H-22.

9. Click the **Cancel button, close** on the task pane, click the **Save button** on the Standard toolbar, then exit Publisher

PUBLISHER 186 USING SPECIAL FEATURES

FIGURE H-21: BorderArt applied to text box

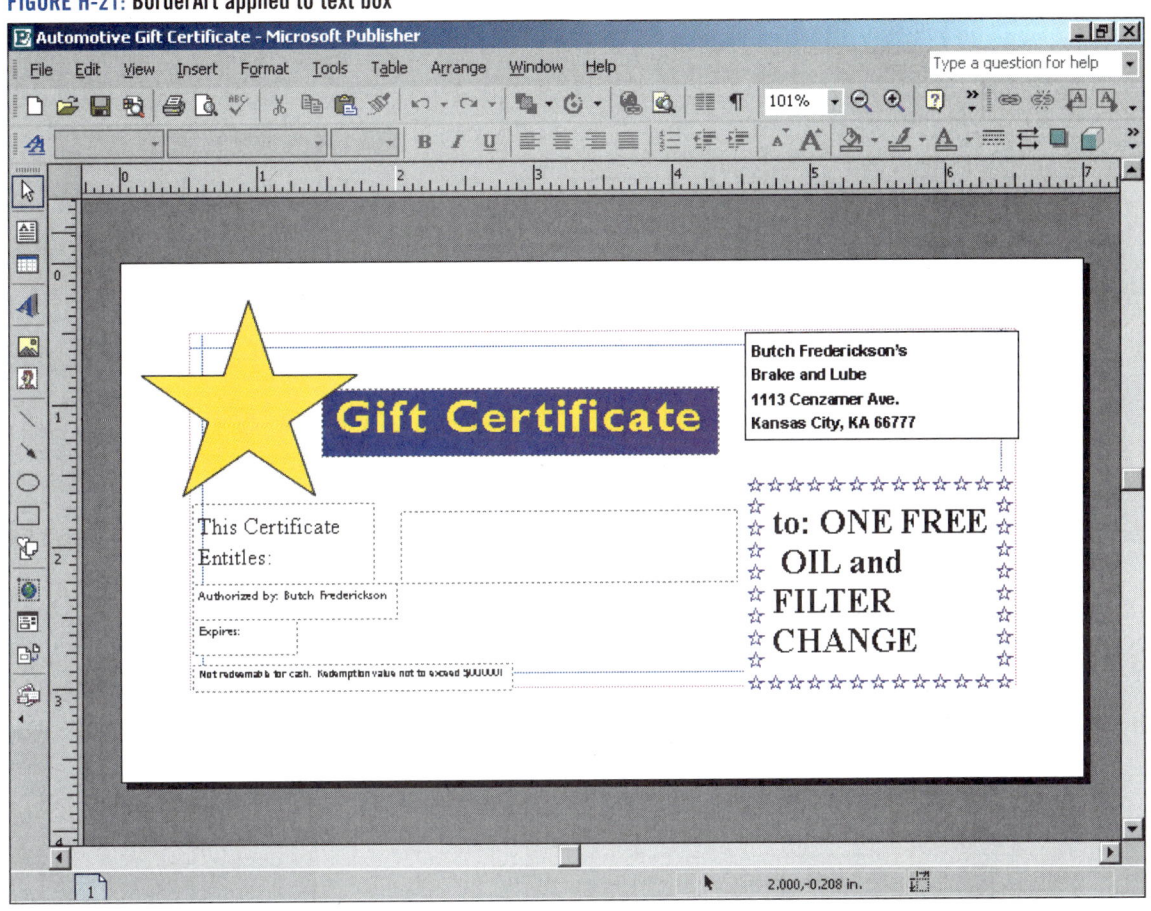

FIGURE H-22: Test publication

USING SPECIAL FEATURES   PUBLISHER 187

Publisher 2002 Practice

▶ Concepts Review

Label each of the elements in the Publisher window shown in Figure H-23.

FIGURE H-23

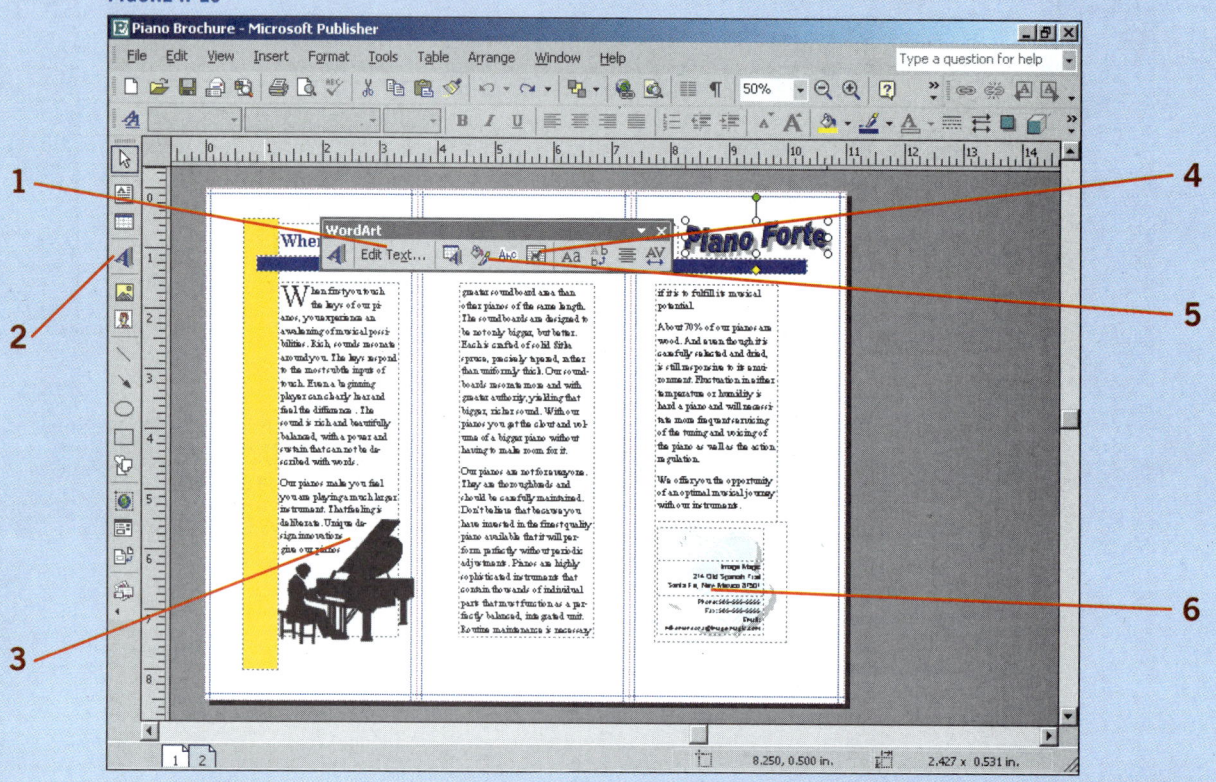

Match each of the buttons with the statement that describes its function.

7.
8.
9.
10.
11.
12.

a. Displays WordArt Gallery
b. Displays WordArt shapes
c. Formats WordArt
d. Edits irregular shape
e. Changes line color
f. Inserts WordArt

Select the best answer from the list of choices.

13. BorderArt can be:
    a. Customized.
    b. Colored.
    c. Changed in point size.
    d. All of the above

14. Each of the following is true about WordArt, except:
    a. WordArt has a text wrapping menu.
    b. Character spacing in WordArt cannot be changed.
    c. WordArt can be resized like any other object.
    d. WordArt can be edited.

▶ PUBLISHER 188   USING SPECIAL FEATURES

Practice

15. Which button is used to insert WordArt?
    a. [icon]
    b. [icon]
    c. [icon]
    d. [icon]
16. Which button is used to change a WordArt shape?
    a. [icon]
    b. [icon]
    c. [icon]
    d. [icon]
17. Which button is used to change how WordArt is aligned?
    a. [icon]
    b. [icon]
    c. [icon]
    d. [icon]
18. Which feature blends two information sources together?
    a. File Blender
    b. Mail Marriage
    c. Mail Merge
    d. WordArt
19. A file that contains information about the recipients of a mail merge is called a:
    a. Field.
    b. Record.
    c. Data source.
    d. Blend source.
20. Which button is used to edit wrap points around a picture?
    a. [icon]
    b. [icon]
    c. [icon]
    d. [icon]

▶ Skills Review

Throughout these exercises, use the Zoom feature where necessary.

1. **Add BorderArt.**
    a. Start Publisher.
    b. Open the file Pub H-4 from the drive and folder where your Project Files are located, then save it as **Gym Flyer**.
    c. Right-click the text box at 1" H / 2" V, click Format Text Box, then click the BorderArt button.
    d. Scroll through the list of Available Borders, then click Hearts.
    e. Click the Always apply at default size check box to deselect it, then click OK.
    f. Change the Line weight to 15, then click OK.
    g. Save your work.
2. **Design WordArt.**
    a. Click the Insert WordArt button on the Objects toolbar, then click the second box in the second row of the WordArt Gallery.
    b. Click OK, type **We Want You Back!** in the Text text box.
    c. Change the font size to 36 if necessary, make the text bold, then click OK.
    d. Reposition the WordArt so that its top-left corner is at 1½" H / 2" V.
    e. Apply the Double Wave 1 (the seventh WordArt shape in the third row).
    f. Add the Accent 2 (yellow) fill color to the WordArt.
    g. Save your work.
3. **Wrap text around an object.**
    a. Add the Heart AutoShape (first column, sixth row)
    b. Create an image of a heart whose top-left corner is at 1½" H / 5" V, and whose dimensions are 2½" H × 2½" V.
    c. Experiment by moving the wrap points to alter the shape of the wrapped text, then click the Undo button.
    d. Use the Fill Color list arrow and More Fill Colors to fill the heart with any shade of red you choose.
    e. Save the publication.

Publisher 2002 Practice

4. **Rotate a text box.**
   a. Draw a new text box anywhere that has the dimensions 1¾" H × ½" V.
   b. Type **We Miss You** in the text box, then change the font size to 20.
   c. Click the Bring to Front button on the Standard toolbar.
   d. Place the text box so that the top-left corner is at 1¾" H / 5¾" V (superimposed over the heart).
   e. Rotate the text box 25 degrees.
   f. Save your work.

5. **Create a Mail Merge.**
   a. Start the Mail Merge Wizard.
   b. Select the file Pub H-2 from the drive and folder where your Project Files are located as the data source, confirm that your first and last names and preferred title are in the first record, then click OK.
   c. Click Next: Create the publication, click the text box at 1½" H / 3" V to select it, press [F9], put the insertion point at the beginning of the text, click More items on the task pane, insert the Title and Last Name fields, then click Close.
   d. Insert a space between the Title and Last Name merge fields.
   e. Go to the next task pane, then verify that your preferred title and last name are the first words in the text box.
   f. Go to the next task pane, click Print in the Merge section of the task pane, make sure that the correct printer is selected, then print a test. Click Cancel in the Print Merge dialog box.
   g. Save your work.

6. **Use the Pack and Go Wizard.**
   a. Open the Pack and Go Wizard to take files to a commercial printing service.
   b. Use a blank, formatted floppy disk, if necessary.
   c. Answer "Next" to each of the Wizard dialog boxes, then click Finish in the last dialog box.
   d. Close the publication.
   e. Exit Publisher.

▶ Independent Challenge 1

As office manager for your company, you decide to make customized monthly calendars for the employees.
   a. Start Publisher and use the New Publication task pane to select the full page, Layers design in the Calendar section of the Publication Gallery.
   b. Use Personal Information sets to add appropriate information, and the color scheme of your choice.
   c. Save the publication as **Monthly Calendar** to the drive and folder where your Project Files are located.
   d. Add BorderArt of your choice, sized to 16 pt around the text box containing the month and year.
   e. Use the WordArt feature to create vertical text that reads **Go Team**. (*Hint*: The right side of the WordArt Gallery contains several vertical text templates.) Change the font size to 24 pt.
   f. Superimpose the WordArt over the filled text box to the left of the calendar.
   g. Modify the fill color of the WordArt to Accent 1.
   h. Type your name in the text box located at 2" H / 1½" V.
   i. Save and print the publication, then exit Publisher.

▶ Independent Challenge 2

The Believe It or Not Bookstore asks you to design a postcard announcing an upcoming book-signing event.
   a. Start Publisher and use the New Publication task pane to select the Schedule design in the Event Postcards section of the Publication Gallery.
   b. Use Personal Information sets to add appropriate information, and the color scheme of your choosing.

Practice

c. Save the publication as **Believe It or Not Postcard** to the drive and folder where your Project Files are located.
d. Add BorderArt around the Activities text box.
e. Modify the text at 2" H / 2" V with your own text.
f. Delete the object at 1" H / 1¾" V.
g. Delete the contents of the Activities text box.
h. Write appropriate text in the text box.
i. Add your name as the contact person.
j. Change any text as necessary to fit the theme of a book signing at the Believe It or Not Bookstore. Make up a suitable event title.
k. Save and print the publication, then exit Publisher.

▶ Independent Challenge 3

Your Publisher skills convince you that you can open your own design shop, Design Center. First, you'll need business cards for you and your employees, which demonstrate your talents. You will use mail merge to personalize the cards.

a. Start Publisher, then use any design of your choice in the Plain Paper Business Cards section of the Publication Gallery.
b. Use Personal Information sets to add appropriate information, and add any color scheme you choose.
c. Save the publication as **Design Center Business Card** to the drive and folder where your Project Files are located.
d. Open the Mail Merge Wizard, then select the file Pub H-2 from the drive and folder where your Project Files are located as the data source.
e. Insert First and Last Name merge fields where you wish the names to appear on your business card.
f. Make sure the First and Last Name merge fields are separated by a space.
g. Preview the business card to make sure that your name appears. Make any necessary corrections.
h. Use the Print Merge dialog box to test print your business card.
i. Save the publication and exit Publisher.

e Independent Challenge 4

Your employer is traveling to Toronto, Canada. She is interested in having a publication printed by a commercial printing service there so she can travel light. You tell her that Publisher makes it easy to hand off files to such a printer, and you decide to investigate this capability and create an informative flyer.

a. Connect to the Internet and use your browser to go to www.microsoft.com/office/publisher/. From there, look for information on commercial printing with Publisher.
b. Find out the key features and benefits of this Publisher feature, and print out any necessary information from the Microsoft Web site. You can add to this information by using the Publisher Help feature offline, and searching Commercial Printing if needed.
c. Start Publisher if necessary.
d. Use the Publication Gallery to create a flyer. Save the file as **Publisher Printing Options** to the drive and folder where your Project Files are located.
e. Use bulleted lists to briefly describe the benefits of the commercial printing features of Publisher.
f. Add BorderArt to call attention to a text box within the page.
g. If necessary, make space for a new text box by deleting placeholder artwork.
h. Find at least one commercial printing service in Toronto that accepts Publisher files, and include its address on your flyer. (*Hint*: Look on Publisher's home page for directions on how to find a printing service.)
i. Save and print the publication, then exit Publisher.

Publisher 2002 Practice

▶ Visual Workshop

Use the New Publication task pane and Publication Gallery to create an Accessory Bar Price List Brochure as the initial design of a brochure for Tom's Toy Shop. Save this publication as **Toy Shop Brochure** to the drive and folder where your Project Files are located. Use Figure H-24 as a guide. The BorderArt around the text box at 9" H / 1½" V has a zigzag pattern. The style for the "Specializing In Model Airplanes" text comes from the WordArt Gallery—second row, fifth from the left. Replace the store manager's name with your name. Save and print the first page.

FIGURE H-24

Publisher 2002

Unit I

Working
Efficiently

Objectives

- ► Integrate with Office products
- ► Import a Word document
- ► Use AutoCorrect
- ► Record images
- ► Embed and link objects
- ► Use Design Checker
- ► Understand speech recognition
- ► Capstone Project: Dinner Invitation

Choosing the right tool for the right job, and choosing to do tasks in the best order helps you increase your effectiveness. By increasing efficiency, you can increase not only the quantity of your work but the quality too; when you spend more time on the most difficult tasks, the quality of your work improves. Understanding how to integrate Publisher with other Office programs and peripheral devices means that you can join their strengths and work around their limitations. Learning how to use additional features, such as AutoCorrect and Speech Recognition, can speed up your work. AutoCorrect automatically fixes your typing errors as you type. Speech recognition software lets you create text and vocally give computer commands. Image Magic is holding a two-day computer-training course for its employees. The goals of the training are to introduce the employees to efficient methods of working with Publisher and other Microsoft applications, as well as to use peripheral devices to enhance and speed up their work. Mike Mendoza will create some course materials.

Integrating with Office Products

Publisher 2002 — Unit I

All Office programs are designed to work together. Because the Office suite programs have a similar look and feel, your familiarity with one program can help you use other programs. You can also transfer information or objects created in one program to another. Mike wants everyone to appreciate what business productivity software can do, and which programs are best suited to individual jobs. To make the training interactive, he will ask those most familiar with specific programs to speak about how they are used at Image Magic.

Details

▶ Microsoft Word

Everyone at Image Magic uses Word, a **word processing** program, to create letters, memos, reports, and the stories that go in publications. Mike will show how a Word document, such as the one shown in Figure I-1, can be imported into a publication, letting you take advantage of some of the features of Word, such as grammar checking and word count, which aren't available in Publisher.

▶ Microsoft Excel

Employees also use Excel, an **electronic spreadsheet** program that automatically calculates and analyzes data and creates powerful charts. A **chart** is a graphical representation of data. Ricardo Fernandez, Image Magic's office manager, uses Excel to create budgets and financial statements, and to track customer billing and invoices. Figure I-2 shows an Excel worksheet with data and a chart. This chart is also shown in Figure I-3, after it was pasted into Publisher.

▶ Microsoft PowerPoint

When they need to present information to a group of people, Image Magic employees create professional visual presentations using PowerPoint. A **presentation** is a series of projected slides and/or handouts that a speaker refers to while delivering information. Together, Publisher and PowerPoint can make for an impressive and cohesive presentation using a slide show from PowerPoint and supporting documents from Publisher, which share similar fonts and colors. Maria Abbot, Image Magic's president, will use PowerPoint to create a slide show summarizing the company's growth and financial performance; she will give the presentation during the training session, and later at an annual meeting of investors, creditors, and clients.

▶ Microsoft Access

Complex data can be organized, tracked, and updated using an Access database. A **database** is a collection of related information that is organized into tables, records, and fields. Information entered into a database can be sorted and retrieved in a variety of ways, and then used to make business decisions. Access databases can be used as a data source for Publisher mail merges. Nancy Garrott, Image Magic's marketing manager, uses Access to create and maintain a customer information database. She shares this information with the accounting department so it does not have to re-enter information about new customers and sales.

▶ Microsoft Outlook

Employees use the Outlook personal information manager to keep track of business contacts and schedule appointments. Outlook contact lists are often used as data sources for mail merges in Publisher. Nancy Garrott uses Outlook to stay in touch with Image Magic's customers and employees. She considers it crucial to maintain the company's relationships with customers.

Office tools

▶ All Office programs include **online collaboration**, the ability to share information over the Internet. Employees can schedule online meetings and have discussions over the World Wide Web. **Speech Recognition** lets them enter data and give commands verbally using a computer microphone.

FIGURE I-1: Word document

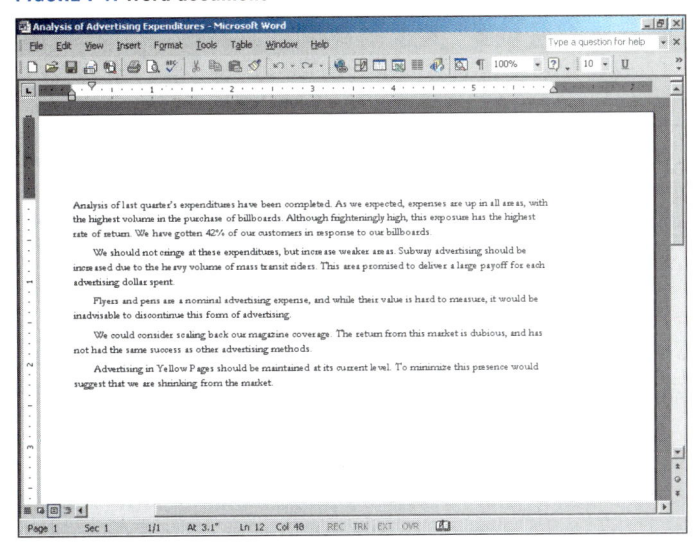

FIGURE I-2: Excel worksheet containing a chart

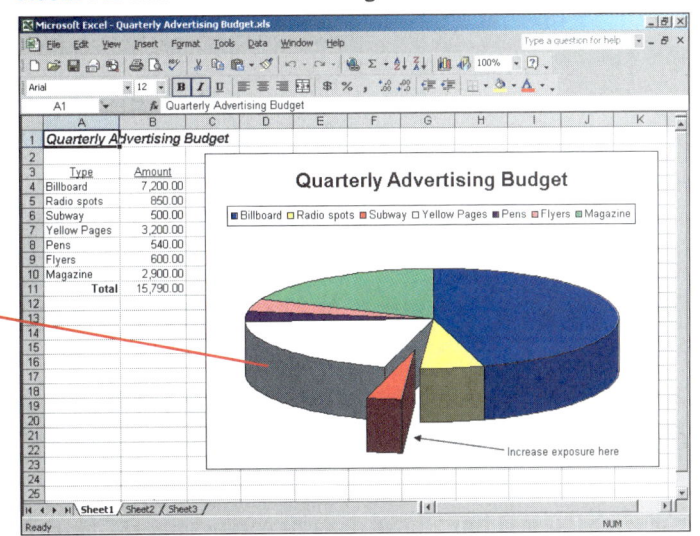

The pie chart is just one example of the chart types that can be generated in Excel

FIGURE I-3: Excel chart and Word story in publication

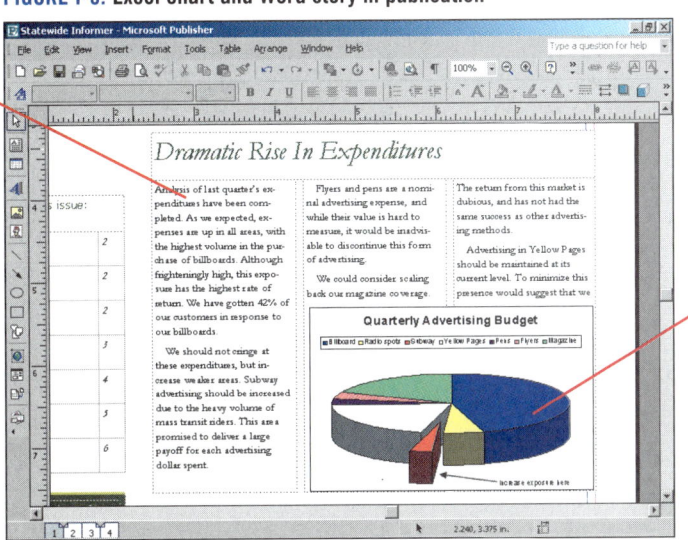

The Word document imported into a Publisher newsletter

The chart is a colorful design element that supports the publication text

Publisher 2002

WORKING EFFICIENTLY   **PUBLISHER 195**

Importing a Word Document

Publisher 2002 — Unit I

You have already imported Word documents into text boxes. You have also edited a Publisher story in Word and returned it to Publisher. However, Publisher also lets you import Word documents directly into a publication, where you can automatically add design elements to ensure that all of your documents have similar designs and maintain the same look and feel. It also provides an easy way to enhance an unformatted Word document. Mike wants to include a book review in the pre-course materials. This publication will be distributed one week before the training session and will be designed to raise questions about job effectiveness and to spark discussion.

Steps

1. Start Publisher, click **Word Documents** in the By Publication Type list in the New Publication task pane, then click the **Layers Word Document** in the Publication Gallery
   The Import Word Document dialog box opens, as shown in Figure I-4.

   Trouble?
   If you get a warning box that you need a converter, contact your instructor or technical support person.

2. Open the file **Pub I-1** from the drive and folder where your Project Files are located, click **OK** in the Import Word Document dialog box, then save the publication as **Book Review**
   The Word document is imported into a Publisher text box and the Word Import Options task pane opens. You think a two-column format will make the document easier to read.

3. Click the **2 Columns button** in the task pane
   The two-column format looks great. Now you will add a title to the document.

4. Click the **Close button** on the task pane, press **[F9]**, click the **Document Title placeholder text**, then type **Sources of Power: How People Make Decisions**
   The title of the book review is inserted, but you want the text to be larger.

5. Press **[Ctrl][A]** to select the text, click the **Font Size list arrow** on the Formatting toolbar, then click **16**
   The font size of the title is now larger. Compare your page to Figure I-5.

6. Right-click the **text box** whose top-left corner is at 6¾" H / ¾" V, then click **Delete Object**
   Page numbers are not necessary since this is a single-page publication.

7. Press **[F9]**, click the **Save button** on the Standard toolbar, then close the publication

WORKING EFFICIENTLY

FIGURE I-4: Import Word Document dialog box

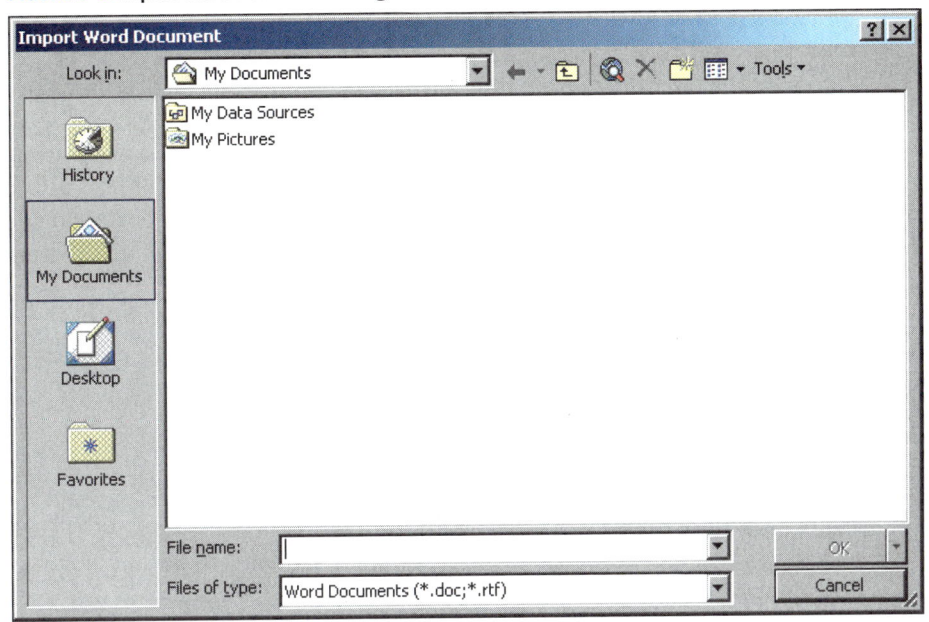

FIGURE I-5: Imported Word document

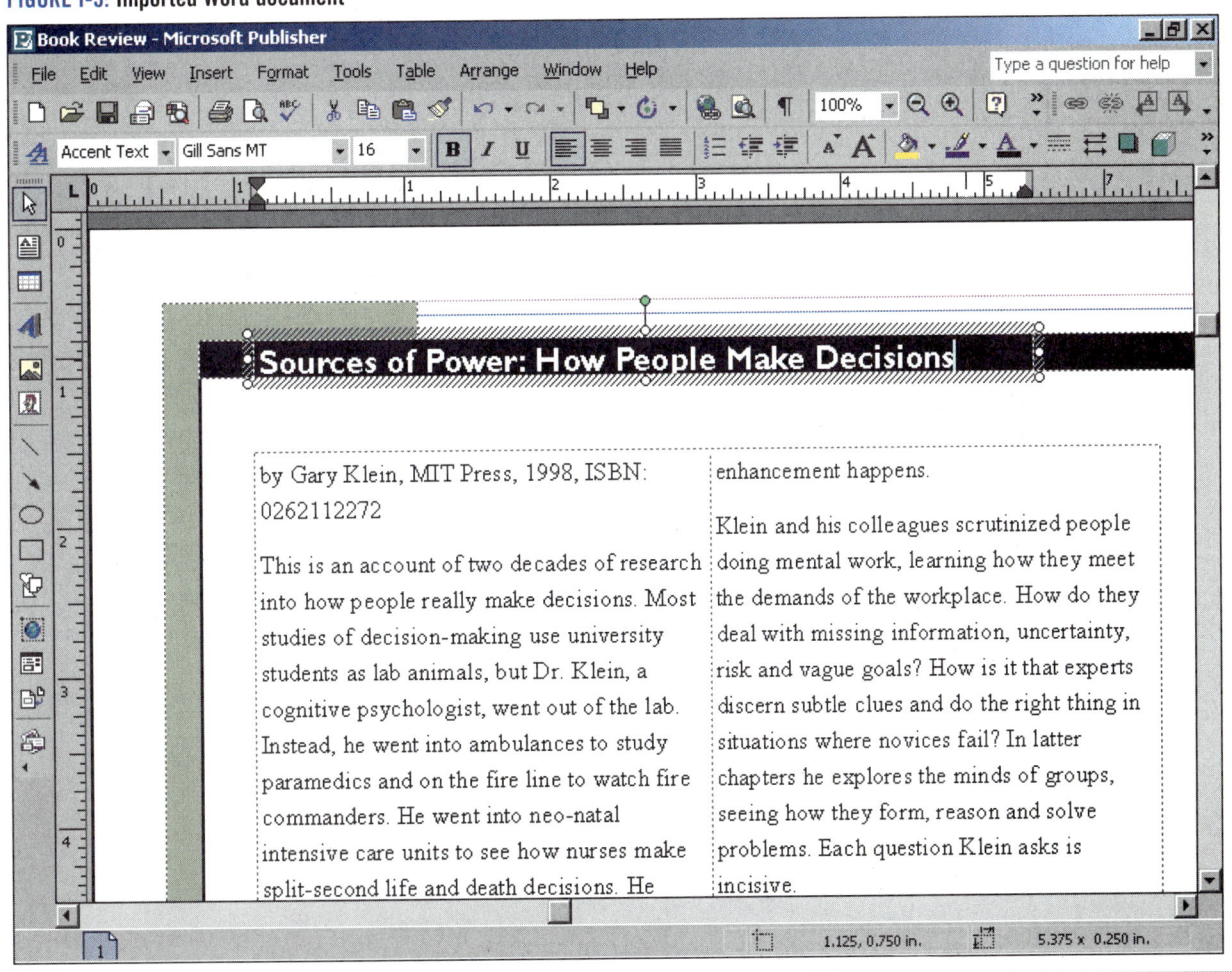

Using AutoCorrect

Publisher 2002

The **AutoCorrect** feature can detect and correct misspelled words, typos, and errors in capitalization and grammar as you type. For example, if you type "yuo" followed by space, AutoCorrect replaces the incorrect word with "you." In addition, AutoCorrect lets you quickly insert text, graphics, or symbols. For example, you can type "(tm)" to insert ™, or customize AutoCorrect to automatically replace abbreviations such as "potus" with President of the United States. Mike wants to change his AutoCorrect settings to speed up his work and help him avoid spelling errors as he generates the training material for the course. He reviews how AutoCorrect works and how it can be modified.

Details

> **QuickTip**
>
> There are different versions of Microsoft Office depending on your dialect or language. Each has its own AutoCorrect feature and dictionary.

▶ Add to or change AutoCorrect entries

AutoCorrect uses AutoCorrect entries, a list of commonly misspelled words and typos, to detect misusages and automatically correct them. It also contains some common symbols, such as ©, that can be substituted for specific keystrokes. You can easily add your own custom AutoCorrect entries or remove unwanted ones. You can make additions or changes to AutoCorrect by clicking Tools on the menu bar, then clicking AutoCorrect Options. The AutoCorrect: English dialog box opens. You can add an entry to AutoCorrect by typing the text you want replaced in the Replace text box, and the text that will replace it in the With text box. Once you create your entry, click Add, and the new AutoCorrect entry will be in effect. Figure I-6 shows a new entry added to AutoCorrect. You can delete an AutoCorrect entry by clicking the entry you want to delete, then clicking Delete. You can also use AutoCorrect to format as you type. By clicking the AutoFormat As You Type tab in the AutoCorrect dialog box, shown in Figure I-7, this feature can be programmed to automatically apply bullets and numbers to your text.

▶ Use AutoCorrect to correct errors of capitalization

AutoCorrect recognizes words that are commonly capitalized and corrects them when they are entered incorrectly. For example, the first word in a sentence, or the days of the week, are recognized and corrected if they are not capitalized. AutoCorrect also recognizes when the first two letters of a word have been capitalized incorrectly and makes the second letter lowercase. You can also add names or words that you want capitalized or in lowercase to the AutoCorrect entries.

▶ Use AutoCorrect to correct spelling errors

The Publisher Spell Checker does not automatically correct all of your spelling errors. After it identifies potential misspellings, it underlines the words with a red wavy line. As you edit your publication, you then decide if the words it identifies are truly misspelled. AutoCorrect makes spelling corrections automatically. With AutoCorrect, you enter your common misspellings and the proper replacement spellings. It then identifies the misspellings and makes the replacements as you type.

▶ Prevent AutoCorrect from making specific corrections

To modify AutoCorrect, you can turn options on and off, or edit the AutoCorrect entries. For the AutoCorrect capitalization and Spelling Checker options, you can also create an exceptions list that specifies which words should not be changed. For example, you can prevent AutoCorrect from capitalizing a word that you want to appear in lowercase characters for stylistic reasons.

FIGURE I-6: Entry added in AutoCorrect dialog box

List of capitalization errors and AutoCorrect options

AutoCorrect entries appear alphabetically

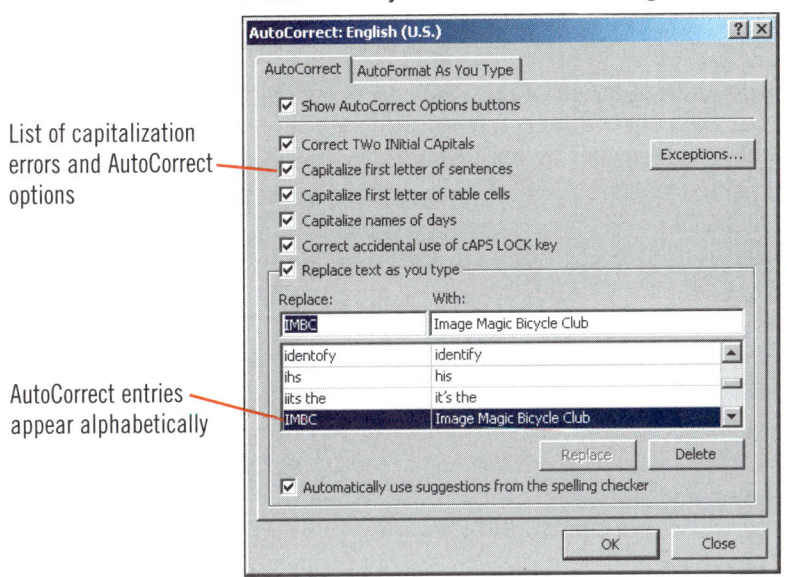

FIGURE I-7: AutoFormat As You Type tab in the AutoCorrect dialog box

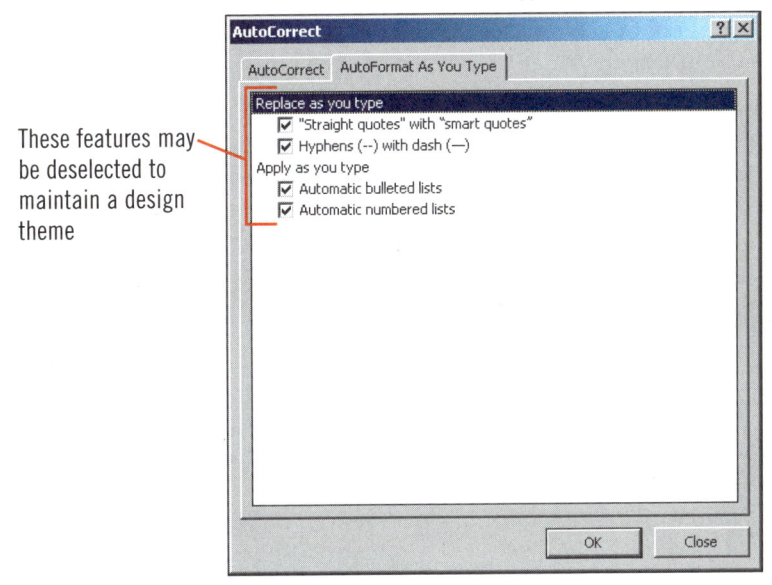

These features may be deselected to maintain a design theme

Design Matters

Using tools wisely

AutoCorrect is a powerful tool. However, like all tools, it is important to recognize appropriate uses and limitations. There may be occasions when, for design or literary reasons, you want to turn off AutoCorrect features. Consider how the works of Mark Twain, James Joyce, e. e.Cummings, Lewis Carroll, and other English-speaking authors would have been altered by the tools found in software products. Knowing how and when to use a tool is vital. Knowing when and how to dispense with a tool is important too.

WORKING EFFICIENTLY   PUBLISHER 199

Recording Images

Publisher 2002

Details

Publisher is a powerful program because of its ability to handle both text and graphics. As your publications become targeted to a specific audience, your choice of graphic images will become targeted as well. Instead of relying on digital images created by others, you may wish to create your own. A **digital image** is a picture in an electronic file. The two most common methods of creating digital images are using a scanner and digital camera photography. Mike wants the training materials to foster a sense of inclusion and help all employees get to know each other. He decides to ask each employee to provide a favorite photo for him to scan, or to pose for a photograph that he will take with a digital camera.

▶ Types of scanners

There are many kinds of scanners in use today, each with advantages and disadvantages. By far, the most popular scanners are the flatbed and sheetfed variety. Some common features to both types are that they come with their own software that must be loaded on the computer, and they must be connected to a computer. Most scanners come with **optical character recognition** (**OCR**) software for scanning and translating text documents.

- #### Using a flatbed scanner
  A **flatbed scanner** has a flat surface from which the image is scanned, and it is the best type for creating digital images from photos and printed materials. To scan an item, you place it face down on the scanner's glass surface, just as you would on a copy machine. Since you can remove the scanner's lid, you can scan large objects, such as books, because you can place the object face down on the glass. The biggest disadvantage of a flatbed scanner is that it takes up space on your desk because of its large flat glass surface. Figure I-8 contains an example of software used to scan information into a computer.

- #### Scanning with a sheetfed scanner
  The best feature of a **sheetfed scanner** is its size. Commonly the size of a portable printer, it takes up little space on a crowded desktop. Instead of placing a document on a flat piece of glass, you feed the document into the scanning system using rollers. This limits sheetfed scanners to scanning single sheets of paper, which makes scanning a page from a book impossible without cutting it. Most sheetfeds are more adept at scanning text than photos.

▶ Digital cameras

Unlike other cameras, a **digital camera** does not require film; it stores images on a memory device. Pictures are stored on the device until they are transferred to another storage medium or are deleted. The memory device can then be used again to take and store more images. The number of pictures a camera can save depends on the **resolution** (the density of **pixels**, or color dots) and the capacity of the memory device. Generally, the higher the resolution, the fewer pictures can be stored. Some digital cameras can store four times as many low-resolution pictures as high-resolution images.

Once you take the pictures that you want, you must download them using a software program that comes with the digital camera. As with scanners, the software program must be installed on your computer to download the pictures. In addition, you need a way to transfer the images from the camera to the computer. Some cameras use a floppy disk to transfer the images, while some connect to a computer using a cable. Many digital camera software programs let you organize your images in digital photo albums; an example is shown in Figure I-9.

▶ Copyright laws

Images that you take with either a digital camera or film camera are your property to use as you want. However, images from other sources, including magazines, books, and the Internet, are the intellectual property of others and may be copyrighted and have limitations placed on their use. Permission for you to use an image may be granted by the copyright holder; sometimes permission is received just by asking, and other times you may be required to pay a fee. It is your legal and ethical responsibility to only use images that belong to you or that you have permission to use.

FIGURE I-8: Visioneer PaperPort Scan Manager dialog box

FIGURE I-9: Image Expert photo album

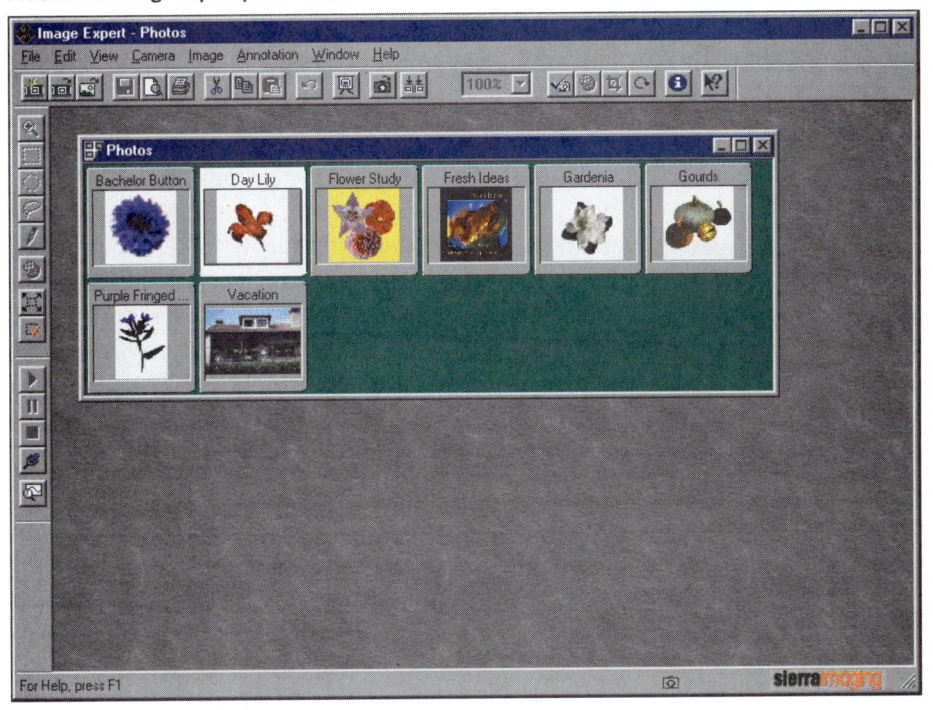

Studying color

Color is one of the most difficult areas of design to master for a variety of reasons. Color perceptions and descriptions are subjective since the human eye can detect several million hues. Adding to that complexity is the limitation of language to deal meaningfully with so many shades of color. Also, between five to eight percent of males have some defect of color vision (females are much less affected since color-blindness is a male dominant trait). Considering the limitations of language and perception, a good way to study color is by using a color wheel. **Color wheels** teach color relationships by organizing colors in a circle so you can visualize how they relate to each other.

WORKING EFFICIENTLY

Embedding and Linking Objects

Objects from other programs can be embedded or linked into a publication. An **embedded object** is a copy that is pasted into a publication. It maintains no ties to the original, so that if the original is modified, the copy does not change. A **linked object** is a copy that is connected to the original. When the original is modified, the copy is updated to reflect those changes. For example, you might want to include an Excel chart that shows corporate quarterly sales. You could include it in promotional literature for potential investors, or informational literature for employees. Instead of creating new publications and charts each quarter, it is more efficient to link the chart to a publication so that the chart is automatically updated when new data is entered into the Excel workbook. As part of the training literature, Mike wants to include a chart of Image Magic's growth in a publication that documents the history of the company. Since Mike anticipates using the publication in the future with only minor changes, he wants to explore different ways of importing the chart from Excel.

Details

▶ Embedded objects

An **embedded object** is created in another program and copied to a publication in Publisher. The **source file** contains the original information, and the **destination file** is the recipient of the information. There is no connection between the two programs, so if you modify the information in the source file, the information in the destination file does not change.

The advantages of embedding are permanence and portability. You do not have to worry that a source file will be deleted, moved, or renamed, which would render the link between the files useless, or that its contents or formatting will change. Because the object is contained within your publication, it will stay the same unless you change it. An embedded object can always be edited using its original program by double-clicking it, but once the editing is done, the connection is again severed. To embed an object in any Office program, click the object, then click the Copy button on the Standard toolbar. You can embed the object by clicking the Paste button on the Standard toolbar, or by clicking the copied item on the Office Clipboard, as shown in Figure I-10.

The disadvantages of embedding an object are that it increases the size of the publication, and if any changes are made to the source file, they are not updated in the destination file.

▶ Linked objects

A **linked object** has a connection to the original object. When the object is updated in the source file, it is automatically updated in the publication (the destination file).

Linking has two advantages over embedding. First, the publication file is smaller because it contains only links to the objects, not the objects themselves. Second, if changes are made to the source objects, they are automatically reflected in the publication when you view the objects. You can link an object in any Office program by clicking the object to select it, then clicking the Copy button on the Standard toolbar. Once the object is copied, click Edit on the menu bar, then click Paste Special. The Paste Special dialog box opens, showing the source of the copied data. Click the Paste Link option button, as shown in Figure I-11, then click OK.

The disadvantages are that the contents may change and those changes will not be reflected in the surrounding text; the formatting may change and be disruptive to your design; and if you move, delete, or rename the source file, the link is broken.

▶ PUBLISHER 202 **WORKING EFFICIENTLY**

FIGURE I-10: Objects copied onto the Office Clipboard

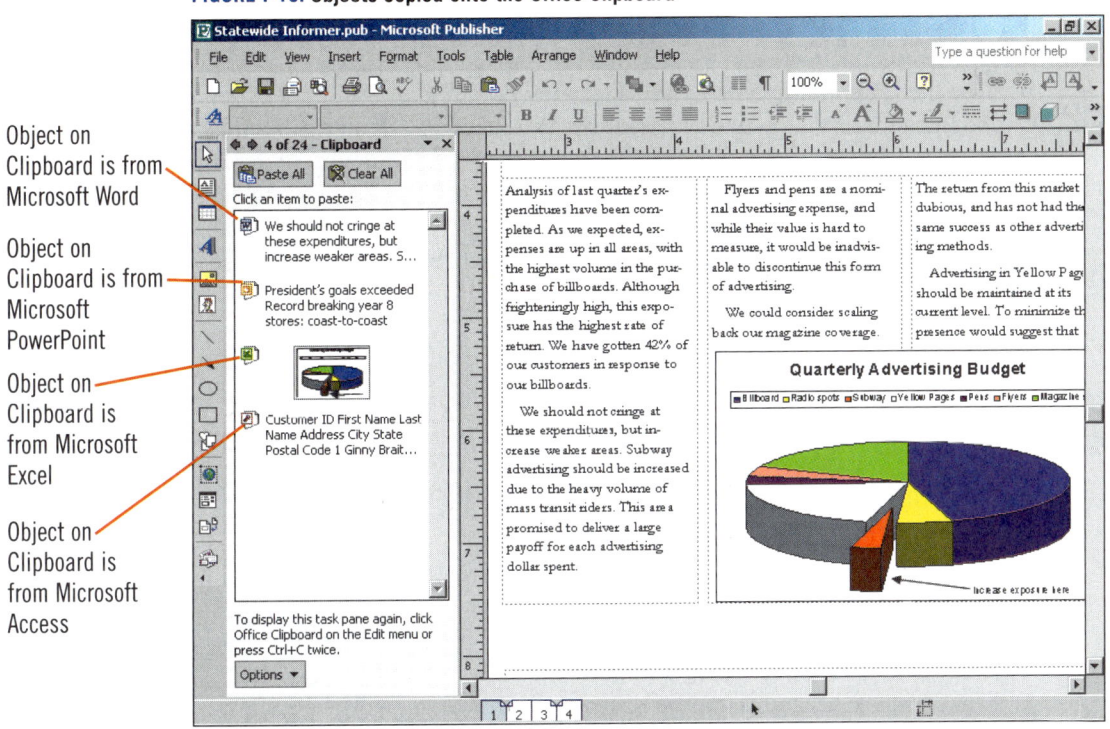

Object on Clipboard is from Microsoft Word

Object on Clipboard is from Microsoft PowerPoint

Object on Clipboard is from Microsoft Excel

Object on Clipboard is from Microsoft Access

FIGURE I-11: Paste Special dialog box

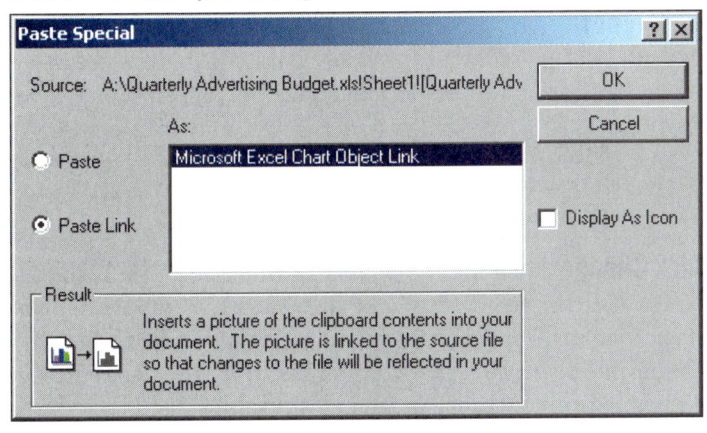

WORKING EFFICIENTLY   PUBLISHER 203

Using Design Checker

Publisher 2002

Because there are multiple elements of text and graphics in most publications, design problems can be introduced that may be missed in a casual review. **Design Checker** looks for errors in layout, alerts you, and suggests changes, but it does not fix the problems automatically. There may be times when the unity of your design may cause you to reject the Design Checker suggestions, but most often, it helps you find areas of your publication that can be improved.

Mike created a flyer containing intentional errors that can be used to dramatize the capabilities of the Design Checker feature. He wants to use this publication so others can see how Design Checker works.

Steps

1. Open the file **Pub I-2** from the drive and folder where your Project Files are located, then save it as **Training Flyer**

   The flyer appears on the screen. It has areas of color on two sides of the text.

2. Examine the publication to check for any obvious design problems, click **Tools** on the menu bar, then click **Design Checker**

   The Design Checker dialog box opens. By default, it will check all pages, as well as the Master Page.

3. Click **Options**, read all the selected features that Design Checker will examine, then check the check boxes in the Design Checker dialog box to match the options selected in Figure I-12, if necessary

   The Design Checker Options dialog box lists all the design areas the feature will examine.

4. Click **OK**, then click **OK** in the Design Checker dialog box

   Design Checker finds that part of the e-mail address went into the overflow area. Design Checker makes suggestions about possible remedies in the lower-left corner of the text box. You decide to proceed with the rest of the check and fix the problem later.

5. Click **Ignore**

   Design Checker finds that the Image Magic logo does not have its original proportions, as shown in Figure I-13. You decide to take the suggestion.

6. Click **Change**, then click **Continue**

   The logo is resized to its original proportions and Design Checker finds there are two spaces after a punctuation mark in the text box.

7. Click **Change**, click **OK**, then click anywhere in the **scratch area** to deselect the text box

   Design Checker removed one of the spaces and the design check is complete. The Image Magic logo in the lower-right corner had its proportions altered and the logo was narrowed. The tag line or motto text box is now disproportionate to the logo. You decide to fix this and the text in overflow problem later.

8. Create a text box in the upper-right corner of the publication, type your name, click the **Print button** on the Standard toolbar, click the **Save button** on the Standard toolbar, then exit Publisher

▶ PUBLISHER 204 **WORKING EFFICIENTLY**

FIGURE I-12: Design Checker Options dialog box

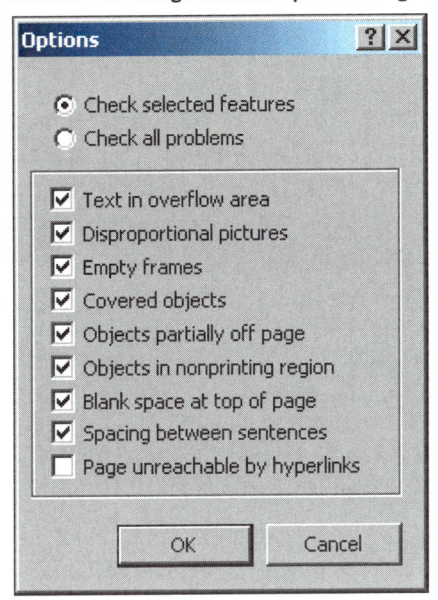

FIGURE I-13: Design Checker results

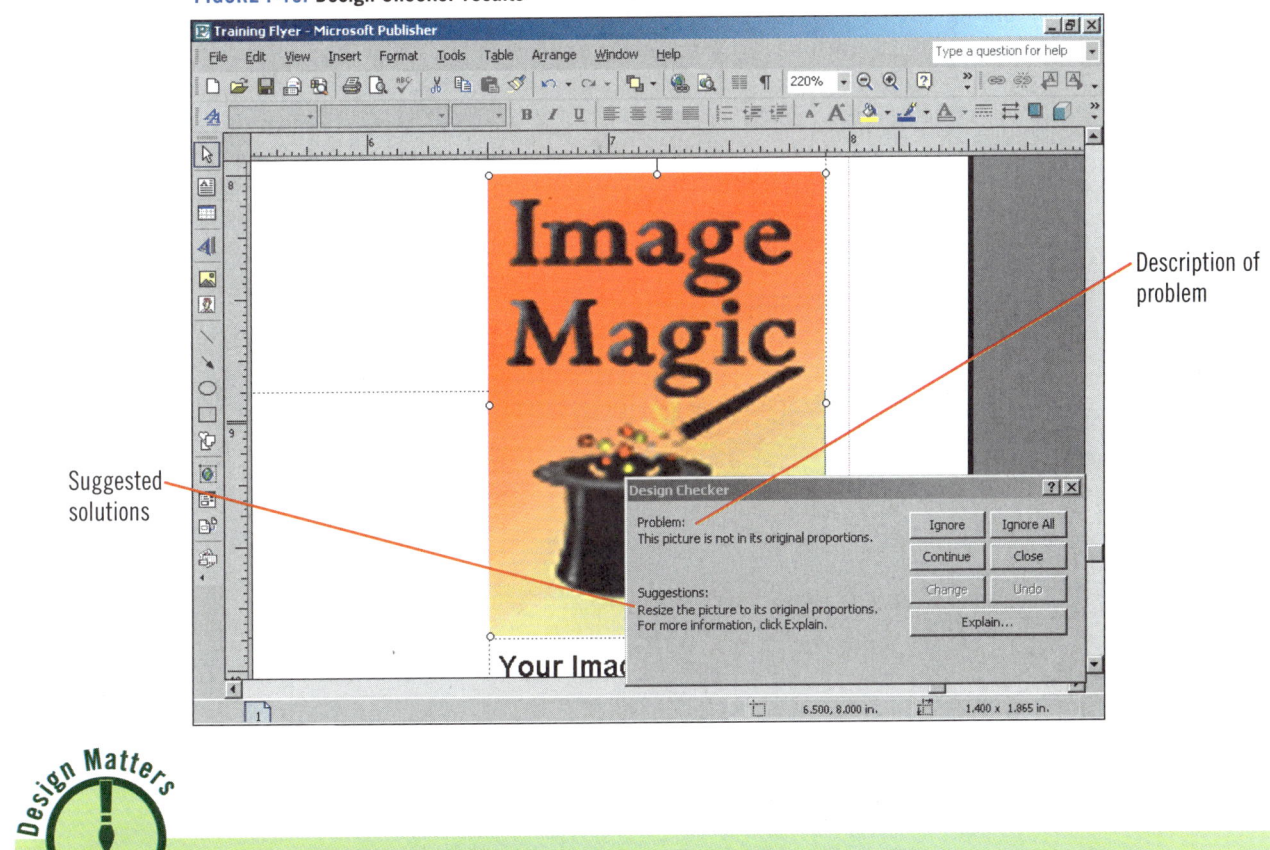

Description of problem

Suggested solutions

Working with Design Checker

Design Checker is a good and valuable tool, but it is crucial to recognize its limitations. Once you learn what the limitations are, you can reduce the number of unrecognized errors in a publication by carefully checking for them. For example, Design Checker does not recognize WordArt as text; instead, it considers it an object, and does not recognize it when it is placed on an otherwise empty text box. It does not recognize color clashes, or insufficient white space in a publication. These and other design concerns must be addressed by visual inspection of the publication. There may be occasions when you wish to ignore the Design Checker suggestions in order to achieve a design goal. For example, you may want to change the proportions of an image to create an interesting visual effect, or simply to fill a space.

WORKING EFFICIENTLY   PUBLISHER 205

Understanding Speech Recognition

Publisher 2002 — Unit I

Speech recognition is an emerging technology that translates spoken language into computer commands or text. When you talk into a microphone connected to a computer, your words are converted into a text file by a software package. Mike has heard a lot about Speech Recognition technology. He thinks a brief overview of the technology would be a good addition to the training program, and will open a discussion about further enhancements to the Image Magic computer system.

Details

▶ Installation
Installation of the Speech Recognition component may require the installation of additional software from your Publisher CD, and does require answering some simple questions in several dialog boxes.

▶ Training sessions
The first time Speech Recognition is started, you will be taken through the Training Wizard, as shown in Figure I-14. The Training Wizard is a series of paragraphs that you read into your computer's microphone. Figure I-15 shows an explanatory dialog box that appears before the training session. The training sessions teach the software's speech module to recognize your voice, and teach you the correct speed and clarity that are understandable to the program, as shown in Figure I-16. Training sessions can be completed more than once, and repetition results in improved performance of the Speech Recognition module.

▶ Using Speech Recognition
Once the Speech Recognition component is installed in Word, it is available for all Office applications (except Office Designer) and can be turned on by clicking Tools on the menu bar, then clicking Speech. With Speech Recognition turned on, the language bar appears in the application title bar.

FIGURE I-14: Welcome to Office Speech Recognition dialog box

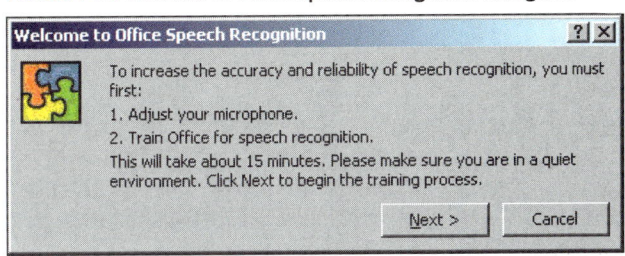

FIGURE I-15: Voice Training dialog box

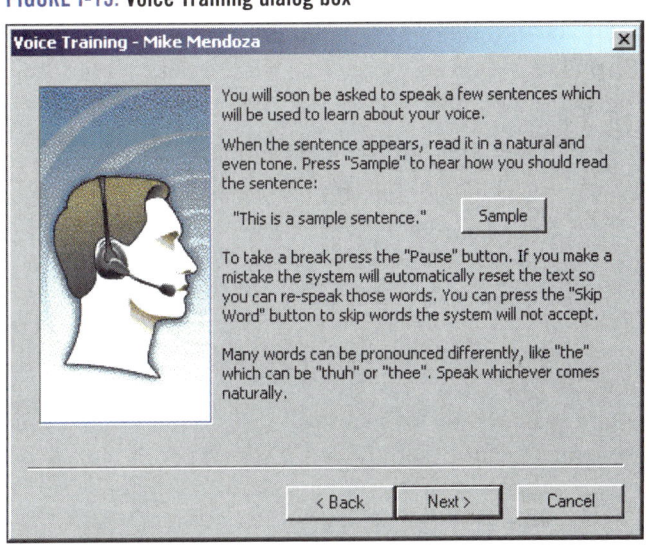

FIGURE I-16: A dialog box screen shot

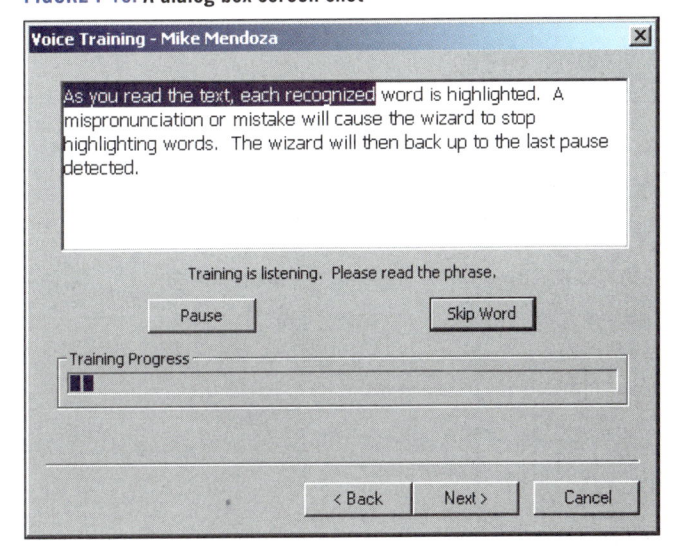

WORKING EFFICIENTLY PUBLISHER 207

Capstone Project: Dinner Invitation

Publisher 2002

You have learned the skills necessary to transform Word documents into publications. You have learned about and used Design Checker. You have also learned about using alternative input devices: scanners, digital cameras, and speech recognition, in addition to learning about linking and embedding objects. The president is inviting the staff of Image Magic to a formal dinner. The invitations will be engraved so Mike wants them to be perfect when he hands the file over to the printer. He decides to use Design Checker.

Steps

1. Start Publisher, open the file **Pub I-3** from the drive and folder where your Project Files are located, then save it as **Dinner Invitation**
   The invitation appears on the screen with two elements of color alongside the text at the top and bottom.

2. Closely examine each page of the publication looking for any obvious design problems, when you finish click **Tools** on the menu bar, then click **Design Checker**
   The Design Checker dialog box opens. By default, it will check all pages, as well as the Master Page.

3. Click **OK**
   Design Checker finds that the Image Magic logo is not in its original proportions. Slight modifications to a picture or an object's proportions may be a useful way to fill a space with color and maintain the overall design of a publication. Design Checker makes suggestions about possible solutions in the lower-left corner of the text box. You decide to proceed with the rest of the design check and look at this problem later.

4. Click **Ignore**
   Design Checker finds that there is more than 1 inch of blank space at the top of page 3. This white space is intentional since it allows you to personalize the invitations with a quick note of thanks to each employee, recognizing their hard work.

5. Click **Ignore**
   Design Checker finds two spaces in the text after a punctuation mark. It does not find the other spaces that occur between the words "some" and "business" in the same sentence because they do not occur after a punctuation mark.

6. Click **Change**
   Design Checker removes one of the spaces and the design check is complete.

7. Click **OK**, click the **page 3 icon**, then delete the extra spaces between the words "some" and "business"
   Compare your work to Figure I-17.

8. Create a text box at the top-right corner of page 3, type your name, click **File** on the menu bar, click **Print**, then click **OK**
   Examine your printed page. If you find any mistakes, go back and correct the mistakes. If necessary, print the pages again.

9. Click the **Save button** on the Standard toolbar, then exit Publisher

WORKING EFFICIENTLY

FIGURE I-17: Completed dinner invitation

PLEASE JOIN US
IN CELEBRATION

The pleasure of your company is requested for a formal dinner party being held for Image Magic employees. Please attend and bring one guest.

RSVP

Mike Mendoza 555 555 5555
Date: 12/08/2003
Time: 8 pm

La Petite Chou Chou Café
at 214 Canal Street.

It has been a momentous year for Image Magic. We moved to a new location, employed some new folks and have set some business records. Please join us in celebrating what has been a fabulous year and in celebrating the great people we work with.

WORKING EFFICIENTLY

Publisher 2002 Practice

▶ Concepts Review

Label each of the programs that created the Office Clipboard elements shown in Figure I-18.

FIGURE I-18

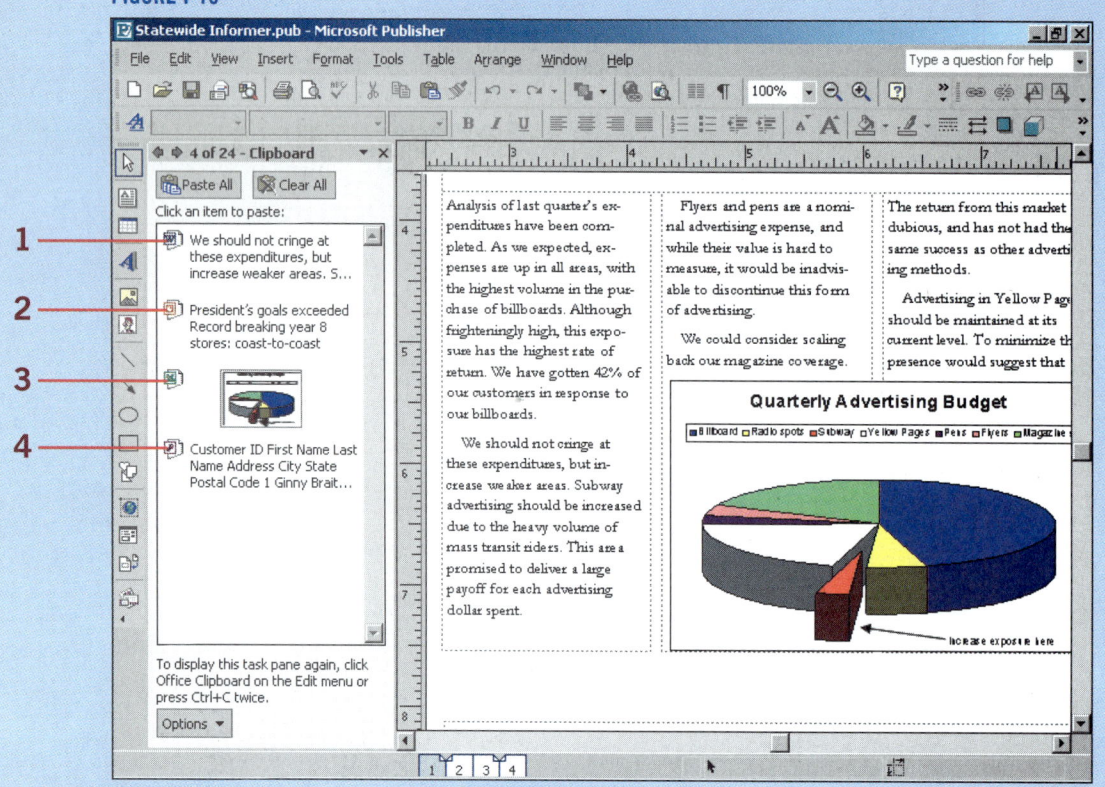

Match each of the features with the statement that describes its function or attribute.

5. Design Checker
6. Digital cameras
7. Embedded object
8. Flatbed scanner
9. AutoCorrect entries
10. Linked object

a. Finds problems such as an object in non-printing areas of the page
b. Maintains a connection to the source file
c. Creates images free of copyright restrictions
d. List of common misspellings
e. Transforms images or text into electronic files
f. Must be double-clicked for editing

Practice

Select the best answer from the list of choices.

11. **Microsoft Excel is used to:**
    a. Create presentations.
    b. Create charts.
    c. Write e-mails.
    d. All of the above

12. **Each of the following is true, except:**
    a. Word documents can be imported directly into Publisher.
    b. Word can be used to edit stories written in Publisher.
    c. Stories written in Word are created in text boxes by default.
    d. One reason to import Word documents into Publisher publications is to maintain design consistency by adding design elements.

13. **Which Microsoft product is used to exchange e-mail across the Internet?**
    a. Access
    b. Excel
    c. Outlook
    d. PowerPoint

14. **Which Microsoft product is used to organize data into tables, records, and fields?**
    a. Access
    b. Excel
    c. Outlook
    d. PowerPoint

15. **AutoCorrect is used to do everything listed below, except:**
    a. Correct misspelled words.
    b. Find and correct typos.
    c. Correct errors in capitalization.
    d. Correct layout and design errors.

16. **To detect and correct misspellings, AutoCorrect uses:**
    a. A list of AutoCorrect entries.
    b. The main dictionary.
    c. The custom dictionary.
    d. A thesaurus.

17. **Design Checker is used to:**
    a. Correct misspelled words.
    b. Find and correct typos.
    c. Correct errors in capitalization.
    d. Correct layout and design errors.

Publisher 2002   *Practice*

18. Design Checker can check for:
   a. Text in the overflow area.
   b. Blank pages.
   c. Subject verb agreement.
   d. Clashing colors.

19. A copyrighted image can be used if:
   a. You ask permission of the copyright holder.
   b. You copy it from the World Wide Web.
   c. You credit the copyright owner in a footnote.
   d. You get permission from the copyright holder.

20. An embedded object:
   a. Can never be updated.
   b. Is updated automatically.
   c. Is updated by double-clicking on the object.
   d. Has to be removed from the publication for updating.

21. A linked object:
   a. Can never be updated.
   b. Is updated when the source file is changed.
   c. Is updated by double-clicking on the object.
   d. Has to be removed from the publication for updating.

▶ Skills Review

1. Import a Word document.
   a. Start Publisher, then create a new publication using the Bars Word Document in the Publisher Gallery.
   b. In the Import Word Document dialog box, select the file Pub I-4 in the drive and folder where your Project Files are located, click OK, then save the publication as **Astronomy Story**.
   c. Make the publication two columns, close the task pane, then press [F9].
   d. Replace the Document Title placeholder text with **Doing Astronomy Right**.
   e. Change the title font size to 18 point.
   f. Click the Save button on the Standard toolbar, then close the file, but do not exit Publisher.

2. Use Design Checker.
   a. Open the file Pub I-5 from the drive and folder where your Project Files are located, then save it as **New IM Newsletter**.
   b. Start Design Checker.
   c. In the Design Checker dialog box make sure that the All option button is selected, then click OK.
   d. Ignore the Design Checker warning box that says "Problem: The picture (the Image Magic logo) is not in its original proportions."
   e. The second Design Checker warning box says "Problem: Part of this object (the selected line) lies off the page," click the Ungroup Objects button, resize the line so that it lies on the page, then click Group Objects. (*Hint*: Press and hold [Shift] while resizing the line.)
   f. Click Continue in the Design Checker dialog box.

Practice

  g. The third Design Checker warning box says "Problem: This object (the blue lightning bolt) is in the printer's non-printing region," click Edit on the menu bar, click Delete Object, then click Continue.
  h. The fourth Design Checker warning box says "Problem: This object is covered by another object," click Ignore.
  i. The fifth Design Checker warning box says "Problem: This frame (the selected text box) is empty," click the text box, type your name, then click Continue.
  j. The sixth Design Checker warning box says "Problem: This frame (the selected text box) is empty," click Delete Frame, then click Continue.
  k. The seventh Design Checker warning box says "Problem: Part of this object (the selected line) lies off the page," click Edit on the menu bar, click Delete Object, then click Continue.
  l. The eighth Design Checker warning box says "Problem: There are two spaces after a punctuation mark," click Change, then click OK.
  m. Print page 3 of the publication.
  n. Save the publication and close Publisher.

▶ Independent Challenge 1

As the office manager for your local Chamber of Commerce, you decide to spend time working with employees to improve their skills. One of the employees needs help with a postcard announcing an upcoming event. You will use Design Checker to find and fix problems.

  a. Start Publisher, then open the file Pub I-6 from the drive and folder where your Project Files are located.
  b. Save the publication as **Potluck Supper Postcard**.
  c. Use Design Checker to find any problems.
  d. Adjust the text point size so that all of the text is visible.
  e. Click Continue.
  f. Read the Design Checker suggestions for the next problem. Use one of those suggestions to fix the problem.
  g. Continue using Design Checker throughout the publication, applying one of the suggested solutions to each problem encountered.
  n. Substitute your name for the e-mail address.
  i. Save and print the publication, then exit Publisher.

▶ Independent Challenge 2

Some friends from an art school are giving a party with the theme "Bad Taste is in Your Face". You agreed to make a flyer in the worst taste you can imagine to announce the party.

  a. Start Publisher, then open the file Pub I-7 from the drive and folder where your Project Files are located.
  b. Save the publication as **Party Flyer**.
  c. Use Design Checker to find and correct at least three problems with the flyer. (*Hint:* There are more than three design problems.)
  d. Correct any text spacing problems not found by Design Checker.
  e. Correct any typos.
  f. Substitute your name for the e-mail address.
  g. Save and print the publication, then exit Publisher.

WORKING EFFICIENTLY

Publisher 2002 Practice

▶ Independent Challenge 3

You created a document in Word that you want to print with the formatting and color accents provided by Publisher.

a. Start Publisher, then click Word Documents in the By Publication Type list in the task pane.
b. Click the Blocks Word Document in the Publisher Gallery.
c. In the Import Word Document dialog box, open the file Pub I-8 from the drive and folder where your Project Files are located, click OK, then save the publication as **Color Psychology Story**.
d. Click the One-sided printing button on the task pane, then click Yes in the warning box.
e. Close the task pane, then press [F9].
f. Delete the page number text box.
g. Click the Document Title placeholder text, type **The Psychology of Color, by**, then type **your name**.
h. Select the text, click the Font Size list arrow on the Formatting toolbar, then click 20.
i. Save and print the publication, then exit Publisher.

❋ Independent Challenge 4

You consider yourself artistic with good instincts about design, but wish you knew more about colors and how to choose them. Use your browser and search engine to explore articles about color wheels on the World Wide Web. Create a brief description of color wheels in Word, then import it into Publisher.

    a. Connect to the Internet, then use your browser and favorite search engine to explore the term "color wheel."

    b. Find out the key features and benefits of color wheels and print out any information that will help you write a brief Word document about the subject.

    c. Use the information you gathered online to write a short Word document about color wheels, then save it as **Color Wheel Story** to the drive and folder where your Project Files are located.

    d. Use the New Publication task pane and Publication Gallery to pick any Word document template of your choosing in Publisher.

    e. Import your Word document into Publisher.

    f. Save the publication as **Color Wheel Story** to the drive and folder where your Project Files are located.

    g. Change the title to **About Color Wheels, by**, then type **your name**.

    h. Select the one-sided printing option.

    i. Save and print the publication, then exit Publisher.

Publisher 2002 Practice

▶ Visual Workshop

Use the New Publication task pane and Publication Gallery to create the Crossed Lines Word Document publication. This is the initial design of a story you are importing from Word. Import the file Pub I-9 into the publication, save the publication as **Presenting Designs Story**. Use Figure I-19 as a guide. Move any of the objects on the page to make the publication easier to read. Create a text box at the bottom of the page and type your name in it. Save and print the first page.

FIGURE I-19

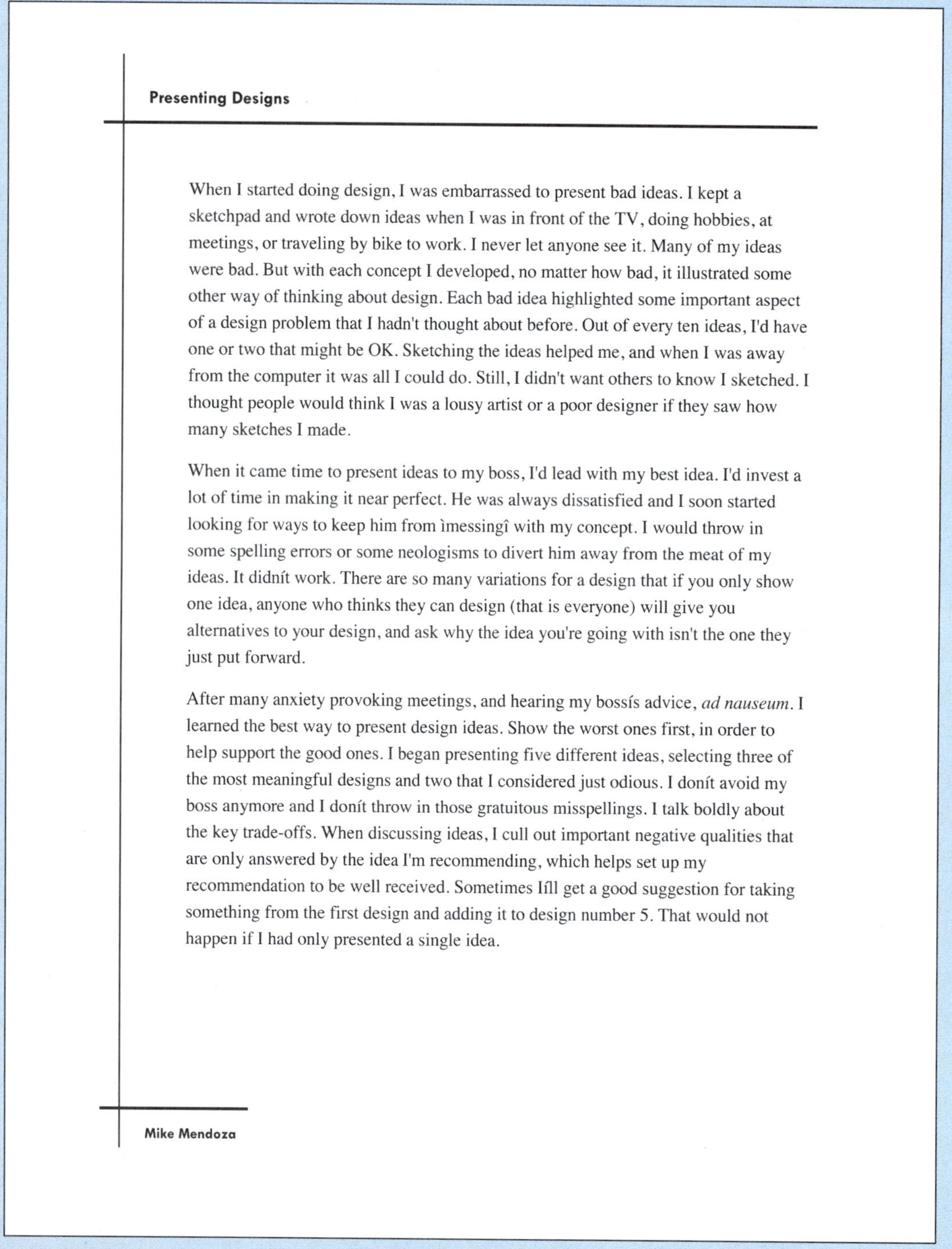

Presenting Designs

When I started doing design, I was embarrassed to present bad ideas. I kept a sketchpad and wrote down ideas when I was in front of the TV, doing hobbies, at meetings, or traveling by bike to work. I never let anyone see it. Many of my ideas were bad. But with each concept I developed, no matter how bad, it illustrated some other way of thinking about design. Each bad idea highlighted some important aspect of a design problem that I hadn't thought about before. Out of every ten ideas, I'd have one or two that might be OK. Sketching the ideas helped me, and when I was away from the computer it was all I could do. Still, I didn't want others to know I sketched. I thought people would think I was a lousy artist or a poor designer if they saw how many sketches I made.

When it came time to present ideas to my boss, I'd lead with my best idea. I'd invest a lot of time in making it near perfect. He was always dissatisfied and I soon started looking for ways to keep him from ìmessingî with my concept. I would throw in some spelling errors or some neologisms to divert him away from the meat of my ideas. It didnít work. There are so many variations for a design that if you only show one idea, anyone who thinks they can design (that is everyone) will give you alternatives to your design, and ask why the idea you're going with isn't the one they just put forward.

After many anxiety provoking meetings, and hearing my bossís advice, *ad nauseum*, I learned the best way to present design ideas. Show the worst ones first, in order to help support the good ones. I began presenting five different ideas, selecting three of the most meaningful designs and two that I considered just odious. I donít avoid my boss anymore and I donít throw in those gratuitous misspellings. I talk boldly about the key trade-offs. When discussing ideas, I cull out important negative qualities that are only answered by the idea I'm recommending, which helps set up my recommendation to be well received. Sometimes Iíll get a good suggestion for taking something from the first design and adding it to design number 5. That would not happen if I had only presented a single idea.

Mike Mendoza

Publisher 2002

Unit J

Working
on the Web

Objectives

- Plan a Web site
- Design a Web site
- Create a Web site
- Add hyperlinks
- Modify a background
- Test a Web site
- Publish a Web site
- Convert a publication into a Web site
- Capstone Project: Personal Web Site

Publisher has Web capabilities and graphics tools that make it easy to create multi-page Web sites. You can create professional-looking Web sites with attractive backgrounds, useful navigation bars, and interesting links. You can test a finished site with a browser, and publish it to the Internet so that others can access it. Before you create a Web site, you must identify your goals and resources. Frank Gonzalez is in the Web department at Image Magic and is experimenting with design ideas for the company's Web site. The primary purpose of the Web site is to describe Image Magic, including what they do for customers and how they can be contacted.

Publisher 2002

Planning a Web Site

Just like any other publication, creating an effective Web site requires planning. The steps in planning a Web site are similar to planning a publication, but with one exception. You must begin by considering how much time, money, and expertise are available for your Web site. This is dictated by the differences between Web sites and paper publications. For example, paper publications are a form of one-way communication, where the reader does not interact with the document. Web sites, on the other hand, are interactive. Here, the reader navigates the site, uses hyperlinks to find information they consider most important, while skipping past information that's less relevant to them. Another difference is that print publications do not change once they are printed, but Web sites must be maintained and their content updated to attract multiple visits. Frank recognizes the constraints of Web sites, and thinks about the key questions necessary to plan a Web site.

Details

▶ What are the constraints?

Time, money, expertise, and competing needs are the limiting factors in most enterprises. Being aware of budgetary, scheduling, and technical limits may influence your selection of a target audience and consequently, your design. A few of the things you should consider before designing a Web site are shown in Figure J-1.

▶ Who is the target audience?

The more narrowly you can define the characteristics of your audience, the more you can tailor the content, design, and access to your Web site so that the site appeals to the target group. The Internet makes it difficult to identify who is actually visiting your site since anyone can access it. You may never know who visits your site and whether their impressions are good or bad. In addition to the traditional ways to segment populations (age, sex, geography, etc.), access to the Internet and the technical abilities needed to find and use Web sites also segment your audience.

▶ What is the desired effect of the Web site?

Are you trying to sell something, persuade, teach, motivate, inform, or solicit a contribution of time or money? Deciding what effect you want is the first step to obtaining it. The answers to those questions will help you decide whether the site should give technical support, or be a clearinghouse of information, an electronic catalog, or another type of site.

▶ What response do you want?

Do you intend the site to be a one-way communication of information, or do you desire feedback? If you want people to interact with your site, what structure should the feedback take? Do you want to solicit and register people for attendance at an event? Do you want e-mail inquiries for additional information, such as a catalog? Do you want multiple visits to your Web site? If you plan to collect money, do you want to collect credit card information? How will you deal with tariffs and taxes and other barriers to international trade? Your answers to these questions will help you to reexamine and reevaluate the constraints and the desired effect of your Web site.

▶ What will you do with the responses?

If you offer people a product in exchange for money, or offer some free service such as additional information by mail, or an e-mail response, you must be able to deliver on your offer. If you don't have enough merchandise or other materials prepared for a timely response, you risk alienating customers and potential customers who show interest in your products or services. If you don't have adequate resources to deal with the potential responses your Web site will generate, then you should adjust your goals accordingly.

FIGURE J-1: Web site planning constraints

Web Site Planning Constraints

- Budget limitations
- Limiting technologies
- Staffing needs (current and future requirements)
- Development staff (programmers, designers, etc.)
- Maintenance staff (e-mail responses)
- Security issues (prevention of hacking)
- Privacy issues (guarding clients' personal information)
- Web site transactions (credit cards, order processing)
- Customer service issues (pre-sales questions, customer support, warranties, returns, etc.)
- Foriegn language services

Planning for customer service

One of the most problematic areas of planning is customer service. Even with earnest research efforts to try to anticipate the need for your product or service, the marketplace determines the demand for a product or a service. Underestimating demand for a product or service can lead to outstripped supply. Overestimating demand can lead to idle capacity, underutilized workers, and eventually, perhaps, layoffs and/or bankruptcy. When developing a Web site, carefully consider the developmental and maintenance costs. Unless there is value in a return visit, either to purchase additional product, or read updated content, the number of visits to a site will drop off. Changing content requires an investment of time and energy on the part of developers and management. You must plan for direct contact with visitors to your site too. While e-mail responses can be standardized and automated to respond to customer needs, someone has to make sure that the responses are timely and accurately answer the customers' questions. If you do not satisfy your customers' needs, someone else will.

Designing a Web Site

Publisher 2002 — Unit J

Before creating a Web site, it's a good idea to decide on the design of the site, including how you want elements to appear on the pages. Although you'll probably make many modifications to your initial design over time, a master design with a list of required elements can help you work more effectively. The elements may include a logo, colors, font selections, and other items that support you or your business's identity. As Frank plans the content of Image Magic's Web site, he wants to present the company in the best possible light. To accomplish this, he wants to incorporate success stories and accolades from credible outside sources, as well as positive visual images.

Details

▶ Create an outline or a sketch

The first step in preparing a Web site is to prepare an outline. The outline should include a list of the elements to place on each page. Information you might want to have on a page includes: a title, introductory paragraph, contact information, links to other sites and other pages, and graphic images. For the Image Magic Web site, you want the primary page, or **home page**, to briefly describe Image Magic, including what they can do for customers and how they can be contacted. You also want a page for the company's success stories, or **testimonials**, in the form of a list of satisfied clients and some of their comments.

▶ Decide how many pages are necessary

Before you work on the Web site, you should consider the number of pages for the site. Each page should be linked to the home page, and it should be easy for a reader to jump from page to page. Figure J-2 illustrates relationships that often exist among Web pages.

▶ Add links to other sites

In addition to linking associated pages within your site, you can also provide helpful links to other Web locations of interest to your readers. If you have a page that lists Image Magic's clients, you might include links to the clients' Web sites. By including your clients on your corporate Web site, they become ambassadors for your company. These links also serve to promote your corporate clients. While there is no legal requirement to ask permission to link to another site, it is a good idea to seek the cooperation of clients, and keep them updated on how you represent their interests.

▶ Add graphics, backgrounds, and design elements

A few well-placed graphic images can enhance your Web site by breaking up blocks of text and making your pages more attractive. You can use any Clip Gallery images on your pages, and Publisher provides over 300 **animated GIFs**—images with movement—for Web page use. Using one of the over 200 backgrounds available can make your pages eye-catching. The Design Gallery contains a variety of elements designed specifically for Web pages. Additional buttons appear on the Objects toolbar to add Web-related elements, and the Web Site Options task pane lets you quickly add response forms and navigation bars to your Web pages.

▶ Critically examine the page

Because Publisher shows you exactly how your page looks by letting you see it through a browser, you can monitor your progress as you work. The Image Magic site consists of four pages. Figure J-3 shows the sample Image Magic home page, and Figure J-4 shows the Design Clinic page. Pages 2, 3, and 4 are linked to the home page, and the vertical navigation bar is present on each page, making it easy for a reader to jump to any page on the site. It's a good idea to occasionally step back and imagine that you're seeing your work for the first time. Ask yourself if you find the pages easy to read and navigate. See if the pages look attractive.

▶ Preview the Web site and test the links

If your pages include links to other Web sites, make sure that the links are correct. Periodically check the links to make sure that they work as intended. There is software available that can test links automatically, but you must still manually test them to make sure that the content on the sites to which you are linking is still relevant and appropriate.

WORKING ON THE WEB

FIGURE J-2: Possible relationships between Web pages

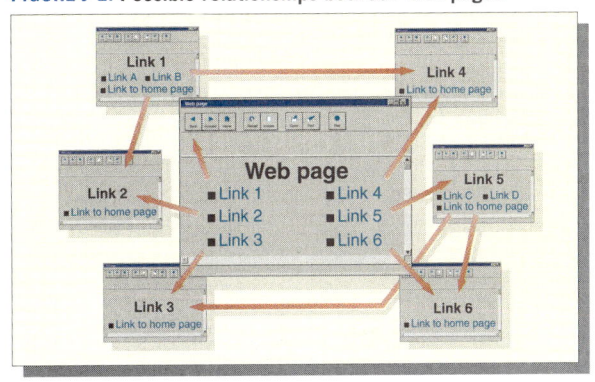

FIGURE J-3: Image Magic home page

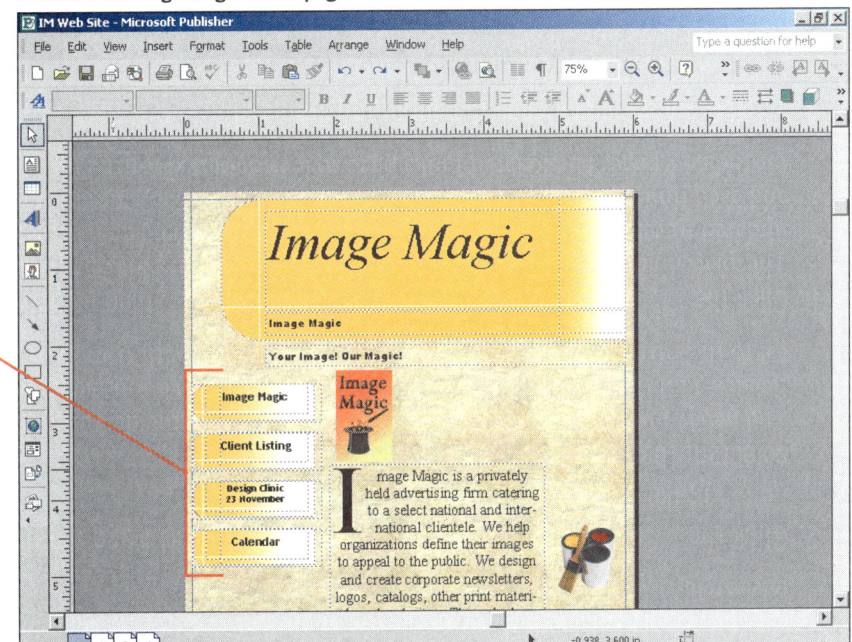

Navigation bar to pages on the site

FIGURE J-4: Design Clinic page

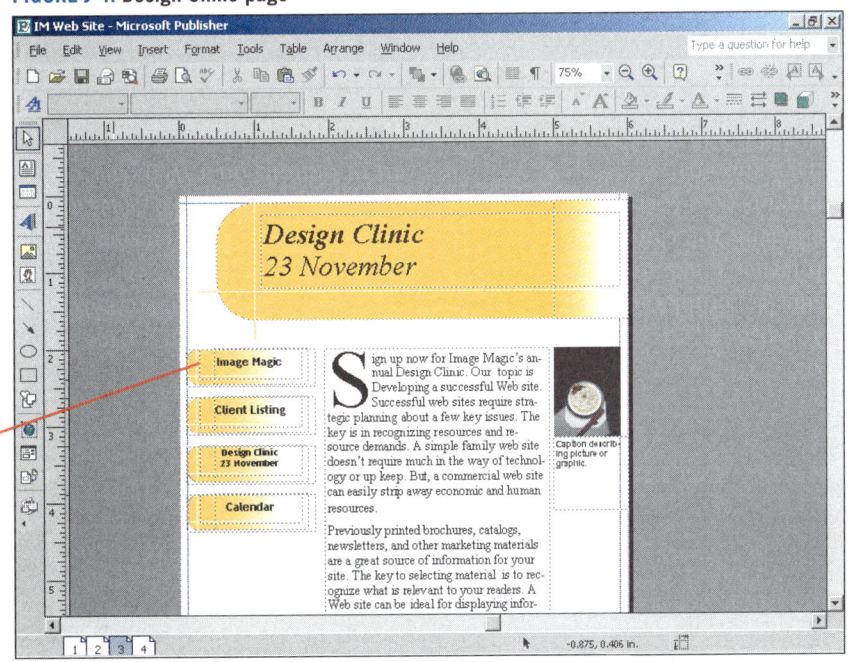

Link returns to home page

WORKING ON THE WEB PUBLISHER 221

Publisher 2002 — Unit J

Creating a Web Site

The New Publication task pane contains many options for creating Web sites. Like other publications, Web sites created using the New Publication task pane have coordinated colors and placeholders for graphic images and text. Additionally, the Web Site Options task pane offers navigation bar choices, inclusion of forms, background sounds, and background textures. Frank will use the New Publication task pane and the Publication Gallery to get a quick start on his new design ideas. Using Personal Information Sets will speed up his work.

Steps

1. Start Publisher, click **Web Sites** in the New Publication task pane, then click the **Crisscross Web Site** in the Publication Gallery

   The Web site appears on the screen. Now you will add Personal Information.

2. Click **Edit** on the menu bar, click **Personal Information**, click **Secondary Business**, if necessary type **Mike Mendoza** in the Name text box, type **Account Executive** in the Job or position title text box, type **Image Magic** in the Address text box, press **[Enter]**, type **214 Old Spanish Trail**, press **[Enter]**, type **Santa Fe, New Mexico 87501**, in the Phone/fax/e-mail text box type **Phone: 505-555-5555**, press **[Enter]**, type **Fax: 505-555-4444**, press **[Enter]**, type **E-mail: mikemendoza@imagemagic.com**, type **Image Magic** in the Organization name text box, type **Your Image! Our Magic!** in the Tag line or motto text box, click the **Include Color Scheme** check box if necessary, click the **Color Schemes list arrow**, click **Wildflower**, then click **Update**

3. Save the publication as **IM Web Site** to the drive and folder where your Project Files are located

   You can easily replace text placeholders on this Web page as you would in any publication.

4. Click the text frame at **2" H / ½" V**, press **[F9]**, then type **Image Magic**

   The home page title placeholder is replaced, as shown in Figure J-5. Web sites for a company should include the company logo, so you will add Image Magic's logo.

5. Right-click the **picture frame** at **2½" H / 3" V**, point to **Change Picture**, click **From File**, click the file **Imlogo** from the drive and folder where your Project Files are located, then click **Insert**

   The Image Magic logo replaces the picture placeholder on the page. You can also use images from the Clip Gallery on a Web page to add visual interest and convey your message.

> **Trouble?**
> If this image is not available, choose a similar image.

6. Scroll until the picture at **5" H / 5" V** is visible, right-click the **picture**, point to **Change Picture**, click **Clip Art**, type **paints** in the Search text text box in the Insert Clip Art task pane, press **[Enter]**, point to the image shown in Figure J-6, click the **list arrow**, then click **Insert** on the menu

   The placeholder image is replaced with the image of the paint cans. You can already see how a combination of text and images builds a Web page.

7. Right-click the **text frame** at **4" H / 4" V**, point to **Change Text**, click **Text File**, click the file **PUB J-1** from the drive and folder where your Project Files are located, then click **OK**

   The document file replaces the placeholder text. Drop caps work well as a design element on a Web page, as they do in any publication.

> **Trouble?**
> A warning box appears when you add a drop cap if the insertion point is not in the paragraph.

8. Click anywhere in the paragraph, click **Format** on the menu bar, click **Drop Cap**, click the choice beneath the current selection, then click **OK**

   Compare your page to Figure J-7. The Web Site Options task pane helped you to set up the page easily, and you were able to replace the placeholders with images and text appropriate for your needs.

9. Click the **Save button** on the Standard toolbar

▶ PUBLISHER 222 **WORKING ON THE WEB**

FIGURE J-5: Home page placeholder replaced

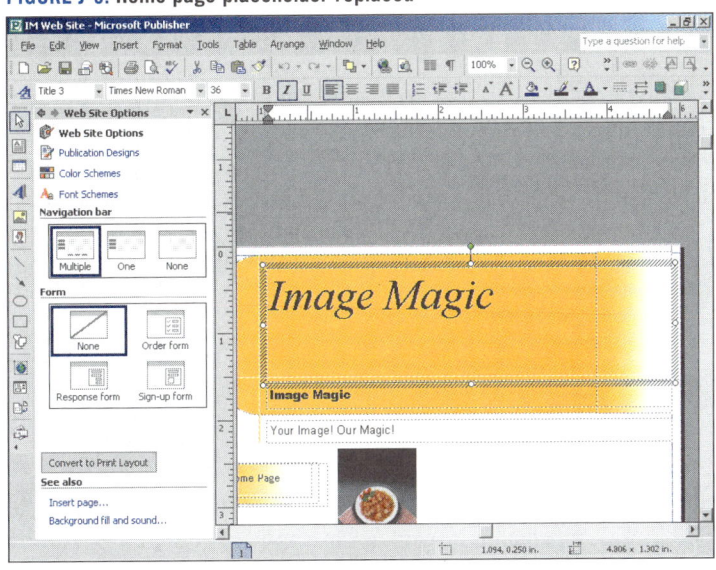

FIGURE J-6: Insert Clip Art task pane

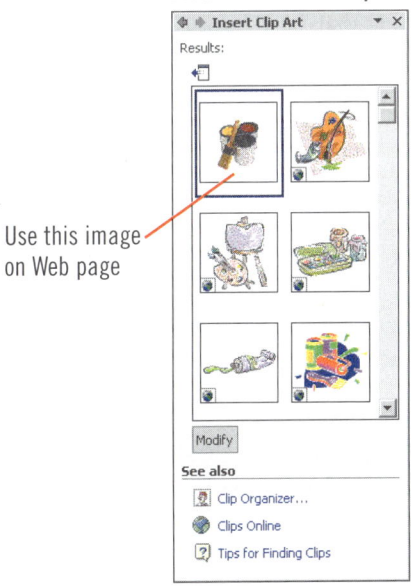

Use this image on Web page

FIGURE J-7: Home page with images and text replaced

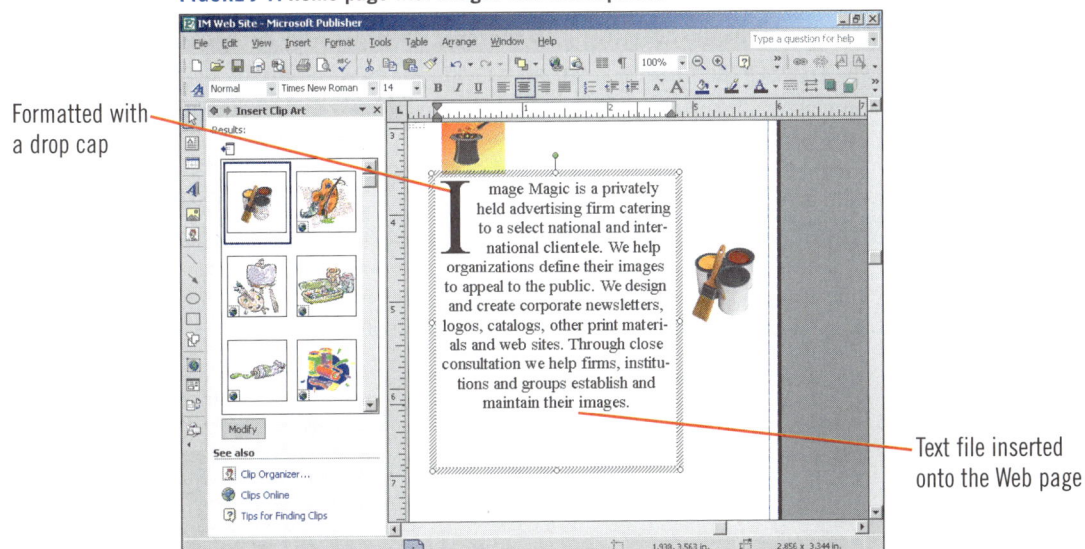

Formatted with a drop cap

Text file inserted onto the Web page

WORKING ON THE WEB PUBLISHER 223

Unit J
Publisher 2002

Adding Hyperlinks

You use **hyperlinks**, or **links**, each time you click an area on a page and jump to another Web site. Hyperlinks are electronic connections to locations within your Web site, or elsewhere on the Internet. Links are included on Web pages to make the reader's experience more pleasurable and efficient. You can create links to your own or other pages, Web sites, e-mail addresses, and documents on a specific computer. Publisher automatically links pages added to a Web site with a navigation bar. A **navigation bar** is a row of buttons on a Web page containing links to each of the site's sub pages. Frank wants to add an additional page to the Web site, and include a link to a client's Web page.

Steps

1. Close the task pane, click **Insert** on the menu bar, then click **Page**
   The Insert Page dialog box opens, as shown in Figure J-8. You can choose from a variety of page styles.

2. Click the **Available page types list arrow** in the Insert Page dialog box, click **Related links**, make sure that the **Add hyperlink to Web navigation bar check box** is selected, then click **OK**
   The newly inserted page 2 is now the current page, and the default heading is "Directory of Related Links". There is now a second entry on the navigation bar whose heading is identical to the current page title, which you want to replace with your own text.

3. Click the **text frame** at **2" H / 1" V**, type **Client Listing**, then press **[Esc]** twice
   The placeholder text is replaced with the new heading. Notice that the navigation bar is updated to reflect the new heading. Each page on this Web site has the same navigation bar, and each time a page is added to the site, the navigation bar is updated to include a hyperlink for the new page. The Related Links page style is designed for the inclusion of hyperlinks.

4. Scroll down so you can see the entire text frame at **2½" H / 4" V**, select the text **Web site name and address hyperlink**, then type **Course Technology**
   The company name, Course Technology, will contain the hyperlink.

5. Select the text **Course Technology**, then click the **Insert Hyperlink button** on the Standard toolbar
   The Insert Hyperlink dialog box opens.

6. Make sure that the **Existing File or Web Page button** is selected, click the **Address Box**, type **http://www.course.com** as shown in Figure J-9, then click **OK**
   The Course Technology text changed color and is now underlined, indicating that it is a hyperlink.

7. Click the text beneath the Course Technology link, type **A publisher of high-quality technology textbooks and other electronic training materials.**, then press **[Esc]** twice
   Compare your page to Figure J-10.

8. Click the **Save button** on the Standard toolbar

► PUBLISHER 224   **WORKING ON THE WEB**

FIGURE J-8: Insert Page dialog box

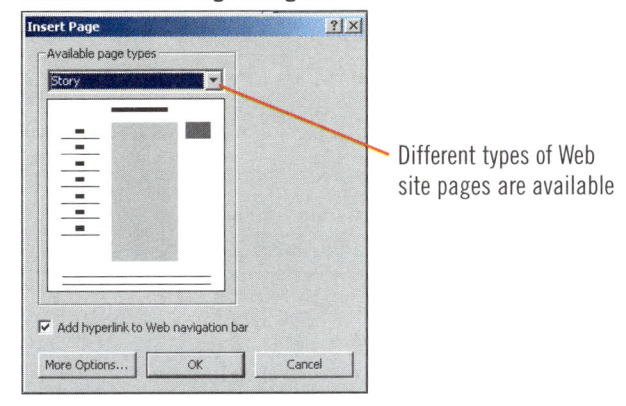

Different types of Web site pages are available

FIGURE J-9: Insert Hyperlink dialog box

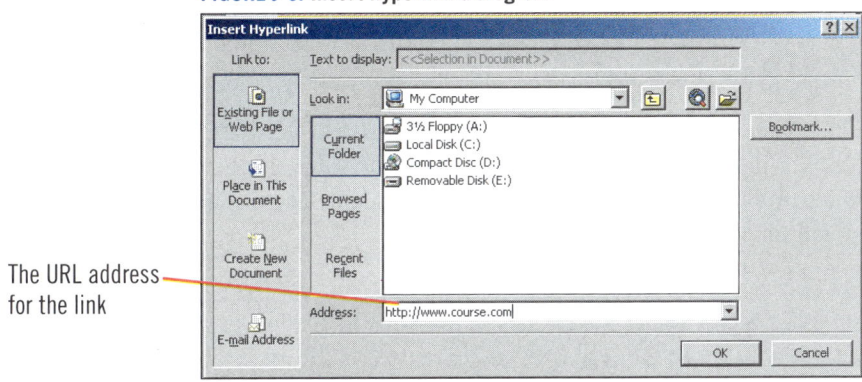

The URL address for the link

FIGURE J-10: New page with hyperlink added

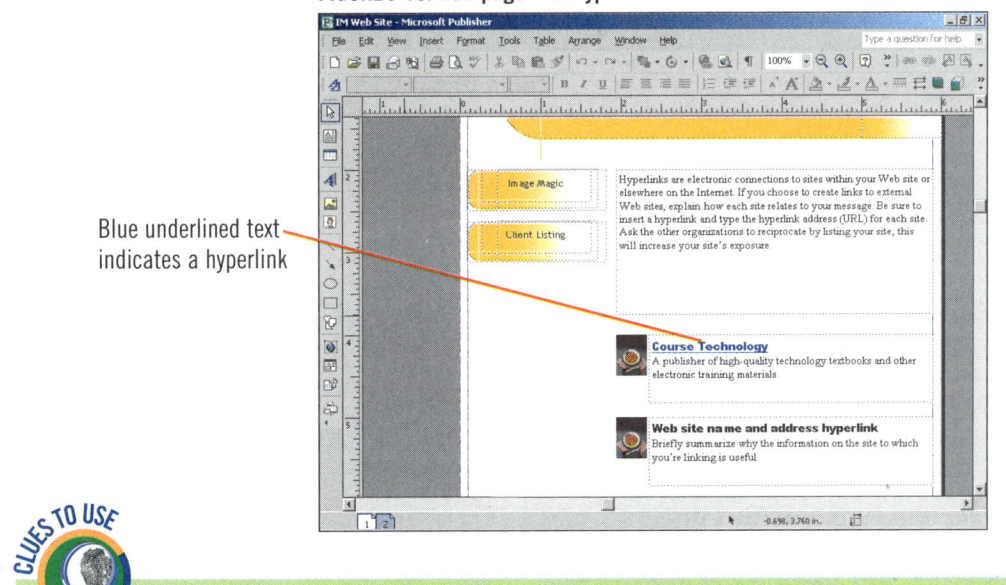

Blue underlined text indicates a hyperlink

Clues to Use

Adding a hyperlink to an e-mail address

By adding a hyperlink to an e-mail address, you can make it easy for your readers to keep in touch. Because the Internet is a fairly anonymous medium, this kind of contact with readers can be invaluable. It can lead you to new ideas, and new sources of content, and expand your network. Complaints can be particularly valuable because they help you identify problems that might otherwise escape notice. To establish a hyperlink to an e-mail address, first select the text that you want to be the link, open the Insert Hyperlink dialog box by clicking , click the E-mail Address button, then enter a valid address in the E-mail address text box. If you wish to identify that the message is coming through the hyperlink, you can place an entry in the Subject text box, then click OK.

WORKING ON THE WEB PUBLISHER 225

Modifying a Background

The background of the pages on the Web site can be modified to have different colors and textures, or no texture at all. The addition of carefully chosen background colors and textures enhances a Web site's design by adding visual interest and an illusion of depth. You can easily modify the background colors and textures individually on each page, or on all the pages, using the Master Page view. Frank wants to modify the background texture so that it is patterned, but still allows the text to be legible.

Steps

1. **Click View on the menu bar, then click Master Page**
   With the Master Page view selected, the design elements are no longer visible.

2. **Click Format on the menu bar, click Background, click More backgrounds in the Backgrounds task pane, then click the Texture tab in the Fill Effects dialog box**
   The Texture tab appears. You want to select a light, warm shade for the background—one that will make the text stand out.

3. **Click the selection in the upper-right corner**
   A sample appears in the lower-right corner of the dialog box, and the name of the texture, "Stationery," appears underneath the selections, as shown in Figure J-12.

4. **Click OK**
   The Master Page has a beige, textured background that will add visual interest and an illusion of depth when the design elements are visible.

5. **Press [Ctrl][M], then click the page 1 icon on the status bar**
   With the design elements visible, the colors all seem to complement each other, and the texture creates a pleasing appearance, as shown in Figure J-13.

Creating a custom color scheme

You can create your own custom color schemes, just like those included in the Publisher Color Scheme list. Custom color schemes include main, accent, and hyperlink colors, as well as background textures. You create a custom color scheme by making selections in the Color Schemes task pane. Click Custom color scheme at the bottom of the Color Schemes task pane. Click the Custom tab in the Color Schemes dialog box, shown in Figure J-11, if necessary. You can now change the color scheme selections. Click the list arrows for any of the Scheme colors in the New column, then click a color from the palette. When all your selections are made, you can name the scheme by clicking the Save Scheme button, typing a name for the scheme, then clicking OK.

FIGURE J-11: Custom tab in the Color Schemes dialog box

Blue hyperlink is selected; click arrow for other choices

Blue hyperlink text sample

PUBLISHER 226 WORKING ON THE WEB

FIGURE J-12: Texture tab in Fill Effects dialog box

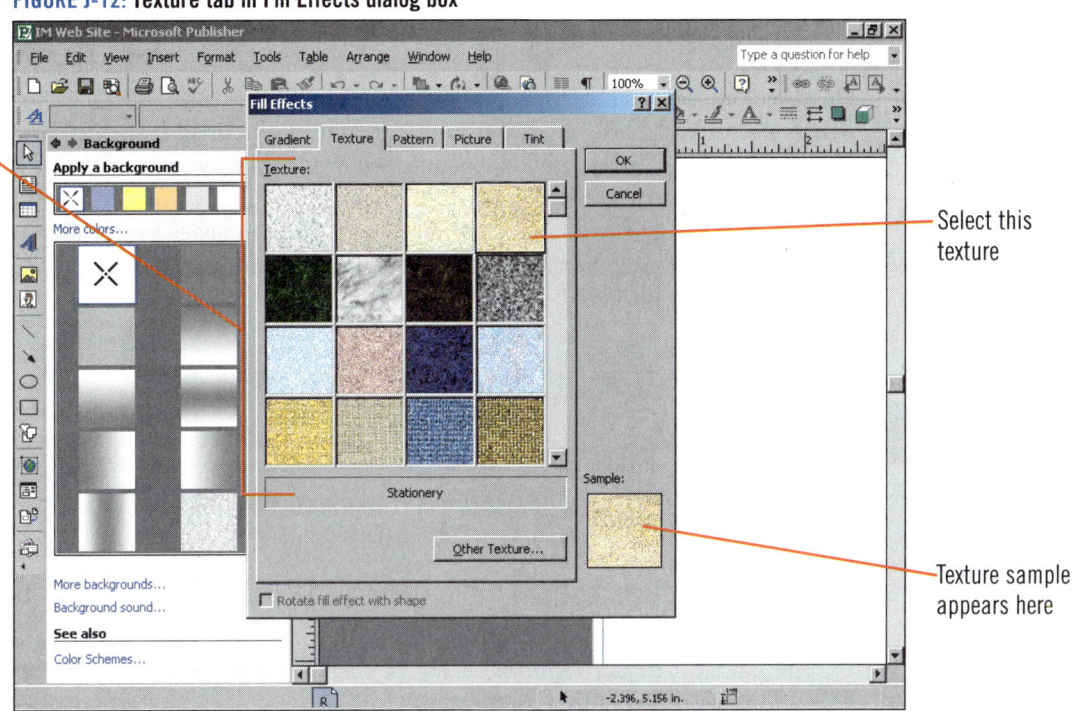

Available textures
Select this texture
Texture sample appears here

FIGURE J-13: Web page background texture modified

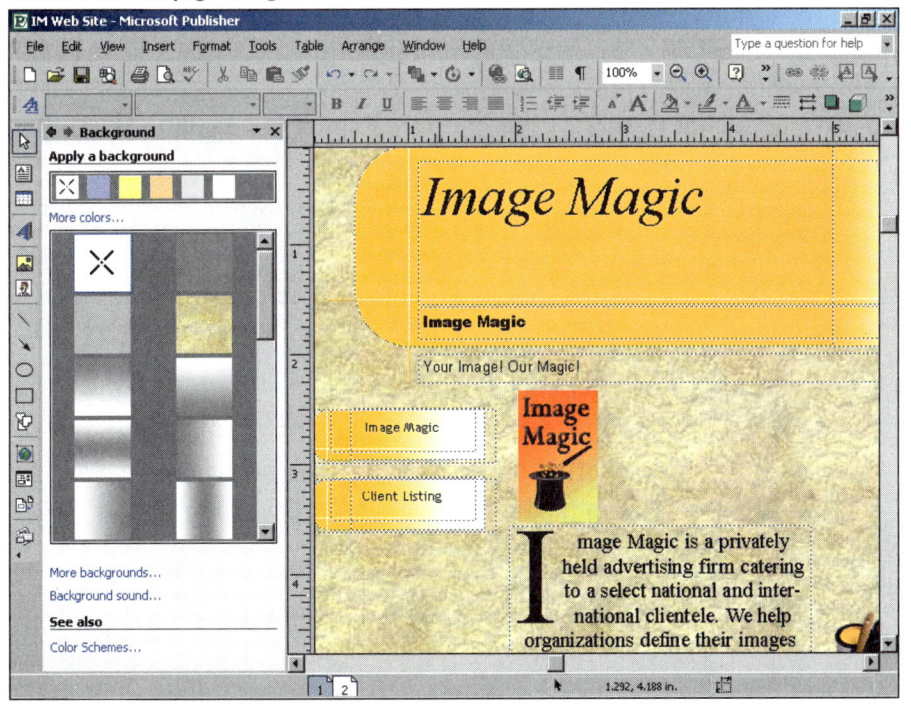

WORKING ON THE WEB PUBLISHER 227

Publisher 2002

Publisher 2002

Testing a Web Site

On a Web site, the potential for embarrassment caused by typos, misspellings, and awkward or poor design is worldwide. It is important to test and critique your Web site before publishing it to the Internet. Careful examination of the publication, first using Design Checker, and then the Web Page Preview feature, can help you identify and correct errors long before they are public. ✒ Frank wants to correct any errors, and make sure that the additional elements and changes to the background of the Web site do not distract from the overall design. He decides to use Design Checker first, then preview the publication in Internet Explorer.

Steps

1. **Close the task pane, click Tools on the menu bar, then click Design Checker**
   The Design Checker dialog box opens. By default, it will check all pages, as well as the Master Page.

2. **Click the Options button in the Design Checker dialog box, then read the selected features that Design Checker will examine**
   The Design Checker Options dialog box is shown in Figure J-14. Note that some of the options are different than in print publications.

3. **Click OK in the Options dialog box, then click OK in the Design Checker dialog box**
   Design Checker finds that there are two spaces after a punctuation mark.

4. **Click Change, click OK, then click on the Scratch area to deselect the textbox**
   Design Checker found no other problems.

> **Trouble?**
> Your page may look different depending upon which browser is installed.

5. **Click the Web Page Preview button on the Standard toolbar, make sure the Web site option button is selected in the Web Page Preview dialog box, then click OK**
   The Web page opens in your browser. The first page of the Web site appears, as shown in Figure J-15.

6. **Click Client Listing on the navigation bar, then scroll until the Course Technology link is visible**
   Page 2 of the IM Web site appears on the browser screen, as shown in Figure J-16.

7. **Connect to the Internet**
   If you are unsure how to connect to the Internet, contact your instructor or technical support person. If you are unable to connect to the Internet, skip Steps 7 and 8.

> **Trouble?**
> You will not be able to test the hyperlink if you cannot connect to the Internet.

8. **Click the Course Technology link**
   The Course Technology Web site now appears on the browser screen.

9. **Click the Close button on the browser window, click the Save button on the Standard toolbar in the Publisher window, then close the file**

▶ PUBLISHER 228   **WORKING ON THE WEB**

FIGURE J-14: Design Checker Options dialog box

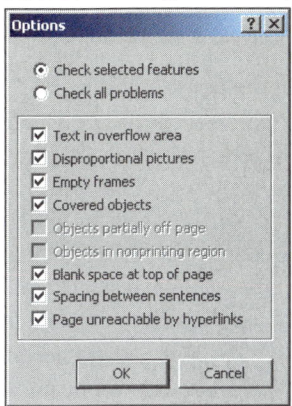

FIGURE J-15: Page 1 of the IM Web site in Web Page Preview.

Web page previews in Internet Explorer or other browser

Appearance of background and other elements may differ

FIGURE J-16: Page 2 of the IM Web site in Web Page Preview

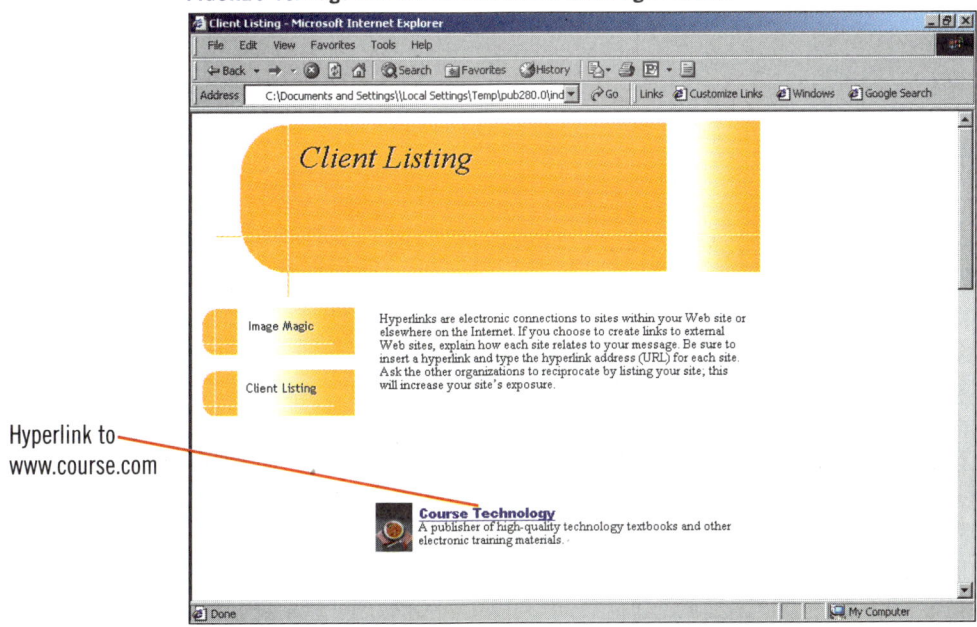

Hyperlink to www.course.com

WORKING ON THE WEB PUBLISHER 229

Publisher 2002

Publisher 2002 — Unit J

Publishing a Web Site

Once your Web site is finished, you will want to publish it to the Internet so that others can see it. Publisher offers several ways to do this. The procedures are different for Windows 2000 and Windows Millennium Edition operating systems versus Windows NT and Windows 98. The instructions below are for Windows 2000 and the Millennium Edition so if you are using another operating system, your instructions will be different. Before you can publish a Web site to the Internet, you must create a Network Place for the site. A **Network Place** is a shortcut to a location on a Web server where your pages will reside. Before beginning the publishing process, you must get a **Uniform Resource Locator (URL)** from your **Internet Service Provider (ISP)**. Once the Image Magic Web site is complete, it will need to be published to the Internet. Frank researches the steps required to do this so that he will be familiar with the procedure.

Details

Read below to understand how to publish a Web site, but do not follow the instructions.

▶ **Create a Network Place**

The first step in creating a Network Place is to contact your ISP and get an address for your files. Once this is complete, click File on the menu bar, then click Save as Web Page. Click the My Network Places button in the Save as Web Page dialog box, as shown in Figure J-17. Double-click Add Network Place, then use the Add Network Place Wizard, shown in Figures J-18 and J-19, to establish a connection to the URL.

▶ **Save the publication as a Web page**

To save the publication as a Web page, you must use the Save as Web Page dialog box shown in Figure J-17, which is available from the File menu. Open My Network Places, double-click the site you want, double-click the folder in which you want your files published, then click Save.

Design Matters

Adding design elements

There is a wide variety of design elements for Web pages, which can be found in the Microsoft Design Gallery Live, including some that create movement and sound. The animated GIFs and sound clips will not be visible or heard within Publisher. They are only displayed or played with a browser. You can attract attention by creating moving images or using an animated GIF. The **Graphics Interchange Format (GIF)** is commonly used on the Web because of its small file size, which makes it quick to download. Additionally, you can add sounds to your Web pages so that people with sound-capable computers will be able to hear them when the page opens. You can install most commonly used sound formats by clicking Background fill and sound at the bottom of the Web Site Options task pane, clicking Background sound, then typing the name of the sound file in the File name text box of the Web Options dialog box.

▶ PUBLISHER 230   **WORKING ON THE WEB**

FIGURE J-17: Save as Web Page dialog box

Add Network Place button

My Network Places button

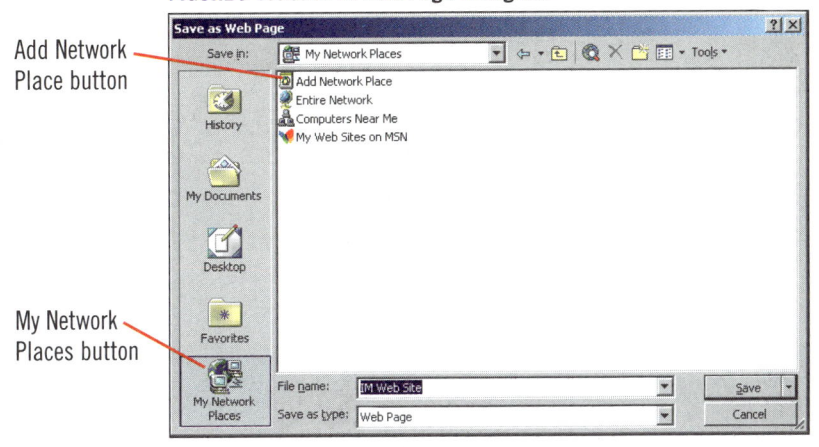

FIGURE J-18: First page of the Add Network Place Wizard

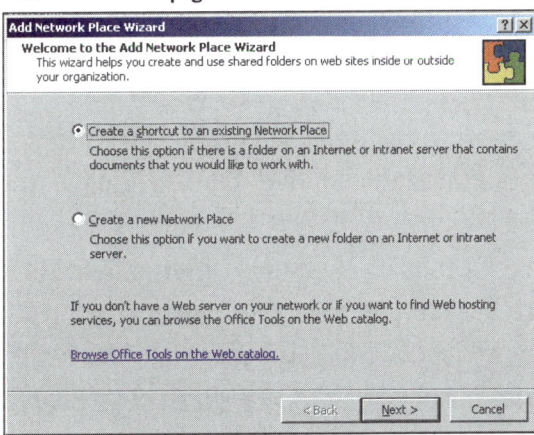

FIGURE J-19: Second page of the Add Network Place Wizard

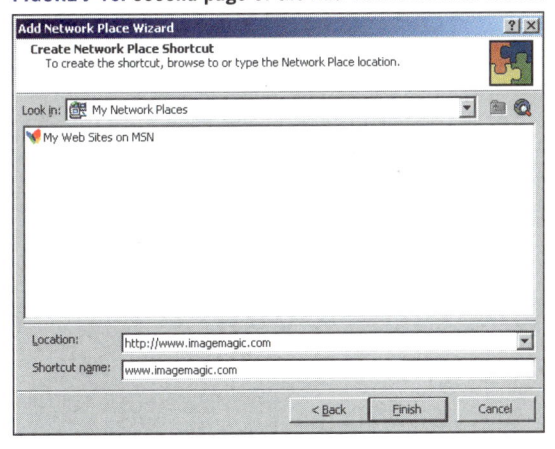

Increasing Web site traffic

The key to a successful Internet site is its accessibility to all Web users. After all, if no one sees your site, the caliber of its design is irrelevant. At minimum, you want to contact interested parties by e-mail to let them know of your site. You also want to register your Web site with several **search engines**, special Web sites that search for and report on information found on the Internet. Since many search engines compile their indices using **keywords**, the descriptive reference words found on a page, it is important to include those words. Additionally, there are several listing services on the Internet that will make submissions to the search engines, and provide information on maximizing the amount of traffic to your site.

WORKING ON THE WEB

Converting a Publication into a Web Site

Publisher 2002 — Unit J

Making relevant information readily available is the Internet's strong point. By using prior printed material on a Web site, you can increase your site's usefulness to a reader, and increase the usefulness of your written work. Using Publisher, it is easy to convert a newsletter or brochure to a Web page. It even stores design elements that must be removed to fit the Web site design. Those removed design elements from the conversion process are added to the Extra Content tab in the Design Gallery so they can be retrieved if needed elsewhere. Once a publication is converted to a Web site, you can modify the design and create your own hyperlinks. Any newsletter or brochure Frank develops may ultimately be converted to a Web page. Frank knows this and wants to test the conversion process. He uses the New Publication task pane and the Publisher Gallery to quickly create a brochure he can use for practice.

Steps

1. Click **File** on the menu bar, click **New**, click **Brochures** in the New Publication task pane, click **Informational**, then click the **Blends Informational Brochure**
   The brochure is created and appears on the screen.

2. Apply the **Secondary Personal Information set**, then save the publication as **Brochure Conversion** to the drive and folder where your Project Files are located
   Use of the same color scheme in all of your publications helps build and maintain your identity.

3. Click **Color Schemes** in the task pane, click **Bluebird**, then click **Brochure Options** on the task pane
   Adding just a few identifiers to the brochure will help you determine how the conversion process will affect the appearance of the brochure.

4. Click the text frame at **9" H / 3" V**, type **Image Magic Brochure**, then press **[Esc]** twice
   Compare your screen to Figure J-20. The last button in the Brochure Options task pane is Convert to Web Layout. You can use this feature to turn your brochure into a Web site.

   > **QuickTip**
   > If you get a warning box asking if you want to save your publication, click Yes.

5. Click the **Convert to Web Layout button** at the bottom of the task pane
   The Web Site Options task pane appears, and the publication is converted to a Web site, as shown in Figure J-21.

6. Save the publication as **Converted Brochure** to the drive and folder where your Project Files are located, click **File** on the menu bar, then click **Exit**

FIGURE J-20: Brochure before conversion to a Web site

Convert to Web Layout button

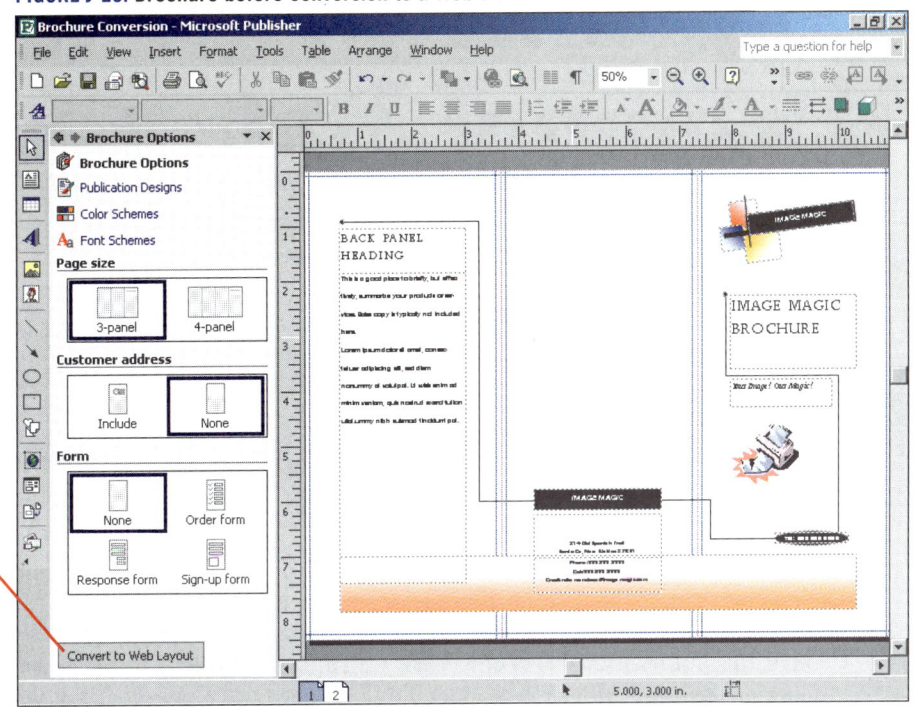

FIGURE J-21: Web site after conversion from a brochure

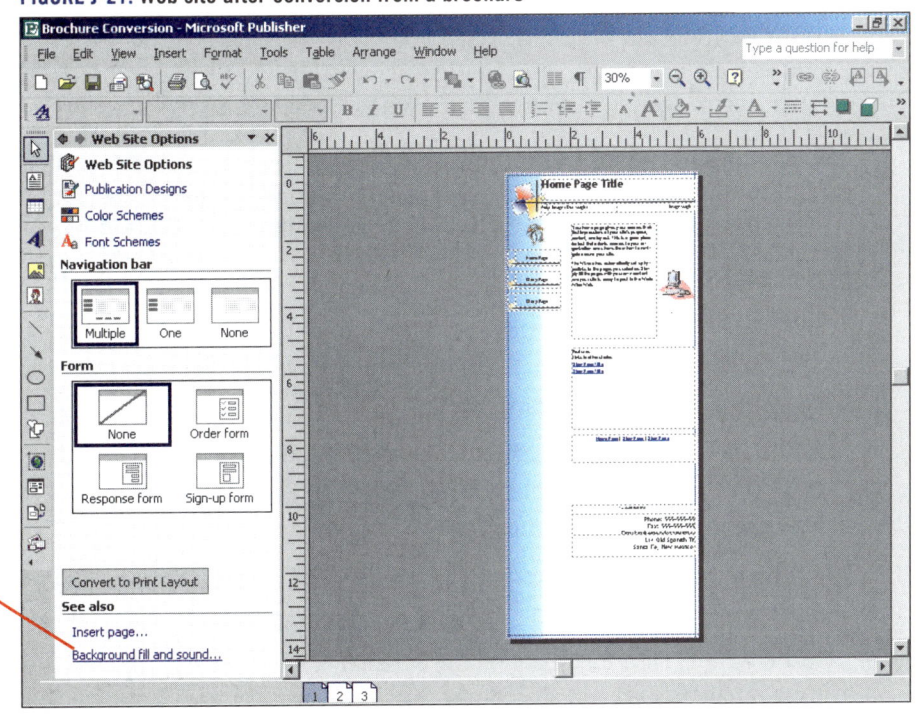

Background fill and sound

Converting a Web site to a print publication

You can also convert a Publisher-designed Web site into a brochure or newsletter. Once the Web site you want to convert is open, and the Web Site Options task pane is open, click the Convert to Print Layout button at the bottom of the task pane, then click the type of print publication you want.

WORKING ON THE WEB PUBLISHER 233

Capstone Project: Personal Web Site

Publisher 2002 — Unit J

You have learned about planning, designing, creating, testing, converting, and publishing Web sites. Additionally, you have added hyperlinks and modified a Web site's background. Frank wants to make it easier for people to get to know him so he created a personal Web site that contains his resume and a calendar. He wants to modify it to make it easier for visitors to the page to contact him by including an e-mail button.

Steps

1. **Start Publisher, then open the file Pub J-2 from the drive and folder where your Project Files are located**
   The Web site appears on the screen. As with all other publications, you can use the task pane to make simple modifications.

2. **Save the publication as Frank's Web Site to the drive and folder where your Project Files are located, then press [F9]**
   The Design Gallery contains many design elements specifically created for use on Web sites. You want to find an e-mail button that will stand out against the blue background of the Web site.

3. **Click the Design Gallery Object button on the Objects toolbar, then click Web Buttons from the Categories list**
   You can easily find a variety of design elements specifically made for insertion on Web pages, as shown in Figure J-22. You think the yellow Email Framed Oval button will attract attention.

4. **Click Email Framed Oval from the Web Buttons list, then click Insert Object**
   The button is inserted onto the Web page. You think it will look best and be most functional if it is placed close to the navigation bar that contains hyperlinks to the other pages.

5. **Using drag the object so that the upper-left corner is at ½" H / 4½" V, then select the text E-mail**
   The e-mail button appears to be well positioned on the page.

6. **Click the Insert Hyperlink button on the Standard toolbar, click the E-mail Address button, type fgonzalez@imagemagic.com in the E-mail address text box, click OK, then click anywhere on the scratch area to deselect the e-mail button**
   The e-mail hyperlink is created.

7. **Create a text box whose top-left corner is at ¼" H / 5½"V with the dimensions 1½" H x ½" V, click the Font Size button on the Formatting Toolbar, click 14, type your name in the text box, then click anywhere on the scratch area to deselect the text box**
   Compare your page to Figure J-23.

8. **Click the Save button on the Standard toolbar, print the first page of the Web site, then close Publisher**

▶ PUBLISHER 234   **WORKING ON THE WEB**

FIGURE J-22: Web Buttons

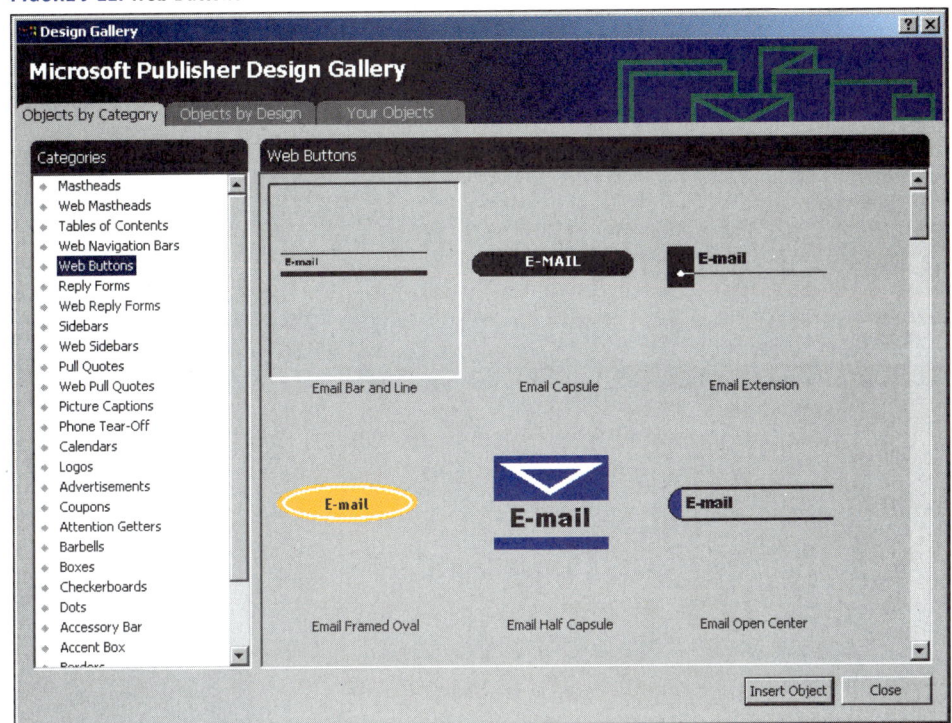

FIGURE J-23: Text box added to Web site

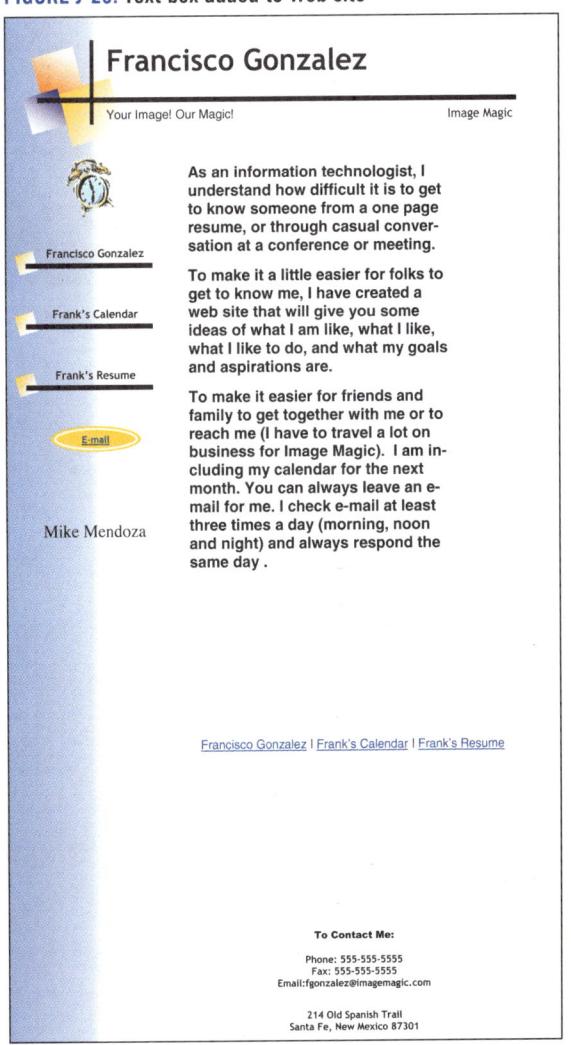

WORKING ON THE WEB

Publisher 2002 Practice

▶ Concepts Review

Label each of the elements in the Publisher window shown in **Figure J-24**.

FIGURE J-24

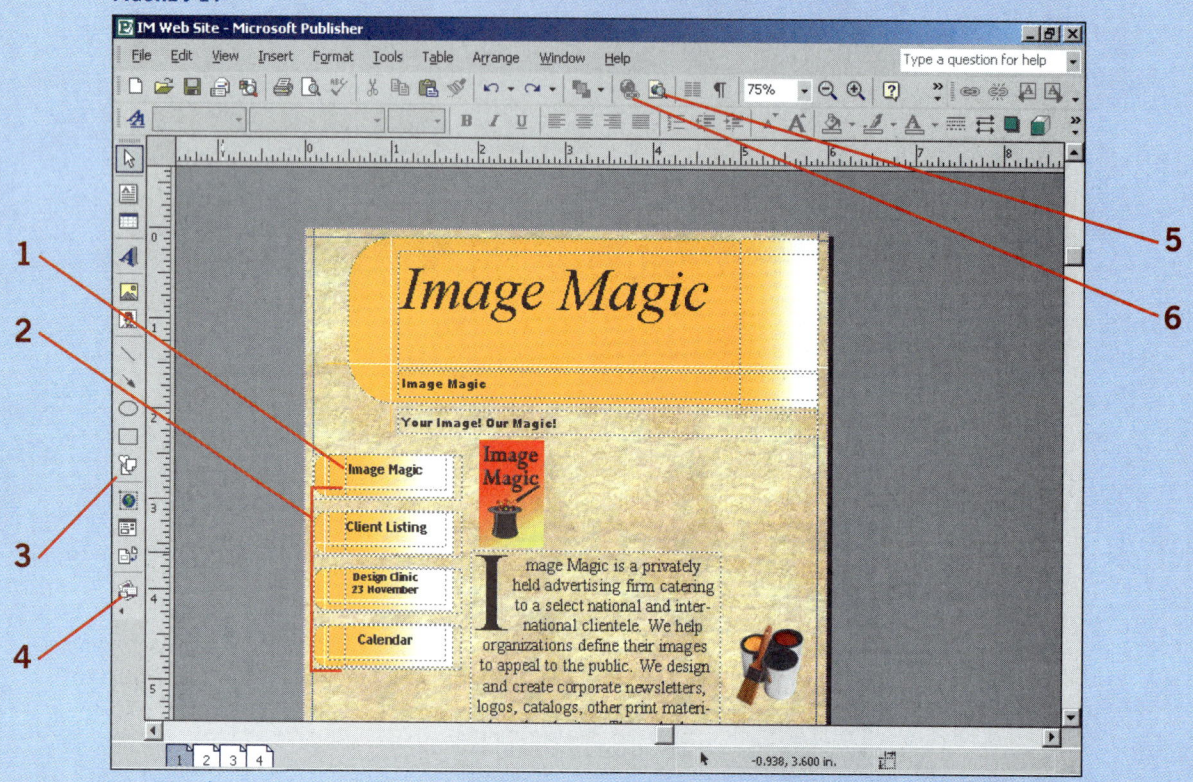

Match each of the buttons or terms with the statement that describes its function.

7. 🖼
8. Animated GIF
9. Navigation bar
10. 🖼
11. Network Place
12. 🖼

a. Views page in browser
b. Creates a hyperlink
c. Image with movement
d. Contains Web design elements
e. Buttons on a Web page containing links to sub pages
f. Shortcut to a location on a Web server where pages will reside

Select the best answer from the list of choices.

13. Each of the following is true about a navigation bar, except:
    a. Publisher creates one automatically as part of a Web site.
    b. It can contain an animated GIF.
    c. It can be horizontal or vertical in design.
    d. It is automatically updated when a page is added.

▶ PUBLISHER 236   WORKING ON THE WEB

Practice

14. Add sound clips to a Web page using the:
    a. Programs menu.
    b. Objects toolbar.
    c. Format menu.
    d. Web site options task pane.
15. Which button is used to add a hyperlink?
    a. [icon]
    b. [icon]
    c. [icon]
    d. [icon]
16. Which of the following can be hyperlinks on a Web page?
    a. Other Web sites
    b. E-mail addresses
    c. Web pages on your own Web site
    d. All of the above
17. You can modify a Web page's background texture using the:
    a. File menu.
    b. Edit menu.
    c. Format menu.
    d. All the above
18. Which statement about hyperlinks is true?
    a. You can add a hyperlink to any object.
    b. The only object to which you can add a hyperlink is an animated GIF.
    c. You cannot add a hyperlink to a text frame.
    d. A hyperlink cannot be used with e-mail.
19. GIF stands for:
    a. Great Image Format.
    b. Graphics Interchange Format.
    c. Good Image Format.
    d. None of the above
20. Which statement is true about animated GIFs?
    a. They only display movement in a browser.
    b. They display movement in Publisher and a browser.
    c. They cannot be added to the Clip Gallery.
    d. They are available for a fee from Microsoft Design Gallery.
21. Which button can be used to add Design Gallery elements?
    a. [icon]
    b. [icon]
    c. [icon]
    d. [icon]

▶ Skills Review

Throughout these exercises, use the Zoom feature when necessary.

1. **Create a Web Site.**
   a. Start Publisher.
   b. Use the New Publication task pane and the Publication Gallery to create a Web site for Ladders By Mail. Select the Bubbles Web Site, use Personal Information Sets to enter appropriate information, then apply the Bluebird color scheme.
   c. Save the file as **Ladders By Mail Web Site** to the drive and folder where your Project Files are located .
   d. Replace the Home Page Title text at 2" H / 1" V with **Ladders By Mail**.
   e. Replace the text in the frame at 5" H / 1½" V with **Your Name, Owner**.
   f. Save your work.
2. **Add hyperlinks.**
   a. Insert a Related links page after the home page. (*Hint*: Make sure that the hyperlink is added to the Web navigation bar.)
   b. Change the title on page 2 at 2" H / 1" V to **Happy Customers**.
   c. Click the text frame at 4" H / 4" V, make sure that the Web site name and address hyperlink text are selected, then type **Microsoft Corporation**.

Publisher 2002 Practice

   d. Select the Microsoft Corporation text, then click the Insert Hyperlink button on the Standard toolbar.
   e. Make sure that the Existing File or Web Page button is selected, enter the Internet address http://www.microsoft.com, then click OK.
   f. Save your work.
3. **Modify a background.**
   a. Click Background fill and sound in the Web Site Options task pane, click More backgrounds, then click the Texture tab in the Fill Effects dialog box.
   b. Click the Papyrus texture in the fourth row of the first column.
   c. Click OK.
   d. Save your work.
4. **Test a Web site.**
   a. Click Tools on the menu bar, click Design Checker, click OK, then fix any problems.
   b. Click File on the menu bar, click Web Page Preview, then click OK. Notice the animated GIF image.
   c. Click the Happy Customers text on page 1.
   d. Click the hyperlink to Microsoft Corporation (*Hint*: If you are not connected to the Internet, you will not be able to view the Microsoft Web site. Skip Steps d and e).
   e. Close the browser.
   f. Print the current page.
   g. Save and close the Web site publication.
5. **Convert a publication into a Web page.**
   a. Use the New Publication task pane and the Publication Gallery to create a brochure for Ladders By Mail. Select the Bubbles Informational Brochure, use the same Personal Information Set as in Step 1. b, then apply the Bluebird color scheme.
   b. Save the file as **Ladders By Mail Brochure** to the drive and folder where your Project Files are located.
   c. Click Convert to Web Layout in the Brochure Options task pane.
   d. Create a text box at 5" H / 1½" V with **Your Name, Owner**.
   e. Save the file as **Ladder Conversion** to the drive and folder where your Project Files are located.
   f. Print page 1 of the Web site.
   g. Close the publication.
   h. Exit Publisher.

▶ Independent Challenge 1

You are the proud owner of a very successful rare comic book store in Binghamton, NY. You decide to expand your store, Comix Alive, by designing a Web site. This way, you will be able to retain all the university student customers who leave town after graduation.

   a. Start Publisher, use the New Publication task pane and the Publisher Gallery to select the Blocks Web Site.
   b. Use Personal Information Sets to enter appropriate information.
   c. Select the Wildflower color scheme.
   d. Save the publication as **Comix Alive Web Site** to the drive and folder where your Project Files are located.
   e. Change the title of the home page to **Comix Alive**.
   f. Insert a Related links page after the home page.
   g. Select the first Web site name and address hyperlink text listed on page 2.
   h. Create a hyperlink to any other comic book site. Use your favorite search engine to find a site.
   i. Add a text box containing your name on page 1.
   j. Save the publication, print the first page of the publication, then exit Publisher.

Practice

▶ Independent Challenge 2

Your family asks you to create a newsletter that can be distributed to everybody, and you know that a request for a Web site isn't far behind. Thinking ahead, you want to prepare a simple mock-up of a family newsletter, convert it to a Web site, then suggest it to the family at your next gathering.

- a. Start Publisher, then use any newsletter design in the Publication Gallery, accepting all the defaults.
- b. Use Personal Information Sets to enter appropriate information, then change the color scheme to your choice.
- c. Save the publication as **Family Newsletter** to the drive and folder where your Project Files are located.
- d. Make modifications you feel are necessary to give family members a feel for the newsletter, but make sure that the newsletter masthead contains your last name. (For example, the masthead might be "Mendoza Family News.")
- e. Place your name in one of the headlines on page 1.
- f. Save your work and print the first page of the newsletter.
- g. Convert the publication to a Web site.
- h. Save the converted publication as **Family Web Site** to the drive and folder where your Project Files are located.
- i. Use the Design Gallery Object button to add a Web button on the home page.
- j. Create a hyperlink to the Web button that allows a user to send e-mail to you.
- k. Delete all but the first four pages of the Web site.
- l. Save the Web site, print the home page, then exit Publisher.

▶ Independent Challenge 3

You are creating a proposal for Jack's Joke Shop, a novelty store. The company's management team is not technologically sophisticated but they believe they need a Web site to be competitive in their local market.

Use Microsoft Word or another word processor to create the proposal that includes these features:

- a. A list of constraints that management should consider before pursuing their planning process.
- b. Two Web site plans. One plan is a listing of their location, phone number and an e-mail link at minimal cost. The other option would, at moderate cost, let them sell a limited number of items over the Internet.
- c. A recommendation of which plan they should choose. Support your recommendation based on management's knowledge of technology.
- d. Include your name, address and phone number on the proposal.

▶ Independent Challenge 4

You have seen how dynamic Web sites look when they contain animated GIFs, or other sources of animation. But you have probably also seen Web sites that go overboard in gimmickry and silly design stunts that distract from their message. In this exercise you are asked to use your own judgment about what is bad design.

- a. Connect to the Internet and use your favorite search engine to search on **bad Web site design** or **worst of the Web**, then locate two examples of poorly designed Web sites.
- b. Start Publisher. Use the New Publication task pane and the Publication Gallery to create a Flyer. Use Personal Information Sets to enter appropriate information, then apply the color scheme of your choice.
- c. Describe the Web sites you chose in the flyer and list the sites by their URL.
- d. Modify the flyer to include your name.
- e. Describe what could be done to improve those Web sites.
- f. Save the publication as **Bad Web Site Design Flyer**, print the flyer, exit the browser, then exit Publisher.

Publisher 2002 | Practice

▶ Visual Workshop

Use the New Publication task pane and the Publication Gallery to create the Southwest Web Site. Save the Web site to the drive and folder where your Project Files are located as **Traveler Web Site**. Use Personal Information Sets and the color scheme of Bluebird so that your publication matches Figure J-25.zzz Using Figure J-25 as a guide, add two additional story pages (Colorado Adventures and New Mexico Adventures). Insert the images Canyon and Train (both included in the drive and folder where your Project Files are located). Replace any text, and rearrange any element, using Figure J-25 as a guide. Include your name in a text box on page one, then print page one.

FIGURE J-25

Project Files List

Read the following information carefully!!

Find out from your instructor the location of the Project Files you need and the location where you will store your files.

- To complete many of the lessons in this book, you need to use Project Files. Your instructor will either provide you with a copy of the Project Files or ask you to make your own copy.
- If you need to make a copy of the Project Files, you will need to copy a set of files from a file server, standalone computer, or the Web to the drive and location where you will be storing your Project Files.
- Your instructor will tell you which computer, drive letter, and folders contain the files you need, and where you will store your files.
- You can also download the files by going to www.course.com. See the inside back cover of the book for instructions to download your files.

Copy and organize your Project Files.

- Use the Project Files List to organize your files either on a zip drive, network folder, hard drive, or other storage device. Note that the Project Files for each unit will not necessarily fit on a single floppy disk.
- Create a subfolder for each unit in the location where you are storing your files, and name it according to the unit title (e.g., Publisher Unit A).
- For each unit you are assigned, copy the files listed in the **Project File Supplied column** into that unit's folder.
- Store the files you modify or create in each unit in the unit folder.

Find and keep track of your Project Files and completed files.

- Use the **Project File Supplied column** to make sure you have the files you need before starting the unit or exercise indicated in the **Unit and Location column**.
- Use the **Student Saves File As column** to find out the filename you use when saving your changes to a Project File provided.
- Use the **Student Creates File column** to find out the filename you use when saving your new file for the exercise.

Unit	Project File Supplied	Student Saves File As	Student Created Files
Unit A	PUB A-1.pub	Grand Opening Flyer.pub PUB A-2.pub PUB A-3.pub	Study Abroad Flyer.pub Sample Business Card.pub Suggestion 1.pub Suggestion 2.pub Suggestion 3.pub Explanation.pub
		PUB A-4.pub PUB A-5.pub	Image Magic Award.pub Image Magic Gift Card.pub
Unit B			IM Newsletter.pub
	PUB B-1.doc IMlogo.tif PUB B-2.doc	*Used in* IM Newsletter *Used in* IM Newsletter *Used in* IM Newsletter	
			Camelback Brochure.pub Mock-up Newsletter.pub
	PUB B-3.doc PUB B-4.doc	*Used in* Mock-up Newsletter *Used in* Mock-up Newsletter	
			Fun Run Flyer.pub Take-Out Menu.pub For Rent Sign.pub Publisher Class Web Page.pub IM Postcard.pub
Unit C			Design Clinic Flyer.pub
	PUB C-1.doc	*Used in* Design Clinic Flyer	
			Book Sale Flyer.pub Company Picnic Flyer.pub
	PUB C-2.doc	*Used in* Company Picnic Flyer	
			Promotion Announcement.pub
	PUB C-3.doc	*Used in* Promotion Announcement	
			International Leadership Certificate.pub Music Program.pub Different Font Flyer.pub Estate Sale Flyer.pub
Unit D	PUB D-1.pub PUB D-2.tif PUB D-3.pub PUB D-4.pub	Fundraiser Flyer.pub *Used in* Fundraiser Flyer Flower Show Web Page.pub Family Reunion Postcard.pub	
			New Business Card Design.pub Gift Certificate.pub Next Month's Calendar.pub
	PUB D-5.pub	Party Invitation.pub	
Unit E	PUB E-1.pub PUB E-2.doc PUB-E-3.pub PUB E-4.doc	Route 66 Traveler.pub *Used in* Route 66 Traveler Solar System Newsletter.pub *Used in* Solar System Newsletter	
			Guanajuato Newsletter.pub
	PUB E-5.doc	*Used in* Guanajuato Newsletter	
			Finance Wizardry Brochure.pub
	PUB E-6.pub	Community Promotion Web Site.pub	
			A Great Place.doc Homeless Shelter Flyer.pub New England Foliage Brochure.pub New England Attractions.doc SW Brochure.pub
	PUB E-7.pub		

Unit	Project File Supplied	Student Saves File As	Student Created Files
Unit F	PUB F-1.pub PUB F-2.pub PUB F-3.pub PUB F-4.pub PUB F-5.pub PUB F-6.pub	Concerned Parent Newsletter.pub Flower Shop Flyer.pub Daily Specials Menu.pub Corporate Business Card.pub Certificate of Appreciation.pub Tour Guide Flyer.pub	Design Techniques-Bad.pub Design Techniques-Good.pub
Unit G	PUB G-1.pub NavajoRug1.tif PUB G-2.doc NavajoRug2.tif PUB G-3.pub PUB G-4.tif PUB G-5.doc PUB G-6.pub NavajoRug3.tif	Rug Catalog.pub *Used in* Rug Catalog *Used in* Rug Catalog Rug Label.pub Jewelry Tools Catalog.pub *Used in* Jewelry Tools Catalog *Used in* Video Store Catalog Rug Collection Binder.pub *Used in* Rug Collection Binder	Video Store Catalog Video Label.pub Play Program.pub School Newsletter.pub Personal Shipping Label.pub Publisher Newsletter.pub
Unit H	PUB H-1.pub Piano1.tif PUB H-2.mdb PUB H-3.pub PUB H-4.pub	Piano Brochure.pub *Used in* Piano Brochure *Mail Merge Source File* Automotive Gift Certificate.pub Gym Flyer.pub	Monthly Calendar.pub Believe It or Not Postcard.pub Design Center Business Card.pub Publisher Printing Options.pub Packed01.puz; Unpack.exe Toy Shop Brochure.pub
Unit I	PUB I-1.doc PUB I-2.pub PUB I-3.pub PUB I-4.doc PUB I-5.pub PUB I-6.pub PUB I-7.pub PUB I-8.doc Pub I-9.doc	Book Review.pub Training Flyer.pub Dinner Invitation.pub Astronomy Story.pub New IM Newsletter.pub Potluck Supper Postcard.pub Party Flyer.pub Color Psychology Story.pub Color Wheel Story.pub Presenting Designs Story.pub	
Unit J	 Paint Can.gif IMlogo.tif PUB J-1.doc	 *Used in* IM Web Site *Used in* IM Web Site *Used in* IM Web Site	IM Web Site.pub Brochure Conversion.pub Converted Brochure.pub

Unit	Project File Supplied	Student Saves File As	Student Created Files
PUBLISHER	PUB J-2.pub	Frank's Web Site.pub	Ladders By Mail Web Site.pub Ladders By Mail Brochure.pub Ladder Conversion.pub Comix Alive Web Site.pub Family Newsletter.pub Family Web Site.pub Joke Shop Web Site.pub Bad Web Site Design Flyer.pub Traveler Web Site.pub
	Canyon.tif Train.tif	*Used in* Traveler Web Site *Used in* Traveler Web Site	

Glossary

Publisher 2002

Align To arrange two or more items along an edge.

Animated GIFs An image with movement; commonly used in Web pages.

AutoCorrect A feature that automatically corrects misspellings and grammar errors as you type.

AutoFit A feature that automatically resizes type and manipulates text to fit within a text box.

Autoflow A feature that automatically places text that does not fit in a text box into the next available text box.

AutoShapes Ready-made design elements, including lines, connectors, basic shapes, flowchart elements, stars and banners, and callouts.

Balance Symmetrical arrangement of design elements in a publication.

Booklet A multi-page publication that is folded or bound.

Border The edge or boundary line of an object.

BorderArt Decorative borders that come with or can be created using Publisher, for placement around most objects.

Browser A program that locates and displays data from the Internet, such as Web pages, and other networks.

Bulleted list Used to illustrate items that can occur in any order or that are of equal importance.

Camera-ready artwork Graphic illustrations that have been fully prepared for the printing of a publication.

Catalog A publication that presents a list or display of items.

Chart A graphic representation of numerical information.

Clip art Electronic artwork available for use on a computer.

Clipboard Temporary holding area in Windows into which as many as 24 objects can be copied and pasted.

Color schemes Coordinated sets of matched and complementary colors that may be applied to a publication.

Color wheel Circular illustrations where primary and intermediate colors are arranged so that related colors are next to each other and complementary colors are opposite.

Continued on/Continued from notices Text that tells on what page a story is continued on or from, and automatically updates if the story is moved.

Copyfit To make text fit into a space within a publication.

Crop To conceal portions of an image.

Data source Files in which names, addresses and other contact information are stored to be used in a mail merge.

Database A collection of information arranged for easy search and retrieval.

Design The layout and choice of colors, fonts, and artwork that enhance a publication.

Design Checker A feature that searches publications for specific layout problems.

Design Gallery A collection of formatted elements, such as pull quotes, sidebars, and logos that can be added to an existing publication.

Design Gallery Live A Microsoft Web site that continually offers new downloadable images.

Design Sets Groups of matching elements in the Design Gallery that contain common themes, colors, or objects.

Desktop publishing program A program that lets you manipulate text and graphics to create a variety of publications including multi-page catalogs and single-page flyers.

Destination file The file that into which an object is embedded or linked.

Digital camera A camera that captures and stores images as digital electronic information instead of on photographic film.

Publisher 2002 Glossary

Digital image A pictorial representation generated, stored or displayed electronically.

Drag and drop Moving or copying technique in which an object, or a copy of an object, is dragged to a new location.

Drawing tools Toolbox buttons that let you create geometric designs.

Drop caps A formatting feature that lets you change the size and appearance of a paragraph's initial character.

Electronic spreadsheet Software in which data is arranged in rows and columns and mathematical operations and charting functions are performed.

Embedded object An object created in a source file that is transplanted to a destination file. The object then becomes part of the destination file.

Field An element of a database record that contains one piece of information.

Fill To add a color, pattern or texture to a design element.

Fill color The hue added to shade a design element.

Flatbed scanner A type of digital scanner that has a sheet of glass where the page is place to be scanned. The optical sensor then passes along the glass.

Flip To rotate an Object 180 degrees horizontally or vertically using a toolbar button.

Font schemes Coordinated sets of matched and complementary fonts that may be applied to a publication.

Footer Text that repeats on the bottom of each page.

Foreground The section of a publication where non-repeating information is placed, such as textboxes or images.

Formatting toolbar Buttons on a toolbar that change the appearance of objects within a publication.

Frame An object in a publication containing a photographic image, a table, or any combination of these.

GIF (Graphics Interchange Format) A commonly used file format for graphics used in Web pages due to its small size; displayed by most browsers without the use of additional programs.

Graphic image A piece of artwork in electronic form.

Group To turn several objects into one, which is an easy way to move multiple items.

Handles Small hollow circles displayed around the perimeter of a selected object.

Hand-off format The final digital electronic format of a publication that is conveyed to a commercial printer.

Header Text that repeats on the top of each page.

Home page The first page, or primary page, in a Web site.

Horizontal ruler Measuring guide that appears above the publication window.

Hyperlink A connection, either text or an object, in a document that when clicked connects with another page or object. Hyperlinks connect Web pages together on the Internet. Also called a Link.

ISP (Internet service provider) An entity that provides companies or individuals with access to the Internet.

Kerning A form of character formatting that adjusts the spacing between character pairs.

Keywords Words used to search for specific pages, objects or images within applications.

Layer To change the position of objects in relation to one another so that one appears to be on top or behind another.

Layout guides Horizontal and vertical lines place on a publication's Master Page and visible on all pages that help you accurately position objects within a page.

Glossary

Leaders Dots or dashes in a row that make it easier to read a table of contents or other information by guiding the eye across a page.

Link *See Hyperlink.*

Linked object An object created in a source file that is shared in a destination file. The object retains its connection to the source file.

Logo Distinctive shape, symbol, or color that is visibly recognized as belonging to a company or product.

Mail merge A feature that combines a destination document, such as a personalized brochure, with a data source, such as an Excel or Access file containing names and addresses.

Mail Merge Wizard An interactive set of dialog boxes that guide the user in creating a mail merge.

Margin guides Lines that repeat on each page, separating the margins from the other design elements.

Margins White space between the edge of design element and the edge of a page.

Master page The section of a publication where objects are placed so that they are reproduced on every page.

Masthead The banner at the beginning of a newsletter with its name, volume, issue, and date, which remains consistently formatted from issue to issue.

Measurements toolbar Toolbar that lets you more precisely move, resize, or adjust objects.

Menu bar Contains menus from which you choose Publisher commands.

Microsoft Clip Organizer The artwork organizer in Publisher.

Mirrored guides Layout guides and margins on left and right facing pages that appear to be mirror images.

Mirrored image A type of two-page layout where either page appears as if viewed in a mirror, with right and left reversed.

Navigation Bar A row of buttons on a Web page containing links to information on the site's sub pages.

Network Place Shortcut to a location on a Web server where pages will reside.

Nudge To move a selected object a defined distance by pressing an arrow key.

Numbered list Used to list items that occur in a particular sequence.

Object shadow Gives an object the illusion of depth by adding a shadow behind it.

Objects toolbar Contains buttons used to create and enhance publication objects.

Online collaboration Participants working together on a project across the Internet.

Optical Character Recognition (OCR) A software application that transforms scanned images of text into digital electronic documents.

Orientation Direction in which paper is printed.

Pack and Go Wizard Feature that compacts all the files (fonts, graphics, and essential design elements) needed by a commercial printing service onto your choice of media.

Page icons Located at the bottom of the workspace, one page icon displays for each page in the publication. Click a page icon to go to a specific page.

Page numbers The numbers assigned in sequence to pages of text in a publication.

Personal Information sets Four distinct sets of information that can be used to store frequently used information such as names, addresses, and phone numbers, which can be placed automatically in publications.

Pixel The fundamental unit of an image on a television screen, computer monitor, or similar display.

Placeholders Design elements created by the Publication Gallery that you can later replace with your own information.

Publisher 2002 Glossary

Point size The measurement of the height of a character. 1/72 of an inch equals one point.

Postscript file A page description format developed by Adobe Systems that is widely supported by both hardware and software vendors.

Pour To move text that will not fit in a text box to an empty text box from Overflow.

Pre-press work Process in which a commercial printer verifies the availability of fonts and linked graphics, makes color corrections or separations, and sets the final printing options.

Proof print Approximation of how your final printed publication will look.

Publication A document created in Publisher.

Pull quote A short statement extracted from a story and set aside from the body of the text.

Record A group of related fields, such as the name, address, and title of a customer.

Resolution A measure of the fineness of detail that can be distinguished in an image.

Response Form A printed or electronic arrangement of blanks for the insertion of information that invites a reply.

Reverse text To format text so that light characters appear on a dark background.

Rotate Changes the position of an object in degrees from a horizontal plane.

Rotation An object's position measured in degrees from a horizontal plane.

Ruler guidelines See Ruler Guides.

Ruler guides Created in the foreground of individual pages by dragging a ruler by holding [Shift]. Also referred to as ruler guidelines.

Rulers Horizontal and vertical scaled displays beneath the toolbars and to the left of the workspace.

Sans serif font A typeface that has no small strokes at the end of main stroke of the character.

Scaling Stretches or shrinks the widths of characters.

Scanner Hardware that enables you to turn information on paper into an electronic file format.

Scratch area Area surrounding the publication page that can be used to store design elements.

Serif A small cross stroke at the end of the main stroke of the letter.

Sheetfed Scanner A type of digital scanner that uses rollers to pulls single sheet of paper past the optical scanning device.

Sidebar Information not central to a story in a publication, placed to the side of the regular text to create interest.

Signatures A large sheet printed with four or a multiple of four pages that when folded becomes a section of a book or catalog.

Smart objects An object category in the Design Gallery that can be modified by clicking the associated Wizard button.

Snap To commands When turned on, this feature has a magnet-like effect that pulls whatever is being lined up to an object, a guide, or a ruler mark.

Speech recognition Software used to transform human speech into computer commands or text.

Spelling checker Used to check a story or publication for spelling errors.

Standard toolbar Toolbar containing buttons for common tasks, such as saving and printing.

Status bar Located at the bottom of the Publisher window; provides information relevant to the current task.

Story Text in a publication.

Style Defined set of text formatting attributes.

Style by example To name an existing set of text attributes as a style.

Symmetrical Having parts in proportional dimensions.

Glossary

Tab A location that the insertion point advances to when [Tab] is pressed, defined using rulers.

Table Arrangement of information in columns and rows.

Table AutoFormat Pre-existing designs used to quickly format an existing table.

Table of contents A sequential list of the contents and associated page numbers of a publication.

Task pane A collection of tools that appears on the left side of the screen from which users can perform searches, open or start a new document, view the contents of the clipboard, or format publications.

Testimonial An affirmation of an entity or product's worth by a non-involved party; a recommendation.

Text box Object in which text is typed.

Text overflow Text that does not fit within a text box.

Text wrapping The automatic placement of text around design elements.

Title bar Where the program name and the filename of the open publication appear.

Toolbars Contain buttons for frequently used Publisher commands, and are organized by subject, such as Formatting, Measurement, or Objects.

Tracking The spacing between characters.

Two-Page Spread View that enables you to see two pages at once.

Ungroup To turn one combined object into individual objects.

URL (Universal Resource Locator) A Web page's address.

Vertical ruler Measuring guide that displays to the left of the page.

Washout A faint, lightly shaded image that appears behind other images.

Web folder A shortcut to a location on a Web server where your pages will reside.

White space Blank space in a publication.

Word processor A software application used to generate and edit electronic documents.

WordArt An object containing curved or wavy text.

Workspace The area where a new or existing publication appears and it's surrounding scratch area.

Zero point The location of zero on both the vertical and horizontal rulers that can be moved and lets you make precise measurements.

Zoom To make the page scale larger or smaller so that you can move in or away from page objects.

Index

special characters
(pound sign), Publisher 154

▶ **A**

Access, Microsoft, Publisher 194
adding
    border art, Publisher 170
    drop caps, Publisher 112
    graphics, Publisher 34–35
    headers, footers, Publisher 152
    page numbers, Publisher 154
    pages to publications, Publisher 146–47
    tables, Publisher 64
Add Network Place Wizard (fig.), Publisher 231
Address block, Publisher 180
advertisements
    experimenting with design elements, Publisher 136
    working with, Publisher 135
aligning
    images, objects, Publisher 82
    text, Publisher 105
animated GIFs, Publisher 220
applying styles, Publisher 102
Arial font, Publisher 101
Arrowhead Attention Getter object, Publisher 60
arrows, drawing, Publisher 88
art
    in advertisements, Publisher 135
    aligning and grouping, Publisher 82
    border, adding, Publisher 170
    clip. *See* clip art
    graphics. *See* graphics; images
    rotating, Publisher 86–87
    scanning, Publisher 83
    WordArt, Publisher 172-73
    working with, Publisher 75–98
Attention Getters, Publisher 60
attracting readers' attention, Publisher 115, Publisher 126

audience, target
    publications, Publisher 26, Publisher 218
    Web sites, Publisher 218
authors, working with, Publisher 127
AutoCorrect, using, Publisher 198–99
AutoFit Text command, Publisher 39, Publisher 156
autoflow, Publisher 108
AutoFormat, using, Publisher 65
AutoShapes button (fig.), Publisher 84

▶ **B**

background, modifying for Web pages, Publisher 226
balancing objects on pages, Publisher 132
Basic Shapes, Publisher 88–89
bitmaps. *See* graphics; images
BorderArt, Publisher 170–71, Publisher 187
borders
    adding, Publisher 170
    adding to text boxes, Publisher 54
Brick Attention Getter, Publisher 66
Bring to Front button, Publisher 85, Publisher 128
brochures, Publisher 42, Publisher 66, Publisher 233
bulleted lists, Publisher 56
bullets, adding, Publisher 56–57
business cards, Publisher 22, Publisher 142

▶ **C**

callouts, Publisher 84, Publisher 86
cameras, digital, Publisher 83, Publisher 200
capitalization, using AutoCorrect, Publisher 198
catalogs, Publisher 146, Publisher 162
.CDR files, Publisher 35
Center button, Publisher 138
certificates, creating, Publisher 71, Publisher 186
Change Style dialog box (fig.), Publisher 103
characters
    adjusting spaces between, Publisher 103
    drop caps, Publisher 112
    kerning, Publisher 103
    reversed text, Publisher 114

Character Spacing dialog box, Publisher 103
charts, Publisher 194, Publisher 195
checking
    design, Publisher 204
    spelling, Publisher 58–59
Check Spelling dialog box (fig.), Publisher 59
clip art
    described, Publisher 34
    inserting, Publisher 76
    Insert task pane (fig.), Publisher 223
    results of search (fig.), Publisher 93
    using in story (fig.), Publisher 137
Clipboard
    Office, using, Publisher 79
    using for copied or cut images, Publisher 79
Clip Organizer, Publisher 76, Publisher 92
closing
    files, Publisher 16
    Picture tool, Publisher 132
    publications, Publisher 16
    WordArt, Publisher 128
collaboration, online, Publisher 194
Color/Grayscale button, Publisher 12, Publisher 18
colors
    Color/Grayscale button, Publisher 12, Publisher 18
    creating custom scheme for Web pages, Publisher 226
    design considerations, Publisher 201
    filling shapes with, Publisher 90–91
Color Schemes dialog box (fig.), Publisher 226
Colors dialog box (fig.), Publisher 91
color wheels, Publisher 201
columns
    creating multiple, Publisher 107
    creating text, Publisher 106
    and leaders, Publisher 158
    page design considerations, Publisher 134
    table, Publisher 64
    vertical lines between, Publisher 135

Index

Columns dialog box (fig.), Publisher 107
commands
   Bring Forward, Publisher 85
   Rotate, Publisher 86
   Save, Publisher 9
   Send Backward, Publisher 85
commercial printing
   packaging files for, Publisher 184
   preparation, Publisher 182
Connect Frames, Publisher 108
contact information, inserting, Publisher 19
Continued on/from notices, adding, Publisher 110–11
contrast in publication design, Publisher 137
converters, Publisher 108, Publisher 196
converting publications into Web sites,
   Publisher 232–33
Copy button (fig.), Publisher 78
copyfitting text, Publisher 156
copying objects, Publisher 78
copyright laws, Publisher 200
corrections, preventing spelling, Publisher 198
cover art, Publisher 127
cover text, Publisher 130
Create New Style dialog box, Publisher 101
Create Styles By Example dialog box, Publisher 105
Create Table dialog box (fig.), Publisher 65
Create Text Box Link button (fig.), Publisher 108
creating
   columns, Publisher 106
   headers, footers, Publisher 152
   labels, Publisher 160
   mail merges, Publisher 180
   Network Place, Publisher 230
   publications, Publisher 25–48
   reversed text, Publisher 114
   styles by example, Publisher 104
   text boxes, Publisher 10, Publisher 12, Publisher 18
   text columns, Publisher 106
   Web sites, Publisher 222–23, Publisher 226
creative deletion, Publisher 63, Publisher 81
critiquing Web sites, Publisher 228
Crop button (fig.), Publisher 80, Publisher 132
cropping images, Publisher 80–81

custom BorderArt, Publisher 170
custom drop caps, Publisher 113

D

databases, Publisher 194
data sources, using mail merge, Publisher 178
defining styles, Publisher 99–124
Delete Page dialog box (fig.), Publisher 149
deleting
   drop caps, Publisher 113
   pages, Publisher 148
   text boxes, Publisher 131
Design Checker
   testing Web sites with, Publisher 228–29
   using, Publisher 204–205
design elements
   adding to Web pages, Publisher 230
   colors, Publisher 201
   contrasting, Publisher 137
   critiquing, Publisher 126
   rearranging, Publisher 130
   Web sites, Publisher 220
Design Gallery
   Smart Objects, Publisher 60
   using, Publisher 38–39
   Web Buttons (fig.), Publisher 235
   Web site design elements, Publisher 234
Design Gallery Live Web site, Publisher 77
designing publications
   adding emphasis with contrast, Publisher 137
   Attention Getters, using, Publisher 60
   catalogs, Publisher 162
   creative deletion, Publisher 63
   critiquing publications, Publisher 126
   cropping as creative deletion, Publisher 81
   Design Checker feature, Publisher 204
   design elements, experimenting with, Publisher 136
   design sense, Publisher 27, Publisher 29,
      Publisher 126
   fonts, choosing, Publisher 100–101, Publisher 115
   font schemes, using, Publisher 112
   generally, Publisher 28–29
   margins, using, Publisher 55, Publisher 105

mastheads, strengthening, Publisher 128
page refinements, Publisher 134
rearranging elements, Publisher 130
recognizing bad design, Publisher 29
refining pages, Publisher 134–35
rotating text boxes, Publisher 176
templates, using, Publisher 37
Web sites. *See* Web sites
designing WordArt, Publisher 172–73
destination file, linked objects, Publisher 202
dialog box views, using, Publisher 9
dialog boxes. *See specific dialog box*
diamond bullets, Publisher 57, Publisher 66
dictionary, adding words to, Publisher 58
digital cameras, Publisher 200
digital images, recording, Publisher 200
dinner invitation (sample), Publisher 209
documents. *See* files; publications
dot leaders, Publisher 159
drawing perfect shapes, Publisher 89
drawing tools, using, Publisher 88
Drop Cap dialog box (fig.), Publisher 113
drop caps
   adding, Publisher 112, Publisher 135–36,
      Publisher 222
   creating custom, Publisher 113
   moving from Word to Publisher, Publisher 156
   in story (fig.), Publisher 157
DTP/HTML Tutorials Plus Web site, Publisher 143

E

Edit Wrap Points, Publisher 174
editing
   shapes for text wrapping, Publisher 174
   stories, Publisher 156
electronic mail, adding hyperlinks, Publisher 225
electronic spreadsheets, Publisher 194
elements. *See* design elements
email addresses, adding hyperlinks to, Publisher 225
embedding and linking objects, Publisher 202–203
enhancing publications, Publisher 99–124
entering text in text boxes, Publisher 10
.EPS files, Publisher 35

Index

error messages
    converter not installed, Publisher 58
    printer can't be initialized, Publisher 8
    Publisher can't import format, Publisher 32
errors, spelling
    and AutoCorrect, Publisher 198
    catching, Publisher 179
example, style by, Publisher 104
Excel, Microsoft, Publisher 194
exiting Publisher, Publisher 16

▶ F

fields (mail merge), Publisher 178
file formats
    graphic, common, Publisher 35
    importing, Publisher 32
    PostScript, Publisher 182–83
File menu (fig.), Publisher 17
files. *See also* publications
    opening and closing, Publisher 8
    opening in Publication Gallery, Publisher 15
    packaging for another computer, Publisher 184
Fill Color list arrow (fig.), Publisher 90
fill drawn shapes, Publisher 90–91
Fill Effects dialog box (fig.), Publisher 227
flatbed scanners, Publisher 200
flipping objects, images, Publisher 78–79
flyers
    creating with focal points, Publisher 66
    flower shop example, Publisher 138–39
    sample (fig.), Publisher 3, 91
    Study Abroad, Publisher 18
Font and size button (fig.), Publisher 100, Publisher 102
Font dialog box (fig.), Publisher 63
Font Size list arrow, Publisher 130
fonts
    attracting readers' attention with, Publisher 115
    choosing, Publisher 101
    drop caps, Publisher 112
    font schemes, Publisher 112
    limit on number per page, Publisher 115
    ornate, and good design, Publisher 29
    packaging, Publisher 184
    point size, Publisher 10
    readability and, Publisher 99
    sans serif, Publisher 101
    sizing, Publisher 100
    WordArt effects, Publisher 172
Fonts dialog box (fig.), Publisher 183
footers, Publisher 152, Publisher 155
Format AutoShape, Publisher 90, Publisher 128
Format AutoShape dialog box, Publisher 87
Format Paint button, Publisher 62
formats
    changing into styles, Publisher 104–105
    painting, Publisher 62–63
Format Text Box dialog box, Publisher 55, Publisher 111
formatting text boxes, Publisher 54–55
Formatting toolbar, Publisher 6
frames
    described, Publisher 33
    linked, Publisher 108
    resizing, Publisher 33
framing elements with white space, Publisher 131

▶ G

geometric shapes, Publisher 88
GIFs
    animated, Publisher 220
    .GIF files, Publisher 35
    using on Web pages, Publisher 230
gift cards, Publisher 24
gift certificates, Publisher 186
Go to Frame button (fig.), Publisher 110
Go to Next Frame button (fig.), Publisher 108
Go to Previous Frame button (fig.), Publisher 108
graphics. *See also* art; images
    adding to publications, Publisher 34–35
    aligning and grouping images, Publisher 82
    animated GIFs, Publisher 220
    backgrounding behind text, Publisher 151
    .BMP files, Publisher 35
    common formats, Publisher 35
    copying and moving, Publisher 78
    creating with drawing tools, Publisher 88
    cropping images, Publisher 80
    file formats, Publisher 35
    flipping, Publisher 78
    layered images (fig.), Publisher 85
    layering objects, Publisher 84
    layout experimentation, Publisher 136
    manipulating on Web sites, Publisher 92
    margins, using around, Publisher 55
    nudging, Publisher 61
    packaging, Publisher 184
    repositioning (fig.), Publisher 35
    resizing, Publisher 35
    rotating art, Publisher 86–87
    rotating images, Publisher 78
    smart objects, Publisher 60
    washout images, Publisher 150–51
    wrapping text around, Publisher 174
Graphics Interchange Format. *See* GIFs
Graphics Manager dialog box (fig.), Publisher 183
grayscale. *See* Color/Grayscale button
green rotation handle, Publisher 86
grouping
    images, Publisher 82
    objects, Publisher 40–41, Publisher 43
Group Objects button (fig.), Publisher 41, Publisher 82
guides
    layout, Publisher 50–51
    margin, Publisher 50
    ruler, Publisher 52

▶ H

handles
    described, Publisher 10
    displaying, Publisher 174
    green rotation, Publisher 86
    grouped objects', Publisher 41
hand-off format described, Publisher 182
Header and Footer toolbar (fig.), Publisher 153
headers, creating, Publisher 152
heart shapes, Publisher 88
Help
    accessing, Publisher 14
    Office Assistant topics, Publisher 15
home page, Publisher 220
horizontal text alignment, Publisher 105

Index

hyperlinks
   adding, Publisher 224
   checking on Web sites, Publisher 220
   color of, Publisher 226
   testing, Publisher 228

I

Ignore button, Publisher 58, Publisher 59
Image Export photo album (fig.), Publisher 201
images. *See also* graphics
   aligning and grouping, Publisher 82
   animated GIFs, Publisher 220
   clip art. *See* clip art
   copyrighting, Publisher 200
   cropping, Publisher 80
   digital, Publisher 200
   moving backward or forward, Publisher 85
   recording, Publisher 200
   rotating, Publisher 86
   wrapping text around, Publisher 174
importing Word documents, Publisher 196
Import Word Document dialog box (fig.), Publisher 197
Indents and lists button (fig.), Publisher 100–102
indents and Lists dialog box (fig.), Publisher 57
Insert Address Block dialog box (fig.), Publisher 181
Insert Clip Art task pane (fig.), Publisher 76–77, Publisher 223
Insert Hyperlink, Publisher 225, Publisher 234
Insert Page dialog box (fig.), Publisher 147, Publisher 225
Insert Pages dialog box (fig.), Publisher 147
Insert Picture dialog box (fig.), Publisher 35
Insert Table button, Publisher 64
inserting
   clip art, Publisher 76
   contact information, Publisher 19
   dot leaders, Publisher 159
   tables, Publisher 64
   WordArt, Publisher 172
Internet. *See* World Wide Web
Internet Service Provider (ISP), Publisher 230
ISPs, Publisher 230

J

JPEG files, Publisher 35
.JPG files, Publisher 35
justified text, Publisher 105

K

kerning, Publisher 103
keywords on Web sites, Publisher 231

L

labels, creating, Publisher 160
law, copyright, Publisher 200
layering objects, Publisher 84–85
layout
   experimenting with design elements, Publisher 136
   guides, using, Publisher 50–51
   mirrored guides, Publisher 150
Layout Guides dialog box (fig.), Publisher 51, Publisher 150
leaders, Publisher 158
letters, fancy, Publisher 112
Line button (fig.), Publisher 89, Publisher 134
line leaders inserted (fig.), Publisher 163
lines
   between columns, Publisher 135
   drawing, Publisher 88
linked frames, Publisher 108
linking
   objects, Publisher 202–203
   to other Web sites, Publisher 220
links. *See* hyperlinks
lists, bulleted and numbered, Publisher 56
logos, Publisher 2

M

mail merge
   creating, Publisher 180
   described, Publisher 178
Mail Merge Recipients dialog box (fig.), Publisher 181
Mail Merge Wizard, Publisher 180
margin guides, Publisher 50–51
margins
   text alignment and, Publisher 105
   using to create white space, Publisher 55
Master Pages
   general, Publisher 50, Publisher 146
   modifying background, Publisher 226
   working with, Publisher 150–51
mastheads, improving, Publisher 128
matte, Publisher 137
Measurement toolbar
   choosing measurement tools, Publisher 53
   moving and resizing graphics, Publisher 87
   rotating callouts with, Publisher 86
measurement tools, choosing, Publisher 53
menu bar described, Publisher 6
Microsoft Access, Publisher 194
Microsoft Design Gallery Live Web site, Publisher 77
Microsoft Excel, Publisher 194
Microsoft Outlook, Publisher 194
Microsoft PowerPoint, Publisher 194
Microsoft Publisher. *See* Publisher
Microsoft Word, Publisher 156, Publisher 194
mirrored layout guides, Publisher 51, Publisher 150
misspelled words, Publisher 58, Publisher 179, Publisher 198
modifying
   backgrounds, Publisher 226
   Master Pages, Publisher 150
   objects, Publisher 132
   styles, Publisher 102
Move Both Rulers button, Publisher 52
moving
   objects, Publisher 78
   pages, Publisher 146
   rulers, Publisher 55
multiple pages, working with, Publisher 145–68

N

naming styles, Publisher 100
navigating through tables, Publisher 64
navigation bars, Publisher 224
negative space. *See* white space
Network Place, creating, Publisher 230
Next Frame button, Publisher 110
New Publication task pane, Publisher 5, Publisher 30, Publisher 222
newsletters
   columns in, Publisher 106

Index

creating, Publisher 30–31, Publisher 116
   masthead design, Publisher 128
   sample (fig.), Publisher 29
notices, Continued, Publisher 110–11
nudging objects, Publisher 61
numbered lists, Publisher 56
Numbering button, Publisher 56
numbers, page, Publisher 154

O

objects. *See also specific object*
   aligning, Publisher 82
   copying and moving, Publisher 78
   described, Publisher 11
   embedding and linking, Publisher 202
   graphics. *See* graphics
   grouped (fig.), Publisher 41
   grouping, Publisher 40–41
   inserted Design Gallery (fig.), Publisher 43
   layering, Publisher 84–85
   modifying, Publisher 132–33
   nudging, Publisher 61
   pictures. *See* graphics
   rotated (fig.), Publisher 87
   rotating or flipping, Publisher 78
   saving, Publisher 149
   smart, Publisher 60–61
   understanding, Publisher 11
   wrapping text around, Publisher 174
Objects toolbar, Publisher 6
OCR, Publisher 200
Office Assistant, Publisher 14–15
Office Clipboard
   objects copied onto (fig.), Publisher 203
   using, Publisher 79
Office Collections, Publisher 2
Office products, integrating, Publisher 194
online collaboration, Publisher 194
opening publications, Publisher 8–9
Open Publication dialog box (fig.), Publisher 9
optical character recognition (OCR), Publisher 200
Outlook, Microsoft, Publisher 194
Oval button (fig.), Publisher 89

oval callouts (fig.), Publisher 85
ovals, drawing, Publisher 88
Overflow button (fig.), Publisher 108
overflows, text, Publisher 108
overlapping graphics, Publisher 79, Publisher 83, Publisher 84–85

P

Pack and Go Wizard, Publisher 184
Pack and Go Wizard dialog boxes (fig.), Publisher 185
page
   layout design elements, experimenting with, Publisher 136
   navigation icons, Publisher 6
Page Content task pane, Publisher 106, Publisher 107
Page Numbers dialog box (fig.), Publisher 155
pages
   adding, Publisher 146–47
   adding hyperlinks to, Publisher 224–25
   background, modifying, Publisher 226
   columns, adding, Publisher 106–107
   deleting, Publisher 148
   master. *See* Master Pages
   moving, Publisher 146
   multiple page spreads, Publisher 149
   page numbers, adding, Publisher 154
   rearranging elements within, Publisher 130
   refining, Publisher 134–35
   Web site, types, Publisher 225
   working with multiple, Publisher 145–68
   zooming in and out of, Publisher 10
pages, multiple, Publisher 145–68
painting formats, Publisher 62–63
Paste button (fig.), Publisher 78
Paste Special dialog box (fig.), Publisher 203
pasting images, objects, Publisher 78
patterns, filling drawn shapes with, Publisher 90–91
.PCX files, Publisher 35
personal information, changing, Publisher 14
Personal Information Sets, Publisher 14–15
personal Web site, creating, Publisher 234
photographs. *See* graphics; images
pictures. *See* graphics; images

Picture toolbar, closing, Publisher 81, Publisher 132
pie charts, Publisher 195
pixels, Publisher 200
placeholder text, replacing, Publisher 32–33
placeholders
   described, Publisher 10
   sidebar, Publisher 37
   using, Publisher 28
planning
   publications, Publisher 26–27
   Web sites, Publisher 218–19
point size, Publisher 10
positioning objects, Publisher 40–41
postcards, Publisher 70
PostScript file format, Publisher 182
pound sign (#), Publisher 154
PowerPoint, Microsoft, Publisher 194
pre-press work, Publisher 182
presentations, Publisher 194
previewing
   mail merge, Publisher 181
   Print Preview, Publisher 12–13
   Web sites, Publisher 220
Preview pane, Publisher 9
Print button, Publisher 12
Print dialog box (fig.), Publisher 13
printers
   error messages, Publisher 12
   uninitialized message, Publisher 8
printing
   commercial preparation, Publisher 182
   multi-page documents, Publisher 147
   packaging files for commercial, Publisher 184
   publications, Publisher 12–13
   tips, Publisher 13
Print Preview, Publisher 12–13
programs
   desktop publishing, Publisher 2
   integrating for efficiency, Publisher 193–216
Programs menu (fig.), Publisher 5
Publication Gallery
   opening file created in, Publisher 15
   options, Publisher 31

Index

publications
- adding graphics to, Publisher 34–35
- adding pages to, Publisher 146–47
- adding tables to, Publisher 64
- adjusting text overflows, Publisher 108
- brochures, Publisher 42
- closing, Publisher 16
- completed newsletter (fig.), Publisher 117
- converting into Web sites, Publisher 232
- creating, Publisher 25–48
- creating with task pane, Publisher 30
- defined, Publisher 2
- editing, Publisher 156
- embedded and linked objects, Publisher 202
- enhancing, Publisher 99–124
- experimenting with layout, Publisher 136
- layout guides in, Publisher 50–51
- mail merge, using, Publisher 178
- Master Pages, working with, Publisher 150–51
- opening and saving, Publisher 8–9
- packaging for commercial printing, Publisher 184
- planning, Publisher 26–27
- printing, preparing for commercial, Publisher 182
- printing tips, Publisher 13
- rearranging elements in, Publisher 130
- saving, Publisher 8–9
- saving as Web pages, Publisher 230
- spanning pages, Publisher 110
- spell checking, Publisher 58
- templates, using, Publisher 37
- types (table), Publisher 4
- viewing and printing, Publisher 12–13

Publisher
- Design Checker feature, Publisher 204
- drop caps in, Publisher 156
- exiting, Publisher 16
- Help, Publisher 14
- imported Word documents (fig.), Publisher 197
- integrating with Office products, Publisher 194
- program described, Publisher 2
- special features, using, Publisher 169–92
- starting, Publisher 4
- window (fig.), Publisher 7
- World Wide Web site, Publisher 16

publishing Web sites, Publisher 230–31
pull quotes
- adding, Publisher 39, Publisher 136–37
- described, Publisher 38
- design element, use as, Publisher 136
- moving, Publisher 42
- placing in stories, Publisher 137
- reversed text in, Publisher 115

▶R

readability, enhancing, Publisher 99
recognizing speech, Publisher 206–208
recoloring objects, Publisher 90–91
recording images, Publisher 200–201
records described (mail merge), Publisher 178
Rectangle button, Publisher 88, Publisher 128, Publisher 138
rectangles, drawing, Publisher 88
red lines under misspellings, Publisher 10, Publisher 198
replacing text, Publisher 32
repositioning graphics, Publisher 35
resizing
- clip art, Publisher 76
- frames, Publisher 33
- graphics (fig.), Publisher 35
- grouped objects, Publisher 41
- images, text boxes, Publisher 87
resolution described, Publisher 200
reversed text, creating, Publisher 114–15
rotating
- art, images, Publisher 78, Publisher 86–87
- text boxes, Publisher 176–77
ruler coordinates, Publisher 50
ruler guides
- added (fig.), Publisher 53
- described, Publisher 10
- using, Publisher 52–53
rulers, Publisher 6, Publisher 50

▶S

sans serif fonts, Publisher 101
Save As command, Publisher 8–9
Save as PostScript File dialog box (fig.), Publisher 183

Save as Web Page dialog box (fig.), Publisher 231
Save command, Publisher 9
saving
- objects on pages, Publisher 149
- publications, Publisher 8–9
- and undoing, Publisher 62
scanner types, Publisher 200
scanning artwork, Publisher 83, Publisher 200
scratch area described, Publisher 6
searching for clip art, Publisher 92–93
Select Zoom Mode button, Publisher 32
Send Backward, Publisher 128, Publisher 132
Send to Back button, Publisher 85
serifs described, Publisher 101
Shadow Style button, Publisher 36
shapes
- AutoShapes, Publisher 84
- drawing, Publisher 88
- fill drawn, Publisher 90–91
sheetfed scanners, Publisher 200
sidebars
- adding, Publisher 36
- described, Publisher 28
- pull quotes, Publisher 38
- using for emphasis, Publisher 36
signatures described, Publisher 147
smart objects
- inserted (fig.), Publisher 67
- modifying, Publisher 60–61
source files for linked objects, Publisher 202
spaces between characters, Publisher 1–3, Publisher 180
speech recognition, Publisher 206–208
spelling
- catching errors, Publisher 179
- red lines under misspellings, Publisher 10
- using AutoCorrect, Publisher 198
Spelling Checker, Publisher 58
spoken language, converting to written, Publisher 206
spreads, multi-page, Publisher 148–49
spreadsheets, Publisher 194
Standard toolbar, Publisher 6

PUBLISHER 255

Index

starting Publisher, Publisher 4
Start menu (fig.), Publisher 5
status bar, Publisher 6
stories
    editing, Publisher 156
    Excel chart in (fig.), Publisher 195
Study Abroad flyer, Publisher 18
styles
    changing formats into, Publisher 104
    continued notices, Publisher 110
    defining, Publisher 100–101
    modifying and applying, Publisher 102
    Tight Wrapping, Publisher 174
    WordArt, Publisher 172
Styles and Formatting task pane, Publisher 100–101, Publisher 106

▶ T

Table Autoformat feature, Publisher 65
tables
    adding to publications, Publisher 64
    described, Publisher 64
    using AutoFormat, Publisher 65
tables of content, Publisher 158–59
tabs, Publisher 158
Tabs dialog box (fig.), Publisher 159
target audience
    for publications, Publisher 26
    for Web sites, Publisher 218
task panes
    New Publication, Publisher 222
    Page Content, Publisher 107
    Styles and Formatting, Publisher 100, Publisher 106
    using, Publisher 4–5, Publisher 7
    Web Site Options, Publisher 222
templates, Publisher 2, Publisher 37
testimonials, Publisher 220
testing Web sites, Publisher 228–29
text
    adding drop caps, Publisher 112
    adding files to publications, Publisher 150–51
    adjusting overflows, Publisher 108

adjusting spaces between characters, Publisher 103
applying formats to, Publisher 62
boxes. *See* text boxes
checking spelling, Publisher 58
columns, creating, Publisher 106
copyfitting, Publisher 156
creating reversed, Publisher 114
defining styles, Publisher 100–101
entering in text boxes, Publisher 10
foregrounding against image, Publisher 151
horizontal alignment, Publisher 105
overflow, Publisher 109
placeholder, Publisher 28, Publisher 32–33
pull quotes, Publisher 115
replacing, Publisher 32
reversed, creating, Publisher 114
shaping, Publisher 172
speech recognition software, Publisher 206
spell checking, Publisher 58
title (fig.), Publisher 131
working with, Publisher 49–74
wrapping around objects, Publisher 174–75
Text Box button, Publisher 18, Publisher 107
text boxes
    adding bullets or numbering to, Publisher 56-57
    continued notices, turning on, Publisher 110
    creating, Publisher 10, Publisher 12, Publisher 18
    formatting, Publisher 54–55, Publisher 110–11, Publisher 133
    lists in, Publisher 57
    moving, Publisher 87
    overflow text in, Publisher 109
    in publications (fig.), Publisher 11
    resized (fig.), Publisher 129, Publisher 135
    rotating, Publisher 176
    selecting, Publisher 33
    white space in, Publisher 129
text columns (fig.), Publisher 107
Text in Overflow button, Publisher 33
Texture tab in Fill Effects dialog box (fig.), Publisher 227
.TIF files, Publisher 35

Tight Wrapping Style button, Publisher 174
title bar described, Publisher 6
toolbars
    header and footer buttons, Publisher 152–53
    Measurement, Publisher 53
    moving, Publisher 80
    picture, Publisher 81, Publisher 132
    standard, Publisher 6
    WordArt, Publisher 128, Publisher 173
tools
    drawing, Publisher 88
    measurement, choosing, Publisher 53
    Office, Publisher 194
    Spelling Checker, Publisher 58
trimming graphics, Publisher 80
type, kerning, Publisher 103
typos, correcting, Publisher 58, Publisher 179, Publisher 198

▶ U

Undo button, Publisher 62, Publisher 148
Ungroup Objects button (fig.), Publisher 82
Uniform Resource Locator. *See* URLs
URLs
    adding to Web sites, Publisher 224–25
    publishing Web sites, Publisher 230

▶ V

vertical lines between columns, Publisher 135
viewing and printing publications, Publisher 12–13
views
    dialog box, Publisher 9
    Master Page, Publisher 150
Visioneer PaperPort Scan Manager dialog box (fig.), Publisher 201
Voice Training dialog box (fig.), Publisher 207

▶ W

washout images, Publisher 150, Publisher 163
Web. *See* World Wide Web
Web Buttons, Design Gallery (fig.), Publisher 234–35
Web pages
    completed (fig.), Publisher 93
    Flower Show, Publisher 92

Index

Web sites
    adding hyperlinks, Publisher 224
    background, modifying, Publisher 226
    converting publications into, Publisher 232
    creating, Publisher 222–23
    creating personal, Publisher 234–35
    design elements, adding, Publisher 230
    Design Gallery Live, Publisher 77
    designing, Publisher 220–22
    increasing traffic to, Publisher 231
    manipulating artwork on, Publisher 92–93
    Microsoft Publisher, Publisher 17
    navigation bars, adding, Publisher 224
    planning, Publisher 218–19
    publishing, Publisher 230–31
    testing, Publisher 228–29
white space
    cropping, Publisher 81
    Design Checker, Publisher 205
    general, Publisher 28
    and horizontal text alignment, Publisher 105
    margins, using to create, Publisher 55
    in mastheads, Publisher 125
    negative space described, Publisher 28
    and text alignment, Publisher 105
    text wrapping and, Publisher 174
    using to frame elements, Publisher 131
Wizard button, Publisher 61
wizards
    Mail Merge, Publisher 178
    Pack and Go, Publisher 184
.WMF files, Publisher 35
Word, Microsoft
    editing in, Publisher 156
    importing documents, Publisher 194, Publisher 196
WordArt
    and Design Checker, Publisher 205
    designing, Publisher 172
    toolbar, opening and closing, Publisher 128
WordArt Gallery (fig.), Publisher 173
words, checking spelling of, Publisher 58, Publisher 179, Publisher 198
working
    with art, Publisher 75–98
    with text, Publisher 49–74
workspace described, Publisher 6
World Wide Web
    Design Gallery Live site, Publisher 77
    DTP/HTML Tutorials Plus Web site, Publisher 143
    Publisher site, Publisher 17
    working on, Publisher 217–40
wrapping text around objects, Publisher 174
writers, working with, Publisher 127

▶ Z

zero point, Publisher 52
Zoom box (fig.), Publisher 106
zooming in and out, Publisher 10, Publisher 32
Zoom list arrow, Publisher 108